A Dictionary of Synonyms & Antonyms

B.B. Sinha

UNICORN BOOKS

Publisher
UNICORN BOOKS
F-2/16, Ansari Road, Daryaganj, New Delhi-110002
☎ 011-23262683, 23250704, 45644782
E-mail: info@unicornbooks.in • *Website:* www.unicornbooks.in

Branch : Mumbai
23-25, Zaoba Wadi, Thakurdwar, Mumbai-401002
☎ 022-22010941, 022-22053387
E-mail: unicornbooksmumbai@gmail.com

ISBN 978-81-7806-340-9
A Dictionary of Synonyms & Antonyms

Edition 2026

Printed at : Unique Color Carton, New Delhi-110064

PREFACE

The ability to express oneself with a precise word, having the appropriate meaning is what differentiates a proficient practitioner from a casual user. It is essential that we understand the subtle variations of English before we can claim a good command over it.

Synonyms or 'similar meaning words' are hence essential for all of us. It is for this reason that all competitive exams contain a lot of questions on synonyms. The same has been explained in the beginning of the chapter on synonyms to give emphasis to this point.

I have written this book, giving sufficient question sets of all kinds that are asked in such exams so that the students are able to practise properly for them.

In the Antonyms section, the opposites of a large number of words have been listed again, with sufficient practice exercises.

I hope the readers will find this book useful, especially for the practice question sets given there in.

– B.B. Sinha

CONTENTS

PART-A

SYNONYMS

PART-B

ANTONYMS

Part A

SYNONYMS

- **Words Beginning with A to Z**
- **Multiple Choice Questions-Answers**
- **Exercises on Synonyms (with Answers)**

By the same author

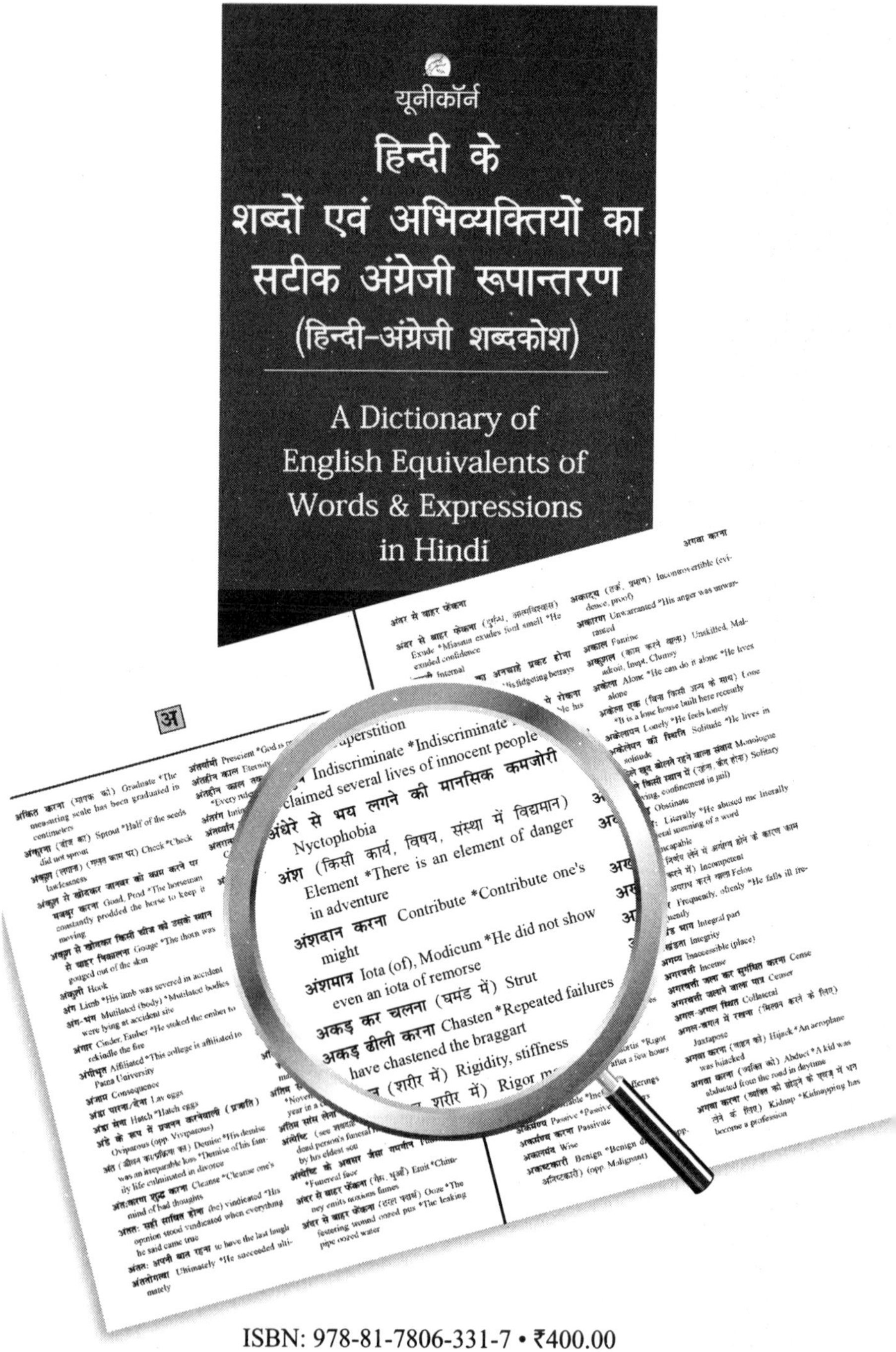

ISBN: 978-81-7806-331-7 • ₹400.00

Synonyms

It should be clearly understood that synonymous words carry same meanings broadly, but they cannot be oftenly used interchangeably in sentences. It is so because each of the synonymous words differs from the rest. So far as its application is concerned, uses depend on nuances of situations in which it is appropriately used.

For example

Renounce – The king renounced his throne and went in search of peace.

Abdicate – The king abdicated his throne and fled in exile. These two synonymous words broadly carry same meaning of leaving one's possession.

But 'renounce' is used for leaving possession for a lofty cause.

Whereas, 'Abdicate' is used for deserting or leaving possession in favour of someone else for being unable to carry on with it.

1. **Abandon** – leave someone alone and uncared
   Abdicate – leave power, duty, authority **Abdicate responsibility* **King abdicated throne*
   Abjure – leave something voluntarily
   Desert – leave someone alone **He deserted his friends*
   Forsake – leave comfort, luxury, bad habit
   Forswear – leave something in violation of pledge **Forswear allegiance*
   Renounce – leave something as a supreme sacrifice**Renounced his wealth and luxury for working for world peace*

2. **Abandoned** – left discarded **Abandoned house*
   Neglected – left out of care **Neglected child*
   Discarded – left alone and got rid of due to being worthless **Discarded furniture thrown in lumber room*

3. **Abase** – degrade someone by shameful acts **Leaders have abased themselves*
   Degrade – downgrade in rank
   Deprave – morally abased (corrupt)

4. **Abash** – make someone ashamed by shameful acts **The son abashed his family*
   Mortify – make someone acutely ashamed due to humiliation **Boss' reprimand has mortified him in the presence of colleagues.*

5. **Abate** – become less in intensity of fury **Anger soon abated*
   Allay – become less in intensity of fear, anxiety
   Alleviate – become less in intensity of pain
   Assuage – become less in intensity of ego; to reprieve the hurt feeling
   Mitigate – become less in intensity of harshness, severity **Mitigate harsh speech with juicy anecdotes* **Mitigate crime by repentence* **Mitigate the effect of disaster through Management.*

6. **Abject** – in humiliating condition **Abject poverty.*
   Ignoble – lacking in dignity **Ignoble behaviour*
   Sordid – degrading baseness **Corruption is rampant, which is a sordid state of affairs.*

7. Aborigine – a person belonging to original race living in a place

Indigenous – a product which is produced in a place (locally/domestically) **Indigenously manufactured product*

Native – a person who is born in a place (own country).

Autochthon – flora and fauna which is original to a place

8. **Abound (in)** – be in large amount **Market abounds in*

Glut – be in large excess of demand **There is a glut of vegetables in market.*

Teem – be in large numbers in a place

Swarm – **The market teems with people*

9. Abrade – scrape soft surface by rubbing with hard surface

Excoriate – wear away skin by rubbing with hard surface

Chafe – rub skin make it painful

Fret – wear away surface by constant rubbing **Dripping water frets away hard surface beneath*

Gall – rub surface of skin so as to make blisters due to friction **Shoes galled his toes*

10. Abscond – to flee from getting caught

Escape – to flee confinement

Elope – to flee secretly with someone to marry

Elude – to flee from someone by evading him

Skive – to flee from a place quietly

Bunk – play truant, flee from workplace or school

11. Absorb – soak a liquid (by a solid surface)

Imbibe – soak knowledge/learning through mind **Imbibe knowledge* **Imbibe respect for Values*

Assimilate – absorb and make one's own **Assimilate alien culture*

12. Abstain – to keep off from indulging in something harmful **Abstain from smoking*

Desist – to keep off from doing something **Desist from violence*

Eschew – to keep off from doing something on moral or practice ground **Eschew bad companion*

Refrain – to keep off from doing something, despite feeling urge to do so **Refrain from laughing on sombre occasion*

Shun – to keep off from someone abhorrent or repulsive **Shun lepers*

13. Abstemiousness – self-control on eating, drinking

Abstinence	–	self-denial in indulging in sensual gratification, *viz.* drinking alcohol
Continence	–	self-control in indulging in sex **Continence rather than abstinence is advisable in case of married people, but unmarried ones are advised abstinence*
14. Absurd	–	ridiculously devoid of any sense
Bizarre	–	absurd because of having incongruous combinations, *e.g.*, of old & new, tragic and comic **A bizarre dress *A bizarre plan*A bizarre incident*
Grotesque	–	having laughable quality **Grotesque face*
Preposterous	–	having misplaced positions of parts **Preposterous plan; completely contrary to nature.*
15. Abundant	–	present in large quantity
Excessive	–	present in excess of requirement
Superfluous	–	in more amount than required, which goes waste
Plenty	–	sufficient in amount **Plenty of eatables*
Surfeit	–	excess amount of consumption causing disgust
Legion	–	a large number of troops
Host	–	a great number of something **A host of people gathered there*
Plethora	–	*excess of something which must be reduced * Plethora of laws are existing but their implementation is tardy.*
Galore	–	in plenty **Food galore is available*
16. Abysmal	–	of endless depth/low **Abysmal conduct*
Fathomless	–	of endless depth/low which is beyond means of measurement **Fathomless cruelty*
17. Accept	–	agree to have done something **Accepted his mistake*
Acknowledge	–	accept the fact **Acknowleged the presence hitherto concealed of error in the plan*
Admit	–	accept the fact reluctantly **He admitted his fault*
Confess	–	accept one's crime **He confessed his role in hatching a conspiracy*
18. Acclimatize	–	adjust oneself to a changed climate
Accustom	–	adjust oneself to a changed custom
Inure	–	adjust oneself to a dangerous situation **Workers were inured to work in hazardous situation (e.g., tunnel workers)*
Habituate	–	adjust oneself to follow a habit or routine **He became habituated to following hygiene*

19. Accursed – cursed to suffer
Damed – cursed to go to hell
Doomed – cursed to be ruined

20. Accuse – blame for wrong-doings
Charge – blame for committing offence
Incriminate – blame for criminal act
Indict – blame for legal violation (by courts)
Impeach – blame for abuse of office of high position (by parliament)
Arraign – blame for wrong-doing and call for explanation

21. Acerbic – bitter in taste **Acerbic food*
Acrid – bitter and pungent in smell **Acrid smell*
Mordant – bitter and corrosive **Mordant liquid*
Vitriolic – extremely bitter (speech)

22. Adamant – rigid in one's own opinion
Resolute – rigid in one's own decision

23. Adjourn – stop and shift for a later day or time (meeting etc.)
Defer – stop and shift for a later day or time (decision)
Postpone – stop and shift for a later day or time (an event)
Prorogue – stop and shift for a later day or time (parliament session)

24. Admire – praise for good work/achievements
Acclaim – praise publicly with enthusiasm
Applaud – praise by clapping
Compliment – praise by showering congratulations
Commend – praise by making appreciation
Hail – praise by showing/expressing gratitude

25. Admirer – one who praises good work of art, etc. **Admirer of art works*
Aficionado – one who praises a particular sport **Aficionado of bull-fight*
Aesthete – one who praises the beauty of something **Aesthete of Nature*
Dilettante – one who praises particular music **Dilettante of classical music*
Fan – one who praises a famous person **Fan of Amitabh Bachchan*
Gourmet – one who praises good food **Gourmet of Chinese dishes*

26. Ado – excited movement or flurry without much to do worthwhile **People were abuzz with ado about nothing * Without any further ado, the speakers were invited by the chairman for panel discussion.*

Bustle – excited movement in great hurry around a place

Flurry – excited movement in nervous agitation **Flurry of officials on arrival of minister on the ground was was pleasing to the aggrieved public.*

27. Adroit – skillful in doing something

Adept – skillful in handling a situation

Deft – skillful in doing something quickly

Dextrous – skillful in doing something with hands

Proficient – skillful in doing something with efficiency

28. Adulterate – to mix something of lower quality with superior one for making more profit on sale

Contaminate – to mix something with impure things so as to make it injurious

Taint – to mix something in small amount to a substance so as to impart a foul smell

Tinge – to mix something in small amount to impart colour

Pollute – mix contaminants with natural resources, *e.g.,* water, air etc. so as to make it harmful to health.

29. Advent – coming to a place of someone/something important **Advent of Mahatma Gandhi on national scene gave impetus to freedom struggle*

Arrival – coming to a place of destination

30. Affect – to show false feelings

Feign – to affect ignorance, injury

Malinger – to affect illness

Pretend – to affect emotional display **Pretend sympathy*

31. Affirm – to say something firmly or emphatically

Assert – to say something confidently

Aver – to say something thought to be true

Avouch – to say something openly

Avow – to say something with guarantee

Declaim – to say something passionately **He declaimed his innocence*

32. Affix – to fix with a paste **Affix stamp on the envelope*

Adhere – to stick to a party, religion

Cling – to stick to the body of someone **Kid clings to the mother*

Hug – to stick to someone by taking in one's arms

Embrace – to stick to someone by catching shoulders

33. Afflict – to hurt as by disease, harmful condition **Ill-fate has afflicted him*

Inflict – to hurt by attacking with weapon **Inflict injury on someone*

34. Aggravate – make situation worse

Intensify – make something intense/acute

Recrudesce – make situation worse again after improvement

35. Agitate – disturb mentally to make one lose calm

Discomfit – disturb mentally, making one feel uneasy **Heckling by audience discomfited the speaker*

Disconcert – disturb mentally, making one lose composure

Rattle – disturb mentally, making one utterly nervous **Defeat rattled the politician*

Faze – (used in negative) disturb mentally causing shame **No amount of criticism can faze him*

36. Agitated – mentally disturbed

Disconsolate – mentally disturbed without something to consolate

Distraught – mentally disturbed, making worried

Disconcerted – mentally disturbed, losing peace of mind

37. Agnate – descendant of same male ancestor (male) **Agnate brothers*

Cognate – descendant of same female ancestor **Cognate brothers*

Consanguineous – descending from the same blood **Consanguineous brothers*

Kindred – descending from blood relations

38. Aid – help given to needy

Grant – aid given on certain condition

Subsidy – aid given in part of total expenses

Subvention – aid given to cultural or literary institution to meet expenses. Interest subvention is provided to exporters earning foreign exchange for the country.

39. Alibi – a fact mentioned as evidence to prove that one was not present at the place of occurrence of crime **He showed his absence from the town as an alibit to prove his innocence*

Excuse – a fact put forward as a ruse to avoid something **Fever came handy as an excuse to avoid work*

Plea – a fact put forward to justify failure to do something **Delay in project was justified on the plea of civil unrest*

Pretext – a fact put forward as an excuse **Use pretext of paucity of funds*

40. Alienation – loss of affection in relationship **Alienation of people from politicians*

Disaffection – loss of bondage in relationship

Estrangement – loss of bondage resulting in complete separation **Estrangement between husband and wife living separately*

41. Allegiance – firm adherence to party, group

Devotion – firm adherence to religion

Esprit de corps– firm adherence to comradeship of professionals

Fealty – firm adherence to feudal lord

Fidelity – firm adherence to faith towards someone

Loyalty – firm adherence to a person

42. Allot – distribute by apportioning something to each one **Allot quarters*

Allocate – distribute by apportioning resources for each purpose

Assign – distribute by apportioning work/duty to a person

Apportion – distribute by apportioning amongst claimants **Father apportioned the family's property amongst his sons*

43. Alone – indicates physically isolated **He is alone in the house*

Solitary – indicates without companion **The convict was kept in solitary confinement*

Lonely – indicates longing for companionship **He is feeling lonely in a place away from home*

Forlorn – indicates dejection due to separation**Forlorn lover*

Desolate – indicates sad due to being left bereaved **Desolate widow*

44. Amaze – bewilder someone with surprise

Astonish – make one too surprised to believe

Astound – make one surprised beyond wildest expectations

Flabbergast – make one surprised greatly

45. Amend – make correction for improving **Amend law*

Emend – make correction for removing errors **Emend a text of speech (edit)*

Expunge – make correction by removing objectionable portion of write-up. * *The speaker expunged the remarks of legislative member after the debate.*

46. Amends – to compensate for wrong-doings by rectifying **Apologise to make amends*

Atone – to compensate for wrong-doing by acts of goodness **Make charity to atone himself*

Expiate – to compensate by inflicting self-punishment **Mahatma Gandhi frequently went on fast to expiate*

Repent – to compensate by feeling sorry for wrong-doing

47. Anathema – someone or something intensely disliked **Lying is anathema to me*

Bete noire – someone/something to which one feels aversion **He is my bete noire*

Pariah – someone who is hated, abhored like untouchable

48. Ancestor – one from whom a person is descended

Forefathers – is more distant in lineage from whom one has descended.

Forbear/forebear – is distant in lineage

Progenitor – is just preceding in lineage, *e.g.* father

49. Anger *(noun)* – expression of displeasure

Rage – violent, uncontrollable anger

Outrage – strong anger

Fury – extremely violent anger

50. Anger *(verb)* – make one angry **My accusation angered him*

Enrage – make one violently and uncontrollably angry

Outrage – make someone very angry

Infuriate – make someone extremely angry

Incense – make one angry, akin to burning incense.

51. Announce – inform public of important issue **Exam results are announced*

Declare – announce officially **Declare holiday*

Herald – announce imminent arrival of someone important **Nip in the air heralded onset of winter season*

	Proclaim	– announce official decision **Proclaim curfew*
	Promulgate	– Announce official order **The ordinance promulgated by the Government is still in force*
52.	**Announcer**	– one who announces something on public address system.
	Herald	– one who or which announces the imminent arrival. on the scene of someone/something very special
	Harbinger	– one who or which announces the imminent arrival of something unpleasant **Lull in the harbinger of storm*
53.	**Annoy**	– irritate someone mentally
	Exasperate	– vex, irritate intensely
	Chagrin	– **Foolish mistakes committed by him chagrined him*
	Irk	– irritate because of being tiring
	Irritate	– agitate mentally due to discomfort
54.	**Annoyance**	– feeling of mental irritation over someone's foolishness
	Chagrin	– feeling of mental irritation over own foolishness **Chagrin of committing ridiculous mistake*
	Huff	– feeling of annoyance over petty matters
	Exasperation	– vexation, intense annoyance
55.	**Annul**	– cancel validity of a contract
	Abrogate	– cancel validity of an act, law
	Countermand	– cancel validity of an order
	Revoke	– cancel validity of a decision **Revoke arrest warrant*
	Repeal	– to revoke, to quesh, repress, set aside.
	Rescind	– to cut away, abrogate
56.	**Anthem**	– song in praise of country, school, organisation **School anthem *National anthem*
	Alleluia	– Hallelujah, praising song for God
	Epithalamium	– song of praise of bride and groom in wedding ceremony. Epithalamion
	Encomium	– high commendation and eulogy
	Hosannah	– An exclamation of praise to God **Cry hosannah to God*
57.	**Anxiety**	– feeling of distressing uneasiness due to apprehension
	Angst	– unfounded feeling of fear, dread
	Hypochondria	– unfounded anxious feeling of affliction of diseases

Paranoia – unfounded feeling of being persecuted

Snafu – unfounded feeling chaos everywhere

Worry – show concern for something or someone

58. Apotheosis – symbol of highest state of greatness **Mahatma Gandhi became apotheosis of human-beings*

Paragon – symbol of highest quality **He is the paragon of virtue*

Non-pareil – symbol of being unparralel *He is a human-being non-pareil

Epitome – symbol of a given quality **He is an epitome of laziness*

59. Apparent – appearing to be so **Apparent calm*

Conspicuous – clearly visible to be so **Conspicuous absence*

Distinct – sharply visible **Distinct characteristics*

Manifest – openly visible **Grief on his face is manifest*

60. Appeal – request earnestly to do something required

Plead – request arguably

Exhort – request emotionally

Urge – request insistently

61. Appease – to make one pleased by agreeing to demands **Voters are appeased by politicians by announ- cing freebies to people*

Placate – to make one pleased by pacifying anger

Propitiate – to make one pleased by trying to win one's favour

Assuage/Mollify – to make one pleased, who has been emotionally hurt

62. Apposite – appropriate for given occasion **Apposite quotes*

Cogent – appropriate for the topic of discussion **Cogent argument*

Germane – appropriate to the issue at hand

Relevant – appropriate to the matter at hand **Relevant informations*

Pertinent – appropriate to the question **Pertinent reply*

Apropos – Appropriate to opportunity **Appropos remark*

63. Appraise – evaluate the work of someone or something as by an expert **Experts appraise employee's performance*

Assess – evaluate quantum of gain or loss **Income is assessed for taxation* **Damage is assessed for compensation*

Evaluate – decide on worth of something **Exams' answer-sheets are evaluated*

Estimate – evaluate accurately cost, number or quantity **Estimate population of a place*

64. Apprehension – fearful feeling of something bad to happen

Suspicion – feeling of something bad which might be possible to happen

65. Appropriate – suitable **Appropriate action*

Befitting – suitable to the occasion **Befitting reply*

Condign – suitable to meet demand **Condign punishment*

Cogent – (in argument) suitable logically **Cogent point*

Germane – suitable to the subject's relevance **Germane to topic*

66. Approve – permit to go ahead **Approve the plan*

Endorse – permit to do something by putting one's signature on the back of the paper **Endorsed payment on the slip*

Sanction – permit as by govt. or a person in authority

67. Aquit – discharge from accusations, criminal charges

Absolve – discharge from responsibility or guilt

Exculpate – discharge from charges by declaring not guilty

Exonerate – discharge from onus of duty-lapse

68. Archaic – belonging to old time **Archaic custom*

Antiquated – having become outdated **Antiquated fashion*

Primitive – belonging to the past, undeveloped time **Primitive technology*

Pristine – belonging to old time, but still existing in its original form **Pristine religious scriptures*

69. Aroma – distinguishing smell of something **Aroma of coffee*

Bouquet – savoury smell of wine or meat **Bouquet of meat cooked in spices*

Flavour – savoury smell of tasty food

Fragrance – sweet smell of flowers

Redolence – mixed smell of flowers as in a garden

70. Arrogance – haughtiness

Audacity – disregard of restraint

Temerity – open & bold disregard of restraint

Hardihood – daring disregard of restraint

Gall – arrogant disregard of restraint

71. Arrogant – haughty
Audacious – showing undue boldness in disregarding others
Impudent – showing disrespect to others
Impertinent – showing improper behaviour

72. Arrogate – to snatch unjustly someone's credit for good work
Usurp – to snatch unjustly someone's power or authority
Supplant – to snatch unjustly someone's place and take it oneself **A whore supplanted his wife*
Pre-empt – to snatch unjustly somene's chance before he could do it or take it

73. Ascend – to go upward **He ascended to the top of hierarchy*
Levitate – to go up in the air floating **The saint levitated*
Soar – to go up in the sky continuously **The missile soared up towards moon*

74. Aspect – specific considerable matter of a fact
Dimension – specific considerable direction of a problem
Facet – specific considerable side of something **We should consider all facets of a proposal*
Ramification – specific considerable consequence arising out of a problem or fact **The problem has a serious ramification for the security of the country*

75. Assent – agree to someone's idea or proposal
Consent – agree to someone's request
Accede – agree to someone's request unwillingly
Acquiesce – agree to someone's request by keeping quiet instead of refusing it
Subscribe – agree with open support

76. Assiduous – continuingly and deeply engaged in work **Assiduous worker*
Diligent – delightfully engaged in work
Persistent – resolutely, determinedly engaged
Persevering – resolutely engaged, despite failure or difficulty

77. Assignation – a place for secret meeting **Lovers' assignation*
Rendezvous – a place for pre-fixed meeting together or assembly **Parks are popular rendezvous of retired people*
Tryst – a place for pre-fixed meeting with someone **I have to keep a tryst with him*

78. Atrabilious – depressed by ill-founded anxiety
Hypochondriac– depressed by ill-founded illness or anxiety
Melancholic – depressed by persistent sadness

79. Attempt – try to achieve goal in face of difficulty & failure **He attempted thrice to succeed*
Endeavour – try to do something with great offort **He endeavoured to keep himself composed*
Strive – try to do something/succeed with persistent effort **He strove hard to lift a heavy load*
Struggle – try with great effort to fight resistance

80. Attrition – feeling of sorrow for wrongdoing
Contrition – feeling of heart-rending sorrow for sinful acts
Compunction – feeling of sorrow while doing wrongful act
Penitence – feeling of sorrow with desire to make amends for wrongdoing
Remorse – feeling of sorrow and deep regrets

81. Augur – to indicate good outcome as by an event **Increasing terror activities do not augur well for the country*
Portend – to indicate bad outcome as by an event **Global warming portends disasters*

82. Auspicious – favourable by God and, hence, able to bring luck **Auspicious occasion to do something*
Benign – favourable by good nature of someone **Benign stars*
Benevolent – favourable by kindness of a person **Benevolent person*
Propitious – favourable by supernatural powers of something **Propitious luck*

83. Austere – strict in look **Austere face*
Harsh – strict in punishing or cruelty
Severe – strict and intense **Severe punishment*
Tough – strict and uncompromising **Tough administrator*

84. Authorise – to allow someone do something as by an authority **The boss authorised him to take action*
Accredit – to allow to do something recognising someone's competence **Government's accredited press reporters are invited to the press conference*
Delegate – to allow someone work on own behalf
Franchise – to allow someone do business by a company on its behalf

85. Autocrat – one who exercises power imposing one's will

Despot – one who exercises power imperiously

Tyrant – one who exercises power in an oppressive m anner

86. Avenge – to take revenge, vengeance on behalf of others

Retaliate – to take on to settle scores

Revenge – to take revenge for oneself

87. Avert – prevent what is unpleasant **Avert accident*

Obviate – prevent the necessity of something

Ward off – prevent what is dangerous

Stave off – ward off problems temporarily

Preclude – prevent occurrence before its possibility

Parry – Prevent attack by turning the weapon aside

88. Avoid – to keep away so as to remain safe **Avoid oily food*

Eschew – to keep away from something **Eschew violence*

Avert – to keep by taking appropriate measures beforehand **Avert student's agitation by assuaging their grievances*

Evade – to keep away by employing tact **Evade arrest*

89. Awesome – inspiring owe of someone great, learned etc.

Formidable – inspiring fear of someone powerful **Formidable enemy*

Menacing – inspiring fear of some action **Menacing flood*

Minatory – inspiring threat

90. Awkward – indicates lack of grace or convenience in doing something **Awkward handling*

Clumsy – indicates lack of ease

Inept – indicates lack of appropriateness **Inept handling of situation*

Maladroit – indicates lack of tact

Words beginning with — B —

1. Babel – noise made by confused people in crowd

Bedlam – uproar and confusion

Brouhaha – overexcited uproar

Chaos – noisy disorder and disturbance

Commotion – noisy hustle-buste in crowd

Melee – noisy scuffle in crowd

Pandemonium – noisy disorder in assembled mass of crowd

Rumpus – noisy disturbance

Uproar – noisy protest

Clamour – noisy shouting of crowd

2. **Backtrack** – to go back from one's taken stand on a matter

Forswear – to go back on promise or oath **Swear today, forswear tomorrow*

Recant – to go back from one's stated belief or opinion

Retract – to go back on one's given words

Welsh – to go back from honouring obligation, debt payment

3. **Backward** – moving in back direction **Move backward*

Retrograde – moving in inferior condition **Retrograde society*

Retrogressive– opposite of progressive, going back in previous inferior state of something

Regressive – returning to previous position

4. **Bad smelling**– smelling offensive

Fetid – smelling bad and be hazardous to health

Noisome – bad smelling, causing revulsion, disgust

Putrid – bad smelling due to rotting of garbage, corpse

Rancid – bad smelling and tasting offensive (said of cooking oil)

Fusty – due to uncleanliness of place

Musty – due to dark, unventillated condition

5. **Baffle** – confuse due to complexity

Perplex – Bewilder

Befuddle – confuse due to difficulty in understanding

Bemuse – make unable to think

Bewilder – make unable to think due to confusion

Daze – make unable to think due to blow on head

Stun – make unable to think due to shock

Stupefy – make unable to think due to drunken state

6. **Bait** – the thing which is used to lure prey **Earthworm is used as bait for fishing *Rebate and discount are used as bait to attract customers in shops*

Decoy – the which is used to divert attention of prey so as to become unaware of impending danger **Dummy parachutes are dropped at a place away from the place to be attacked by troops as a decoy to divert enemy's attention*

Feint – trick employed to divert other's attention from the real intention of the one who used trick

Ruse – trick used to divert attention from truth

7. Ban – official forbidding for public from doing something **Public assembly on roads has been banned *Ban on strikes has been announced*

Prohibit – forbidding by law **Smoking in public place is prohibited*

Inhibit – to stop one from doing something *Thyroid inhibits kids' growth

Forbid – not allow to do something undesirable

8. Banish – expel from a place by authority *The *criminal was banished out of town*

Excommunicate – expel someone out of his religion for anti-religious activities

Outcaste – expel from one's own caste

Exile – expel from one's own country and force to take refuge in another country **The dethroned king was exiled*

Extradite – expel from a country to another one to face trials by courts for offence committed there

9. Bark – outer covering of a tree

Peel – outer covering of banana or else which can easily be peeled off or stripped off

Rind – hard outer covering on some fruits, *viz.* watermelon

10. Baron – the most powerful person in a given field of business. **He is a publishing baron*

Magnate – the biggest influential businessman in a trade. **Tata is a steel magnate*

Tycoon – the most wealthy businessman in a given trade. **A shipping tycoon*

11. Beat – to strike someone's body to injure or punish

Bash – beat thoroughly with smashing blows

Batter – beat repeatedly.

Bludgeon – beat with thick stick at its one end

Box – blow on the head or ear with the hand or first

Clobber – beat with heavy blows

Clout – beat with careless, playful strokes **Clout kids on their back*

Cuff – beat with open palm on head

Pound – beat with legs by laying in ground
Pummel – beat with fists repeatedly
Slog – beat with forceful strokes
Slug – beat with hard knock
Smite – beat with hammer
Swat – beat with a flat object as a fan or book
Thrash – beat violently and repeatedly
Thresh – beat crops in order to separate grains from chaff.

12. **Beg** – ask humbly for getting something **Beg for alms*
Beseech – ask by repeated persuasion **Beseeched him for help*
Entreat – ask by earnest requesting
Implore – ask with anxious urgency
Importune – ask for something so repeatedly as to annoy someone, entreat causing annoyance
Supplicate – ask for something by praying before someone **Supplicate before deity in prayer*

13. **Behaviour** – manner in which one treats others **His behaviour is pleasing*
Conduct – one's manner of behaving in a particular situation **He conducts himself coolly in face of provocation*
Comportment– behaviour in a specified manner akin to a class of people **Comportment of an aristocrat*
Deportment – behaviour showing etiquette
Demeanour – behaviour in accordance with one's status **An aristocrat's demeanour*

14. **Belief** – acceptance as true **I have no belief in the rumours*
Faith – acceptance in tenets of religion or party to which one belongs **His faith in party is unshakable*
Credence – acceptance in what someone said **People lend credence to whatever he says*
Credit – acceptance of someone's reputation as being worth relying upon **He is a man of unblemished credit amongst people*

15. **Benumb** – deprive of physical movement due to loss of sensation **Biting cold benumbed his fingers*
Petrify – deprive of physical movement due to sudden fright **Encountered by a ferocious dog, he was petrified*
Stun – due to shock
Stupefy – due to amazement

16. Bequeath – leave property to someone by making a will

Legate – hand over property to posterity

Demise – leave property by transferring it to someone

17. Bias – inclination to or against someone or something as per one's liking or disliking **He has a bias for sweets *His bias against people of other castes is well-known*

Disposition – inclination towards something due to inherent mental tendency

Predisposition – inculcated disposition in someone to create tendency in someone so that he behaves in specified manner

Predilection – disposition shown in advance *i.e.,* in early stage of life

Stance – inclination to take a specified posture in a given situation

Tendency – inclination to feel or do something in a particular manner

Trait – mental inclination/disposition to think or act in a specified manner

18. Bigot – a person who is an admirer of a religion or sect, and does not tolerate contrary opinion of an opponent

Chavinist – a person who is an admirer of one's own gender or group, and looks down upon people of opposite gender or group

Fanatic – admirer of one's religion or party with excessive zeal

Zealot – admirer of one's own party, religion, etc. with excessive commitment

19. Blend – to mix ingredients to prepare an agreeable mixture

Concoct – to mix ingredients to prepare a drink

Taint – to mix ingredient in small quantity to make something foul smelling

20. Block – to stop passage by putting obstacle

Clog – to stop passage by something sticky **Silt and mud clog drains*

Hamper – to impede; to derange

Interrupt – to break in between; to stop or hinder

Hinder – to put up obstacle and impede progress

Jam – to stop traffic movement by overcrowding

Obstruct – to put up obstacle and hinder movement

21. Bogus – not genuine **Bogus claim*

Erastz – not a genuine substitute of a valueable thing **Ersatz work of art*

Placebo – (medicine) not genuine – looking like genuine and used to be given to a patient suffering from imaginary diseases

Sham – not genuine – only appearing to look genuine

22. **Boredom** – loss of interest in something due to excess exposure to it

Cloyness – loss of interest in something causing revulsion

Doldrums – loss of interest due to prolonged indulgence in an activity

Ennui – loss of spirit due to lack of occupation

Tedium – loss of interest in some work due to lacking variety

23. **Bounce** – to jump up after hitting a surface

Rebound – to return back after hitting a hard surface

Reverberate – to return back from a hard surface repeatedly to make an echo

Repercuss – (water waves) to return after hitting shores

24. **Boundary** – protective wall around a building

Rampart – protective wall around a fort or castle

Parapet – protective wall around edge of roof or balcony

Moat – protective ditch around a fort or castle

Stein – protective wall around the dug portion of a well

25. **Boycott** – expel from the group and refuse to socialise with

Ostracise – expel from society and refuse to socialise with

Excommunicate – expel from religion

Outcaste – expel from caste by castemen

26. **Brat** – a person who habitually boasts

Braggart – a person who brags

Braggadocio – a boastful person

27. **Breach (*n*)** – braking of a rule by failing to obey it **Breach of traffic rules*

Violation – breaking of accepted social norms **Violation of etiquette*

Contravention – breaking of a rule by acting against it

28. **Breach (*v*)** – to break a rule by failing to observe it

Violate – to break social norms

Contravene – to break rule by acting against it

29. **Buckle** – to bend under unbearable load

Sage – to bend in the middle of length of a beam due to its own weight

Prolapse – to slip down from position by becoming loose

30. Bump – move forward so as to strike something ahead **A moving car bumped into another car ahead*

Collide – bump into something with hard knock

Crash – bump into something with immense force

Dash – bump into something violently

31. Bunch – a number of keys hung together

Cluster – a number of grapes hung from a stem

Skein – a length of thread wound around a reel

Tassel – hanging decorative threads

Tuft – hanging mass of hairs, grass from one end

32. Bundle – tied mass of something

Bale – bundle of cotton

Faggot – bundle of dried wood or sticks

Sheaf – bundle of grass, paper, etc.

Swag – bundle of personal effects hung on shoulder of a traveller or labourer

Wad – bundle of currency notes

33. Burn – hurt in fire

Scald – hurt or injure with steam or hot liquid **Scald fingers with hot milk accidently*

Singe – hurt or injure superficial hairs on skin in open flame

Scorch – hurt or injured with extreme heat (as the surface of skin in intense sun)

Words beginning with — C

1. Cadaverous – looking pale like a corpse due to illness and imaciated body

Careworn – looking pale due to tiredness or worry

Haggard – looking pale due to exhaustion and tiredness

Pinched – looking pale due to mental tension

Wasted – looking pale due to emaciated physique

Worn – looking pale-faced due to weariness

2. Calm – not showing mental agitation

Placid – (a person) not easily agitated, nor excited by provocation

Serene – (atmosphere etc.) without any disturbance **A serene valley – a calm and quiet area.*

Tranquil – in a state of peace **Tranquil mind*

3. Cant – language spoken by people of a particular trade which is unintelligible to others **Hawkers cant* **Thieves cant*

Argot – language spoken by a close nit group **Argot of smugglers*

Jargon – language used by people of technical profession which is full of technical words **Doctors jargon*

Lingo – language too strange to be understood

4. Caper – jump around in enjoyment **Children caper on field*

Cavort – jump around in excitement **Winning players cavorted on the ground*

Frolick – jump around cheerfully, lively **Kids frolicked around*

Gambol – jump around playfully

5. Caprice – swinging mood without any pattern **Capricious mood of boss was beyond the guess of subordinates*

Vagary – swinging of weather which is unpredictable **Vagary of climate. The farmers' hopes are subjected to the vagaries of nature.*

Vicissitude – swinging of luck or fortune which turns unpredictably

6. Caress – touch and strike gently and lovingly **Caressed his hairs*

Fondle – touch and strike sexually

Pet – touch and strike erotically

Preen – touch and caress feathers with beak (used for birds)

7. Casual – (event etc.) occurring without pre-meditation **Casual event/occurrence*

Accidental – involving chance **Accidental meeting with a friend*

Fortuitous – happening without any cause *i.e.* luckily

Incidental – happening unforeseen **Incidental event*

8. Catch – take hold of **Catch the ball*

Grasp – catch firmly **He grasped my shoulders with hands to hug me*

Hold – grasp and continue to do so **He held my hand until I pulled it off.*

Nab – catch a person while fleeing **Nab the thief*

Sieze – hold something by confiscating from someone **Siezed stolen goods*

Apprehend – catch someone red-handed

Grab – catch someone/something by hand

9. Catholic – of wide variety **Catholic taste* **Cutholic faith – not restricted to a particular one*

Cosmopolitan– of wide variety of residents **Cosmopolitan city*

Cosmic – of wide universe **Cosmic event*

Ecumenical – of widespread scale **Ecumenical destruction*

Universal – of as wide as universe **Universal appeal of non-violence philosophy* **Universal truth*

10. Cautious – ready to avoid potential danger. **He stood there cautious*

Circumspect – ready to avoid danger by looking around alertly

Chary – cautious in doing something due to being harmful

Aware – ready with the knowledge of what is happening around

Wary – cautious due to possible problems

11. Cede – give up territory to another country

Demise – give up property to someone

Demit – give up post held by someone

Relinquish – give up property voluntarily

12. Celebration – observance of gaiety on the occasion of some importance **Birthday celebration*

Ceremony – observance of gaiety on the occasion of social or religious rites **Marriage ceremony*

13. Chafe – wear away surface by rubbing with something hard **Collar of shirt chafed kin of nape*

Abrade – scrape by rubbing with hard surface

Excoriate – wear away skin by whipping

Fret – wear away surface by constant rubbing

Gall – make blisters by rubbing on skin

14. Chant – recite slogan in unison

Recite – sing song, prayer, etc. loudly

Dithyramb – recital of a poem or speech passionately

Drivel – recital of meaningless speech

Harangue – recital of speech forcefully

15. Chatter – to speak incessantly

Babble – to speak foolishly

Blabber – to speak too much

Jabber – to speak rapidly and incoherently

Twaddle – to speak in a trivial manner

Drivel – to speak nonsense

Prattle – to speak too much unnecessarily

16. Cheat *(n)* – one who deceives by playing tricks

Con – one who deceives by lying to make one convinced

Fraud – a cheat who dispossesses someone of money by dishonest means

Impostor – a cheat who deceives by assuming false identity

17. Cheat *(v)* – to deceive someone by playing trick

Con – to deceive by lying

Defraud – to deceive by dishonest means

Swindle – to cheat by imposture *i.e.* assuming identity of someone else

Dupe – to cheat by employing tricks

Gull – to cheat

Hoodwink – to cheat by making a person unable to see or realise the trap

18. Chew – grind food in mouth

Chomp – chew noisily *i.e.* ,with making sound of chewing

Munch – chew crisp food noisily

Ruminate – chew cud (by animal)

19. Chide – speak angrily for doing wrong

Scold – chide bitterly

Berate – scold angrily

Castigate – scold severely

Chasten – chide so as to discipline erring person by giving punishment

Chastise – scold with beating

Reprehend – scold and condemn/criticize

Hector – scold like a bully

Remonstrate – scold and protest against wrongdoing

20. Circadian – (biological activities in our body) occurring on daily basis **Sleeping is a circadian process*

Diurnal – (a process) occurring on daily basis **Diurnal earth's rotation causes day and night*

Quotidian – (work) done on daily basis **Quotidian household chores*

21. Class – group of persons distinct from others on the basis of status in social divisions **Aristocratic class of people*

Category – group of things distinct on the basis of quality or characteristics

Denomination – group of things on the basis of name assigned to the whole group

Gender – group assigned on the basis of sex of birth

Genre – group of art or literary work assigned on the basis of distinct nature

Genus – category of creatures on the basis of species

22. Classify – separate on the basis of class

Categorize – separate into categories

Segregate – separate from a group isolated from others

Sort – separate papers, documents, letters according to subject matters, titles, addresses etc.

Assort – separate bills, reeipts according to related matter

23. Clean – remove dirt and dust

Cleanse – make thorough cleaning of undesirable such as soul from sin, moral from blemish

Emunge – clean bowels of stool, secreted mass from nostrils

Flush – clean toilet with large amount of water

Lustrate – clean with holy water for ceremonial purpose

Mop – clean floors with bundle of rags soaked in water

Scour – clean something by rubbing

Swill – clean by swirling with water

Wash – clean clothes, utensils, etc. with water

24. Clever – able to see someone's attempt to befool

Shrewd – having acute sense of cleverness, cunning

Crafty – having the ability to befool others

Astute – having the ability to save oneself from being befooled

Sagacious – having the ability to take decisions with farsightedness

Perspicacious – having the ability to take decisions with farsightedness

25. Cliche – (slogan etc.) over used and, hence, uninteresting anymore

Bromide – (slogan etc.) over used and, hence, ineffective in impressing people

Platitude – (remark etc.) oft-repeated and hence, uninteresting

26. Climax – state of extreme excitement in story

Bliss – state of extreme happiness in life

Culmination – state of extreme end of a process

Orgasm – state of extreme sexual passion

Trance – state of extreme absorption in pleasurable enjoyment, *e.g.*, listening to music or divine song

27. Climb – go up a slope, stairs, ladders

Clamber – climb laboriously on a slope, using hands and feet both

Board – to go inside a transport vehicle for travelling

Mount – to ride on a horse, bicycle etc.

Embark – to get in a ship for journey

28. Clique – group of experts in specified areas of knowledge

Claque – group of hired audience to clap the speaker

Choir – group of singers

Panel – group of experts for decision making/discussion

Troupe – group of artistes

29. Closeness – nearness in relationship

Vicinity – nearness in space, being in the neighbourhood **His house is in vicinity of mine*

Propinquity– nearness to almost in touching contact **Sit in propinquity with each other*

Proximity – nearness in distance

Contiguity – nearness with mutual touching

Intimacy – nearness in personal relations.

30. Clot – (liquid) form a thick, sticky mass

Congeal – (liquid) become semi solid on cooling

Coagulate – become semi solid by chemial process

Curdle – (milk) change into curd

31. Cogitate – to consider deeply over a topic

Introspect – to consider one's own past actions to find out lapses

Retrospect – to consider about past events to find out if anything went wrong

Ruminate – to think about deeply

Meditate – to think carefully about something

Mull – to consider at length about something

32. Collect – to pick up and keep at one place

Accumulate– to collect and store **Accumulate water* **Accumulate wealth*

Cull – to pick up by plucking as inferior in quality

Garner – to pick up and keep in a storage place

Gather – to collect in a place

Summon – to pick up courage to face challenge

Marshall – to collect in an orderly manner **To marshall facts before arguing a case*

Muster – collect troops or workers for putting on job

33. Colossal – of large in size **Colossal waste*

Monolith – of a large single piece as of a stone **A monolith organization*

Mammoth – of large size physique **A mammoth elephant*

34. Commit – hand over to other's charge **This case was committed to superior court *Commit parcel to railways*

Consign – hand over to someone for disposal or send forward **Consign goods to transporter *Deadbody was consigned to pyre*

Confide – hand over personal secrets to someone you have trust in

Entrust – hand over something to someone you trust **He entrusted valuables to his neighbour*

Relegate – hand over someone/something to inferior place **He was relegated to oblivion*

35. Companion – one who moves in someone's company **He has gone there with his two companions*

Consort – one who accompanies with someone, and shares common destiny **He always moves with his female consort wherever he goes*

Spouse – one who accompanies someone, and is formally married to him

36. Compare *(with)* – to consider both liken-ness as well as difference with something else **Compare life in Delhi with that in Mumbai*

Compare *(to)* – to consider only liken-ness of one to another **This year summer's intensity is comparable to that in a desert*

Contrast *(with)* – to consider only the difference **Contrast the luxury of aristocrats with the penury of the peasants*

37. Compensate – to make up for loss or deficiency

Recompense – to make up as reward for rendering service

Indemnify – to guard gainst any possible loss, and compensate in case of damage or loss incurred

38. Complacent – well satisfied and pleased with one's own achievements

Smug – complacent with a sadist arrogance for those who are less fortunate in this matter

39. Complain – air grievance about something **Complain against water supply problems*

Carp – complain by finding fault deliberately

Cavil – complain about petty problems

Grumble – complain in muted voice and sullen face

40. Complicity – active participation in conspiration/wrongdoing

Connivance – passive participation in conspiracy by means of acquiescing in wrongdoing

Collusion – active participation in wrongdoing in secret manner **Collusion with perpetrators of crime*

Indulgence – active participation in some activity to fulfil desire **Indulgence in share marketing*

Involvement – active participation in some activity by means of grossly absorbed in it

41. Concession – privilege of paying less **Students get concession in bus fares*

Discount – deduction in price of an article on sale **Store sold articles on 10% discount in prices*

Rebate – deduction in payable amount allowed to the payee **Rebate of 5% on the bill was allowed for early payment*

Exemption – freedom allowed from fulfilling obligation or liability which others have to fulfil **Exemption in tax payment for those earning less*

Relaxation – application of rules less strictly **Relaxation of 5 years in upper age limit was allowed to the tribal candidates for entry in jobs*

42. Confine – keep within specified limit of space, scope or time **Discussion was confined to corruption* **He confined himself in the house*

Immure – keep within the boundary of a place/house **Saints immure themselves in hermitage*

Incarcerate – keep within the four walls of a room, or prison cell **They incarcerated themselves for private talks*

Intern – keep within a specified space without allowing to cross it **War prisoners are interned in tents surrounded by barbed fences*

43. Confiscate – seize with legal authority **Contraband goods were confiscated*

Distrain – seize property of someone for paying his liability

Escheat – seize unclaimed property (by the state)

Forfeit – seize property, privilege, etc. as a penalty for wrong doing **Property of fugitive was forfeited*

Impound – seize something and retain in custody **His car was impounded by police after it met with an accident*

44. Confute – prove a statement to be wrong

Refute – prove an accusation to be wrong

Disprove – Prove a claim to be wrong

45. Congenital – (disease, defect) present since birth **He is suffering from congenital hernia*

Inborn – (habit, merit) present since birth **Talent in a person in inborn*

Innate – (quality, virtue) present since birth **Compassion is an innate virtue in human beings*

46. Conserve – prevent wasteful use of reserved resources so as to last long **Conserve water*

Preserve – prevent valuable things from getting damaged **Preserve heritage*

Eke out – use/consume in less amount of resources so to last longer **Eke out a living on alms*

Stint – use in limited amount which is available by restricted allotment **Stint on rationed foods*

47. Consult – consider something with the advisors.

Confer – consider with one's equals or peers **Senior executives confer on company's affairs*

Advise – consider with someone on personal matters **He advised with his friends on matters of his career*

Parley – consider with others on matters which are contentious **Govt. parleys with the opposition leaders on the passage of legislation*

Treat – (belligerent countries) consider on negotiating terms for truce and finalise treaty.

48. Contemporary – (two things or persons) existing during the same period of time *C*ontemporary poets/leaders/art & cultures*

Contemporaneous – existing during the same time period as the existence of something else **Our friendship was contemporaneous with the period of our college days together*

Coeval	–	existing during the same period in the long past **Coeval cultures which are extinct now*
Coetaneous	–	existing with the same time of birth or origin **Coetaneous mounains*
49. Contempt	–	feeling of dishonour for something
Disdain	–	contempt for being worthless/unworthy
Scorn	–	derisive contempt
Spite/spleen	–	a feeling of hate
50. Contingent	–	(something) dependent upon something else **Success is contingent upon hard work*
Incumbent	–	(duty, responsibility) dependent upon someone expected to discharge **Care of elderly people is incumbent upon progeny*
Recumbent	–	something reclining upon something else for support **He is recumbent upon the pillow*
51. Continuously	–	without break **He slept continuously for 6 hours*
Constantly	–	very often – again and again **He is constantly bothering me*
Continually	–	at short intervals **He lost his temper continually in the meeting*
Perpetually	–	endlessly **Poor people suffer perpetually*
52. Controversial	–	causing controversy **Controversial decision*
Contentious	–	likely to become a matter of arguments between contenders **Census on caste basis has become a contentious issue in the country*
53. Cooperate	–	work jointly to achieve common goal **They cooperate with each other*
Collaborate	–	to work jointly on a plan
Collude	–	to work jointly on a conspiracy
54. Courage	–	quality in character to face extreme difficulties without fear
Fortitude	–	quality in character to endure problems
Guts	–	stamina to endure or face challenges
55. Coward	–	lacking in courage
Timid	–	lacking courage to venture in unknown area or mix with unknown person *Too timid to talk to strangers **Too timid to invest in shares*

Timorous – lacking courage in taking bold action on one's own accord **Too timorous to take on a challenge*

56. Crack – narrow split in surface

Chasm – profound gap in opinions, friendship

Cleavage – wide split

Crevice – narrow split in surface which runs deep

Fissure – a long and narrow split

Gape – opening gap as in open mouth **He yawned with a gape*

Hiatus – a gap with continuity

Rent – large split as by tearing **A rent in cloth*

57. Crave – desire overwhelmingly for something **Crave for wine*

Covet – desire to possess what someone else is having **I covet his success*

Hanker – strongly desire for something

Long – strongly desire for something which is not easily achieved **Long for name and fame*

Yearn – desire impatiently or eagerly **Yearn to meet family members*

Suspire – desire strongly indicated by taking deep breath

58. Crawl – move slowly along the ground with the help of hands and knees

Creep – move slowly with the body lying on the ground

Slither – move slowly on the ground with turning and twisting the body alternately in the opposite directions

59. Craze – excessive liking for something **He has a craze for sweets*

Fad – excessive arbitrary habit of doing something

Mania – excessive tendency to do something **He has a mania of talking*

Obsession – excessive pre-occupation with something **Obsession for watching television*

60. Create – to bring something into existence by using skill **God created the unverse*

Generate – to bring into existence by producing something by using a process **Generate electricity*

Engender – to bring into existence in someone like emotion **Engender wonder/interest/anger in someone*

Breed – to bring offsprings into existence by giving birth by animals **Animal breeds calf*

Beget – to bring into existence offspring by humans **He has begotten four kids*

61. **Credit** – to acknowledge that someone has done something appreciable

Attribute – to give credit for something **Success was attributed to his efforts*

Assign – Attribute something to someone

Impute – attribute a bad motive to someone **Imputed motive to him for helping others*

62. **Cringe** – to bow before someone in flattering

Cower – to bow before someone in fear

Grovel – to bow before someone mighty

Truckle – to bow before someone in submission

Crouch – to bow one's body

Stoop – to bow one's head and shoulder and keep rest of the body erect

63. **Criticise** – speak against someone unfavourably

Harangue – criticise single forcefully or emotionally

Inveigh – criticise with intense hostility

Vituperate – criticise in disparaging manner

Objurgate – denounce, upbraid someone harshly

64. **Criticism** – act of criticising

Diatribe – criticism in bitter language

Harangue – criticism in emotional manner

Obloquy – strong-worded criticism

Invective – criticise abusively

Philippic – bitter criticism

65. **Cruel** – ruthless

Ferocious – violently cruel

Savage – furiously cruel

Barbarian – lacking civility in behaviour

Inhuman – lacking pity

Truculent – fierce and brutal

66. **Cry** – weep in loud voice

Keen – cry in grief for dead person

Wail – cry very loudly

Weep – shed tears

67. **Curse** – wish divine punishment for wrongdoing

Anathematise – (religious head) pronounce curse for something anti-religious *Pope anathematised violence against humanity*

Imprecate – curse by praying God to make someone suffer

Words beginning with —— D ——

1. **Damage** – harm something **Damage machine* **Flood damaged the standing crops*

Impair – harm someone's or something's natural ability to do something **Impaired hearing power of ears*

Hurt – harm to cause physical injury

2. **Danger** – possibility of happening something unwelcome, unpleasant or harmful **Going out in jungle is full of danger*

Risk – something full of danger

Hazard – chance of suffering unwelcome consequences. **Hazard of pollution*

Jeopardy – even chance of suffering harm as a consequence **Working without safety gears can put you in jeopardy*

Peril – chance of exposing someone to immediate harm as a consequence **Peril of war*

3. **Dazzle** – shine brightly with intense light **Sun dazzles* **Dazzling gems*

Glitter – shine with reflecting light impressively **Gold glitters.*

Coruscate – shine with sudden flash of light

Sparkle – shine with flashes of light as electric spark

Gleam – shine with a brief flash of light

4. **Dead body** – body of a dead person

Mortal remains – deadbody of an important personage

Cadaver – corpse of a dead person

Carcass – deadbody of an animal

Carrion – deadbody of an animal which is decaying

5. **Deadlock** – a situation of no progress in talks or negotiations due to rigid attitude

Disruption – disturbing condition in which no progress is possible

Hindrance – condition of delay in progress

Interruption – breaking continuity in progress

Obstruction – disruption due to blocking the way of progress

6. Dearth – absence of something desirable **There is a dearth of good politicians*

Lack – unavailability of something needed **Lack of nutrition in children affects their timely growth.*

Scarcity – unavailability of resources in sufficient amount **Scarcity of vegetables in the market causes price rise and inflation.*

7. Depris – broken pieces of something demolished **Debris of demolished buildings*

Rubble – broken pieces of stones, bricks etc.

Wreckage – broken pieces of something damaged **Wreckage of aeroplane damaged in an accident*

Flotsam – wreckage of a ship floating on water

Lagan – wreckage of a ship settled on the sea-bed

8. Deceive – befool someone by making him accept false as true

Delude – by making someone unable to see truth

Ditch – by getting rid of someone, and leave him in the lurch

Beguile – by tricking into doing something **Beguile someone to lend money*

Betray – by aiding someone's enemy, or by becoming disloyal to him

9. Declare – let people officially or formally know something important **Declare examination results*

Announce – let people know by addressing publicly

Herald – let people know of something important to happen soon by indicating an event **Chill in the morning heralds arrival of winter*

Proclaim – let people know of official decision to be imple- mented **Proclaim curfew in the city*

10. Decorate – to beautify something not looking attractive **Decorate tent for the wedding ceremony*

Adorn – to beautify to add on the attractive-looking

Garnish – adorn a food dish before serving to diners

Embellish – make a speech more attractive by adding on juicy anecdotes

11. Decrepit – (a thing) in worn out condition **Decrepit chair/house*

Dilapidated – in ruined state due to neglect **Dilapidated building*

Ramshackled – in a condition of severe disrepair

Rickety – in a condition of distorted shape **Rickety furniture*

12. Defalcate – steal money by removing a part of it under one's care, and falsely reconcile the account

Embezzle – remove a part of money kept under one's control

Misappropriate – to remove a part of fund for own use un authorisedly

13. Defame – spoil someone's good reputation by spreading lies

Slander – by false statement about him

Libel – by writing false accusations in newspapers

Calumniate – by speaking false things about him

Vilify – by speaking in scurrilous manner, or by name -calling

Asperse – by indirect accusation made against him

Malign – by speaking evil things about him

14. Defeat – to win victory over someone

Rout – to defeat by making enemy retreat or flee from the scene

Vanquish – to defeat enemy thoroughly

15. Defect – lacking in perfection **Defect in a machine*

Flaw – defect impairing soundness **Flaw in proposal*

Drawback – lacking in desirable features

Shortcoming – lacking in what is required

Deficiency – lacking in completeness **Deficiency in plan*

Fault – defect in character, system

Lacuna – defect due to a part missing; gap

Handicap – defect that restricts ability to function normally

16. Defector – one who changes his party to join another one

Apostate – one who changes his party or religion without harbouring ill will against it

Renegade – one who changes his party or faith/religion with rancour against it

Proselyte – one who is converted to another faith

Turncoat – one who changes party or faith for one's convenience or selfgain instead of any principle

17. Defile – make a place dirty

Desecrate – make a sarcd place dirty – spoiling its sacredness

Contaminate – make something dirty by allowing germs or harmful things mixed up

Soil – make dress dirty as with dirt, mud

18. Degenerate – to revert to poor condition **Moral degeneration of people*

Deteriorate – to become worse than the earlier condition

Depreciate – to decline in value **Prices of buildings have depreciated*

Impoverish – to decline in richness reducing to poor state **Lavish spending impoverished a rich man *Cultivation on land leads to impoverished fertility*

19. Delicate – too fine to distinguish or detect **Delicate touch*

Subtle – too fine to realise or describe **Subtle distinction*

Subliminal – too delicate to be sufficient to be felt or to affect

Naunce – too delicate difference to make differentiation as in colours, words' meanings

20. Deliverance– setting someone free from guilt or sin

Salvation – setting someone free from mundane/temporal life

21. Delve – search something in a heap of it **Delve out the required book from a heap on the floor*

Forage – search usable things in heap of garbage **Pigs forage for eatables in the garbage*

Frisk – search the body of a person to find anything objectionable on him by moving hands all over him

Grope – to search for something in dark by moving hands so as to feel for it

Rummage – search for something in haphazard manner by throwing things around **He rummaged contents of almirah for a document*

Scrabble – search something by blindly moving fingers or legs' toes all over a surface as if scratching it **A hill climber scrabbles slope with his toes to find a foothold on it *He scrabbled his pocket with his fingers to find out coins in it.*

22. Demise – to give, relinquish power, property to someone by will

Bequeath – to give property to someone by will

Defray – to give money to someone to meet specified expenses, *viz.*, college fees

Bestow – give gift, shower praise on someone

Confer – give title, degree, etc. to someone

Impart – to give special quality, characteristic to someone

Endow – give money as a regular source of income to someone

Endue – give someone power or position or rights **Endue voting rights on the non-resident Indians*

23. Demolish – to break a building down
**The building was demolished*

Destroy – to ruin by damaging **Destroy public property*

Raze – to knock down an erected structure by hammering

Wreck – to break a ship, vehicle etc. down to ruin by damaging **Storm wrecked the building *Vehicle was wrecked in an accident*

24. Demonstrate – to show something by practical action **Effect of gravity was demonstrated by the teacher to students*

Show – to make something visible to others

Exhibit – show something interesting by displaying publicly **Exhibit works of art*

Evince – to make something obvious by indirect indication **His lack of interest in studies is evinced by his truancy from school*

Flaunt – to display something proudly or boastfully
**He flaunted his costly pen to his friends*

Manifest – to make something obvious to others **Talent manifests itself in a child at early age*

Display – show something by placing in the open to be seen by all

Parade – to show one's possession to others by demon-strating it **He paraded his knowledge*

25. Denounce– declare something to be wrong by openly criticising it **Denounce negligence in public works*

Objurgate – denounce in harsh language

Deplore – express strong disapproval **Falling snorality is deplorable*

Deprecate – express disagreement with something wrong

Decry – denounce publicly

Assail – denounce severely

Execrate – denounce something for being loathsome

26. Deny – refuse to accept truth or existence of something **Deny involvement in crime*

Decline – refuse to accept politely **Decline someone's offer*

Disavow – refuse to accept being responsible

Reject – refuse to accept suggestion, advice and counselling

Repudiate – refuse to accept, to own up something
**Repudiate loan of the bank *Repudiate one's own son. *The insurance company has repudiated the claim of the policy-holder.*

Spurn – reject with disdain **Spurn someone's offer of help*

27. Deplete – (stock) become less due to consumption

Diminish – become less in intensity, size

Decrease – become less in number, value

Dwindle – become less gradually in stock

Wane – become less gradually in size

28. Deprive – take away opportunity to do or to have something **He was deprived of taking part in competition*

Deny – to refuse to give something which is due to someone **He was denied promotion*

Disenfranchise – to take away the voting rights

29. Deride – express contempt

Ridicule – express contempt by laughing at someone

Lampoon – to ridicule publicly

Scoff – to deride scornfully

Sneer – to deride laughingly/contemptuously

Pillory – to ridicule by abusing

Mock – to ridicule by making fun of someone

30. Descend – to come down from a height **Descend from a hill *Plane descends on the airport*

Dive – to jump down in water, or jump down headlong

Plummet – to come down from a height by falling rapidly **Prices of commodities plummetted*

Plunge – to come down uncontrllably

Swoop – come down rapidly to catch a target below **Predator bird swooped to catch its prey*

31. Descendant – one who has descended from the lineage of an ancestor **Descendant of a noble family*

Progeny – offspring of a progenitor *i.e.,* parents

Posterity – person of future generation **Heirloom of a family passes on to posterity*

32. Desire – strong liking to have something **He expressed his desire to eat something*

Will – inner desire in one's heart **He has a strong will to achieve what he wanted*

Wish – strong desire to see something happen **His wish to see the country prosper came true *He prayed God to grant his wish*

Conation – desire to achieve supreme objective in life **Salvation is everyone's conation*

Volition – strong desire to do something on one's own choice or free will

33. Destroy – damage to ruin something **Old civilizations were destroyed*

Annihilate – destroy to the state of making non-existent **Bombing annihilated the city*

Devastate – to ruin completely by damaging as by large scale violence, colanity disaster **War devastated country's economy*

Ravage – to ruin extensively as by disease grief, worries **Flood ravaged the area as by dieare, grief, worries*

34. Determination – quality of remaining firm in pursuing goal

Resolve – act of determination with firmness in purpose

Grit – courageous determination

Mettle – determination with the ability to cope up with the diffculties

Tenacity – determination with no sign of laxity

35. Devalue – to lower the value of something

Debase – to lower the quality, character **Adulteration debases purity* **Moral depravity debases a person*

Demean – to lower dignity **Demean someone's reputation*

Degrade – to lower rank, position

Abase – to lower dignity

Belittle – to lower someone's importance

36. Deviate – go off the course/path **Deviate from the right path and go elsewhere*

Digress – go off the main topic in writing or speech

Divagate – digress

Diverge – to go off the straight line by turning aside in a different direction **The road ahead diverges in different directions*

37. Devise – to prepare a plan, contrivance, etc. using skills

Contrive – to make something using tact, trick **Contrive a plan to befool someone*

Concoct – to make something by mixing ingredients **Concoct a slanderous lie to defame*

Fabricate – to make something by joining parts **Fabricate a machine*

Fashion – to make something by giving it shape using various materials with skill **Fashion a lamp with bamboo sticks*

Forge – to make something by the process of heating, casting or other things *Forge an alliance by talking to the allies*

38. **Devour** – to swallow hungrily

Gorge – to swallow food greedily in large morsels

Gobble – to swallow quickly

Raven – to swallow voraciously as an animal

39. **Difference** – dissimilarity between two which is visible **Difference in colours of two pens*

Distinction – difference which can be perceived, analysed but not seen **Distinction in fragrance of flowers*

Discrepancy – difference between contents of two statements or facts

Disparity – difference between conditions of two things expected to be similar

40. **Differences** – disagreements in opinions of two persons

Dispute – disagreement over a matter of discussion **Dispute over wage revision*

Dissent – differences over a decision made

Discord – differences in harmonious relations

41. **Dig out** – to take out something by digging the ground

Excavate – to dig out to remove soil

Exhume – to dig out a grave to take out a burried deadbody

Disinter – to dig out something that had been kept burried **Disinter items of archaeological value*

42. **Dilemma** – a situation in which it is difficult to take a dicision about what to do because of two equally undesirable alternatives

Plight – a situation which puts a person in unfavourable, sorry state of affairs

Predicament – an unpleasantly perplexing situation about what to do under the circumstances

Quandary – state of uncertainty about what to do

43. **Dilly-dally** – to avoid a job by delaying in doing it **Govt. is dilly-dallying over the decision in tackling price inflation*

Dawdle – to avoid doing work by doing it slowly or lazily

Procrastinate – to avoid doing a work by deliberately postponing to a later time causing inordinate delay.

44. Din – prolonged unpleasant noise of talking or shouting **Din in classroom*

Murmur – loud-pitched continuous noise

Hum – low-pitched continuous noise

Drone – low-pitched continuous noise as produced by striking a musical instrument's strings

45. Dip – to put something under water or oil **Dip a wick in oil before lighting it. Dip the tea bag in the cup containing boiled water*

Dunk – to put an eatable in liquid' *viz.* milk, to make the eatable soft **Dunk bread in milk before eating*

Immerse – dip something in water so as to disappear **Idols are immersed in the river*

Inundate – dip something in excess of or large amount of **Houses were inundated in flood water *Letters of protests inundated the office*

Submerge – dip something under overflowing water **Low-lying areas were submerged in water*

46. Disaffection – (see Alienation)

47. Disagree – to have a different opinion from that of another person

Disapprove – to have unfavourable opinion about something

Differ – to have unlike opinion

Dissent – to have different opinion at an agreed or accepted decision

48. Disappear – cease to be visible

Vanish – disappear suddenly

Evanesce – disappear gradually, fade away

49. Disappointment – loss of hope

Dejection – loss of hope causing sadness

Despair – complete loss of hope

Despondence – loss of hope causing low spirit

50. Disaster – unfortunate event/destruction causing wides -pead damage

Apocalypse – unfortunate event causing great damage

Cataclysm – ....causing great upheaval

Catastrophe – ....causing great damage

Calamity – ....causing distress, misery

51. Disbelief – mental inclination of refusing to accept as true **Disbelief in rumours*

Unbelief – disbelief due to being not fit to be accepted as true

Distrust – disbelief due to being not fit to be trusted

Mistrust – refusal to trust someone

Incredibility – inclination of refusing to accept as true because of the impossibility of being true, of being beyond belief

Cynicism – inclination to refuse to accept selfless motive of anyone

52. Discard – throw off what is useless **Discard the peels of banana*

Dispose of – get rid of something

Jilt – cast off the lover by breaking relationship **The girl jilted her lover*

Moult/Molt – cast off feathers, horns by birds/animals before new ones grow in place naturally

Shed – cast off leaves (by trees) before new ones grow

Slough – to cast off dead skin (by snakes) and take on new grown skin in that place

Jettison – to cast off goods from ship to reduce load overboard to save it from sinking

53. Discharge – set free from accusations, hospital etc.

Absolve – set free from duty, responsibility

Acquit – set free from charges by courts

Deliver – set free from burden of something, guilt, etc. **Pray god to deliver from the nightmare of guilt*

Enlarge – set free from captivity

Enfranchise – set free from political subjugation to decide for oneself

54. Disclose – make a concealed information, secret known

Divulge – dislose official secrets

Betray – disclose internal emotional feelings through expression **He took deep breath betraying his frustration*

Reveal – disclose something by removing veil from it

55. Discourage – dishearten someone from doing something **Insurmountable difficulties discouraged him from doing something desirable*

Dissuade – persuade someone to desist from doing something due to being undesirable

Daunt – to make one lose hope by putting dificulties in the way of something done by him

	Deter	– discourage from doing something by threatening with consequences
56.	**Disgorge**	– expel from mouth something eaten
	Eructate	– (volcano) expelling lava
	Regurgitate	– expel ingested food back into mouth (by birds, animals) for feeding fledglings, or for chewing again (cows).
	Reek	– expel billowing smokes from chimney
	Ooze	– expel pus, fluid from a wound
	Vomit	– expel ingested food out due to nausea
57.	**Disguise**	– alter appearance to conceal identity **Disguised himself as a woman to escape from a place*
	Impersonate	– alter identity by assuming name of another person in order to cheat someone **A thug impersonated as an income tax officer to take bribe from a business man*
	Masquerade	– to alter identity by pretending to be someone else **Rich man masqueraded as a beggar*
58.	**Disintegrate**	– to break up into small parts
	Shatter	– to break up into broken fragments
	Fragment	– to break up into a small piece from a large whole of something
	Split	– to break up into pieces by cracking under impact
59.	**Disobedient**	– who habitually disobeys
	Contrary	– who is too self-willed to obey
	Recusant	– who refuses to obey orders
	Froward	– insolently disobedient
	Refractory	– who openly defies command
60.	**Disobey**	– refuse to obey
	Defy	– openly refuse to obey
	Rebel	– refuse to obey by challenging authority of command
	Revolt	– refuse to obey by violent defiance
	Baulk	– (horse) refuse to obey rider's command to go ahead
	Jib	– refuse to obey by showing reluctance to obey
61.	**Disorderly**	– without being in order or arranged manner **Books are kept in the shelf in a disorderly manner*
	Dishevelled	– in disorderly appearance (hairs, dress etc.)
	Untidy	– in scattered manner **Untidy room*
	Unkempt	– (hairs) scattered, without combed
	Ruffled	– (feathers) scattered, unpreened

62. Disperse – (mob) spread away in different directions from a place

Diffuse – (gas, scent etc.) spread away over a large space by passing through air **Foul smell diffused in a short time*

Dissipate – to scatter wastefully in different forms **Youth's energy dissipates in meaningless activities.*

63. Dissatisfied – not satisfied–causing displeasure **I am dissatisfied with his performance*

Unsatisfied – not fully satisfied–wanting more, being inadequate **Unsatisfactory performance*

Discontented – not contented – failing to feel fulfilment in heart, or to quench the desire

Disgruntled – not satisfied – causing resentment

64. Dissociate – break off association with someone

Secede – break off from a group by withdrawing from it **Secede from an organization/alliance *Rebel state seceded from the country and declared independence*

Separate – break off by stopping staying together **Couple separated due to differences *A hall was separated from the adjoining room*

65. Distress – extreme mental/physical suffering due to being in dangerous situation

Dismay – extreme mental suffering due to being disheart- ened **I was dismayed at his behaviour*

Anxiety – mental suffering due to worries

66. Dodge – to evade attack by stepping aside from the line of attack **Dodge a blow/missile*

Duck – to evade attack by sitting, bending down

Parry – to evade verbal attack by making counter attack

Stave off/Ward off – to evade attack by deflecting missile aside

67. Domain – area under rule of a ruler **Law & order comes under the domain of the state government*

Bailiwick – area under the control of a person **Everyone is the master of his house, which is his bailiwick *Regional parties are personal bailiwick of local satrap*

Jurisdiction – area under the legal authority

Ken – area of knowledge of an individual **Science is beyond my ken *His idea is beyond my ken*

Province – area of one's competence, authority *Mathematics is not my province **This decision is beyond my province*

Realm – area under the influence of supreme authority of a sovereign power **Realm of the nature is replete with wonders*

68. Dominance – commanding influence on someone

Hegemony – dominance of a country over another one

Clout – influence due to the power to control others

Influence – the effect of one's states, position, wealth over other

Sway – control over others' opinions

69. Dominate – exercise commanding influence over others

Domineer – exercise command in an overbearing manner arbitrarily

Prevail – dominate by imposing one's will, opinion on others

70. Dormant – lying inactive with possibility to become active anytime **Dormant volcano* **A dormant disease*

Latent – of hidden activity which is not manifested **Talent in a child is latent in early age*

Hibernating – remaining inactive, almost lifeless in winter **Hibernating toad remains burried in mud during winter (said about cold-blooded insects)*

Aestivating – remain inactive during summer

71. Dregs – worthless remanents left at the bottom of a liquid *e.g.,* in a tea cup

Scum – worthless matters which cover upper layer of a liquid

Lees – sediments left at bottom of a barrel containing wine

72. Dress – clothes which are used to wear

Costume – dress appropriate to the role of an actor in a drama

Garment – clothings of several kinds prepared for sale **Garment factory*

Garb – clothing for distinct identity **Garb of a priest*

Habiliment – clothes suitable to a person's work **Habiliment of a crusader*

Regalia – dress with attached decorative medals **He is dressed up in his regalia*

Robe – dress suitable to a profession **Lawyers' robe*

Trousseau – dress of bride to be worn in wedding

Weeds – dress to be worn by mourners/widows

73. Dribble – (saliva) run down from mouth

Drool – (saliva) run down excessively from mouth

Drivel – (saliva) run down from nose, mouth

Salivate – (saliva) fill the mouth in anticipation of tasty food

74. **Drink** – to swallow liquid

Sip – drink slowly in small amount at a time

Guzzle – drink greedily in large amount

Quaff – drink heartily

Gulp – drink with making sound of swallowing

75. **Droop** – to hang down as from weariness

Wilt – (plant leaves) hang down limpily due to loss of moisture

Lop – hang down limpily as of ears of rabbits due to absence of stiffness

76. **Drown** – to go under water and die due to suffocation **A boy drowned in river*

Sink – to go under water and settle on the water bed *Ship sank in the river

77. **Dull** – not stimulating, inspiring interest because of being routine work **Discussion in the meeting was a dull affair*

Dreary – charmless and depressive **Dreary life of a poor person*

Humdrum – dull because monotonous without change **Humdrum daily household chores*

Lackadaisical – dull because of lacking enthusiasm

Lacklustre – lacking vividness, vitality

Monotonous – lacking variety

Pedestrian – lacking quality of work–being quite general, usual **Pedestrial movie*

78. **Dwarf** – abnormally small person than usual

Midget – extremely small person

Pigmy – human race of small stature

Words beginning with —— E ——

1. **Eager** – strongly want to do or have something **He is eager to meet his family*

Agog – strongly eager to know about something **We are agog with the election results*

Curious – very eager to know something unusual or interesting **Curious to know about strange things*

Inquisitive – very eager to know by enquiring about **Inquisitive about*

Keen – very eager to know about something

2. Effect – change brought about by something accomplished *Exposure to the sun has a bad effect on the skin*

Result – final outcome brought about by something accom plished

Consequence– the outcome which happens as a sequence to something accomplished

Implication – result of some action which is inherent in the action **War has a very serious implication for the belligerent countries*

3. Effective – capable of showing its effect as desired or expected **The new law is very effective in curbing lawlessness*

Effectual – capable of achieving desired purpose **Immunization programme proved effectual in eradicating polio*

Efficacious – capable of showing desired results **Efficacious remedy for curing tuberculosis is now available *Efficacious solution is needed to tide over problems assuming dimensions*

4. Effigy – a crudely made figure of a disliked person for ridiculing him, or for showing contempt **An effigy of the chief minister was burnt in public place by the protestors*

Mannequin – a human figure which is erected in a shop to exhibit dresses by putting on this figure

Marionette – a figure of man, woman or animal which is attached to strings in order to manipulate it to move like a living one in an enterainment show

Puppet – a figure of man or animal which is manipulated by someone with his hand inserted into its cavity for an entertainment show

Doll – a figure of pretty girl made for a kid to play with

Toy – a figure of an animal or object made for a kid to play with **A toy dog*

Scarecrow – a terrifying object's figure clothed in tattered dress erected on cultivated land to frighten birds away to protect crops from being eaten by birds

5. Egregious – (Something) extraordinarily (ex = out, gregare = flock) bad or offending which stands it alone out of others of its kind **Egregious behaviour/liar/mistake*

Blatant – (Something) offensively bad which hurts someone seeing or hearing it **Blatant behaviour error/noise/coloured dress*

Flagrant – outrageously bad, which hurts someone who sees it **A flagrant crime*

Wanton – maliciously, unjustifiably bad **Wanton attack/cruelty*

6. Elevate – to take something up in vertical height *Elevate the height of a wall *Elevate rank, standard

Raise – to make something stand erect in vertical position **Raise a pole *Raise one's hand*

Rear – to raise oneself or one's part of body **The horse reared its head*

Hoist – to lift something heavy with the help of machine **Crane hoisted cargo on to a ship*

Heave – to lift something by pushing it Supward from under its bottom **He heaved his chest by drawing air in his lungs *Waves heaved the boat up during storm in the sea*

Boost – to lift the value, morale, etc. of someone **Boost spirit/ sales of products*

Enhance – to raise to a higher degree, intensity etc. **Enhance the beauty, value*

Lift – to take something upward from the ground **He lifted his luggage on to his shoulder*

7. Eject – throw forth something with a force
**Pilot ejected himself from the plane before it crashed*

Ejaculate – throw forth in stream of fluid **Snake ejaculates venom into victim's body*

Spout – throw forth a fluid through a narrow opening of something in a stream of jet of liquid **He swilled his mouth with water and spouted it out of the opening of lips*

Spurt – to throw forth a fluid in a sudden gushing stream

8. Elicit – to draw out information from someone using tact **Elicit a response from someone *Elicit facts from a boy*

Educe – to draw out something latent within someone **Educe talent in a kid *He educed a reply from his memory*

Evoke – to draw out *e.g,* soul of a dead person from grave **Evoke demon lying within someone *Evoke sympathy in someone*

9. Elongate – to draw out something to increase its length **A metal piece was elongated into wire*

Lengthen – grow into length **His body has lengthened with age*

Prolong – to increase the time of, duration of something to longer duration **His stay was prolonged *His illness prolonged*

Protract – to draw out something to increased length (Pro = forward, Tract = stretch) **The bird protracted its wings before starting to fly*

10. Embrace – to draw someone close to one's chest within arms as a sign of affection **He embraced his old friend when they met*

Hug – hold someone tightly in one's arms **A bear hugged his trainer*

11. Emit – to give out light, sound, etc. from within **Fluorescent tube emits bright light*

Emanate – to come out from a source, give out as a source **Flowers emanate fragrance *His face emanates happiness*

Discharge – to send forth liquid or gas from storage **Water was discharged from a dam*

Exude – to send forth smell, confidence etc. by its source **He exudes confidence *Rotten vegetation exudes bad smell*

Transude – to send forth sweat through pores of skin, or moisture through pores of tree leaves **Skin transudes sweat*

Belch – (stomach) send forth ingested air through mouth with a loud sound **He belched loudly after taking food *He belched gas accumulated in his stomach*

Fart – to send forth/expel accumulated gas inside the intestine through the anus.

12. Emphasize – to lay importance to something significant **Emphasize on the importance of ethics in behaviour*

Accentuate – lay stress on a part of syllable of a word while pronouncing

Stress – lay importance on a point of argument, opinion, etc. **Stress upon the need of curbing corruption*

13. Emulate – to copy or try to copy someone's achievements **The son emulated his father in doing social service*

Ape – copy mechanically actions of someone as a monkey does

Imitate – to copy the work of art which exactly resembles original

Replicate – reproduce what has been done by someone else

Mimic – to copy the voice of someone else in order to befool, or to deride him

Mime – to copy the gesture of someone else without speaking as an entertainment

Simulate – to copy by producing similar conditions for study or experiment under the same situation as required **Simulate scenery in studio for the shooting of a film*

14. Encounter – sudden confrontation with hostile persons **Criminals were killed in encounter with police*

Confrontation – face-to-face coming in front of a problem, difficult situation **He successfully handled several confron tations with problems*

Rencontre – suddenly meet old friend face-to-face after a long time

15. Encroach – violate other's territory **The outer wall of his compound has encroached into my land adjoining his land *This law encroaches people's rights*

Infringe – violate law, rules, normal behaviour **His acts infringe upon the rules of etiquette *Infringe a business contract*

Outrage – violate someone's modesty, dignity, causing hurt feelings **Wanton acts of ruffians outraged public*

Transgress – violate by crossing over limits of one's authority, moral codes etc. **The official was accused of transgressing his authority*

Trespass – to enter into someone's house without authority **The dog jumped on the person who txespassed into his master's house*

16. Enshrine – give something a place of sacredness as an idol of worship is given in a shrine **Memory of my friend is enshrined in my heart *Right of freedom of speech is enshrined in our constitution*

Sanctify – give a place of reverence by appropriate religious rituals

Consecrate – give a place of sacredness

17. Ensnare – to catch in a snare, a trap * *The bird was ensnared in a net*

Implicate – to make someone involved in an undesirable situation **Implicate someone in an act of crime*

Entangle – to make someone enmeshed in something **The cow entangled its horns in a bush*

Entwine – to make slender thread-like things twisted together– making them unable to get separated **Locks of her hairs entwined together*

Entrap – to take someone in a trap

18. Enter – get inside something **Enter a house*

Ingress – to walk into a place **Flood water ingressed into the low-lying areas*

Intrude – to enter a place forcibly **Intrude upon others' privacy *Mob intruded into his office*

Invade – to enter others' territory with the intent to cause harm *The enemy forces invaded the neighbouring country *Pathogens invade our body to make us ill

Trespass – enter others' or territory property unlawfully without permission *Trespassing the prohibited area is a crime

Infiltrate – enter into another group, area, territory and get mixed up with people there with the intent to cause harm, violence *The enemy spy infiltrates the sensitive area or protected establishments to collect information

19. Entertain – to extend hospitality with amusements *He entertained his friends with juicy anecdotes

Regale – to extend hospitality with choice food and drink

Treat – to extend hospitality with the intent to make the guests pleased *The visiting dignitaries were given a treat in lavish surroundings of the hill town

20. Enthusiasm – absorbing interest in some pursuit *He evinced great enthusiasm for his studies

Ardour – burning enthusiasm *Ardour of patriotism

Fervour – great warmth and earnestness in enthusiasm or other feelings *Fervour of a religious devout in performing rites

Zeal – enthusiasm for a lofty objective *Zeal of a missionary

Passion – uncontrollable enthusiasm *Passion for reading books

21. Entice – to mislead someone by promising exciting offer *He was enticed by the lure of big city life *Discount offered on sales is a ploy to entice customers

Beguile – to mislead by employing tricks *Multitude of attractions beguiles the tourists *A ghost beguiles its prey to a lonely place by mimicking his friend's voice

Inveigle – to mislead by persuasion or flattery *He inveigled me into giving loan to him

Seduce – to mislead into committing itticit activity, or away from right path.*Seduce to indulge in corruption

Suborn – to mislead someone by inducement to commit perjury

22. Ephemeral – lasting for just one day, *i.e.*, for a very short time *Ephemeral joy of childhood *Ephemeral flowers

Evanescent – lasting for short duration before vanishing *Evanescent apparition of ghosts

Fleeting – (time) passing off quickly *Fleeting moments of holidays

Transitory	–	(mood, anger, etc.) lasting for a shortwhile **Transitory anger turned into compassion*
Transient	–	(guest) staying for a brief period **Transient hotel guests*
23. Epithet	–	a name given by people which is attributed to his habit, quality in a well known personality **He is famous by the epithet of Mr. Joker*
Appellation	–	a name given to someone by people which is based on his appealing manners/work **Gandhiji earned appellation of Mahatma*
Sobriquet	–	a name given to someone by people on the basis of his achievements **Bose was known as the sobriquet of Netaji*
Nickname	–	a name by which someone is lovingly called
24. Equality	–	state of being equal in magnitude rank with others **Gender equality*
Equivalence	–	state of being equal in value with something else **Equivalence in various currencies*
Parity	–	state of being equal in status **Parity in post, power, or pay with those in other services*
Resemblance	–	state of being equal in appearance
Analogy	–	state of being equal in comparison with something else **Analogy between heart and pump*
Commensuration	–	state of being equal in measure
25. Eradicate	–	root out (radi = root) something that has taken root **Eradicate malaria/superstitions*
Exterminate	–	(ex = out, terminate = end) end, finish something by killing **Exterminate mosquitoes by fumigation*
Extirpate	–	finish something by depriving its source of sustenance to exist **Deforestation extirpates wild species of flora and fauna*
26. Erect	–	become straight and rigid in shape **Dog's ears become erect when it is alerted*
Upright	–	become erect in vertical direction **He is sitting upright*
Bristled	–	(hairs) become erect as in fear, excitement **His hairs bristled with excitement* **Bristled hairs of pigs are used for making brush*
27. Essential	–	what is required as the very essence of something **Breathing is essential for living* **Discipline is essential for the armed forces*

Necessary – what is required to meet the needs of something *Attending meeting is necessary *A new law is necessary to check terrorism*

Compulsory – what is required as compulsion **Compulsory qualification for a job*

Indispensable – what is required as one cannot do without it **His services are indispensable to his organization *Courage is indispensable to face challenges*

Reqisite – what is required to meet a given situation good physique is a requisite to join the army

28. Ethics – standards of priciples adopted in one's profession **He observes the highest norms of ethics*

Morals – standards of principles adopted in one's character **A man of loose morals*

Morality – standards of principles adopted by someone in his or her social conduct **His conduct is against social morality*

29. Examine – to test knowledge, facts by question

Check – to verify facts

Investigate – to verify the facts, cause of an occurrence **Investigate a crime*

Inspect – to look into something to check carefully

Audit – inspect accounts

Scrutinize – to check details of a problem through close observations

Vet – to scrutinize a document, manuscript, proposal, etc. for its quality, usefulness

30. Example – which serves as a lesson to others **Severe punishment serves as an example to prospective offenders*

Instance – which serves as an example to show the character or intention of someone **Tough punishment awarded by the courts is an instance of judiciary's intolerance to crimes*

Paradigm – which serves as an example of a pattern in some thing **Changing allegiance for personal gains is contemporary paradigm in politics*

Precedent – (rules, judgements) which serves as an example in similar cases to follow suit **Earlier judgements serve as precedents for judging subsequent cases of similar nature*

31. Exclusive – excluding others **Exclusive school for the rich people*

Exquisite – excluding others in a group of similar things **Exquisite beauty/art*

Exotic – excluding locals – belonging to foreign origin *Exotic dress/design*

32. Exhausted – drained of energy due to excessive work **Heavy work exhausted him* **Exhausted due to excessive work in office*

Fatigued – tired due to long duration of working hard **Fatigued of long drive*

Haggard – having an exhausted appearance as with prolonged tiredness, anxiety etc. **A haggard face/eyes*

Languid – drained of vigour due to fatigue, weakness **Languid gait*

Weary – tired excessively of hard work

33. Explain – to describe in detail

Expatiate – explain at length **Expatiate on one's theme/idea*

Elucidate – to explain so as to make lucid (clear), especially with illustrations

Expound – explain something in a learned manner **Expound the secrets of the universe*

34. Exquisite – impressive in quality **Exquisite art*

Elegant – impressive in grandeur **Elegant mansion/decolouration*

Dainty – impressive in taste, beauty **Dainty woman*

35. Extempore – (do something) on the spur of moment **Reply to questions extempore*

Extemporaneous – (do something) without preparing oneself **Extemporaneous lecture*

Impromptu – (do something) promptly **He made an impromptu speech in response to the audience's request*

Instantly – (do something) at once **Give relief instantly*

36. Extenuate – to make seriousness of a crime, fault less serious/light **Extenuate seriousness of his crime*

Mitigate – to make seriousness of something light **Mitigate punishment*

Palliate – to make seriousness light by concealing facts of crime

Gloze/Gloss (over) – make light of a seriousness by extending excuses

37. Extinguish – put out fire

Douse – put out fire by throwing water on it

Quench – put out thirst

Quell – put out rebellion

Quail – put out enthusiasm, courage, spirit **Failures quailed his enthusiasm*

Snuff – put out light **He snuffed out the candle's flame*

38. Extraordinary – unusually extra or good **Extraordinary power/ talent*

Phenomenal – remarkably outstanding **Phenomenal performance*

Prodigious – outstanding in size, degree, extent **A prodigious worker*

Outstanding – exceptional, making something different from others, above others **Outstanding performance*

39. Extravagant – spending much more unnecessarily

Spendthrift – wastefully extravagant

Prodigal – recklessly extravagant

Wastred – a person who spends wastefully

Words beginning with — F —

1. Face – a person's frontal part of head

Muzzle – an animal's projected part of head consisting of jaws, nose, eyes, etc., *e.g.*, of a cow, horse

Countenance – a person's face with a specified emotional expression on it **A sad countenance of a person*

Facade – frontal part of a building **Castle's magnificent facade*

Mien – face indicative of a specified demeanour **Mien of an aristocrat*

Physiognomy – face with specified features indicative of person's race **A man of mongoloid physiognomy*

Visage – a person's face with reference to specified shape **He has a round visage/wide visage*

Facet – one of several faces of a polygonal shape

2. Facetious – (remark) lacking serious intent **Facetious remark*

Flippant – (remark) lacking in gravity of attitude **Flippant remark about patriotism*

Frivolous – lacking in seriousness of purpose, worth or importance **Frivolous conduct/suggestion. His case has been rejected by the court as frivolous.*

Triffling – (manners) playfully non-serious **Triffling manner of dealing with a serious matter*

3. Failure – not succeeding in doing something

Futility – not succeeding in producing useful outcome

Debacle – not succeeding in attempt due to sudden collapse **Our team suffered a debacle in the tournament*

Miscarriage – not succeeding in delivering as expected **Punishment to an innocent is a serious miscarriage of justice system*

4. **Fake** – (something made) which is not genuine, and is prepared for fraudulent purpose **A fake report/signature*

Counterfeit – (something) imitated to look alike genuine one for fraudulent purpose **Counterfeit currency*

Ersatz – (something) which is made or imitated to serve as a substitute for the real one **Ersatz ornaments*

Sham – (something) which is not as it is purported to be **A sham sympathy/illness*

Spurious – (something) which is not genuine **Spurious automobile bearings have been seized by the authorities*

5. **Falter** – become unsteady in speaking or doing something due to losing control **He faltered in speech* **The old man faltered on the stairs*

Flounder – become unsteady in walking as when passing through sticky mud or pool of water **He floundered while crossing a muddy field*

Fumble – become unsteady in using one's hands so as to catch a ball **The fielder fumbled and dropped the ball*

Stagger – become usteady in walking as if about to fall due to weak ness or stumbling on a rough surface **He staggered when someone pushed him from behind*

6. **Famous** – widely known for good virtues or possessions **This town is famous for its forts* **He is famous for his bravery*

Renowned – widely known by one's name **He is a renowned person in this town*

Popular – widely admired by people **He is a popular leader*

Reputed – widely respected for having good reputation as a person **A reputed person in the society*

Eminent – widely known for superiority in a particular field **An eminent scientist*

7. **Fanciful** – beyond practicality **Fanciful ideas*

Fantastic – extravagantly fanciful **Fantastic story/idea*

Chimerical – absurdly impractical **Chimerical idea*

Quixotic – beyond realisation, too ideal to be realised **Quixotic ideas*

8. Fare – money chargeable for travelling by public transport **Train fare*

Freight – money chargeable for transporting goods by public transport **Goods' transportation freight*

Rent – money chargeable from tenant for house given to him to live in/from users of machinery, materials by the owner

Tariff – listed amount of money payable for various types of hotel rooms

Charge – money payable for hiring services **Charge of hiring a taxi* **Charge of a hired carpenter*

Fee – money payable by school, doctor, lawyer for rendering services to the beneficiaries

9. Fastidious – (someone) very critical of imperfection in work, cleanliness, taste etc.

Fussy – critical of minor details about work

Finnicky – excessively fastidious

Supercilious – habitually critical of others by raising one's eyebrows while frowning

10. Fatal – causing death **Fatal accident*

Lethal – liable to cause death **Lethal dose of poison* **Lethal weapons*

Deadly – liable to kill **Deadly disease*

11. Fear – nervous feeling of threat, danger

Awe – nervous feeling of fear from the greatness of a person **Awe of God/learned person*

Dread – intense feeling of fear by anticipating danger **Dread of death shook him*

Fright – intense feeling of sudden fear **Fright of encountering a ferrocious dog*

Horror – intense feeling of fear caused by a shocking, gruesome sight **Horror of seeing a corpse*

12. Fertile – (land) producing abundantly

Fecund – (woman) producing offsprings abundantly

Prolific – (writer, free) abundantly producing books/fruits

13. Fight – engaged in physical asaults or angry arguments **They fought over a point of discussion*

Scuffle – engaged in pushing and jostling

Fisticuff – engaged in trading blows with fist

	Financial	– money matters of a company institution **Financial management of a company is in shambles*
	Fiscal	– of government treasury **Fiscal dficit*
	Pecunary	– money matters of a person **Pecuniary condition of a person*
14.	**Fit**	– violent, uncontrollable bout of anger, epilepsy **He flew in a fit of anger.*
	Attack	– violent fit of pain, melancholy etc. **Attack of pain in the stomach.*
	Paroxysm	– uncontrolled bout of coughing, laughing etc. **He turned blue due to prolonged paroxysm of coughing*
	Convulsion	– uncontrolled bout of involuntary spasm in body
15.	**Flag**	– a piece of cloth which is the symbol of a country **Flag of India is a tricolour*
	Colours	– a flag which is the identity of a regiment **Regimental colours*
	Standard	– flag representing a sovereign power **Presidential standard*
	Pennant	– long, tapered triangular-shaped flag
	Banner	– flag with slogans written on it, which is carried by the demonstrators
16.	**Flatter**	– to please someone by showering praises on him **Sycophants flatter someone for personal gains*
	Fawn	– to please someone with servile demeanours towards him **Courtiers fawn on the king* **His dog fawns on his master's feet in a display of affection*
17.	**Flexuous**	– bending in alternating turns **Flexuous river*
	Meandering	– bending in irregular turns **Meandering water stream*
	Sinuous	– bending in frequent turns at short distances
	Tortuous	– bending several times in large number of turns
	Winding	– bending in turns like a coil **Winding mountain roads*
18.	**Flinch**	– to shake one's body/to shake off what give uncomfortable feelings **Flinch at gory right*
	Wince	– to shake one's body due to being in pain or disgust **His body winced in pain*
	Blench	– to shiver at the fearful thought **Blenched at the very thought of death*
	Quail	– shiver/shake one's body under the threat of someone as a mark of losing courage to face him **Students quail in front of the headmaster*

19. Follower – a person who is loyal to and always follows someone *Followers of a political leader*

Cohort – a group of followers **She has a cohort of admirers*

Henchman – a trusted follower of a gangster who is eveready to commit crime at his (gangster's) bidding

20. Folly – foolish weakness in character **To act before giving a thought is his folly*

Foible – pleasant weakness in habit **Speaking innocent truth is kids's foible*

Fraility – weakness in character **Yielding to temptation is our major fraility*

21. Forbid – warn someone not to be something **Workers were forbidden to leave workplace*

Inhibit – to forbid by one's inner conscience or sense of propriety **Fear of contracting cancer inhibits him from smoking*

Prohibit – to forbid by authority *Smoking in public places is prohibited

Proscribe – to announce a warning against doing something **Doctor prescribed his patient not to take fatty foods*

22. Foresight – ability to judge things to happen in distant future

Clairvoyance – ability to see or perceive events in a distant place which is beyond the range of normal vision

Vision – ability to think or plan with imagination or wisdom about future course of action **Vision of an entrepreneur*

23. Foretell – to announce something to happening in future

Forecast – to announce weather conditions obtaining in future **Forecast rains/storm*

Augur – to foretell outcome of an omen **Sighting an owl is supposed to augur well*

Portend – foretell something bad to happen in future **Portend a disaster*

Predict – foretell future events **Predict a war to take place*

Prophesy – foretell supernatural events happening in future which requires knowledge of an oracle/saint **Prophesy doom of this world*

Prognosticate – (doctors) foretell about the onset of a disease in near future on the basis of symptoms in a patient

24. Foster – to bring up a child who is deprived of parents **Foster a child who lost his parents*

Cherish – to take loving care of a child **Cherish one's child*

Nurture – to take care of a growing child by providing nourishment, encouragement to promote his growth and development **Nurture poor children*

Rear – to take care of a growing animal until attaining maturity for meat, milk, fur etc. **Rear farm animals for meat*

25. **Free** – having the ability to do what one likes to **He is free to go wherever he wants to*

Independent – being free from others' command to manage own affairs, free from other's control **Autonomous organization is free from govt. control*

Autarky – freedom from economic dependence

Sovereign – having supreme authority in one's own domain **Parliament is sovereign in democracy*

26. **Friend** – a person with good comradeship

Chum – a close childhood friend

Crony – an intimate friend

Alterego – a close friend who is one soul, two bodies

27. **Frighten** – to fill someone with fright **Encounter with a snake frightened him*

Terrify – to fill someone with terror

Threaten – to warn of consequences

Horrify – to fill someone with horror **Ghastly scene of the accident horrified him*

Scare – to fill someone with nervousness due to fear

Panic – to fill someone with nervous agitation due to fear **Bomb scare panicked people, who began to flee from the place*

Intimidate – to fill someone with fear by threatening to make him timid (coward)

Rattle – to fill someone with worries due to fear **A bad news rattled him*

Words beginning with —— G ——

1. **Garbage** – unwanted disposable matters from kitchen and household

Rubbish – unwanted disposable matters thrown as useless

Litter – scattered rubbish **His room was filled with waste-paper litter*

Trash – unusable portion of something after the removal of its usable portion **Sugarcane trash after extraction of juice*

Refuse – something discarded as worthless **Refuse of vegetables*

Sullage – mud, silt, sediments collected in sewage

2. Gaze – to look at something fixedly for long **Gaze the stars in the night sky*

Glance – to look for a brief period to catch a glimpse of **He glanced at a girl furtively*

Glare – to look in anger with wide eyes

Peer – to look with partly-closed eyes **He peered at me in an attempt to recognize me*

Stare – to look with wide-open eyes

Gape – to stare with one's mouth open in disbelief, wonder

3. Genocide – deliberate masskilling of people of a particular race

Carnage – mass-killing of people in a battle

Butchery – mass-killing of people or animals with wanton brutality

Massacre – mass-killing of people indiscriminately in revenge

Pogrom – planned massacre

4. Get – to possess **Get hold of*

Obtain – get by putting in efforts

Acquire – get by putting in prolonged efforts

Procure – get by caring to search

5. Get rid of – be relieved of someone/something unwanted **Get rid of his presence with me*

Dispense with – make oneself relieved of compulsion of having to do with something undesirable **Facility of an A.T.M. has enabled us to dispense with carrying cash*

Dispose of – be relieved of liability of, or unwanted possession **He disposed of his old house*

6. Gorge – overfeed oneself to the extent of chocking **He gorged himself with chocolates*

Satiate/Sate – overfeed oneself to one's satisfaction and desiring no more

Surfeit – overfeed oneself until felt nausea or aversion to taking anymore **He surfeited himself with sweets*

7. Gradation – gradual/graded difference in quality

Shade	– graded & delicate/minute difference in colours, opinions etc. **There is a shade difference in meanings of synonyms *It is a shade better than others*
Nuance	– very delicate/minute subtle difference in colours, meanings etc. **Nuance of expressions changed on his face*
8. Grind	– to break into powdery mass
Comminute	– to break into minute particles
Levigate	– to grind in a mortar
Pulverise	– to grind to fine powdery mass
Triturate	– to grind to powdery mass by crushing or thresshing
9. Growl	– (animal's) produce deep guttural sound of expressing anger **The dog growled at the intruder in the house*
Snarl	– (dog's) produce loud threatening sound aggre- ssively with exposed teeth, as if it would jump on the victim **Dog snarled viciously*
Purr	– to produce low continuous sound as a cat does
Grumble	– (person's) produce low sound of voice of expressing discontent
10. Guess	– to conclude on basis of incomplete knowledge
Conjecture	– to conclude on basis of insufficient information
Surmise	– to conclude without any information/knowledge
Speculate	– to make wild guess at the risk of being wrong
11. Guide	– who leads tourists around a place/who shows the right path to others
Pioneer	– who explores path for others to move ahead in a field of knowledge. **A pioneer in cancer research*
Trailblazer	– who shows path to others in a new field of knowledge **A trailblazer scientist*
Usher	– who shows people their seats in a hall to sit on by escorting them to that place

Words beginning with — H —

1. Harass	– annoy someone by constant provocation
Bother	– to annoy by constantly disturbing
Badger	– to annoy, harass persistently by ragging
Harry	– to harass by attacking repeatedly **To harry the enemy forces by repeated incursions*

Persecute – to harass by hostile activity

Tantalise – to harass by not allowing someone to get something present within reach

Torment – harass by teasing **Reporters tormented him with uncomfortable questions*

2. **Hasty** – (action) done in a haste – without consideration **Hasty action/decision*

Impatient – (person) lacking patience due to eagerness for something **He is impatient to hear the news*

Impetuous – (person, action) done quickly and rashly **Impetuous decision/person*

Rash – without waiting for thinking about **Rash action*

Impulsive – (action, person) involving emotional action taken in involuntary impulse **Impulsive action*

3. **Healthful** – which promotes health **Healthful diet*

Hygienic – which promotes health through cleanliness **Hygienic surroundings/habits*

Sanitary – which promotes health through preventing infections **Sanitary precautions*

Salubrious – which promotes health through healthy climate **Salubrious climate*

Wholesome – which promotes health by giving helpful effects on health **Wholesome food* **Wholesome exercises*

Salutary – which promotes moral health **Salutary advice* **Salutary punishment reforms an erring behaviour*

4. **Herd** – a group of animals moving together

Flock – a group of birds moving together

Drove – a group of animals being driven together

Gaggle – a group of geese

Bevy – a group of young girls/women

Clutch – a group of young chicks

Brood – a group of newly hatched fowls

Hirsel – a group of sheep/lambs

Litter – a group of newly born mammals

Rabble – a group of rats/insects

Rout – a group of revellers

Shoal – a group of fishes moving together

Swarm – a group of bees

5. **Hesitate** – be reluctant to do something due to indecisive mind

Balk/Baulk– ....due to facing difficulties/obstacle **He balked at making a speech*

Demur – ....due to having doubt/objection **Students demurred at accepting new syllabus*

Dither – ....due to fear of consequences

Jib – ....due to unwillingness

Qualm – ....due to anxiety of doing wrong or feeling guilty **He has no qualm about lying*

Scruple – ....due to feeling uneasy about being unethical on moral grounds

6. **Hide** – to keep off others, sight, knowledge **He is hiding himself behind a bush*

Conceal – to keep off from others' knowledge **Conceal truth*

Cache' – to keep something secured in a hidden place **The thief cache'd booty in a lonely place*

Camouflage– to hide something by covering with paints or materials matching with the surroundings **Tanks were camouflaged with tree twigs*

Disguise – to conceal identity by altering appearance **The king disguised himself as peasant to walk on the streets*

Dissemble – to concel one's emotions/true intentions by behaving otherwise/feigning differently **He dissembled innocence*

Ensconce – to hide something in safe, comfortable place **He ensconced himself in a closet *He ensconced himself in the armchair*

Mask – hide one's face by covering with a mask

Secrete – hide in a safe place **Rats secreted grains in burrow*

Veneer – to cover/hide an ugly or coarse surface by furniture by covering it with attractive surface **Veneer furniture's exposed surfaces with sunmica sheets*

7. **Hint** – indirect indication **I got a hint of his involvement in crime*

Allusion – (verb is Allude) indirect reference. **Facts allusion to his involvement made him a suspect*

Innuendo – indirect disparaging reference **His speech carried innuendo against me*

Clue – indirect hint to solve a problem, mystery

Cue – hint from behind someone to do something needed **He gave a cue to his accomplice to flee*

Insinuation– indirect insulting remark **Flattery turned into insinuation when his objective of gaining was not realised from his boss*

8. Hold – to restrain from moving away by capturing **He held my hands in his arm*

Captivate – to hold attention of someone with charm **Her beauty captivated who saw her*

Enthrall – to hold someone as a slave **Women in households are enthralled by husbands*

Fascinate – to hold someone in spellbinding attention **His speech fascinated audience*

Engross – to hold attention by a work someone is doing **The task engrossed him for hours*

9. Holy – what is revered by devotees **Holy river/saint*

Divine – what is related to God

Sacred – dedicated to religious purpose, revered **Sacred monument*

Sacrosanct – inviolably sacred

10. Horrible – (act, scene) engendering horror in others **Horrible accident*

Ghastly – which shocks others **A ghastly murder*

Gruesome – making someone shudder with fear

Grisly – engendering with extreme horror **Grisly monster*

Macabre – horrible because of being associated with death, ghost etc. **Macabre rituals*

11. Hurl – to throw upward in air

Lob – throw in an arc or projectile in air **Lob a ball to someone in front to catch it*

Pelt – throw forward in air to aim at the target **Mob pelted stones on the policemen*

Toss – throw upward in air in casual manner **Toss a coin*

Words beginning with ——— I ———

1. Idea – a mental impression formed about something **His idea about me is not good*

Notion – vague idea **He harbours a strange notion about life in America*

Concept – mental picture made about a subject, plan **He has a clear concept about the marketing strategy to boost sales*

Perception – idea formed in one's mind on the basis of under standing about something *Police is not people friendly in the perception of general public

2. Ignoramus – an ignorant person

Agnostic – a person who does not claim to have knowledge of God or other mystery in absence of experience

Cad – a person who is ignorant of social etiquette, or knowledge of a trade

Liaty – people who are ignorant of a subject as opposed to professional practising in that field of subject **Professional jargon is beyond the ken of laity*

3. **Ignore** – deliberately avoid to pay attention **He ignored me when we met in the meeting*

Disregard – ignore due to being unimportant **His suggestions were disregarded by others*

Neglect – deliberately avoid to pay attention due to being indifferent to it **He neglected his studies/duty/ appearance*

4. **Impassive** – not reacting to stimulus, emotions

Phlegmatic – hard to be aroused, not showing emotions **Phlegmatic person*

Stoic – indifferent to pain or pleasure, cool to joy or grief both

Stolid – of blank / expressionless countenance showing no emotional expression

5. **Impertinent** – offensive to someone's privacy **Ask impertinent questions*

Intrusive – thrusting oneself into others' affairs unsolicited **Intrusive person*

Obtrusive – thrusting into others' affairs, which is unwelcome

Meddlesome – thrusting into others' affairs which becomes interference to them

Officious – offering one's good offices to others without being asked for **Officious advice. Meddlesome *Officious neighbour becomes a nuisance*

6. **Impinge** – to give sharp pressure on something **His shoes impinge on his toes*

Prick – to give sharp pressure by a pointed object so as to enter into it painfully

Prickle – to give sharp tingling sensation **Skin eruptions in summer prickle*

7. **Impious** – not showing reverence to God

Profane – given to show irreverence in acts for sacred one **Profane acts*

Sacrilegious – given to violate sacredness, holiness **Sacrilegious person* **Sacrilegious conduct*

Blasphemous – (speech) not showing reverence to God, religion **Blasphemous speech*

8. Imprison – to keep someone confined in prison

Incarcerate – to keep someone confined in a room or restricted space **They incarcerated themselves to confer*

Immure – to keep confined in a walled area **She immured herself in the house to nurse her ailing father*

Intern – to keep confined within a specified area **War prisoners were interned in a field enclosed with barbed wires*

Impound – to keep confined in an enclosure as stray animals or vehicles are kept

9. Inclination – mental tendency to do something **Inclination for acting*

Attitude – mental bent **Helping attitude*

Disposition – inherent inclination **Disposition to pick up quarrel*

Pre-disposition– made prepared to be inclined to **Pre-disposition to love for country was infused in him in his childhood*

Predilection – mental state of preferring **He has a strong predilection for sports*

Propensity – natural inclination **Propensity for earning money*

Proclivity – habitual inelination

Penchant – strong liking for

Bias – frame of mind favouring someone/something

Tendency – prevailing inclination

10. Inculcate – to fill someone with good habits, values in life by repeated instructions **Inculcate patriotism in children/ respect for elders*

Indoctrinate – fill someone with the lessons, principles, ideology of a religion, group by preaching **Indoctrinate devotees in religious lessons*

Infuse (*in*) – fill someone with values by pouring these values in their mind **The team was infused in enthusiasm by the coach* **Infuse loyalty in the followers*

Imbue (*with*) – fill someone with good values by soaking them with these values **Imbue the disciples with spartan living*

Instil – to fill someone with values by slowly pouring **Instil good habits in children*

Insinuate – to fill into the mind of someone with some idea, suggestions etc. using skill, by suftle means **Propaganda insinuates doubt in people's mind*

11. **Indecent** – in bad taste (behaviour) **Indecent behaviour*

Risque – (behaviour) very close to being indecent **Risque behaviour*

Ribald – (speech) indecent in language **Ribald speech*

Scurrilous – indencent, abusive **Scurrilous remark*

Vulgar – indecently coarse devoid of sophistication **Vulgar scene in pictures*

12. **Indemnify** – to make up for any loss caused by one's action, to ensure to guard against anticipated loss

Compensate – to pay back for loss, injury, or suffering **Insurance cover is taken because it compensates for any damage to the insured*

Recompense – to pay back for a service rendered, trouble taken etc. **He was adequately recompensed for the trouble he took to help someone*

Reimburse – to pay back the expenses incurred by someone, refund

Reparation (*n*)– compensation paid by a defeated country to the victor for the cost of war. Germany paid reparation to the U.S.A. after the second world war.

Repay – to pay back loan

Pay damages – pay back money to compensate for causing injury of loss to someone

13. **Indiscriminate** – without caring to select/choose **Kill people indiscriminately* **Indiscriminate firing*

Haphazard – without caring to arrange in order**Haphazard arrangement of books on self*

Random – without taking care of aim, direction **They threw balls randomly*

14. **Infamy** – loss of reputation, disrepute **Outrageous conduct caused his infamy*

Ignominy – contemptuous disrepute

Odium – heteful disrepute

Opprobrium – severe disrepute earned by shameful conduct

Stigma – blot on reputation

Obloquy – disrepute resulting from public blame, deunciation

15. Infer – arrive at a conclusion/opinion on the basis of reasoning **His absence from the meeting was inferred as his displeasure*

Interpret – arrive at an opinion on the basis of explanation **Interpret hidden meaning of an omen*

Conclude – arrive at an opinion by judging/on the basis of judgement **He concluded that I was innocent*

Construe – arrive at an opinion on the basis of explanation in a specified way/particular context **His abstention from voting was construed to be diefiance of party whip*

Deduce – arrive at an opinion/conclusion on the basis of assumption **The detective deduced from the evidence that the servant was involved in crime*

16. Influence – effect on others' cast by someone's character or bahaviour **He has great influence on people*

Clout – effect on others of someone's authority

Impression– effect on others of image, behaviour of someone **His gentle conduct cast good impression on others*

17. Inform – to let someone know about something **He was informed of the arrival of his friend*

Advice of to let someone know about the situation which is prevailing **Investors were advised of the risk involved*

Acquaint – to let someone know about situation to get familiar or conversant with it **To acquaint someone with the plan*

Apprise of– to let someone know about something by making him understand about it **He was apprised of worker's performance*

18. Inherent – (a quality) be present in someone inseparably **Arrogance is inherent in him*

Immanent – be present within someone **Gold is immanent in everyone*

Intrinsic – be present with someone associated by its very nature **Heat is intrinsic with the sun *Antique has intrinsic value*

19. Injurious – likely to cause injury

Deleterious – likely to cause harm, harmful in effect **Deleterious to public health*

Detrimental – likely to cause harm to one's interest **Detrimental to our health*

Disastrous – likely to cause great damage, loss **Disastrous war*

	Inimical	– likely to cause harm as an enemy causes
	Insidious	– likely to cause harm in subtle manner
	Noxious	– likely to cause harm as a poison does **Noxious fumes*
	Pernicious	– likely to cause harm by ruining as death destroys
20.	**Inkling**	– vague feeling or hint about something to happen **I had an inkling of what was going to happen*
	Intuition	– instinctive feeling of something to happen
	Apprehension	– ominous feeling of something to happen
	Anticipation	– prior feeling of something to happen **Anticipation of a favourable decision*
	Foreboding	– fearful apprehension
	Hunch	– feeling of suspicion about what will happen
	Premonition	– uncanny feeling of what will happen **To have a premonition of imminent danger*
	Presentiment	– impression of something evil to happen
	Prescience	– feeling of knowing beforehand about what is to happen
21.	**Innovate**	– make changes in the existing form of something to give it a new look, to improve **Innovate the bureaucratic system*
	Renovate	– (building) to give it a new look again by repairing **Renovate the old house*
	Retrofit	– (machine) to give a new look by fitting it with extra facilities to match its latest version **Retrofit the old model car with the latest gadgets*
	Revamp	– to give something a new look by total overhauling. **Revamp a project*
22.	**Insert**	– push something inside a gap, hole
	Insinuate	– push something *viz.,* roots by plants, indirect remark against someone cleverly through the gap **Tree insinuates its roots through crevices in rocks *He insinuated himself through the crowd to reach in frontline*
	Penetrate	– push inside by thrusting forcefully **The enemy troops penetrated into the border*
	Pierce	– push a pointed object into something by tearing into it **A needle pierced his finger*

23. Instigate – (external provocation) arouse someone to commit. wrong, undesirable act **Instigate the mob to defy the orders*

Incite – (self-emotion) arouse someone to commit crime, unlawful act **Anger and discontent incite people to indulge in violence*

Foment – to arouse people to create trouble, problem. **Foment the law and order problem.*

24. Instruction – advice, direction given to be obeyed

Directive – official instruction

Injunction – authoritative instruction

Prescription – doctor's instruction given to a patient

25. Insult – loss of respect

Affront – insult as if slapped in the face

Dishonour – loss or violation of dignity

Offense – insult causing hurt feelings

Umbrage – insult causing shadow on reputation

Disgrace – insult lowering reputation

Derogate – insult by belittling someone

Disparage – insult by contempting as being lower in rank

26. Insulting – causing insult

Derogatory – causing insult by trying to belittle someone **Derogatory remark*

Disparaging – causing contempt as if one is lower in rank **Disparaging behaviour*

27. Interject – to insert statement/start speaking in the middle of someone speaking **An audience interjected a question to the speaker*

Intercede – to insert oneself in a dispute on behalf of one party to use one's good offices to settle dispute **He interceded on behalf of his friend and apologised for his mistakes*

Interpose – to insert something in between two other things **Interpose an opaque surface between light source and eyes of someone to obstruct vision *Interpose between two quarreling persons to disengage them*

Intervene – to come between two others forcibly. **Intervene into others' affairs.*

28. Invincible – who cannot be defeated **Invincible enemy*

Unconquerable – that which can't be conquerred **Unconquerable problems*

Indomitable – which cannot be tamed, subdued **Indomitable courage, zeal*

Insurmountable – which cannot be mounted upon **Insurmountable summit*

29. Involved – be engaged in useful activity **To get involved in local politics*

Indulged – be engaged in something to gratify one's desire **He is indulged in activities related to music and art*

Complicit – be engaged in unlawful activities **He is complicit in criminal activities*

Engrossed – be engaged with absorbing attention **Engrossed in listening music*

Embroiled – be engaged in conflict, contentious situation **Embroiled in court cases*

30. Irritable – readily get excited, angered, annoyed **Irritable person*

Cantankerous – readily irritated and start quarrelling **Cantankerous old maid/person*

Choleric – readily get angered **A man of choleric disposition*

Fractious – easily irritated uncontrollably **Fractious person*

Irascible – easily provoked to anger

Fretful – get easily irritated and start gnashing teeth in anger

Peevish – get irritated in discontent **Get peevish on being left out*

Petulant – get irritated and sulking like a child **Petulant nature of a person*

Snappish – get irritated and start speaking or replying in acerbic tongue

Testy – irritable to acute degree

Waspish – get irritated quickly

31. Irritation – feeling of annoyance

Dudgeon – feeling of deep resentment

Huff – a fit of resentment **He left the meeting in a huff when he was not allowed to speak*

Pique – feeling of resentment due to hurt ego, pride **He was piqued at his remark.*

Resentment – feeling of displeasure **Unjust remark caused resentment in him*

1. **Journey** – act of travelling from one place to another **A journey by train*

Cruise – travelling by a ship on sea for pleasing without any destination **Patrol ships cruised along the sea shores*

Excursion – travelling a short distance for pleasure **They went on excursion to forts and musea on city outskirts.*

Expedition – travelling undertaken for a particular purpose **Scientists went on an expedition to the north pole to study environment of that area*

Jaunt – travelling to a place for pleasure **The family went on a foreign jaunt*

Junket – travelling for pleasure at others' expenses/government expenses **Offiials often make a junket to foreign lands*

Pilgrimage – travelling to religious places **He has gone on pilgrimage to Tirupati*

Tour – travelling for official work/to discharge duty

Trip – travelling to a given place **Trip to Delhi*

Voyage – travelling through ship or spacecraft in sea or space for a long distance **Astronauts went on a vayage to Mars in a spacecraft*

2. **Justify** – to show that action is right/just **He justified his decision*

Rationalise – to show that an action is right by specious reasonings put forward **Rationalise one's action to convince others*

Vindicate – to show that an action was right by subsequent evidence/facts **Subsequent events vindicated his prophesy*

3. **Jut out** – extend out from a straight line **Window panes jut out of the wall*

Project – extend outward **A part of beam projected out of the wall*

Protrude – extend out into something else from its place **His swollen eyes protruded *An iron rod protruded through the sand layer*

Protruberate – extend out from the surface of the body **His nose protruberates on the face *A tumour protruberates on his forehead*

Stick out – to extend out by thrusting something **Do not stick your head out of the train's window*

Words beginning with — K —

1. **Kill** – to take life of a person by violent means **Kill someone with weapon/by strangulation*

   Assassinate – to kill an important person **A leader of a prominent party was assassinated*

   Murder – to kill a person by hatching a plot **Murder the enemy by ambushing him*

   Cull – to slaughter birds/chicken selectively

   Slaughter – to kill an animal for meat

   Decimate – to murder one-tenth of people of a race/group

2. **Kind** – (a person) who is considerate and generous to others **He was a kind person*

   Beneficient – who does help and good to others

   Benevolent – who wishes well of others

   Benign – who is not harmful, who does no harm to others

   Humane – who is compassionate in dealing with others

   Magnanimous – who is having a large heart towards others

3. **Kneel** – to bend one's body and rest it on bent knees **Kneel down in punishment *He kneeled down to pick up something lying on the ground*

   Knowtow – to bend on the knees before someone in supplication and put forehead on the ground

   Cower – to bend on the knees in a abject fear/terror before someone

   Genuflect – to bend one's knees as in prayer

Words beginning with — L —

1. **Lament** – to express sorrow **To lament over one's bad luck*

   Bemoan – to wail in grief

   Grieve – to suffer grief, sorrow and endure it alone in silence **Grieve bereavement of one's dear one*

   Mourn – to express grief **Mourn the death of a leader and wear black on the occasion of condolence meeting*

   Condole – to express sympathy with one who is grieving **Condole with a friend over his father's death*

2. **Lamentation** – expression of grief over death of someone

   Condolence – expression of sympathy with someone who has suffered grief of death of his dear one

Dirge – expression of grief in the form of a poem or composition for the funeral of a dead person **Sing dirge for the dead*

Elegy – expression of lamentation in a poem

Requiem – expression of grief on the occasion of public gathering for the repose of the soul of a dead person

Threnody – lamentation for the dead

3. **Laugh** – to voice happiness or amusement

Cachinnate – to laugh loudly

Guffaw – to laugh boisterously

Fleer – to laugh mockingly

Chortle – to laugh delightfully/gleefully

Giggle – to laugh in half-suppressed manner in a silly way as and when feel embarrassed

Chuckle – to laugh in amusement **Chuckle at someone's ridiculous gestures*

Snigger – to laugh in half-suppressed voice in a disrespectful manner

Titter – laugh in half-suppressed manner to express amusement

4. **Lawyer** – one who practises law in courts

Advocate – one who pleads clients' cases in courts, pleader

Advoate-General – highest ranking govt.'s advocate

Attorney – one who represents a litigant by being appointed by him to represent on his behalf

Attorney-General – one who is head of govt.'s law department and represents the govt. in legal matters

Barrister – (in U.K.) a senior lawyer who practises in high courts

Jurist – one who is an expert in law

Solicitor – one who prepares a case for a client and represents a client in lower courts

Solicitor-General – Govt.'s seniormost solicitor – next in rank to Attorney-General

5. **Laziness** – lack of inclination to do something

Languor – laziness due to sensuous pleasure/feeling emotional softness/soft touch **Languor felt on inhaling pleasant scent*

	Lassitude	– laziness due to physical/mental weariness
	Listlessness	– l aziness due to lack of enthusiasm
	Sluggishness	– laziness causing to move slowly
6.	**Lazy**	– not inclined to do something
	Indolent	– habitually lazy (person) who does not want to take pain to do something
	Languid	– feeling dis-inclination to work due to fatigue
	Languorous	– feeling laziness due to sensuous pleasure
	Languishing	– lazy due to illness
	Listless	– lazy due to the lack of enthusiasm
	Sluggish	– slow to move due to laziness
	Enervated	– who is lazy due to luxurious style of living
7.	**Learned**	– (person) having acquired knowledge by study **A learned professor*
	Scholarly	– (person) highly knowledgeable
	Erudite	– (speech) showing full of knowledge **Erudite speech*
	Pedant	– a knowledgeable/learned person, who parades his knowledge
	Cogniscenti	– learned person in a specified field of knowledge **Cogniscenti of literature*
8.	**Lewd**	– (remark) showing vulgarity, indecent, obscene
	Lascivious	– (remark, look) showing sexual expression **Lascivious gesture*
	Libidinous	– (remark) characteristic of libido, complete surrender to sexy desire
	Lustful	– showing lewd desire
9.	**Lie down**	– to rest body on ground or bed
	Lie prone	– to lie down with chest on the ground
	Lie supine	– to lie down with chest upward
	Lie prostrate	– to lie down with limbs outstretched
	Lie recumbent	– to lie down with resting the body on a pillow
10.	**Lift**	– see *elevate*
	Levitate	– to raise oneself above the ground and stay out in the air without support
11.	**Limp**	– drooping because of not being stiff or erect
	Floppy	– drooping, limp as a dog's ears
	Flaccid	– limp and soft

Flabby – limp and loose *Flabby muscles*

Wilted – drooping due to losing moisture as in the case of a plant's leaves

12. Lonely – (place/people) without company *A lonely place *A lonely person*

Deserted – (place) without anyone to take care *A deserted house*

Desolate – (place) without anyone to take care *A deserted house*

Desolate – (place) devoid of people *A desolate place*

Solitary – (living) without anyone in company *Solitary living in prison cell*

13. Look – turn one'seyes in the direction of the object to see *Look at the map*

See – to perceive an image of something with one's eyes' visual power by looking at it *I looked at the map, but could not see its fine prints due to weak eye-sight*

Behold – to hold one's eyes on something and see *Behold the beauty of nature*

Watch – to look at something with full attention *Watch the cricket match on the television.*

Glance – to look at something for a brief period

Espy – to look into distant space as if to detect something

Gaze – to look at something for a long period

Gloat – to look smugly at one's prized possession

Stare – to look at something with wide-open eyes

Peer – to look at something with partly-closed eyes, trying to recognize it *He peered at him from a distance*

Glare – to stare at someone in anger

Leer – to stare at someone lasciviously

Ogle – to stare at someone lecherously

Glower – to stare at someone in sullen mood

Pore – to stare at someone with eyes fixed on it with complete concentration of mind *He pored over the book*

14. Loot – rob, snatch possession of someone

Plunder – loot with open violence *Plunder the travellers on the highway*

Pillage – loot in open violence *Mob pillaged the roadside vendors*

Despoil – loot under the guise of legality *Politicians despoil the public money*

Sack – (victorious army) loot the conquered place and its people's properties

15. **Loud** – (sound) harsh to hear **A loud noise*

Raucous – (laughter, voice) harsh to hear

Stentorian – (sound) exceedingly harsh **Stentorian siren*

Stertorous – (snoring) harsh and loud

Strident – (noise) loud and harsh **Strident traffic noise*

Shrill – (cry) loud and piercing to ears **Shrill cry*

16. **Loyalty** – faithfulness of someone towards a person

Patriotism – faithfulness of someone towards one's own country

Devotion – faithfulness to a cause, religion etc., dedication

Fealty – faithfulness of a tenant to his lord **Servant's fealty to his master*

Fidelity – faithfulness of spouse in conjugal life

Allegiance – faithfulness towards party, group

17. **Lure** – attract by tempting others **Toys lure the children* **Special offers lure the customers*

Entice – attract by a tempting tact **Entice people to join the sect*

Inveigle – attract by employing deceit

Seduce – attract someone to wrong path **He was seduced to crime by the prospect of getting rich overnight*

Tempt – attract too strongly to resist (with advantage) **The offer was tempting* **Tempt someone with bribe*

Words beginning with ———— M ————

1. **Malice** – feeling of ill-will against someone with a desire to hurt him

Malevolence – desire of, wish of evil things about someone **Harbour malevolence towards someone*

Grudge – feeling of resentment against someone **He holds grudge against me*

Grouse – complaining stance against someone in resentment

Despite – (noun of the word 'Despise') feeling of contempt, disdain

Spleen – bad temper, resentful feeling against someone **He poured his spleen against me when I tried to explain myself.*

Spite – feeling of a desire to hurt someone

Rancour – feeling of bitter resentment for a long time

Resentment – feeling of indignation due to hurt emotions

2. **Malodour** – unpleasant, foul smell of something

Stink – unpleasant smell of garbage, sullage etc.

Stench – very unpleasant, unbearable stink as emanating from a rotting mass

3. **Malodorous** – giving out malodour **Malodorous toilet*

Fetid – giving out offensive smell

Fusty – (place) giving out bad smell due to dampness **Musty damp room*

Noisome – giving out bad smell which might affect health **Noisome fumes*

Putrid – giving out bad smell due to rot/decay **Putrid vegetables*

Rancid – giving out foul smell due to decomposed oil and fat **Rancid butter*

Rank – giving out very bad smell **Rank cigar*

4. **Mark** – a sign left by something **Mark of ink on the paper dropped off an inkpot*

Contrail – longitudinal streak of mark left on curtains by fading due to exposure to sunlight/a long streak of white fumes left behind a jet plane passing in the sky **White contrail of a jet plane*

Aftermath – long streak of mowed grass in a field/unpleasant consequences left as mark of disastrous event *War left a ruined town in its aftermath

Rut – mark left by the passing vehicles' tyres on the ground

Spoor – mark left by an animal's hoofs, which is followed by hunters

Trail – mark left by the people passing across a path **Trail is made across a field by the people passing through it daily *An tnjured animal left a trail of blood behind its escape route *He scraped the barks on the trees to make a trail through the jungle to be followed by others of his team*

Wake – mark left on the water surface as a turbulence on the surface behind a ship passing ahead **Failed monsoon left famine in its wake*

5. **Marvel** – something/someone which/who arouses wonder or admiration in others **Universe is a marvel of God's creation*

Miracle – something/someone which/who arouses wonder because of being beyond human experience **This machine is a miracle in efficiency *His surviving the accident was a miracle*

Prodigy – someone who arouses wonder because of being extraordinary in talent **He is a child prodigy showing extraordinary talent early in age*

Phenomenon – someone/something who engenders wonder because of being extraordinary in nature **Total solar eclipse is a phenomenon*Mahatma Gandhi was a phenomenon*

6. **Mash** – to crush into pulp **Mash potato *He mashed his finger with a blow of the hammer*

Squash – to crush into a flat mass as by hitting hard or pressing under a heavy object **He squashed an insect under his shoes *Squash a tomato flat*

Crumple – to crush a cloth into irregular folds **Press a cloth to crumple into the broken creases*

7. **Massacre** – kill a large number of people brutally

Butcher – kill in cruel manner a large number of animals /people

Decimate – kill a large number of people belonging to a particular group or race or community

Slaughter – to kill brutally a large number of people in violent manner

Carnage – act of killing of a large number of people

Pogrom – act of killing of a large number of people of particular ethnicity in organized plot

8. **Mediator** – one who gets a dispute settled by negotiation

Arbitrator – one who gets a dispute setted by his tact/wisdom acceptable to both the parties

Arbiter – one who gets a dispute settled by dictating at his will because of having supremacy **Fate is an arbiter of our destiny*

Intermediary – one who acts as a go-between to settle dispute on the terms of a deal between the two parties

9. **Memento** – small item kept to renew the past memory **Childhood mementos keep one's past memorable*

Memorabilia – item belonging to/associated with someone or an event kept as one's memory

Remembrance– item associated with a dead person/person living far away/an event of distant past, which is kept as a memory

Souvenir – item kept as a memory of a place visited in the past

Token – item which has been gifted by someone and is kept as a sign of his affection

10. Memorial – a structure erected in the memory of an important person/event **Lincoln memorial *War memorial*

Monument – a structure erected in commemoration of an event of historical importance **India Gate is a monument of the martyrs in the war*

Mausoleum – structure of a tomb which is large and magnificent

Tomb – structure erected on the grave of a dead person who has been buried elsewhere

11. Mercenary – (troop, warrior) who takes part in war for a country, army for earning money instead of patriotism/a warrior who fights for money sake for a country, army

Hack – a person who sells his dignity/honour of being an independent writer/artist by working on hire for someone

Hireling – a person who works for someone on payment for services

Venal – (person in authority) who sells his independence/integrity for bribe paid to him **A venal bureaucrat*

12. Mire – soft, sticky, muddy tract of land

Bog – Mire covered with decayed vegetation

Marsh – tract of wetland

Quagmire – mire in which legs go in upon walking

Swamp – marshy land upon which trees and bushes have grown

13. Miser – (a person) who spends money very grudgingly

Frugal – who spends money prudently – who does not spend on unnecessary things, thrifty

Penurious – who is so miser as to live like a poor

Parsimonious – who spends sparingly

Niggardly – who spends too little on his own requirements, too

Stingy – who is unwilling to spend on others

14. Miserable – (condition) deserving pity **Miserable health*

Abject – (condition) extremely undignified, in which one loses self-pride **Abject poverty*

lgnoble – not honourable in character or purpose

Pitiable – (condition) which engenders pity in others

Wretched – (condition) which is extremely contemptible

15. Mistake – wrong committed in judging something **He made a mistake in identifying him*

Error – wrong committed by deviating from accuracy **Made an error in multiplication *Grammatical error*

Blunder – a serious nature of error which appears stupid **Calling A.P.J. Abdul Kalam as Abul Kalam Azad in speech was his blunde*r

Fault – a wrong done by someone knowingly without reck **It was my fault to go out in dead night without regard to risk involved*

Faux pas – error in social etiquette **Shouting abuse in social gathering was a faux pas, which I inadvertently committed*

Gaffe – a blunder which causes embarrassment

Mal-a-prop – an error in using a wrong word in place of a similarly sounding word **Using 'contiguous' for a disease in place of 'contagious' is a mal-a-prop*

16. Motivate – encourage someone to do something by showing cause, purpose and filling him with inner urge

Inspire – encourage by infusing zeal, animated feelings to do something

Encourage – fill someone with courage to do something

Induce – encourage to do something by showing gain, profit, which lures him

Suborn – encourage someone to commit perjury, *i.e.,* give wrong evidence in courts by giving bribe

17. Motive – purpose, cause which fills with inner urges to do something **Patriotism was the prime motive behind joining the army*

Inspiration – purpose etc. which fills someone with animation, zeal to do something **Social iniquities worked as inspiration to him to join social service*

Inducement – gain, greed which spurs one to do something **Pleasure of wielding power was the inducement for him to join I.A.S.*

Afflatus – divine inspiration which urges one to do something

18. Mysterious – (something) which remains unexplained and arouses curiosity and amazement **A mysterious object appeared in the sky which has never been seen before*

Mystic – (symbol, religious rite) which cannot be explained by ordinary people and, hence, arouses curiosity and amazement **Mystic rites* **Mystic formula*

Arcane – (secret) which remains unexplained to persons of average understanding

Abstruse – (something) which is too complex to be understood

Enigmatic – (situation, occurrence) which is perplexing **Enigmatic circumstances surround his death*

Esoteric – (something) which remains unexplained to those who are not having special knowledge **Esoteric poetry*

Recondite – (subject) too profound to be understood by average people

Words beginning with —— N ——

1. **Nap** – a slight, short sleep or dozing

Catnap – a nap in daytime

Siesta – a nap in the hottest part of day in summer

2. **Nascent** – being in the process of taking birth **Nascent rebellion should be nipped in the bud*

Inchoate – being in process of developing imperfect

Rudimentary – being in the state of not fully developed or not matured **Rudimentary knowledge* **Rudimentary stage of a planning*

Incipient – being in the early stage of process/exisence **Incipient tumour is removed by surgery*

3. **Nonsense** (talk) absurd **His nonsense is irritating*

Drivel – nonsense of an idiot/mad person **Drivel of a mad person*

Gobbledygook – absurd talk aimed at confusing others **Pseudo-scientific gobbledygook*

Poppycock – absurd/senseless talking **His poppycock was aimed at impressing others*

Twaddle – absurd talk of an ignorant-in-the-subject person **Cricket watchers indulge in twaddle about intricacy of the game as if they were experts*

4. **Novice** – (person) who is new, inexperienced in a job **A novice carpenter*

Neophyte – (person) who has just joined a group, party etc. **A neophyte has to master rules and procedures*

Greenhorn	–	an inexperienced person
Tyro	–	(person) who has begun to learn
Apprentice	–	(person) who is learning a trade under the supervision of an expert **Apprentice carpenter*

Words beginning with ——— O ———

1. **Object**	–	express opposition to someone's action/statement **They objected his proposal*
Dispute	–	express opposition on account of not being true or correct **He disputed my claim*
Impugn	–	express opposition by challenging **Impugn someone's motive of doing something*
Protest	–	express opposition because of being irrea -sonable **Protest undue criticism*
(Take) exception	–	express opposition because of being offen -ding **He took exception to his insolent behaviour*
2. **Obstacle**	–	something which blocks passage or progress **Wooden bollards are erected on road as obstacle to prevent traffic *Disunity is an obstacle for the party to win elections*
Barrier	–	something put up in the way to block a passage
Blockage	–	obstruction blocking passage **Blood clot creates blockage in the blood circulation*
Blockade	–	obstruction which prevents ingress & egress from a place **Police barricading put up blockade around the office building*
Hindrance	–	obstruction causing delay in progress **Econo -omic slowdown is a hindrance in country's progress*
Obstruction	–	something that obstructs progress **Mob's shouting caused obstruction in the meeting*
Hurdle	–	barrier put up in the way which has to be jumped over in order to go ahead
Impediment	–	difficulty which prevents progress **Lacking in vocabulary is impediment in fluent speech*
3. **Occurrence**	–	an incident which just takes place without apparent connection with anything else **His arrival was an unexpected occurrence*
Event	–	an important occurrence which has a special bearing **A historical event *Total solar eclipse is a rare celestial event*
Happening	–	an occurrence which just takes place

Happenstance – a happening which takes place by chance

Incident – an occurrence of minor nature in connection with something else **An incident of hostility took place on the border*

Incidence – an undesirable occurrence **Incidence of theft in the train shook the passengers *High incidence of heart diseases is caused by faulty food habits*

Instance – a specific occurrence which serves as an example to prove a point **It was an instance of oppression against the weaker section of the society*

4. **Omen** – an occurrence which is indicative of something good or bad to happen soon **End of war is a good omen for the counry *Howling of dogs is a bad omen*

Augury – an occurrence which is indicative of good outcome **Good monsoon is augury of good harvesting season*

Portent – occurrence which is indicative of bad outcome **Seeing a bright object falling from the sky is a menacing portent*

5. **Ominous** – (an event) which gives worry about what bad may happen **Ominous dark clouds*

Inauspicious – which gives fear of unfavourable consequences **An inauspicious event*

Portentous – which gives threatening impression about what may happen **Portentous celestial event*

Unpropitious – what can't be appeased to be favourable or helpful **Unpropitious luck*

6. **Opposite** – Situated at the other end of something **He is sitting opposite to me *Opposite end of the room *He took stance opposite to mine*

Contrary – (a fact, proposition) which is in opposition to another one **Contrary views of members on a matter made it difficult to take decision*

Contradictory – (counter + diction) a statement which is opposite to another one **Contradictory statements of witnesses about what happened makes it obvious that one of them is untrue*

Antithesis – (two things or qualities) which are directly opposite to one another **Water is antithesis of fire *Hell is antithesis of heaven*

7. Order	–	authoritative instruction given to someone
Behest	–	earnest command **He filed a complaint against me at the behest of my detractor*
Command	–	order which must be obeyed **Military command*
Diktat	–	order which is imposed on someone by a superior which is unfair **Boss's diktat*
Edict	–	authority's proclamation – order pronounced publicly
Decree	–	Court's order to litigants
Fiat	–	arbitrary order **A dictator rules by fiat*
Canon	–	religious order of codes of conduct to be observed by the devotees **He violated the canons of etiquette*
Injunction	–	order requiring a person to do or not to do a particular act **Doctor's injuction to refrain from smoking has to be faithfully obeyed by the patient*
Mandate	–	order/command given by people to their represent -atives to manage affairs of the state **The party got the mandate to form government in the election*
Ordainment	–	order prescribed by the destiny for deciding someone's fate in advance **He is ordained to suffer*
8. Outdated	–	belonging to the past – no more now **Outdated fashion*
Antiquated	–	very old, of the past **Antiquated machine*
Ante-diluvian	–	primitive, belonging to very old period **Ante-diluvian civilization*
Archaic	–	of old time and now rarely used **Archaic language*
Obsolete	–	gone out of vogue, no more in use **Obsolete models of cars*
9. Overture	–	initial move towards starting a dialogue, negotiation, relationship **A shy person rarely makes an overture of friendship *My overture to old foe was requited with cold response*
Approach	–	initial move/advance made to an unknown person for friendship **He made a timid approach to his fellow passenger in the journey*
Advance	–	initial move to show one's intention of starting amorous relationship with a person of opposite sex **She rebuffed his advances*

Bid – initial move to getting something from some *He made a bid for others' sympathy

Tender – initial move in the form of indirect hint by actions to show one's intention towards someone **He made several tenders of his attraction towards her in the past, but she did not take the cue*

Words beginning with —— P ——

1. **Paradox** – (a fact, truth) which is contrary to accepted belief, norms

   Anomaly – (fact) which is contrary to general rule, expectations **A reticent person that he is, is anomaly in his family of garrulous persons *People in a free country yet to get freedom from social iniquities is an anomaly*

   Antimony – (conclusion) which is contrary to another conclussion – though both are derived from the same premise

   Irony – (expression) which is contrary to what was intended to convey **Nominating criminals for election, even as proclaiming not to do so, is a stark irony*

2. **Passion** – intense emotional longing **His passion for reading books drew him to the book fair*

   Fervour – intentional emotional devotion **He prays with fervour*

   Ardour – intense emotional zeal like a leaping flame * *Ardour of a neophyte*

3. **Peak** – the highest point as of a mountain, summit

   Apex – the highest point of a pointed object, Acme **Apex of a tree leaf*

   Vertex – the highest point of a rock, career of a person

   Zenith – the highest point in the sky over one's head (opposite Nadir) **His popularity is on the zenith*

4. **Peep** – to look through a narrow slit at something **He peeped into the room*

   Peek – to look at something furtively **He peeked into the room to know what was happening there*

   Pry – to look into others' private life intrusively **Prying into someone's private affairs is a bad habit*

   Voyeur – (a person) who furtively looks at others engaged in sexual activity to derive passive pleasure

5. **Perplex** – to mentally disturb to throw into confusion **Difficult questions in exams perplexed him*

Agitate – to disturb mentally

Discomfit – to mentally disturb to make someone feel uneasy **Hooting and catcalls discomfitted the speaker*

Disconcert– to mentally disturb so as to lose composures

Perturb – to mentally disturb acutely

Rattle – to mentally disturb so as to make one nervous **Sudden explosion rattled people*

Upset – to mentally disturb to bewilder **Bad news about the family upset him*

Vex – to mentally disturb due to annoyance

Faze – to mentally disturb so as to feel ashamed or discouraged **No amount of insult fazed him*

6. **Persuade** – to make one agree to do something by reasoning to convince him **He persuaded me to change my decision*

Coax – to make one agree by gentle persuasion **He was coaxed to agree to the suggestion*

Cajole – to make one agree by flattery

Inveigle – to make one agree by using artful tact **To inveigle someone to accompany to the market*

Wheedle – to make one agree by misleading words or acts **Wheedle someone persistently to consent to the request*

7. **Pierce** – to thrust a pointed object so as to enter into someone's body **Pierce the skin with a needle*

Stab – to thrust sharp weapon into a body **Stab someone with a knife*

Gore – thrust animal's horn or tusker's teeth into someone **A wild bull gored a person*

Impale – pierce a pointed object and keep fixed or unable to move **A snake was impaled on the ground with a bident*

8. **Pillar** – tall, vertical structure to support load

Beam – long, horizontal structure to support load

Pole – long piece of wood, steel or such material

Mast – long pole upon which sails, flag are supported **Flag is hoisted on a mast*

Stake – long piece of wood or steel pointed at one end of it, which is used for fencing.

Pylon – very long, tower-like pole, which is used for supporting high–tension electric wires

	Prop	– long pole which is used as a support for something to prevent it from falling from down
9.	**Politic**	– (action, decision) which is sensible in a given circumstance **It is politic to keep away from dispute*
	Pragmatic	– (action, decision) which is based on practical consideration
	Provident	– (action, decision) which is based on concern for future **Saving money is a provident decision*
	Prudent	– (action, decision) which is based on thought for consequences
	Sagacious	– (action etc.) based on careful considerations, or good judgement
10.	**Poor**	– (person) lacking in the means of living
	Penurious	– extremely poor
	Destitute	– completely devoid of the means of living
	Impecunious	– a poor who lacks in money for sustenance, penniless
	Impoverished	– poor because of losing wealth **Impoverished landlords*
	Indigent	– poor because of lacking means to meet stet
11.	**Pot pourri**	– collection of miscellaneous items of entertainment
	Melange	– collection of miscellaneous items
	Medley	– collection of miscellaneous songs, which are sung in continuity as a single song
	Montage	– collection of miscellaneous photographs placed together to look like a single photograph
	Collage	– collection of miscellaneous newspaper clippings, photographs etc. pasted on the same surface as a work of art
12.	**Poverty**	– state of being poor
	Penury	– state of being penurious
	Indigence	– state of being indigent
	Destitution	– state of being destitute
	Privation	– state of being deprived of means of living
13.	**Powerful**	– having great power **Powerful engine*
	Potent	– having great effect **A potent drug*
	Potentate	– a powerful person having great influence
	Mighty	– having great might/physical strength **Mighty army*
	Puissant	– having great ability (to jump on a horse in a race)

14. Praise – express admiration

Laud – praise by singing or shouting slogans **People lauded their leader*

Extol – highly praise someone

Eulogize – praise a deceased person in a condolence meeting

Commend – praise by naming a person for good work **Commend a soldier for his bravery*

Panegyrize – praise in an oration, writing in paper etc.

Approbate – public praise approving one's good work **Approbate government's policy*

15. Prayer – spiritual communion with God

Matins – morning prayer

Vespers – evening prayer

Paternoster – prayer recitation to the (Pater–) of the universe – supreme father

16. Precedence – preceding another in order of importance, rank in privilege **The President of India takes precedence of all others in official protocol*

Precedent – preceding event/instance which serves as an example to follow in subsequent cases **Precedent of earlier court's judgement helps subsequent decisions*

Antecedent – preceding circumstances of one's life which helps forming an opinion about him **Antecedent of a person is unblemished*

Priority – preceding circumstances of one's life which help forming an opinion about him **Antecedent of a person is unblemished*

17. Pretend – to give false impression by insincere action **Pretend sympathy for someone in trouble*

Profess – to give false impression by insincere speech **Profess loyalty to someone*

Feign – to give false impression by insincere posture **Feign death by lying motionless* **Feign ignorance*

Malinger – to give false impression of being ill in order to avoid duty

Play possum – (insects) to give false impression of death by lying motionless to save itself from the predators

18. Prevaricate – to speak in a round about manner so as to evade speaking the truth

	Equivocate	– to speak ambiguously so that it can be interpreted in equally two meanings to evade truth
	Palter	– to speak insincerely so as to be able to deny later
	Fib	– to speak lie in order to save oneself from embarrassment at that moment and get rid of the situation
19.	**Pride**	– unjustified opinion of one's own worth
	Conceit	– excessive pride which is exaggerated
	Hubris	– excessive pride which becomes the cause of downfall **Hubris of Hitler led to his downfall and death*
	Vanity	– excessive pride in one's ability which is worthless *i.e.,* of no value **Vanity of being a noble descendant*
	Vainglory	– boastful vanity **Vainglory of being a minister/actor*
20.	**Principle**	– fundamental belief governing action **Principle of a party*
	Doctrine	– fundamental belief of a religion/sect which is taught to the followers
	Dogma	– doctrine which is considered inviolable and sacrosanct
	Tenet	– principle held by a group or party truthfully
21.	**Prize**	– thing given to a winner of competition or lottery
	Award	– thing given in recognition of achievement **Award of the best actor*
	Reward	– thing given for services rendered **Loyal partyman was rewarded with the governor -ship*
	Wages	– the thing given for bad acts in return **He is suffering as a wages of sin *Ruined economy of the country was the wages of bad policies*
	Largesse	– thing given in generosity **The government gives largesse to the poor people*
	Bounty	– thing/money given for helping capture a culprit
	Bonus	– thing given to workers for good productivity
	Incentive	– thing given to motivate or encourage
22.	**Profession**	– occupation for which knowledge is a must **Medical profession of a doctor *Teaching profession*
	Occupation	– activity/work in which one is engaged **Writing books is the reired person's occupation*
	Vocation	– main job/employment **His vocation is govern ment service*

	Avocation	– side occupation apart from vocation, which one pursues as hobby
	Metier	– occupation in which one is specially trained and expert in doing it **Marketing is his metier*
	Business	– occupation of commercial nature
	Trade	– occupation in which specific skill is acquired **His trade is carpentry*
23.	**Property**	– things owned by a person **This house is his sole property*
	Asset	– property such as house, land etc. owned by a person who can convert into money by selling if need arises **He has accumulated assets in various towns*
	Chattel	– personal property other than land or money – such as cattles
	Personalty	– personal properties
	Realty	– real estate properties of a person
	Fortune	– great stock of wealth of a person **He spent fortune for his son's education*
	Wealth	– valuables possessed by someone **He lost his wealth*
24.	**Puzzle**	– (game, question) which carries tricky answer/ solution requiring mental agility to solve **Cross-word puzzle*
	Riddle	– question etc. requiring skill to solve because of being full of contradictions
	Enigma	– (something) which is beyond common understanding, giving rise to speculation **He is an enigma to his friends*
	Conundrum	– puzzle or riddle, which is too complex to be solved

Words beginning with ——— Q ———

1.	**Quack**	– a person, who practises a profession and pretends to have qualifications for that **Quack physician* **Quack psychologist*
	Charlatan	– a person who pretends to have knowledge more than he actually possesses
	Humbug	– a person who pretends to be important more than he actually is, a fraud **A humbug in politics* **A humbug politician*
2.	**Quarrel (*v*)**	– to engage in verbal argument over differences
	Altercate	– to engage in heated arguments

Squabble – to engage in petty quarrel

Wrangle – to engage in noisy quarrel

3. **Quarrel (*n*)** – noisy argument over a dispute **Domestic quarrel*

Brawl – quarrel which disturbs the neighbours **A brawl on the road*

Broil – quarrel which annoys others

Fracas – quarrel with uproarious noise

Melee – quarrel which hand-to-hand fighting

Row – angry quarrel which attracts others' attention

Scrap – quarrel with jostling

Scuffle – quarrel with trading blows

4. **Quarrelsome** – a person who is predisposed/inclined to pick up fight with others

Pugnacious – predisposed to engage in fisticuff

Belligerent – (nations) engaged in actual fighting

Bellicose – (a person) who is eager to fight

5. **Quibble** – argue on irrelevant points so as to avoid the real issue

Pettifog – un–necessarily argue on petty points

Words beginning with —— R ——

1. **Reason (*with*)** – to argue with someone to convince him of his fault

Expostulate – to argue with someone to object to his fault **Expostulate with someone of his bad habit of gambling*

Remonstrate (with) – to argue to show one his fault in protest

2. **Rebound** – to spring back after hitting a surface

Boomerang – (a plan, plot) come back on the originator instead of the intended target to harm

Repercuss – (something like action, event) rebound as a bad consequence **A war repercusses on nation's economy*

Reverberate – (sound) rebound several tunes after hitting walls of a hall to make echo **Her shriek reverberated through the hall*

Ricochet – (a flat object thrown forward) rebound by deflecting from the surface several times after hitting it **A flat stone was thrown horizontally, which ricocheted on the smooth surface*

Rebound – to rebound as a credit or discredit someone's good or bad act upon him **Good acts rebound to his credit* **Good upbringing rebounds on one's behaviour*

3. **Rebuff** – bluntly refuse to entertain someone's advances, attempt to come close **The girl rebuffed his advances*

Snub – rebuff disdainfully

Spurn – bluntly refuse to entertain someone's proposal, request

4. **Rebuke** – express sharp disapporoval of someone's wrong action **Rebuked him for disobeying his orders*

Chide – scold for a wrong done

Admonish – scold in a mild manner/goodwill manner **Admonished him to remind him of obligations to his family*

Objurgate – rebuke sharply/harshly, to berate

Upbraid – rebuke sharply **He was upbraided for his cowardice*

5. **Recede** – to go back to a distant position from the point where an observer is looking at **Flood water receded gradually from the inundated road* **His hairline is receding back from his forehead*

Retreat – to go back from a place of trouble to a safe place **Troops retreated from the war zone to safety*

Retrogress – to go back again to earlier inferior condition from a superior one **Religious fundamentalism makes a society retrogressive*

6. **Recrimination** – return accusation with a counter accusation

Repartee – witty reply in return of a witty remark

Riposte – counter-strike to a strike as in the game of fencing **A befitting riposte to an insult*

Retort – quick return in the form of retaliatory reply to a remark

Retaliation – return attack for an attack

7. **Regard** – to consider as a point of view **I regard him useless* **I regard him as my friend*

Recon – to consider as a point of loss or gain on the basis of calculation **Recon the loss*

Deem – to consider as a point of judgement **I deem it fit for selection*

8. **Regret** – to express sorrow for wrong act **He regretted his harsh reply to his elder*

Repent – to feel sorrow for committed sin with change of heart to become the same person *He repented cruelty he had perpetrated on others*

Rue – express sorrow on a past event or action with a wish that it had not happened at all **I rue the day I made friendship with him*

Lament – to express sorrow for something bad that had happened **He lamented his death *He lamented the falling standard of politics*

9. Rehabilitation – action of restoring lost ability to live on one's own **Rehabilitation of those who have been uprooted from their native place enables them to live as before *Rehabilitate amputated persons by prosthetics*

Re-instatement – action of putting a person in the same post he had earlier been removed **The court ordered his re-instatement*

Rapprochement – action of restoring harmonious relations earlier to hostility

Status quo ante – restoration of earlier condition

10. Reject – do not agree to accept due to deficiency **He rejected the bad quality goods *His application was rejected*

Refuse – do not agree because of one's unwillingness **He refused the party ticket for contesting the election *He refused to help him*

Decline – refuse politely **He declined to accept help*

Deny – do not agree to accept because of being untrue **He denied allegations against him *He denied that the earth is flat*

11. Relevant – (matter, argument, etc.) connected with the issue at hand **Relevant remark*

Apposite/Apt – which is suitable for the purpose at hand **Apposite reply *Apt quotation*

Germane – which is significant to the subject **Facts are germane to the issue at hand*

Pertinent – (things) related to the subject matter, which holds good for the topic **Pertinent question *Files pertinent to the case*

12. Relic – remains of a dead person preserved as an object of reverence

Relict – surviving part of something which has become instanct **Relict of instinct civilization*

	Reliquiae	– fossil remains of animal/plant
	Remains	– left-over part of something which does not now exist **Dead body is the remains of a deceased person *Remains of a ruined fort*
13.	**Relief**	– removal of pain, distress, sufferings **Medicine gave relief from pain *Food, shelter were provided to the flood victims as relief*
	Reprieve	– removal of sufferings by means of temporary post-ponement of punishment, temporary relief, respite **Rains brought reprieve from sweltering summer heat *Suspension of tax collection was a reprieve to the people facing financial hardship*
	Riddance	– removal of the situation causing annoyance, annoying or unbearable suffering **Unwanted guest's departure is a good riddance to a host*
14.	**Relieve**	– to give relief, romove suffering **To relieve tension*
	Mitigate	– to lessen punishment, grief etc. by making it milder **Mitigate punishment *Mitigate seriousness of accusation.*
	Assuage	– to lessen hurt feelings
15.	**Repair**	– set right a broken or damaged thing **Repair machine/building*
	Rectify	– set right a mistake
	Mend	– set right what is torn **Mend shoes*
16.	**Repentance**	– feeling of sorrow for sinful acts with change of heart
	Penance	– feeling of sorrow with self–punishment
	Penitence	– feeling of sorrow by expressing regret without intent to make amends
	Compunction	– feeling of sorrow due to hurt conscience while doing sinful act **He had no compunction in deceiving his friend*
	Contrition	– feeling of sorrow with painful heart and intending to confess, so as to unburden his guilt feeling
	Remorse	– feeling of sorrow for sinful acts with intent to do expiation–self-punishment
17.	**Replace**	– to change a defective thing with a right one of the same thing **Replace the fused bulb *The inefficient officer was replaced*
	Substitute	– to change something with another kind **Computer*

*has substituted the typewriters *Card payment has substituted the cash payment*

Supersede – to change a deficient or obsolete thing with more suitable one by setting the former aside **Supersede old law with a new one *Supersede the inefficient officer with another one*

18. Reprimand – (superior authority to subordinate) blame a subordinate in disapproval of his conduct or decision

Reprove – disapprove someone's wrong action by speaking to him

Reproach – censure/blame someone in disapproval of his conduct

19. Request – to beg someone for something

Entreat – request earnestly

Implore – request anxiously due to urgency

Solicit – request repeatedly so as to annoy the person requested

Plead – request by pleading for something

Beseech – request fervently

Importune – request persistently so as to cause harassment to the person requested

Supplicate – request humbly by bending with folded hands before the person requested

20. Restore – bring back to normal condition or former level **Restore peace/lost glory*

Restitute – bring back property, rights which had been taken away **Restitute his conjugal life by reuniting him with his wife*

Retrieve – bring back something which is likely to be lost or destroyed, or from ruin **Retrieve valuable articles from a house on fire *Retrieve one's business*

Replenish – bring back stock to make up what has been consumed **Replenish food stock*

Reclaim – bring back waste/marshy land for use or in a condition of being able to be used for good purpose

Recover – bring back stolen goods, what has been lost **Recover stolen watch *Recover loss in business *Recover sense*

Recuperate – recover lost health due to illness

Rejuvenate – recover youthful vigour which has been lost due to age, weakness **Rejuvenate youthfulness*

Redeem – recover pawned article, sold shares etc. by buying back again **Redeem mortgaged house*

	Ransom	– bring back a captured person by paying demand money for his release **He ransomed his kidnapped son*
21.	**Resurrect**	– to bring back to life from a grave **Resurrect the ancient culture*
	Resurge	– to bring back to activity after lying dormant or from virtual extinction **Resurge economy*
	Revive	– to bring back to life which has ceased to exist **Revive old feud *Revive relationship*
	Resuscitate	– to bring back breathing from asphyxiated state **Mouth–to–mouth blowing air resuscitated stopped breathing in a victim*
22.	**Retaliate**	– return harmful action of someone with harmful action *i.e.,* return in the same coin **He retaliated his hostility in equal measure*
	Reciprocate	– return good gesture/action of someone with similar gesture **Reciprocate favour*
	Requite	– return good action with bad one or vice versa, *ie.,* bad action with good one **He requited my friendship with deceitful action against me*
23.	**Retract**	– withdraw, take back something spread out **Retract the spread wings (by a bird) *Retract one's given statement*
	Recant	– to withdraw statement formally made earlier
	Renege	– withdraw a promise given earlier **He reneged on his promise*
	Backtrack	– withdraw, go back by stepping back from the position, or an undertaking.
24.	**Retrench**	– remove employees in order to reduce expenditure, to ward off financial loss
	Cashier	– remove employees by revoking job contract
	Dismiss	– remove an employee due to his indicipline
	Lay off	– remove employees temporarily because of the shortage of work
25.	**Revenge**	– action of exacting or inflicting punishment on someone for a harm done by the person who has suffered **He took revenge for his insult*
	Retribution	– action of exacting condign punishment on someone for evil doings in the form of divine judgement **Natural*

*calamity is a retribution for neglecting environmental protection *A just retribution of wickedness*

Vengeance – furious, wrathful, vindictive revenge **Police killed the criminal in vengeance for his killing innocent policemen*

Reprisal – retaliatory attack on someone to take revenge for hostile action despite warning to desist **Attack in reprisal *Shops were sealed in reprisal to continued black marketing in essential goods despite repeated warnings*

26. Reverence – gesture of deep devotion **Show reverence to saints*

Deference – gesture of courteous regard **Yield to elders in deference to their wishes.*

Esteem – gesture of giving high regard **I hold him in high esteem*

Homage – gesture of respect **Pay homage to a person in high position*

Obeisance – gesture of reverence by supplication **Supplicate in obeisance to deity*

Tribute – gesture of regard by acknowledging **Erecting statue of a person is a tribute to him*

Veneration – gesture of reverence due to age, wisdom **Show veneration to old persons*

27. Revolt – raising voice of dissent against authority **People's revolt against government's unfair decision*

Coup d'etat – sudden overthrow of established rule

Insurgency – armed rebellion

Insurrection – attempt to overtake government by force

Lese majeste – Treason, crime against a ruler

Sedition – act or speech which incite rebellion

Mutiny – uprising of troops against their own establishment

Putsch – sudden uprising

Rebellion – armed struggle in defiance to the authority of the government

Uprising – rising of people in revolt against established rule

28. Rich – (person) who possesses enough wealth.

Affluent – who is having increasing source of earning money

Opulent – who indulges in ostentatious display of one's wealth

Wealthy – who possesses enough income–generating property

29. Ridicule – laugh at someone to make fun of him **Ridicule a pretentious person* **They ridiculed him for his ugly look*

Deride – make fun of someone by scornful, contemptuous laughter **They derided him for his foolishness*

Mock – make fun of someone by doing his caricature **He mocked my serious thoughts*

Taunt – make fun of someone in a humiliating manner **To taunt someone for his defeat or failure*

Lampoon – make fun of someone by satirical drama, writing articles, etc. **The drama lampooned the political leaders/society for practising absurd customs*

Pillory – make fun of someone by exposing his deeds publicly **He pilloried his opponent*

Scoff – deride scornfully **Scoff him at his attempt to do something brave*

Fleer – deride someone by laughing mockingly

Sneer – make fun of/deride someone by curling lips in smile **They sneered at him when he told some jokes*

Jeer – make fun of someone by shouting/heckling **Crowd jeered the speaker*

30. Ridiculous – which induces laughter due to being absurd **Ridiculous plan*

Risible – which induces laughter due to being contemptible

Ludicrous – which induces laughter due to being preposterous **Ludicrous acts of a jester.*

Droll – which induces laughter due to being amusing in an odd way

Funny – which induces laughter due to being comical **Funny act/ remark*

31. Risk – chance of getting harmed/injured **Jumping in turbulent water involves risk*

Hazard – chance of facing problems **A journey full of hazards*

Jeopardy – chance of getting harmed due to exposing one to dangerous situation **Working without safety gears put workers in jeopardy*

Peril – chance of getting harm due to imminent danger **Landslide puts people in peril*

32. Rude – (person) having offensive behaviour

Insolent – extremely rude

Impolite – having offensive manners

Impudent – showing open defiance boldly

Brash – having overbearing manners

Impertinent – rude towards respectable persons

Churlish – having bad temper/arrogant behaviour

33. **Ruse** – trick, artifice to divert attention from reality **Employ ruse by pretending illness to avoid work*

Ploy – trick employed to turn situation in own favour **Use clever ploys to get others' support*

Feint – trick to divert opponent's attention before attacking him **Feint of skilled fencer*

Gimmick – trick like a magician employs to hoodwink others

Subterfuge – ruse to evade consequences (subter = under, fuge = flee)

Stratagem – trick to deceive enemy or to gain advantage over adversary

Trick – crafty artifice to deceive **Magicians' tricks*

Words beginning with ——— S ———

1. **Sacrilege** – irreligious act of violating sacredness of what is sacred like a temple, for example **Desecration of a holy place is a sacrilege*

Blasphemy – irreligious act of speaking evil about what is sacred **Blasphemy of criticising others' religion*

Heresy – irreligious act of believing in the principles contrary to accepted orthodoxy **Not believing in doing religious rites is heresy*

Profanity – irreligious act of showing contempt or irreverence for what is holy/sacred **Treating sacred thing irreverently is profanity*

2. **Sad** – feeling unhappy, sorrowful **The bad news made him sad*

Desolate – sad due to lonely feeling

Disconsolate– unconsolably sad

Forlorn – sad due to loss of hope

Doleful – sad due to grief

Gloomy – sad with depressed mood

Lugubrious – mournfully sad **Lugubrious mood*

Melancholic– habitually sad **A melancholic person is averse to anything cheerful*

3. **Sarcastic** – (remark) which is in the form of taunting **The sarcastic remark hurt him*

Satirical – (denunciation, riducule) which is taunting on vice, social aberrations etc. **Satirical play on social vices*

Sardonic – (expression) which is disdainfully taunting characterised by bitter smile **Sardonic grin*

Ironic – (statement) which is taunting characterised by speaking opposite to what is intended to say **What a wonderful person you are!*

4. **Satire** – (literary piece of writing) intended to ridicule human follies, social vices **This film was a satire on human pettiness and selfishness*

Skit – (literary writing, play/drama) intended to ridicule in humorous manner

Squib – (a short literary work) intended to ridicule in sarcastic/ malicious manner

Lampoon – (a work, writing) intended to ridicule in a virulent manner **A lampoon on social vices*

5. **Scatter** – throw all around at random **scattering seeds in the field is technically known as 'broadcasting'*

Spread – move a liqid so as to cover space on ground all around **Spread liquid on the floor*

Disperse – move something in all directions at random **Disperse the crowd *Wind dispersed the fog*

Diffuse – disperse gaseous matter through the air **Diffuse fume/ scent throughout the room*

Dissipate – disperse wastefully **Dissipate youth's energy *Plot surface dissipates heat and becomes cool*

Disseminate – disperse by distributing amongst others all around **Disseminate knowledge*

6. **Scrap** – small pieces of paper, metals torn or cut from large size **Metal scraps are lying all around this place*

Fragment – small piece of broken mass/disintegrated mass **Fragments of broken glass*

Shard – fragment of earthenware, crockery

Shrappel – fragment of a shell, exploded bomb

Sliver – long piece of wood, cloth, metal torn from a large size portion **Sliver of wood*

Splinter – small piece of wood, cloth, metal etc., taken out of a large portion

7. Scrape – rub a surface with a rough material so as to remove dirt on it, or its superficial outer layer **Scrape grime off the kitchen wall *Scrape paint from the surface.*A hard stone rubbed his hand to crape its skin*

Graze – (a bullet) rub a surface lightly while passing along it. **A bullet strayed off the course and grazed the arm of a person standing by*

Grate – rub a surface of something with a toothed surface so as to scrape into pieces **Grate the potato into chips*

Scratch – rub a smooth surface with a sharp object so as to tear it off at several places **Nails scratched his face *He scratched his name on the wall with a knife*

8. Scream – loud, piercing sound of a cry as in fear, anger **Scream in fear*

Shriek – loud high–pitched sound as of a cry in pain **Shriek in pain*

Shrill – loud harsh sound of crying

Screech – loud grating sound as produced on applying sudden brakes on a running vehicle.**Vehicle screeched to a sudden halt*

Hoot – loud piercing sound as of a siren, horn.

9. Seclude – to separate from others by keeping away to avoid contact **Aggressive prisoner was secluded from other prisoners*

Segregate – to separate a group of persons or things from other group on the basis of title, nomenclature etc. **Books are segregated on the basis of author's title *Minority communities segregate themselves in ghetto away from the majority community*

Quarantine – to separate an infected person with contagious disease from others, who may get infected (usually for a period of forty days (quarant = forty)

Isolate – separate by taking away from the company **Nitrogen is isolated from the mixture of gaseous elements in the air by cooling *He has been isolated from his group of friends*

Assort – separate things/goods in various sizes, qualities **Assort oranges in various sizes*

Sort – separate the letters according to their destinations **Sort the letters to be sent to different places*

10. Serious – not triffling, sincere in attitude **Serious person*

Grave – having calm or cheerless disposition **Grave mood*

Somber – gloomy, depressed, sad **Sombre occasion of mourning* **He is sitting in somber mood*

Staid – devoid of levity in mood **A staid person*

Solemn – mirthless person, face, mood, occasion **Prayer time is a solemn occasion*

11. Servile – (attitude) of submitting before someone as a servant **Servile bureaucrats*

Subservient– of serving others of important position as an obedient subordinate

Slavish – (attitude) like that of a slave **Slavish obedience*

Obsequious– (attitude) of flattering others in ostentatious submission **Obsequious politeness*

12. Shake – move to and fro **Shake hands* **Shake the tree branch*

Convulse – shake the body uncontrollably and involuntarily as in epilepsy, laughter etc. **He convulsed with laughter*

Rock – shake something violently as in storm **The sea waves rocked the boat*

Teeter – shake the body as if about to fall in drunk condition **The inebriated person teetered home*

Totter – teeter due to weakness **The old man tottered while walking*

Toddle – shake body as when a child begins to learn walking **A child toddled*

Sway – to shake with slight movements as tree leaves and branches do in gentle breeze

Wobble – to shake as does rickety furniture due to loose joints

13. Shameless – (person, act) lacking sense of shame or modesty

Brazen – arrogantly shameless **Brazen denial of having done anything wrong*

Brash – rudely shameless

Impudent – misbehaving shamelessly

Unabashed – unembarrassingly shameless

14. Shelter – place of protection from hostile conditions **A shelter to protect people from rains*

Asylum – place to provide shelter to mentally ill persons or orphans

Harbour – place of protection for ships in the sea, or where the criminals are concealed **A cave is the harbour of* *fugitives *Dark corners in the kitchen provide harbour to insects*

Haven – place which is a natural protection from hostile conditions **Mother's lap is the ultimate haven for a kid from his or her father's wrath*

Lee – (a rock, wall) which provides shelter from storm **Lee of a huge rock protects people from storm or rains*

Refuge – place which provides protection and shelter for people who have fled their houses/homeland **Refuge for people from the war–affected*

15. Shine – to glow with light **The sun shines*

Dazzle – to shine brilliantly **Polished shoes dazzled*

Glare – to glow with intense light **Sun glares in mid–day in summer*

Gleam – shine with sudden flash of light

Glimmer – shine with faint light

Glisten – shine with faint intermittent light

Glitter – shine brilliantly with reflected light **Gold ornaments glitter*

Scintillate– shine with flashes of light

Shimmer – shine with tremulous light

Sparkle – shine with sparkling light

Twinkle – shine like stars

Show – to put/place something in open for other to see

Display – to show in order to attract attenttion **Display skill*

Parade – to show something which is impressive * *To bring into others' knowledge.*

Flaunt – to show prized possession proudly

Flourish – to show something by waving in air to attract attention

Exhibit – to show attractlive things in public place. **Art.*

Brandish – to show by waving in air, gun, weapon etc., to scare away

16. Shrink – to contract to become less in size **The cloth shrinked on washing*

Shrivel – (leaf) to contract in size with wrinkles on it due to loss of moisture **Dried leaf shrivels*

Wither – to shrink on losing freshness **Plucked flowers soon wither*

Wizen – (skin) shrink with wrinkles due to old age **Wizened skin of old man*

17. Shy – feeling nervous and hesitant in company with others

Coy – affectedly shy

Demure – shy in mixing with strangers **Demure woman*

Modest – shy of speaking high of oneself **Modest scholar*

18. Similarity – state of likenness in a particular aspect between two or more **There is no similarity in his behaviour with that of his brother*

Analogy – similarity for comparison between two different things **There is striking analogy between heart and pump*

Commensuration – Similarity in measurement **There is no commensuration between his work and salary, which should justifiably be commensurate with each other*

Conformity – similarity in forms or shapes

Correspondence – similarity in response **My affection for him is not in correspondence with his affection for me*

Parity – similarity in status, level **Salary in a company is in parity with another one in the public sector*

Resemblance – similarity in appearance **Resemblance between the twins in toto*

Equivalence – similarity between two different things in value **An ideal consumer, driven by economically rational mind, always tries to gain equivalent to the money paid by him*

19. Sink – go down under the surface of water **The ship sank in the river*

Drown – go down the surface of water and suffocate **Boys drowned in the river*

Dip – put something in a liquid **Dip a wick in oil before lighting it* **Dip the nib of this pen in the ink*

Dunk – put solid etable in a liquid eatable so as to make it soft to eat **Dunk bread in milk* **Dunk biscuit in tea*

Immerse – plunge something by throwing under water *Image of the Goddess is immersed in the river after the Puja celebration

Overwhelm – to cover something under a mass of something **A huge number of problems have overwhelmed me*

Inundate – to put something under the surface of water by spreading over **Flood water inundated the low–lying areas*

Submerge	–	to put under the surface of something by lowering it down **A water pump is submerged down the bore to pump up water*
20. Slap	–	strike someone's side–face with the open palm
Box	–	strike someone's side–face – below the ears with the fist
Cuff	–	strike someone's head or face with the back of the open palm
21. Smell	–	property of a substance which is perceived by olfactory sense, *i.e.,* nose
Odour	–	bad, unpleasant odour
Stink	–	offensively bad smell
Stench	–	very offensive smell
Aroma	–	distinctive good smell of something **Aroma of coffee.*
Bouquet	–	tasty smell of something being cooked **Bouquet of cooked meat*
Flavour	–	savoury smell of tasty food
Fragrance	–	sweet smell of flower **Rose fragrance*
Redolence	–	sweet smell of mixed fragrance of several flowers **Redolence of flower garden*
Incense	–	sweet smell of burning stet (agarbatti)
22. Smile	–	to broaden one's lips in happiness
Grin	–	to broaden one's lips wide open, exposing teeth
Grimace	–	to smile affectedly in disgust/embarrassment with wry face
Simper	–	smile affectedly in order to please someone
Smirk	–	smile in self–satisfactory expression
23. Speech	–	public lecture **Election speech*
Address	–	speech delivered to a particular class of audience. **Address to the nation by the President. * The President addressed the joint session of both the houses of Parliament.*
Oration	–	eloquent speech **He gave a brilliant oration in the conference*
Talk	–	informal speech
Harangue	–	vehemently passionate speech
Philippic	–	critical speech against a public person or way of life
Sermon	–	religious or moral speech
Homily	–	speech giving practical advice

Discourse – speech on a topic by a scholar

Tirade – abusive speech against someone

24. **Spin** – to rotate something on its axis as a top

Whirl – spin rapidly

Whorl – rotate on spiral path

Rotate – turn around on its axis as a wheel

Revolve – to turn around a circular path **Earth revolves around the sun*

Twirl – to spin rapidly **Twirl a coin*

Gyrate – to spin on a base/fixed point

Pirouette – to spin on one foot or its toe as a dancer

Swivel – to turn around a fixed base as a swivel chair

25. **Spoils** – looted goods **A child brought toffees as spoils from a party *Sleuths discovered huge amounts of currency notes stashed as spoils of office by the corrupt official*

Booty – stolen goods **They apportioned their booty*

Swag – stolen goods taken away in bundles

26. **Spontaneous** – (coming or happening) without pre–meditated effort **Spontaneous laughter/reaction*

Impromptu – (to do something) promptly/without taking time to prepare **He delivered an impromptu speech*

Extempore – (to do something) quickly at the spur of the moment **He replied to the question extempore*

Improvised – (to do) without looking forward for preparation, without the required provisions **He improvised a poem*

27. **Spot** – patch of something undesirable on clean surface **Mud spots on immaculate dress*

Mottle – irregular patches of circular shape in various colours on animal's skin **Variegated mottles on cow's skin*

Speckle – small–sized patches of colour different from that of the surface **Stars speckled the blue sky*

Spangle – patches of glittering circular–sized matter strewn all over the surface., *viz,* glittering glass or metal pieces sewn on a cloth, tiny drops of dews on grass, tiny drops of sweat on the skin of the body **Cold perspiration bespangled his forehead*

Stipple – patches of small dots scattered all over a surface **Stipples of ink on shirt *Stipples of sunrays coming through trees' leaves dotted the side walk of the road*

28. Spread – the area to which a folded material can be unfolded **Spread of the carpet covers the whole room*

Extent – the area to which scope of something covers **Extent of the scope of discussion is limited*

Expanse – vast area of space **Expanse of the universe is infinite*

Tract – the area which a land extends to **A large tract of land*

29. Stay – remain in a place **He stayed in the meeting until it ended*

Linger – remain in a place for longer than expected as if reluctant to leave **Foul smell lingered in the room even after opening the doors and windows*

Torry – remain in a place for longer than intended due to compulsion **He had to tarry in a distant town for few days because of suspended trains due to flood *He tarried on the station due to delay in the arrival of the train*

Stagnate – remain in a place and rot due to obstruction in moving ahead **His career stagnated in the absence of the scope of promotions *Pool of water stagnated in the ditches*

30. Steal – to take away someone's possession surreptitiously

Pilfer – to steal in small portions, in instalments **Cashier pilfered cash totalling lakhs*

Filch – to steal through the window in a quick move as in snatching **He filched my bag and fled*

Purloin – to steal by quietly lifting and pocketing **He purloined my watch kept on the table*

Burgle – to steal by breaking into a house at night **A thief burgled my house at night*

Plagiarize – steal a portion of the written text authored by someone else and claim to have written oneself **Plagiarize data from the journals and include in one's own writing*

Embezzle – misappropriate money kept under own custody

31. Stimulate – cause sensitive part of the body to arouse **Stimulate the taste by savoury food*

Impel – cause to move forward by pushing forward **Impel someone to do as desired*

Actuate – cause to move forward by using force to drive **Machine is actuated by mechanical force*

Arouse – cause passion to awaken

Goad – spur, prod, provoke to move by poking with spikes *Goad the animal to drag the cart*

Provoke – cause to stir anger, annoyance, laughter **Provoke someone to angry retaliation*

32. **Stoop** – to come down below one's dignity to do something mean and selfish **I cannot stoop to lying to my friend* **He can stoop to do anything for selfish reason*

Condescend – to come down from one's exalted status to mix socially with people of lower status **The noble person does not mind to condescend with commoners*

Deign – (used always in negative sentence) coming down below one's status to do something which is not befitting one's status **He does not deign to reply to my accusations* **He does not deign to argue with lowly persons*

33. **Stop** – to prevent someone/something from doing some thing *Stop him from speaking*

Arrest – prevent someone from moving freely by taking into custody by police

Check – prevent from spreading further **Check epidemic*

Curb – prevent horse/animal from moving ahead by controlling with rein **Curb horse/dog*

Detain – to prevent someone/something from leaving a place *Police detained a suspect for questioning him* *The train was detained at the station for searching luggages*

Restrain – stop someone from doing something under pressure, threat **He was restrained from entering the election fray*

Staunch – stop flow of blood from wound **Tourniquet staunched bleeding*

Stem – stop something/condition from worsening **Stem the rot in the education system*

Stymie – stop progress by hindering **Divisive tendencies stymie the progress of the country*

Stunt – stop the growth of or development of **Luck of nutrition stunts physical development of a child*

34. **Strange** – surprisingly unusual **Strange customs/behaviour*

Absurd – logically unsual **Absurd reply*

Antic – amusingly unusual **Antic gesture*

Bizarre – horribly absurd **Bizarre idea*

Fantastic – fancifully unusual – devoid of reality **Fantastic idea*

Grotesque – ridiculously unusual **Grotesque shape*

Preposterous – foolishly absurd–like head of an animal in its back, and tail in the front **Preposterous suggestion*

Queer – obliquely unusual **Queer notion of life in America*

35. Strict – uncompromising in observance or enforcement of rules or principles **Strict laws* **Strict judge*

Austere – (appearance, face) frighteningly strict **Austere face of a strict teacher*

Stern – firmly uncompromising in observance **Stern disciplinarian*

Stringent – (action, rules) severely uncompromising **Stringent punishment*

Rigorous – uncompromising in applying rules **Rigorous observance of rules*

36. Strike – to hit forcefully **Strike ball*

Smite – hit hard **He smote on the back of someone*

Slug – hit with weapon such as rod etc. **Batsman slugged the ball to the boundary*

Slog – hit at random **Slog the haystack*

Swat – hit with a flat weapon **Swat a bee with a flat cardboard*

Clout – hit softly with open palm **Clout a child to reprimand*

Knock – hit by colliding **Knock door* **Car knocked down a cyclist*

37. Struggle – to make efforts to tide over adversity **He struggled the whole life to survive*

Contend – to make efforts to succeed **Sport's participants contended to win*

Cope – to make efforts to deal with difficulties **One has to cope with problems in life*

38. Stub – disposable small part at the end of something usable **Stub of cigarette or pencil*

Stubble – left–over part at the end of something wich is cut above the left over part **Stibble of paddy stalk is left in the ground along with the roots after harvesting the crop* **Stubble of beard wich is crropped above it*

Stump – remaining part of a felled tree **Stump of felled tree remains standing there*

39. Suffocate – deprive breathing due to access of fresh air **Suffocated in closed room*

Asphyxiate – deprive breathing by lack of oxygen in body

Choke – deprive breathing as by pressing or obstructing windpipe

Stifle – deprive breathing as by pressing mouth and nose

Strangle – deprive breathing by squeezing throat

Smother – deprive breathing as by fumes, smoke

40. Suggest – to mention an idea, proposal etc. for consideration **I suggested him to go home.*

Advise – to give counsel **He advised me to be cautious*

Recommend – to suggest something to be worthy of acceptance **I recommended his name for job*

41. Surprise – strike someone with wonder **His sudden arrival surprised me*

Amaze – to greatly surprise someone

Astound – to surprise someone beyond wildest expectation **My friend's testimony against me astounded me*

Astonish – to surprise beyond belief

42. Surrender – to give up resisting someone **Surrender to the will of God.*

Capitulate – give up unconditionally or at agreed terms before the enemy **Capitulate under pressure*

Concede – give up fight and accept defeat **The team conceded defeat*

Defer – give up objecting and surrender before someone out of respect **Defer to the wishes of elders*

Submit – give up resistance and surrender reluctantly **Submit before unjust demand*

Succumb – give up resistance when one becomes unable to keep fighting, especially illness/injury **He succumbed to his illness and died*

Yield – give up resistance due to intense pressure **He yielded to his persistent demand*

43. Surround – to encircle a place **This city is surrounded by hills*

Beleaguer – to surround someone to harass him **Seniors beleaguered a fresher in the college*

Besiege – to surround a person or place to make it impossible to escape away **Beggars besiege pilgrims for alms* **Troops besieged the town*

Cordon – to surround a person or place to make someone

unable to approach or enter **The leader is cordoned by his bodyguards *The meeting place was cordoned off by the police to prevent any outsider from entering*

Maroon – to surround a place/person to isolate or leave helpless **The village was marooned by flood*

Checkmate – to surround a person so as to be unable to make counter attack **Checkmate one's rival*

44. Swell – to become larger in size **His knee has swelled due to injury*

Bloat – to become larger in size due to accumulation of fluid inside **The animal's carcass has bloated*

Distend – to become larger due to pressure inside hollow forcing outer cover outward **Over–eating distended his belly*

Dilate – to become larger in size due to expansion **Medicine dropped in eyes dilated the eyes to facilitate internal examination by the ophthalmist*

Inflate – to become larger in size by pumping air inside **Cycle tryes inflate with air pumped inside the tubes*

Bulge – to become larger in size by protruding from the surface in round shape **A tumour bulged on his forehead*

45. Sycophant – a person who behaves servilely to someone to please him

Flatterer – a person who praises someone insincerely to please him

Toady – a person who is eveready in service of someone to please him

Lackey – a person who follows someone behind servilely **A lackey walks behind a person moving in a vehicle*

46. Sympathy – (sympathise is verb) feeling of sorrow for a sufferer **His sympathy for the oppressed people drove him to fight injustice*

Empathy – feeling of vicarious suffering to realise how a sufferer must be feeling by imagining himself to be in his place

Compassion – deep sympathy

Condolence – expressing sympathy with a person who has lost his near kin who had died **Condole with the son who has lost his father*

Commiseration– feeling of pity for the sufferer **Commiserate with someone in poor health*

Words beginning with —— T ——

1. **Talkative** – (person) who talks too much **A talkative child*
   Loqnacious – who indulges in continuous talking
   Garrulous – excessively talkative without much sense or on trivial matters
   Glib – who talks non-stop, fluently speaks

2. **Tarnish** – to make a shining surface dull by smearing dirt **Tarnished glass panes of windows*
   Besmear – to make dirty by smearing something
   Besmirch – to make dull by discolouring
   Blemish – to make a surface dirty by making or marking with spots **Blemish a clean surface by sprinkling ink or colours*
   Defile – to make a sacred place dirty
   Sully – to make a surface dirty by smearing mud, sullage

3. **Tasty** – pleasantly agreeable to taste
   Delicious – delightfully agreeable to taste
   Luscious – juicy and sweet
   Delectable – highly delightful **Delectable food*
   Succulent – full of juice **Succulent fruit*

4. **Tear** – to force apart a surface of something **A nail tore his shirt*
   Rend – tear into pieces **An explosion rent the body of the victim*
   Sunder – tear apart
   Split – to tear apart lengthwise from a large piece **Split a log with an axe into two parts*
   Cleave – to spearate joint pieces along the joining line **Cleave the cloves of a garlic bulb*
   Rive – tear apart from seam, Rip

5. **Tempt** – (*see lure*)

6. **Terrible** – causing terror due to being extremely bad, depressing **Terrible news*
   Awful – causing fear due to being extremely bad **Awful behaviour*

Enormous – causing fear due to being extremely excessive
Enormous wickedness

Ghastly – causing shock due to being extremely unpleasant
Ghastly murder

Horrible – causing disgust due to being so unpleasant
Horrible living condition in slums

Horrendous – inspiring shudden due to being extremely
Horrendous crime

Horrid – inspiring horror due to being extremely unpleasant

7. **Terrific** – inspiring fear due to being extra ordinarily excellent
Terrific performance

Tremendous – inspiring tremour due to being extraordinarily huge
Tremedous mountain peak

Immense – inspiring wonder, fear due to being extremely large
Immense vastness of sky

8. **Terrifying** – inspiring terror/violent fear caused by being dangerous

Frightening – inspiring fright/sudden fear

Horrifying – inspiring horror/shocking fear as by a gruesome sight
Horrifying sight

Awesome – inspiring awe

Appalling – inspiring horror causing paleness of face

Dreadful – inspiring dread/fear caused by anticipation of danger

9. **Theft** – an act of stealing by a thief **A thief committed a theft in this house*

Burglary – an act of stealing by silently entering someone's house

Heist – an act of stealing by forcibly entering **Heist in a bank*

Larceny – an act of stealing someone's property for own use **He is driving a car obtained by larceny*

Piracy – act of stealing something produced, created by someone and sell it as genuine **Piracy of song records (or C.D. tape) *Pirated print of a new cinema.* Also, *robbery on ships sailing in sea by pirates*

10. **Thrash** – (see Beat)

11. **Threat** – statement of intention to harm someone as retribution
He received a threat on phone

Coercion – threat given to someone who is unwilling to do something desired and force him to do it

Duress – threat of cruel treatment to compel someone do as desired

12. Throw – to send out something with a force in a direction **He threw stones in the pond*

Fling – to throw casually so as to fall on the ground **He flung the note–book in anger*

Hurl – throw missiles upon someone in an attempt to hurt someone **He hurled a shoe on the speaker addressing the meeting*

Jettison – throw materials overboard so as to reduce load on aircraft or ship to prevent from falling down or sinking **Jettison goods to keep aeroplane keep flying*

Lob – throw something on a trajectory **He lobbed the ball towards me*

Pelt – throw missile towards someone so as to hit him **Mob pelted stones on the policemen*

Toss – fling a coin in the air to make head or tail

13. Tie – to bind things together with a rope or cord **Tie the hands of the thief*

Fasten – to tie firmly

Gird – to tie a cloth/loin around waist with a belt

Ligate – tie wound, ruptured skin with surgical cord

Tether – to tie an animal with a longer rope attached to a stake in the ground so as to limit the movement of the animal upto a limited distance from the stake

Yoke – tie animals to a horizontal bar attached to a cart so as to drag it

Harness – tie a horse with the long belts to a vehicle to be dragged by the horse

14. Tolerate – to put up with without reacting against someone's unpleasant behaviour, thing's harmful effect **I can't tolerate his arrogance anymore* **One can tolerate a small amount of poison/bitter taste of capsicum*

Bear – to put up with something painful or inconvenient with patience **Bear acute pain* **Please bear with me until the programme concludes*

Brook – to put up with something objectionable by taking it as usual occurrence **I can't brook factionalism and indiscipline in party*

Endure – to put up with something inconvenient, or unpleasant patiently for a long time **I can't endure his gaffe anymore*

15. Tradition – norms of doing something which has been follow -ed by people from generation to generation **To treat the guest as God is our tradition*

Custom – norms of doing something conventionally **It is our custom to exchange gifts on festivals*

Practice – norms of doing something habitually **Daily walking is his practice*

16. Treasure – wealth of gold and other precious possession accumultated **Treasure of Nizam of Hyderabad*

Treasure-trove – a hidden treasure which is dicovered accidently **He chanced upon an attic which turned out to be a treasure-trove*

17. Treasury – a place where funds of the government are kept deposited

Coffer – a place where funds of an institution, person are kept stored **Company's coffer depleted in the period of lean season of business*

Fisc – place where public funds are stored **Unclaimed property returns to the fisc*

Exchequer – Nation's treasury **Pension is paid to the employees of the government from the exchequer*

18. Tremble – shaking of body as in fear in quick short movements **He stood there trembling *He began to tremble when confronted by a ferocious dog*

Shiver – shake body due to extreme cold. **He was shivering in winter night*

Shudder – shake with convulsive movement due to horror

Quake – shake violently due to shock **Earth suddenly began to quake due to loud explosion*

Quaver – shaking of one's voice as in fear or excitement **His voice quavered in excitement*

Quiver – shaking to and fro as of trees in light breeze; or lips up and down in excitement **His lips quivered*

Flicker – shaking of flame **Candle's flame flickered in the wind*

19. Trick – (see Ruse)

20. Trifle – to treat something in frivolous manner–that is, in non-serious manner **Trifle with one's own career*

Toy – to treat playfully

Flirt – to treat in casual manner–without serious intent **Flirt with future plan*

Dally – to treat in careless manner **Dally with one's duty*

21. Trim – to cut down irregular branches to smooth shape **Trim garden hedges *Barber trimmed hairs*

Truncate – to cut something short **Truncate a long stick*

Lop – to cut off branches, *viz,* of a tree

Pare – to cut outer layer to remove **Pare potato*

Dock – to cut short the tail of an animal

Poll – cut the horn of an animal

Prune – to cut superfluous part of something **Prune stem off the flower*

Crop – to cut away end protion of something **Crop edges of a photograph*

Clip – to cut with scissors **Clip the wings of a bird *Clip wool from the sheep*

22. Try – to make attempt to do something **He tried to run fast to catch up with others*

Endeavour – to try hard to accomplish something **Endeavour to achieve success*

Strive – to try laboriously to accomplish **Strive hard to lift a heavy stone*

Persevere – to try continuously, in spite of failures, to accomplish **He persevered to get selected for the professional course*

23. Turning point – a stage in time when important changes take place in one's life, history etc.

Climacteric – a stage in one's life when important changes in physical conditions take place **Climacteric age marks the changes like menopause in women*

Epoch – a turning point in time of history when important events take place **The treaty ushered in an era of peace *Advent of Gandhi in the freedom struggle marked the epoch-making event in the history of India*

Watershed – turning point, point of time which divides tow phases of events/distinct histories. **Year 2005 was the watershed in Bihar politics which marked the end of lawlessness and beginning of development.*

24. Twist – to turn obliquely **He twisted someone's arm*

Wrench – to turn around by pulling forcefully **Wrench a tight screw*

Wrest – to twist someone's hand or fist to snatch something he had held firmly **Wrest his arm to snatch a pen from his grip*

Wring – to twist a bird's neck, clothes to drain water off **Wring wet clothes* **Wring fowl's neck to kill it*

Distort – twist something out of its shape **Collision distorted the vehicle badly*

Contort – twist lips, face to show cotempt, pain etc. **He contorted his lips in disgust*

Words beginning with ——— U ———

1. **Ubiquitous** – (something ominous) present everywhere **On May Day, the labour movement/demonstration is ubiquitous in the country* **Policemen are ubiquitous in the town on a day of disturbed law and order*

Omnipresent – (God, something divine) present everywhere **God is believed to be omnipresent*

Universal – (something applicable) present everywhere **Universal truth* **Universal law of gravity*

2. **Uncommuncative** – not prone to talking

Laconic – prone to talking in few words

Reticent – not inclined to talking about one's own affairs

Taciturn – prone to be cautious in talking by remaining silent. Taciturn approval of the powerful politician is evident in the serious labour agitations.

3. **Understanding** – mutually tolerant relationship in joint activities **They enjoy perfect understanding* **They have an understanding about who would do which part of the work*

Nexus – mutually helping relationship for unfair purpose **Nexus between the politicians and the criminals is well known*

Coordination – mutual understanding in working together in harmony or tandem **Coordination between various agencies helps smooth progress in work*

4. **Unrestrained** – (activity) without restraint **Unrestrained violence*

Libertine – (immoral activity) unrestrained indulgence **Libertine lecher*

Licentious – unrestrained indulgence in immoral activity without regard to accepted norms **Licentious activities*

Dissolute – unrestrained indulgence in immoral activity without regard to/concerned with the need for control **Dissolute activity.*

Extravagant	–	unrestrained indulgence in spending, praising etc.
Profligate	–	recklessly unrestrained indulgence in immoral activity
Rampant	–	growing unrestrained/unrestricted activity **Rampant corruption*
Wanton	–	willful indulgence in unchecked wrong activity **Wanton cruelty*
5. Untidy	–	(a place) with scattered articles, strewn all around **An untidy room*
Unkempt	–	(hairs) not combed to look smooth **Unkempt hairs*
Dishevelled	–	(hairs) in disorderly condition **Wind dishevelled his hairs*
Ruffled	–	(feathers of bird) in disorderly condition, **Ruffled feathers*
Sloppy	–	(dress) loose and unfitting **Sloppy dress.*
Slipshod	–	(work, workmanship) ill-cared, lacking in details **Slipshod arrangements*
Slovenly	–	(person) with dirty habits/appearance **Slovenly person*
Slatternly	–	(woman) with dirty habits/appearance **A slatternly woman*
6. Untiring	–	(effort) not to get tired of making efforts to achieve something **Make untiring effort*
Unflagging	–	(courage, morale) not to give up or become unvigorous **Unflagging courage*
Indefatigable	–	(person) not to get fatigued **Indefatigable warrior*
7. Upheaval	–	state of violent disorder turning everything agitated **Political upheaval has gripped the nation*
Turmoil	–	state of agitation/disorder
Turbulence	–	(river) the state of agitation in the flowing water **Turbulence in the river capsized a boat*
Topsy-turvy	–	state of agitation turning everything upside down
8. Upset	–	disturbed mentally or emotionally **He is upset because of being badly treated by his friends*
Disconcerted	–	disturbed due to confusion
Disconsolate	–	disturbed emotionally without or beyond consolation **Disconsolate victim of accident*
Distraught	–	Disturbed mentally from grief or worries

Words beginning with — V —

1. **Vacant** – (a place) devoid of its usual occupant **A vacant house is available to let *A vacant niche/seat/chair*

   Vacuum – a place devoid of air or contents

   Void – a vacuum caused by departure of someone **His demise caused a void in politics*

   Empty – (a place) devoid of its usual contents **Empty bottle/jar/wagon*

   Vacuous – (mind) devoid of ideas **A vacuous mind*

2. **Vagabond** – (person) wandering from place to place in the absence of means of livelihood or home

   Vagrant – (person) who wanders idly **Vagrant beggars*

   Tramp – (person) who wanders from place to place by travelling in search of job and means of livelihood

   Rogue – (animal/person) wandering and doing mischief **A rouge elephant on the city roads caused havoc*

3. **Verify** – to confirm the truth of something **Events verified his prediction *Verify the spelling of a word*

   Certify – to confirm to genuineness **Certify a document*

   Vouch – to confirm as by practical evidence **His conducts vouch for his being a gentleman*

   Attest – to confirm something to be true

   Authenticate – to confirm something to be genuine

4. **Violation** – breach of law/rule

   Infraction – breach of rule by mere failure to adhere to it

   Infringement – breach of other's rights or privileges

   Contravention – breach of rule by going or acting against it **Party defection is in contravention of parliamentary democracy*

   Transgression – breach of limits of own authority or propriety **He indulges in occasional transgression in drinking wine.*

Words beginning with — W —

1. **Wander** – move about aimlessly

   Roam – wander for delight

Prowl – (animal) wander in search of prey

Gad – wander even as expected to stay at home *Housewives gad around the marketplace*

Gallivant – wander in search of pleasure or amusement *Gallivant in park, fair*

Traipse – wander from place to place for specific purpose *Leaders traipse around for convassing in the elections*

Rove – wander aimlessly around a place *Rove in the woods*

Loaf – wander lazily to pass time *Loaf along the river*

2. **Warning** – act of making someone aware of danger *He shouted a warning to flee from the house afire*

Caution – act of making someone circumspect of impending danger

Caveat – warning to be wary of something suspect

Caveat emptor – warning to the purchaser to be wary of being duped

Caveat venditor – warning to the seller against indulging in a malpractice

3. **Waver** – change one's opinion/decision repeatedly due to hesitation in remaining firm

Vacillate – change one's opinion/decision repeatedly due to hesitation in remaining firm

Dither – change one's opinion/decision due to being indecisive

4. **Weird** – fearsome due to being supernatural *Weird stillness of jungle at night*

Uncanny – fearsome due to being strangely supernatural *Uncanny feeling*

Eerie – fearsome due to being ghostly *Eerie moaning from a deserted house*

Macabre – fearsome due to being related to death *Macabre rituals of Tantrik*

5. **While away** – to pass time leisurely *While away the day gossiping*

Beguile – to pass time by doing some meaningful work *Beguile time by reading books or coaching the neighbourhood kids*

	Fleet	– to pass time by doing nothing **Fleet one's time sitting in the balcony*
	Idle away	– to pass time by walking around without purpose **Idle away time wandering in the sun*
	Lounge	– pass time by reclining a on support **Lounge by the roadside lamp-post and talk to the passers-by*
	Loll	– to pass time by sitting in laziness **Passengers loll supine on their seats in the train coach*
6.	**Wicked**	– an evil (person)
	Iniquitous	– devoid of just and fair attitude **Iniquitous person*
	Nepharious	– denunciable iniquity **Napharious neglect of the parents*
	Flagitious	– shameful wickedness **Flagitious propaganda*
7.	**Will**	– desire **He has lost his will to fight adversity*
	Conation	– ultimate desire **Salvation from mundane world or one's soul is everyone's conation*
	Volition	– free will **He did it on his own volition*
8.	**Worry**	– (see anxiety)
9.	**Wreckage**	– broken parts of a ship, aeroplane, train destroyed in an accident
	Flotsam	– broken parts of a ship which remain floating on the sea
	Jetsam	– broken parts of a ship or jettisoned goods which are washed ashore and salvaged
	Lagan	– broken parts of a ship which sink to the bottom of the sea
10.	**Writhe**	– to roll or twist one's body in pain **Writhe in pain*
	Squirum	– to roll one's body in embarrassment **He squirmed in his seat due to embarrassment caused by insinuation directed against him by the speech -maker*
	Wriggle	– to twist one's body as in an attempt to pass through a narrow passage
	Wallow	– to roll one's body in something pleasurable **The buffalow wallows in mud *The rich man wallows in the luxury of his richness*
	Welter	– to roll one's body in something difficult to endure **Welter in poverty *Welter in sweltering summer*

❑❑❑

MULTIPLE CHOICE QUESTION ANSWERS

Choose the correct option out of the given options which can replace the word (marked in bold) in the sentence:

1. He is quite **meticulous** in his dealings with others.
   (A) reserved (B) haughty (C) indifferent (D) careful
2. He committed **heresy** by speaking against the religious orthodoxy.
   (A) offence (B) blasphemy (C) sin (D) crime
3. He is **writhing** in pain.
   (A) rolling (B) wresting (C) squirming (D) twisting
4. His **sardonic** grin was quite offending.
   (A) sneering (B) satisfying (C) nicious (D) caustic
5. His **iniquitous** behaviour hurts me.
   (A) unjust (B) unequal (C) uneven (D) unusual
6. He **segregated** bills and vouchers collected over a period.
   (A) assembled (B) filed (C) sorted (D) separated
7. **Vagabond** urchins loiter all day on the street.
   (A) Tramp (B) Stray (C) Astray (D) Discarded
8. He wore a **somber** expression on his face.
   (A) gloomy (B) shadowy (C) sleeping (D) sorrowful
9. **Rampant** corruption has gripped the nation.
   (A) unchecked (B) furious (C) raging (D) running
10. He squandered money in **wanton** manner.
    (A) willful (B) unjust (C) malicious (D) heedless
11. The wild animal **glared** at its prey.
    (A) glowered (B) stared (C) gloated (D) ogled
12. He **abandoned** his old home and shifted to a new one.
    (A) Renounced (B) Demised (C) Deserted (D) Forsake
13. She indulges in flirtations with reckless **abandon**.
    (A) enjoyment (B) unrestraint (C) carelessnes (D) involvement
14. He **abased** his dignity with his questionable deeds.
    (A) degraded (B) lowered (C) reduced (D) depreciated
15. Adulteration **debased** the quality or purity of precious gold.
    (A) devalued (B) depreciated (C) lowered (D) enhanced
16. His son's unbecoming conduct has **abashed** him.
    (A) insulted (B) degraded (C) ashamed (D) humbled
17. His fever has started to **abate** after one week.
    (A) worsen (B) improve (C) decrease (D) vanish

18. A kid was **abducted** for ransom from the kid's family.
(A) kidnapped (B) seduced (C) taken away (D) allured

19. The President of a country **abdicated** to take refuge in another country.
(A) abducted (B) fied (C) renounced (D) resigned

20. He tried to **adduce** a forgotten matter by jogging his forehead with his finger.
(A) deduce (B) to take out from memory
(C) recollect (D) recall

21. He is **adept** in the art of origami.
(A) ignorant (B) clumsy (C) expert (D) recall

22. He earns **adequate** to meet his expenses.
(A) sufficient (B) superfluous
(C) enough (D) just equal to the requirement

23. Mud **stuck** to his shoes.
(A) adhered (B) clung (C) attached (D) affixed

24. Long time **adherent** to the party changed his loyalty in the latter stage of his life.
(A) believer (B) supporter (C) stickler (D) attachment

25. His house is **adjacent** to mine.
(A) contiguous (B) added (C) attached (D) beside

26. The parliament session was adjorned **sine die**.
(A) suspended (B) postponed
(C) deferred (D) without fixing the date of reconvening

27. The position of the political leaders is now a days a **sine cure**
(A) without work (B) cosy
(C) earning income without any care to do something in return
(D) careless

28. The rich man died **sine prole**.
(A) without medicine (B) without money
(C) without offspring (D) without anyone to care about him

29. The father **admonished** his son for wayward activities.
(A) reproved (B) cautioned (C) rectified (D) apprised

30. The **adonis** was the cynosure of all eyes in the party
(A) aphrodite (B) very handsome young man
(C) narcissus (D) don

31. The grand old man **adored** his grandchildren.
(A) loved (B) liked fervently
(C) worshipped (D) disliked

32. The drawing hall was **adorned** with bric-a-brac.
(A) decorated (B) arranged (C) beautified (D) painted

33. He is an **adroit** sculptor.
(A) clever (B) ingenious (C) adept (D) clumsy

34. The **advent** of Mahatma Gandhi on the horizon of freedom struggle gave a shot in the arm of the struggle.
(A) adventure (B) arrival (C) rise (D) return

35. He is my bitter **adversary**.
(A) enemy (B) antagonist (C) critic (D) adviser

36. He takes **adversities** in life in his usual strides.
(A) enemies (B) antagonists (C) hardships (D) annoyance

37. The official **adverted** to the complainant and heard his grievances.
(A) turned his attention (B) turned his face
(C) turned his chair (D) turned his eyes

38. The investors were **advised** of the risk involved in the share market.
(A) cautioned (B) informed (C) suggested (D) consulted

39. The programme was organized under the **aegis** of a voluntary organisation (NGO).
(A) age-old experience (B) shield
(C) arrangement (D) routine activity

40. Mount Everest came into existence **acons** ago.
(A) pre-historic period (B) medieval period
(C) indefinitely long period (D) a few centuries ago

41. The accused **acknowledged** his involvement in the crime.
(A) accepted (B) admitted (C) confessed (D) conceded

42. They **acquainted** the boss with their plans.
(A) informed (B) made conversant
(C) made known (D) familiarised

43. The fighter aircraft displayed brilliant **feats** in the air.
(A) aerobics (B) acrobatics (C) aerobatics (D) aeronautics

44. Their **acrimonious** dispute vitiated the relationship.
(A) acrid (B) harsh (C) sharp (D) bitter

45. He is **actuated** by selfish motives.
(A) incited (B) motivated (C) impelled (D) driven

46. He is endowed with remarkable **acumen** in business matters.
(A) acuteness (B) discernment(C) insight (D) sharpness

47. He lacked the ability to **adapt** to the changed situations.
(A) adjust (B) adopt (C) reconcile (D) conform

48. The parliament was **addressed** by a visiting foreign dignitary.
(A) visited (B) attended (C) lectured (D) advised

49. He is an **affable** and courteous gentleman.
(A) friendly (B) benign (C) pleasant (D) favourable

50. He **affected** ignorance.
(A) feigned (B) adopted (C) preferred (D) assumed

51. He has great **affinity** for sweets.
(A) adherence (B) predilection (C) affectation (D) attraction

52. He **protested** that the newspaper account is misleading.
(A) objected (B) asserted (C) confirmed (D) denied

53. The old man is **afflicted** with crippling gout.
(A) inflicted (B) affected (C) distressed (D) lashed

54. His insinuation was an **affront** to me.
(A) attack (B) criticism (C) directed (D) offence

55. Epidemic struck the people in the **aftermath** of flood.
(A) resultant event (B) consequence
(C) disaster (D) calamity

56. Advance age has **aggravated** his ailments.
(A) annoyed (B) irritated (C) worsened (D) aggrieved

57. The gory sight of the accident left us **aghast**.
(A) amazed (B) frightened (C) horrified (D) shocked

58. The aeroplane was **airborne** on schedule.
(A) afloat (B) aloft (C) flying (D) soaring

59. The door of the room was **ajar**.
(A) shut (B) open (C) wide open (D) partly open

60. He did his job with **alacrity**.
(A) bitter feelings (B) regretfully (C) unwillingly (D) liveliness

61. He has **alienated** his entire family.
(A) estranged (B) deserted (C) antagonised (D) annoyed

62. He **alighted** from the aeroplane with his hand-bag.
(A) descended (B) disembarked (C) dismounted (D) boarded

63. Gossipping is the **ailment** of idle persons.
(A) nutrient (B) food (C) pastime (D) entertainment

64. The court ordered a handsome **alimony** to the divorcee.
(A) maintenance (B) alms (C) sustenance (D) allowance

65. The minister's assurance **allayed** the people's fear of draconian law.
(A) mitigated (B) mollified (C) soothed (D) moderated

66. He often **alludes** to his yeoman's services.
(A) insinuates (B) refers (C) reminds (D) hints

67. The adviser of the president acts as his **alter ego** during his absence.
(A) another self (B) confidant (C) alternative (D) deputy

68. He always takes an **altruistic** approach.
(A) unselfish (B) truthful (C) charitable (D) generous

69. He is **alumnus** of a prestigious college.
(A) student (B) graduate (C) admirer (D) pass-out

70. His personality is a strange **amalgam** of contradictory traits.
(A) alloy (B) combination(C) merger (D) blend

71. He is an **ameteur** of cricket.
(A) aficionado (B) novice (C) dabbler (D) expert

72. The **ambiguities** of modern poetry render it difficult to comprehend.
(A) equivocations (B) complexities
(C) uncertainties (D) explicitness

73. Nomads are **ambulatory** tribes.
(A) walking (B) prehensile (C) moving (D) roving

74. Robbers lurked behind a bush in **ambush.**
(A) waiting to attack (B) concealed (C) hiding (D) waiting

75. Masters like to hire **amenable** servants.
(A) manageable (B) docile (C) tractable (D) stubborn

76. The offender was **amerced** for traffic violation.
(A) punished (B) mulcted (C) penalised (D) fined

77. I think something is **amiss** in your plan.
(A) missing (B) wrong (C) astry (D) offending

78. The government offered **amnesty** if the rebels lay down arms.
(A) permission (B) pardon (C) forgetfulness (D) ignorance

79. He became **amorous** of her on the very first look.
(A) enamoured (B) infatuated (C) passionate (D) loving

80. He is bubbling with **amour patriae**.
(A) love (B) loyalty (C) patriotism (D) fatherhood

81. He refused to compromise with his **amour propre**.
(A) first love (B) self-esteem (C) love affair (D) love

82. People want to get **ample** supply of tap-water in their houses.
(A) adequate (B) abundant (C) overflowing (D) profuse

83. She was **amused** by the children's conversation.
(A) excited (B) pleased (C) aroused (D) happy

84. Using modern sports car in a historical film is **anachronism**.
(A) wrong time reference (B) time matching
(C) obsolete (D) disorder

85. Calmpose tablet is used as an **analgesic**.
(A) pain reliever (B) febrifuge (C) antipyretic (D) tranquiliser

86. I don't see any **analogy** between our problems.
(A) comparison (B) agreement (C) similarity (D) difference

87. His misdemeanour earned his father's **anathema**.

(A) loath (B) hate (C) dislike (D) imprecation

88. Her presence **animated** the party.

(A) enlivened (B) stimulated (C) energized (D) fortified

89. A deep-seated **animosity** between the two sisters was a problem for the family.

(A) opposition (B) hostility (C) enmity (D) antagonism

90. The victorious country **annexed** part of a territory of the defeated country.

(A) appended (B) added (C) attached (D) supplemented

91. The ruling party was **annihilated** in the election.

(A) defeated (B) destroyed (C) decimated (D) vanquished

92. The deity was **anointed** by the priest.

(A) smeared (B) desecrated (C) rubbed with oil (D) annoyed

93. A quiet person was an **anomaly** in his exuberant family.

(A) odd (B) incongruous (C) inconsistency (D) deviation

94. Little is known about his **antecedents**.

(A) precedence (B) anti activities (C) events (D) character

95. He meets his guests in his house's **anterior** hall.

(A) backside (B) internal (C) front (D) posterior

96. Antiquated machines are lying idle in the factory.

(A) old (B) obsolete (C) antique (D) archaic

97. Hot is **antithesis** of cold.

(A) contrast (B) against (C) opposed (D) direct opposite

98. The government seems to be **apathetic** to controlling corruption.

(A) unsympathetic (B) unconcerned (C) against (D) concerned

99. Many **apocryphal** stories about him are doing rounds.

(A) false (B) spurious (C) doubtful (D) unauthentic

100. He is a rowed **apologist** of the government policies.

(A) critic (B) demanding apology (C) defender (D) analyst

101. Movie stars are **apotheosis** of glamour to the fans.

(A) god (B) icon (C) deified symbol (D) symbol

102. He was terrified by ghostly **apparitions** in sleep.

(A) appearance (B) phantom (C) wraith (D) spirit

103. Politicians have unsatiated **appetite** for power.

(A) desire (B) need (C) hunger (D) craving

104. He gave his critics an **apposite** reply.

(A) opposite (B) apt (C) irrelevant (D) adapted

105. The police did not **apprehend** violent mood of the mob.
(A) catch (B) grasp (C) anticipate (D) perceive

106. A huge fund was **appropriated** in the budget for primary education.
(A) made suitable (B) provided (C) justified (D) set aside

107. God is the sole **arbiter** of our fate.
(A) mediator (B) decision-maker (C) arbitrator (D) judge

108. He is my **arch** rival.
(A) cunning (B) sly (C) mischievous (D) chief

109. **Archaic** social traditions have become irrelevant.
(A) antique (B) antiquated (C) old (D) medieval

110. **Ardent** devotees thronged the congregation.
(A) earnest (B) fervent (C) passionate (D) fierce

111. He cunningly **arrogated** the credit of someone who did the job.
(A) appropriated (B) claimed (C) assumed (D) snatched

112. He filed the documents **arsy-varsy**.
(A) topsy-turvy (B) preposterous (C) haphazardly (D) reverse

113. The orator **articulated** his ideas.
(A) jointed (B) enunciated (C) expressed clearly (D) spoke

114. The author **ascribed** innocence to the wife of her cruel husband in the novel.
(A) described (B) imputed (C) indicated (D) attributed

115. He looked **askance** at me.
(A) doubtfully (B) distrustfully (C) disapprovingly (D) obliquely

116. He vehemently aspersed on his opponents.
(A) sprayed (B) traduced (C) sprinkled (D) attacked

117. He is an **assiduous** student.
(A) diligent (B) vehement (C) arduous (D) acerbic

118. The neophyte **assimilated** the party doctrines quickly.
(A) Iearnt (B) imbibed (C) arduous (D) acerbic

119. He passed the evening **assorting** collected bills and vouchers.
(A) arranged (B) sorted (C) distributed (D) classified

120. He **assumed** the style of an aggressive go-getter.
(A) pretended (B) supposed (C) adopted (D) expected

121. He **assured** us that everything would be well.
(A) ensured (B) promised (C) confirmed (D) insured

122. He is an **astute** politician.
(A) arrogant (B) shrewd (C) pragmatic (D) keen

123. One should **atone** for committing sinful deeds.
(A) expiate (B) pardon (C) amend (D) reconcile

124. He attributed his bad temper to his ill health.
(A) allocated (B) contributed (C) assigned (D) credited

125. The student's **audacity** shocked the teacher.
(A) temerity (B) arrogancy (C) recklessness (D) boldness

126. He works overtime to **augment** his income.
(A) add (B) increase (C) enlarge (D) eke out

127. Good monsoon **augurs** bumper harvest.
(A) prognosticates (B) predicts (C) interprets (D) indicates

128. His stoic **aura** crumbled at the slightest provocation.
(A) halo (B) atmosphere (C) character (D) greatness

129. A marriage is solemnised on an **auspicious** day.
(A) opportune (B) favourable (C) propitious (D) holy

130. The principal's **austere** face was enough to quail them.
(A) fiery (B) grave (C) stern (D) strict

131. The harsh punishment **avenged** the crime.
(A) retributed (B) revenged (C) requited (D) reciprocated

132. He is not **averse** to extending amnesty to the rebels.
(A) repugnant (B) disgusted (C) loath (D) opposed

133. Our plan to stage protest against the government went **awry**.
(A) askew (B) distorted (C) lopsided (D) crooked

134. His non-stop **babble** is annoying.
(A) utterance (B) chatter (C) murmur (D) humming

135. The **babel** in the meeting made it impossible to understand who is telling what.
(A) noisy confusion (B) noisy uproar (C) chattering (D) noise

136. The dissidents' plan to attack the policies of the party **backfired**.
(A) rebounded (B) boomeranged (C) recoiled (D) returned

137. The **background** of one's upbringing shapes one's character.
(A) situation (B) milieu (C) environment (D) experience

138. The seats in the coach were **back-to-back**.
(A) front-to-front (B) dos-a-dos (C) round robin (D) face-to-face

139. The dispute engendered **bad blood** between rivals.
(A) enmity (B) hostility (C) animosity (D) bloody war

140. Offers of discount are favourite **baits** to lure customers employed by sellers.
(A) ploys (B) traps (C) ruse (D) hooks

141. The cart-pulling horse suddenly **baulked** at moving ahead.
(A) jibbed (B) stopped (C) refused (D) hesitated

142. They **bamboozed** us into joining their team.
(A) pushed (B) shoved (C) hoodwinked (D) bambooed

143. They were **bandying** accusations upon each other.
(A) trading (B) exchanging (C) throwing (D) bowling

144. He banged the door open in anger.
(A) stroke (B) blew (C) slammed (D) threw

145. The guests were **banqueted** to sumptuous menu.
(A) honoured (B) feasted (C) regaled (D) partied

146. His acerbic **barbs** were pinching.
(A) thorns (B) pointed edges (C) carping remarks (D) beards

147. An inebriate suddenly **barged** into my room.
(A) broke (B) entered (C) forced (D) intruded

148. The vote-seekers **barnstorm** countryside soliciting votes.
(A) raid (B) campaign (C) tour (D) visit

149. The reporters overwhelmed the minister with **barrage** of questions.
(A) volley (B) barrier (C) flood (D) obstruction

150. The police **barricaded** the meeting ground.
(A) blocked (B) obstructed (C) surrounded (D) barred

151. Venal officials **barter** their pride for material gains.
(A) exchange (B) swap (C) trade (D) bargain

152. Nobody **bats** an eye on outrageous behaviour of the present-day politicians.
(A) opens (B) flutter (C) closes (D) casts

153. The spectators **bated** their breaths at the nip-and-tuck race.
(A) held (B) restrained (C) lessened (D) drew

154. A pioneer does not tread on a **beaten** path.
(A) thrashed (B) trodden (C) used (D) defeated

155. This gown **becomes** your personality.
(A) comes for (B) attracts (C) fits (D) befits

156. I warn you stop **badgering** me.
(A) pestering (B) worrying (C) baiting (D) disturbing

157. I **beaconed** him to come near me.
(A) light house (B) warned (C) signalled (D) guided

158. Stop **befudding** the public with misleading propaganda.
(A) muddling (B) stupefying (C) meddling (D) fudgeing

159. He **begrudged** his friend getting the award.
(A) envied (B) reluctantly accepted (C) resented (D) coveted

160. He is used to **beguile** lazy afternoon with reading good books.
(A) pass pleasantly (B) while away
(C) fleet (D) waste away

161. Tourists amusingly **behold** marching sentries on the Wagah border.
(A) catch (B) look (C) regard (D) witness

162. A maverick is **beholden** to no one.
(A) obligated (B) attached (C) responsible (D) look at

163. It does not **behoove** you to be rude to others.
(A) honour (B) suit (C) appropriate (D) honourable

164. The volcano suddenly became active and began to **belch** smoke and fire.
(A) eructate (B) blow out (C) eject (D) emit

165. His trembling hands **belied** his calm voice.
(A) lied down (B) falsified (C) contrasted (D) controlled

166. A peace treaty was formalised by the **belligerent** countries.
(A) hostile (B) bellicose (C) pugnacious (D) warring

167. The injured animal **bellowed** in pain.
(A) roared (B) cried (C) howled (D) wailed

168. The rich man was solicited **benefaction** for earthquake victims.
(A) benefit (B) charity (C) goodness (D) kindness

169. A small **bequest** of a testator made him live comfortably.
(A) donation (B) charity
(C) disposition by will of property (D) will

170. A serious illness **bereaved** them of their mother.
(A) deprived (B) survived (C) killed (D) snatched

171. They **beseeched** him to come home at once.
(A) castigated (B) solicited (C) begged (D) appealed

172. Propaganda was aimed at **besmirching** his good reputation.
(A) smearing (B) tarnishing (C) spoiling (D) besotting

173. Nobel prize is **bestowed** on the renowned achievers.
(A) gifted (B) awarded (C) stowed (D) conferred

174. "Woe **betide** you," He cursed.
(A) gifted (B) awarded (C) stowed (D) conferred

175. He inadvertently **betrayed** a secret.
(A) exposed (B) revealed (C) misled (D) deceived

176. The boy and the girl were **betrothed** recently.
(A) engaged (B) married (C) tied in knots (D) united

177. His tearful plea was designed to bias the judge.
(A) prejudice (B) incline (C) favour (D) bend

178. The couple used to **bicker** as a matter of habit.
(A) flicker (B) quiver (C) argue (D) quarrel

179. He bade **adieu** to his friend going abroad.
(A) good bye (B) bon voyage (C) farewell (D) good wishes

180. He does not earn even to meet his **bare** needs.
(A) naked (B) open (C) minimal (D) bald

181. He expects us to do his **bidding** all the time.
(A) command (B) summons (C) performing (D) subordination

182. He **bided** his time until right opportunity to take revenge on me.
(A) called (B) waited (C) wasted (D) sought

183. Villages agreed to **billet** visiting students from the town.
(A) let enter (B) allow stay
(C) provide requested lodging (D) chase out

184. He is an annoying **blab**.
(A) blabbermouth (B) bore (C) idiot (D) egoist

185. He suddenly **blacked out** due to acute weakness.
(A) became black (B) became unconscious
(C) fell down (D) became dark faced

186. Long illness has **blanched** her face.
(A) dried (B) whitened (C) bleached (D) tanned

187. The loudspeaker **blared** cheap songs all night.
(A) emit (B) sounded loudly (C) shrieked (D) roared

188. He remained **blase** throughout the programme.
(A) bored (B) annoyed (C) cloyed (D) surfied

189. He was **blasphemed** by the critics for airing his frank opinion.
(A) blasted (B) slandered (C) applauded (D) abused

190. Their faces **blazed** with enthusiasm.
(A) fired (B) gleamed (C) burnt (D) glowed

191. His pioneering research **blazed the trail** in the field of space science.
(A) fired (B) triggered (C) showed the new path (D) led

192. His eyes became **bleary** with tears.
(A) blurred (B) filled (C) dim (D) blotted

193. One-year discontinuity in his studies became a **blemish** on his career.
(A) blame (B) blot (C) defect (D) flaw

194. Sky and sea seemed to **blend** in the horizon.
(A) mix (B) combine (C) mingle (D) combine

195. Pests **blighted** the crops in the field.
(A) wilted (B) crippled (C) withered (D) blasted

196. Career promotion has **bloated** his ego.
(A) expanded (B) distended (C) puffed (D) inflated

197. Campaign against corruption proved to be **blockbuster**.
(A) explosive (B) highly effective (C) deadly (D) useful

198. The child has **bloomed** into a handsome youth.
(A) blossomed (B) flowered (C) developed (D) grown

199. A bully **blusters** to cow down others.
(A) threatens (B) flusters (C) rebukes (D) utters empty menaces

200. The spectators **bolstered** the morale of their respective teams with shouting encouraging slogans.
(A) propped (B) raised (C) supported (D) enhanced

201. Bonafides of this person is suspect.
(A) good behaviour (B) goodness (C) faithfulness (D) truth

202. Reduction in the rates of income tax was a **bonanza** granted by the government to the tax payers.
(A) bonus (B) good gain (C) windfall (D) favours

203. He is a minister and a litterateur **to boot**.
(A) bargain (B) help (C) besides (D) extra

204. The dog **bounded** across the field.
(A) leashed (B) tied (C) bolted (D) ran

205. He gave the boy a **box** on his ear.
(A) spar (B) slap (C) strike (D) blow

206. Conceited people use to **brag**.
(A) bark (B) boast (C) shout (D) yell

207. He **braided** strands of twigs in a rope.
(A) twisted (B) branded (C) weaved (D) plaited

208. The desparado **brandished** his gun to scare the people away.
(A) aimed (B) flourished (C) fired (D) shook

209. A midnight **brawl** disturbed the sleeping neighbours.
(A) noise (B) shouting (C) squabble (D) fighting

210. His **brazen** arrogance shocked everyone around.
(A) impudent (B) bold (C) shy (D) brassy

211. The tree's branches swayed in the **breeze**.
(A) whiff (B) slow wind (C) storm (D) gale

212. **Brevity** made his speech impressive.
(A) duration (B) boldness (C) briefness (D) fearlessness

213. A law and order crisis is **brewing** in the town.
(A) concocting (B) fomenting (C) developing (D) steeping

214. Tea was filled in the cup to its **brim**.
(A) edge (B) rim (C) brink (D) top

215. The enraged animal **bristled** up.
(A) ran briskly (B) raised its hairs erect
(C) brushed (D) became stiff

216. I won't **brook** interference in my work.
(A) suffer (B) tolerate (C) allow (D) brood

217. He quickly **browsed** the shelf for something to read.
(A) looked cursorily (B) inspected (C) searched (D) peeped

218. Stormy sea waves **buffeted** ships around aimlessly.
(A) feasted (B) ate (C) pushed (D) blew

219. He used to **bully** his classmates.
(A) intimidate (B) beat (C) pushed around (D) butted

220. His friend always stood by him as a **bulwark**.
(A) bull (B) defence (C) rampart (D) protecting wall

221. A ferocious bull **bunted** a man down on the ground.
(A) chased (B) butted
(C) pushed with its head (D) hanged on its horns

222. A small town **burgeoned** into a city within a decade.
(A) bloomed (B) spurted (C) grew (D) became big

223. The company could not cope with the tough market competition and went **bust**.
(A) broke (B) burst (C) bankrupt (D) ruined

224. The ingenuous boy usually becomes the **butt** of ridicule in the group.
(A) head (B) handle (C) point (D) target

225. She **cached** her valuables in a safe place.
(A) kept (B) enclosed (C) catched (D) hided

226. She is in a habit of **cadging** groceries from the neighbours.
(A) stealing (B) catching (C) begging (D) borrowing

227. A government tends to become **callous** after staying in power for a long time.
(A) hard (B) insensitive (C) apathetic (D) exposed

228. He takes every opportunity to **calumniate** his rivals.
(A) challenge (B) slander (C) insult (D) call upon

229. It has become a trend in films to cast famous actors of the past in **cameo** role.
(A) engraved (B) short scene (C) gem (D) superfluous

230. Military tanks are painted green to **camouflage**.
(A) beautify (B) disguise (C) colour (D) make visible

231. He gave a **candid** reply to the query.
(A) brilliant (B) shining (C) honest (D) frank

232. The **candour** of his speech impressed the audience.
(A) candidness (B) openness (C) fairness (D) impartiality

233. The wrecked car was **cannibalised** of its working parts to fit into another car which needed these parts.
(A) eaten (B) deprived (C) strengthened (D) rehabilitated

234. He is a **canny** businessman.
(A) astute (B) skilled (C) thrifty (D) cautious

235. He violated the basic **canons** of good behaviour.
(A) mortars (B) armours (C) rules (D) fundamentals

236. **Cants** of hawkers are difficult to comprehend.
(A) lingo (B) speech (C) call (D) shouting

237. **Cantankerous** maid was a bane to housewife.
(A) cruel (B) peevish (C) shouting (D) idiotic

238. The auditorium has a large **capacity**.
(A) ability to receive (B) power (C) capability (D) ability

239. Smaller nations **capitulate** to the degemony of America.
(A) buckle (B) sag (C) yield (D) capture

240. A **capricious** person acts to the dictates of his fancy.
(A) unpredictable (B) changing (C) vicarious (D) whimsical

241. Her stunning beauty **captivated** the beholders.
(A) captured (B) fascinated (C) imprisoned (D) caught

242. The **carcass** of once-thriving industrial town is lying desolate now due to the closure of industry.
(A) dead remains (B) deadbody (C) cadaver (D) skeleton

243. Probity in one's personal life is of **cardinal** value.
(A) important (B) fundamental (C) prime (D) cordial

244. The moving car suddenly **careened** besides the road.
(A) turned (B) tilted (C) overturned (D) broke down

245. The train **carriered** towards the destination.
(A) hurtled (B) ran (C) speeded (D) departed

246. The lover **caressed** beloved hairs.
(A) preened (B) tidied (C) petted (D) combed

247. He is fond of **carnal** pleasure.
(A) corporal (B) corporeal (C) sensual (D) human

248. Stinking **carrion** lying on the road nauseated the passers-by.
(A) garbage (B) deadbody (C) rot (D) vegetables

249. He was handed over a **carte blanche** in a deal for his piece of land.
(A) signed document (B) signed blank cheque
(C) white paper (D) full authority

250. Oligopoly is fraught with **cartel** formation to fleece the consumers.
(A) association (B) group (C) business nexus (D) pricing

251. Petrol price-rise has **cascading** effect on the market.
(A) waterfall (B) successive (C) head long (D) falling

252. **Cassandras** of doom of the world are destined to be belied.
(A) prophetesses (B) fortune-tellers
(C) prediction-mongers (D) announcers

253. **Castor** wheels enable the trolley move in all the directions.
(A) rotating (B) swivelling (C) casted (D) small

254. He went out to the market dressed in his **casuals**.
(A) occasional dress (B) irregular dress
(C) informal dress (D) usual dress

255. A missile was **catapultated** in space.
(A) hurled (B) captured (C) launched (D) shot

256. An earthquake caused **catastrophe** in the area.
(A) misfortune (B) deluge (C) triumph (D) calamity

257. Cheap films **cater** for the popular taste of cinegoers.
(A) pander (B) supply (C) provide (D) satisfy

258. He is a man of **catholic** taste.
(A) christian (B) liberal (C) broad-minded (D) whole

259. Boatman **caulked** the seams between jointed planks.
(A) watertight (B) closed (C) filled the gap (D) nagging

260. We all detested his **cavalier** manners.
(A) gallant (B) domineering (C) supercilious (D) nagging

261. Art galleries are **caviar** to the general public.
(A) distasteful (B) detasted
(C) unappreciated by the ignorant (D) unpopular

262. He could not find anything to **cavil** about the arrangements.
(A) object (B) find faults (C) oppose (D) appreciate

263. Newspapers were unanimous in **censure** of the government policy
(A) censor (B) reproach (C) consensus (D) support

264. Orderly meeting suddenly broke into **chaos**.
(A) disorder (B) chasm (C) battle (D) jumble

265. Boiling milk **charred** her fingers.
(A) singed (B) grilled (C) boiled (D) ruined

266. A **charlatan** pretends to be knowledgeable.
(A) pedant (B) quack (C) impostor (D) fraud

267. She is excessively **chary** of her friends.
(A) suspicious (B) trustful (C) confident (D) wary

268. His effort to escape was **checkmated**.
(A) defeated (B) prevented
(C) completely checked on all sides (D) manoeuvred

269. She **chicaned** him into marrying her.
(A) coerced (B) cheated (C) cajoled (D) tricked

270. He is a **chronic** smoker.
(A) habitual (B) constant (C) inveterate (D) incorrigible

271. Arrange the bills and vouchers in **chronological** order.
(A) fixed (B) definite (C) in sequence of time (D) periodical

272. The policeman received a **citation** for bravery.
(A) award (B) quotation (C) censure (D) commendation

273. He **cited** the rules in his defence.
(A) saw (B) quoted (C) censure (D) commendation

274. They **clamoured** their demands in the meeting.
(A) shouted (B) claimed (C) forced (D) announced

275. **Clandestine** meeting of rebels took place in jungle.
(A) underhand (B) secret (C) hidden (D) illicit

276. The doors **clattered** in the wind.
(A) rattled (B) clashed (C) closed (D) collapsed

277. This costume designer has the patronage of wealthy **clientele**.
(A) witnesses (B) customers (C) franchisees (D) followers

278. His career has reached its **climax**.
(A) pinnacle (B) plateau (C) climacteric (D) zenith

279. He was happy to have **clinched** a business deal.
(A) grasped (B) clasped (C) secured (D) bit

280. He conducts his affairs in a **cloak** of secrecy.
(A) caper (B) pretext (C) mask (D) cover

281. The thieves **clobbered** the inmate when he resisted them from collecting the booty.
(A) battered (B) defeated (C) closed in a room (D) pushed

282. The cars **clogged** the road due to heavy traffic.
(A) hindered (B) impeded (C) stuck (D) choked

283. The recluse leads a **cloistered** life.
(A) enclosed (B) confined (C) quiet (D) secluded

284. Over-indulgence in anything soon **cloys** you.
(A) gluts (B) satiates (C) causes aversion (D) disgusts

285. The whole **clutch** of kittens invaded the kitchen.
(A) bevy (B) ensemble (C) brood (D) hatch

286. A loud thunderbolt **curdled** my blood.
(A) congealed (B) clogged (C) coagulated (D) stopped

287. He **cocooned** himself in blankets.
(A) sheltered (B) protected (C) ensconced (D) warmed

288. Family members **coddle** elderly persons who are unable to care for themselves.
(A) ignore (B) molly coddle (C) ameliorate (D) mollify

289. The police resort to **coercive** measures to quell the riot.
(A) corrective (B) forcible (C) compelling (D) intimidating

290. These two mountains are **coeval** in existence.
(A) ancient (B) of same age (C) contemporaneous (D) very old

291. **Coffers** of corrupt officials overflow with slush money.
(A) lockers (B) purse (C) vaults (D) almirah

292. A **cog** of the motor's gear wheel got broken.
(A) clab (B) nail (C) tooth (D) slot

293. The court took **cognizance** suo motu of police atrocity on innocent people.
(A) recognition (B) consideration (C) complaint (D) notice

294. There is no **coherence** in his argument.
(A) sticking together (B) cohession (C) consistency (D) glue

295. A dictionary is an output of long-time **collaboration** of many minds.
(A) nexus (B) connivance (C) combined labour (D) alliance

296. One has to **collate** someone's statement with that of another to know the truth.
(A) arrange (B) inspect (C) attach (D) corroborate

297. The surgeon **colligated** two ends of incision.
(A) collected (B) tied (C) cut (D) combined

298. They **colluded** in hatching a conspiracy.
(A) combined (B) conspired (C) agreed (D) contracted

299. Commit a **colossal** fraud on public.
(A) humongous (B) unusual (C) big (D) nasty

300. The soldier was **commended** for bravery.
(A) recommend (B) mentioned
(C) mention with praise (D) commented

301. Payment was not **commensurate** with the quantum of work I do.
(A) equal in measure (B) measurable (C) equal (D) adequate

302. We **commiserated** with him over the demise of his wife.
(A) felt sorry (B) condoled (C) repented (D) empathised

303. A **complaisant** person will never antagonise anyone.
(A) satisfied (B) complaining
(C) inclined to please (D) obliging

304. He **comports** himself with utmost dignity.
(A) reports (B) supports (C) deports (D) conducts

305. His **comprehension** of physics is amazing.
(A) doubt (B) understanding
(C) dislike (D) vast knowledge

306. He **conceded** defeat in the election even as the counting was halfway.
(A) counted (B) agreed (C) surrendered (D) admitted

307. A brief spell of good performance filled the player with **conceit**.
(A) humility (B) arrogance (C) vanity (D) over-estimation

308. Their **concerted** efforts won them success.
(A) continuous (B) done in collaboration
(C) combined (D) laborious

309. You can **conciliate** the respect of your associates with sincerity of intent.
(A) win over (B) appease (C) restore (D) antagonise

310. He is quick to **concoct** an excuse for not fulfilling his commitment.
(A) mix up (B) juggle (C) imagine (D) cook

311. The teacher **condescended** to the student's intellectual level, in order to enable them to comprehend the subject.
(A) stoop (B) compromised (C) lowered his level (D) assented

312. He **confected** a home remedy from herbs.
(A) contrived (B) concocted (C) sold (D) sweetened

313. The culprit **confessed** his complicity in the crime.
(A) surrendered (B) revealed (C) admitted (D) conceded

314. She **confides** in no one but her husband.
(A) believes (B) reveals (C) trusts (D) commits

315. He **confined** himself in the house the whole day.
(A) limited (B) enclosed (C) immured (D) restricted

316. His property was **confiscated** so that the banks' loans could be cleared.
(A) seized (B) appropriated (C) distrain (D) forfeited

317. Complicated court's jargons **confound** the litigants.
(A) perplex (B) surprise (C) bewilder (D) increase the confusion

318. He successfully **confuted** his opponent's charges.
(A) denied (B) confounded (C) disputed (D) refuted

319. Devotees **congregate** on the banks of the holy rivers on the religious occasions.
(A) flock (B) assemble (C) throng (D) crowd

320. Spectators of the match could merely **conjecture** the outcome.
(A) speculate (B) surmise (C) project (D) conclude

321. The policeman on duty **connived** at the traffic violations.
(A) winked (B) ignored (C) complied (D) conspired

322. He **consigned** unpleasant thoughts to oblivion.
(A) set apart (B) delivered (C) devoted (D) banished

323. He came to the party with his **consort**.
(A) spouse (B) escort (C) group (D) associate

324. He was **conspicuous** by his booming laughter.
(A) seen (B) evident (C) visible (D) noticeable

325. The dais was abuzz with **constellation** of great orators.
(A) brilliance (B) stars (C) group (D) assemblage

326. His moral conscience **constrained** him to abstain from wrongdoings.
(A) curbed (B) forced (C) obliged (D) held

327. He **contemplates** buying a new car.
(A) plans (B) thinks (C) ponders (D) proposes

328. His misdeeds were **contemptible**.
(A) mean (B) pardonable (C) abject (D) admirable

329. He is **contemptuous** of people of lower ranks.
(A) disregardful (B) disdainful (C) condemnable (D) averse

330. This locality is dotted with **contiguous** houses.
(A) closely situated (B) continuous (C) touching (D) dirty

331. He **contorted** his lips in disgust.
(A) bent (B) stretched (C) mangled (D) twisted

332. He is the most **contrary** child I have ever seen.
(A) adverse (B) willful (C) contradictory (D) discordant

333. The threat of dire consequences was **couched** in his police speech.
(A) cushioned (B) folded (C) rapped (D) convoluted

334. Indiscipline should not be **countenanced**.
(A) approved (B) encouraged (C) abetted (D) patronized

335. Condole with someone aggrieved with **counterfeit** grief.
(A) mock (B) fraudulent (C) ersatz (D) sham

336. It was a **crass** misrepresentation of facts.
(A) gross (B) delicate (C) shameless (D) boorish

337. The soldier **crawled** towards the enemy post in darkness.
(A) slithered (B) squirmed (C) creeped (D) strode

338. We did not lend **credence** to the wild rumours.
(A) support (B) belief (C) claim (D) credit

339. Problems **crop** up every now and then in his life.
(A) appear (B) manifest (C) surface (D) grow

340. Fearful of a loud thunderbolt, a boy **crouched** under the table.
(A) crawled (B) hide (C) kneeled (D) covered

341. An argument **culminated** in fisticuff.
(A) concluded (B) developed (C) climaxed (D) grew

342. Workers took up **cudgels** for wage revision.
(A) fight (B) club (C) weapons (D) arguments

343. The director raised his finger to give the actor **cue to start** his dialogue.
(A) clue (B) stimulus (C) suggestion (D) hint

344. The hall is adorned with **curios**.
(A) curious decorations (B) objects of art
(C) precious objects (D) valuable objects

345. He hurled **curses** on his adversary.
(A) malediction (B) swear (C) profanity (D) accusation

346. **Cute** mannerism of the baby was pleasing.
(A) curt (B) pretty (C) cunning (D) keen

347. He is **crazy** about the cricket game.
(A) mad (B) cool (C) sane (D) shaky

348. He is temperamentally a **credulous** person.
(A) suspicious (B) creditable (C) unsuspecting (D) crude

349. It is a very **critical** moment in his life.
(A) hazardous (B) crucial (C) precarious (D) unimportant

350. He was censured for his **culpable** act.
(A) criminal (B) heinous (C) blameworthy(D) praiseworthy

351. He is trying to **cultivate** friendship with me.
(A) till (B) grow (C) neglect (D) improve

352. He is crazy about **accumulating** wealth.
(A) amassing (B) gathering (C) filling (D) squandering

353. Police used force to **curb** violence.
(A) quell (B) check (C) block (D) encourage

354. He is very **curious** about his neighbours.
(A) desirous (B) inquisitive (C) indifferent (D) excited

355. **Current** practice of endogamous marriages is crumbling now.
(A) prevalent (B) running (C) obsolete (D) modern

356. He gave a very **curt** reply to my query.
(A) rude (B) brief (C) abrupt (D) polished

357. He followed **customary** practice of visiting the neighbours occasionally.
(A) habitual (B) conventional (C) uncommon (D) regular

358. He is **cynical** about his colleagues' motives.
(A) insane (B) contemptuous (C) distrustful (D) trusting

359. He deliberately **dallies** with his duties.
(A) procrastinates (B) fondles (C) hastens (D) loiters

360. There is a **dearth** of doctors in the hospitals.
(A) famine (B) abundance (C) plethora (D) scarcity

361. Health gradually **decays** in old age.
(A) rots (B) degenerates (C) decomposes (D) flourishes

362. She has acquired reputation for **deceit**.
(A) deception (B) fraud (C) honesty (D) distortion

363. **Deciduous** trees take on new leaves annually.
(A) permanent (B) shedding (C) evergreen (D) eternal

364. He is a man of **decisive** actions
(A) determining (B) determined (C) conclusive (D) prevaricat

365. He **affirmed** his intention to resign his job.
(A) offended (B) averred (C) denied (D) asserted

366. A **decrepit** old man could hardly walk.
(A) weak (B) infirm (C) emaciated (D) vigorous

367. **Dedicated** workers are the assets of a company.
(A) devoted (B) sacrificing (C) dallying (D) triffling

368. He is a scholar of **deep** knowledge.
(A) profound (B) abysmal (C) shallow (D) drowning

369. The **defective** machine hampered the progress of the work.
(A) imperfect (B) faulty (C) flawless (D) abnormal

370. The meeting was **deferred** due to the lack of quorum.
(A) postponed (B) put off (C) held on schedule (D) yielded

371. He was in a **defiant** mood.
(A) defeating (B) obedient (C) rebellious (D) decorous

372. **Deficit** in money withheld the work on the project.
(A) flaw (B) shortage (C) want (D) surplus

373. The **defiled** house was stinking.
(A) impure (B) sullied (C) impured (D) immaculate

374. He felt **degraded** with their remarks.
(A) defeating (B) obedient (C) rebellious (D) decorous

375. The defeated team members wore a **dejected** expression.
(A) rejected (B) sad (C) despirited (D) elated

376. The guests were treated with **delectable** dinner.
(A) delightful (B) tasteful (C) charming (D) disagreeable

377. Factory chimney spewed **deleterious** fumes.
(A) harmless (B) pernicious (C) stinking (D) unpleasant

378. It was a **deliberate** action.
(A) careful (B) intentional (C) premeditated (D) impulsive

379. He has a **delicate** sense of smell.
(A) crude (B) exquisite (C) fragile (D) delightful

380. She takes great **delight** in teasing me.
(A) charm (B) joy (C) satisfaction (D) distress

381. Oh! God, **deliver** me from these boring people.
(A) throw (B) liberate (C) enthrall (D) save

382. He **demurred** to accept the post offered to him.
(A) wavered (B) hesitated (C) refused (D) agreed

383. The **demure** girl sat aloof.
(A) sober (B) hesitant (C) indecorous (D) arrogant

384. People **denounce** the politicians as morally corrupt.
(A) declare (B) announce (C) condemn (D) commend

385. He **denied** me what was my due.
(A) refused (B) withheld (C) allowed (D) repudiated

386. We all wshould **deplore** the present state of morality.
(A) bemoan (B) denounce (C) rejoice (D) applaud

387. One earnestly **desires** to join family get-together in festivals.
(A) yearns (B) craves (C) solicits (D) loathes

388. Polar regions are **desolate** places.
(A) sad (B) uninhabited (C) populous (D) barren

389. Rescuers made a final **desperate** attempt to save the child.
(A) reckless (B) hopeless (C) hopeful (D) intolerable

390. He has become **despondent** about his failing health.
(A) dependent (B) despairing (C) happy (D) encouraged

391. He is now **destitute** of resources due to reckless squandering.
(A) deprived (B) needy (C) impoverished (D) affluent

392. He could not get a job yet due to his **desultory** attempt.
(A) distressing (B) fitful (C) consistent (D) pertinent

393. He **detected** a theif lurking behind the house in the dark.
(A) descried (B) discovered (C) overlooked (D) missed

394. He is a devout Hindu.
(A) sincere (B) holy (C) pious (D) irreverent

395. He is a **dextrous** artist.
(A) deft (B) clever (C) inept (D) righthanded

396. This creeper is **dextrorse**.
(A) right-handed (B) climbing from right to left
(C) climbing straight up (D) sinistrorse right

397. **Diffident** person shirks from taking the responsibility.
(A) confused (B) defiant
(C) unconfident (D) self-confident

398. Narrow arteries are **dilated** to all blood flow.
(A) expanded (B) expatiated (C) spread (D) constricted

399. The government adopts **dilatory** tactics in taking unpalatable decision.
(A) procrastinating (B) deferring (C) prompt (D) widening

400. He **discarded** the old hat.
(A) rejected (B) cast aside (C) threw (D) retained

401. Hooting by audience **disconcerted** the orator.
(A) ruffled (B) discomfitted (C) calmed (D) confused

402. Bereaved of elder brother, he was **disconsolate**.
(A) unhappy (B) inconsolable (C) soothed (D) sad

403. There is stark **discrepancy** in what you preach and what you practise.
(A) gap (B) contrariness (C) consistency (D) discreetnee

404. He brought **disgrace** on his family with his misdeeds.
(A) insult (B) ignominy (C) respect (D) honour

405. His petty quibblings **disgusted** me.
(A) delighted (B) relished (C) offended (D) annoyed

406. A gust of wind **dishevelled** his hairs.
(A) tidied (B) disarrayed (C) hanged (D) loosened

407. Stashed pot of valuables was **disintered** from the courtyard's underground.
(A) burried (B) exhumed (C) dug out (D) extracted

408. He is **disinterested** in their dispute.
(A) impartial (B) un-interested
(C) having selfish motive (D) indifferent

409. He was in **dismal** mood.
(A) sinister (B) melancholic (C) gay (D) annoyed

410. He **dismantled** the machine's parts for packing.
(A) broke (B) knocked down (C) separated (D) assembled

411. Deadlock in negotiation **dismayed** both sides.
(A) grieved (B) disheartened (C) encouraged (D) pained

412. Wind **dispersed** the cloud in the sky.
(A) dispelled (B) gathered (C) blew (D) drove away

413. His **disposition** towards meticulousness in work is appreciable.
(A) inclination (B) proclivity (C) unwillingness (D) mental

414. He **disregarded** my advice.
(A) ignored (B) heeded (C) disrespected (D) mistreated

415. She **dissembled** crookedness with ingenuous pretention.
(A) betrayed (B) concealed (C) dispersed (D) dismantled

416. **Dissuated** him from leaving the job.
(A) persuaded (B) deterred (C) discouraged (D) dissipated

417. His stomach **distended** with flatulence.
(A) extended (B) protruded (C) bloated (D) shrunk

418. **Distinction** in height helps us identify the twins.
(A) clarity (B) confusion (C) difference (D) resemblance

419. The boy was reading the story of a damsel in **distress**.
(A) agony (B) comfort (C) danger (D) safety

420. **Diurnal** cacophony on city roads subsides in late evening.
(A) daytime (B) nocturnal (C) daily (D) morning

421. Social and cultural **diversity** is the uniqueness of our countery.
(A) divergence (B) dis-similarity (C) difference (D) uniformity

422. Compassion is **divine** virtue in a person.
(A) supreme (B) sacred (C) mundane (D) religious

423. Docile workers readily follow the instructions.
(A) submissive (B) meek (C) intractable (D) stubborn

424. Pet is a d**omesticated** animal.
(A) domestic (B) tamed (C) household (D) wild

425. He is sitting with **dreary** face.
(A) fearful (B) gloomy (C) dreaded (D) cheerful

426. He is a **droll** person.
(A) comically humorous (B) serious (C) boring (D) whimsical

427. He is a person with **dusky** complexion.
(A) shadowy (B) swarthy (C) blond (D) twilight

428. He made an **earnest** appeal to people to help him.
(A) urgent (B) arrogant (C) fervent (D) triffling

429. It is our weakness to run after **earthly** pleasure.
(A) divine (B) mundane (C) ordinary (D) worthless

430. His **egotism** has alienated all his friends.
(A) egoism (B) self-conceit (C) humility (D) selfishness

431. The sun **emerged** from behind the clouds.
(A) cam out (B) emanated (C) immerged (D) mixed up

432. Hordes of technocrats **emigrate** to U.S.A. every year.
(A) leave own country to settle in a foreign country
(B) immigrate (C) move (D) flee

433. He soon rose to **eminence** in his field of expertise.
(A) exclusiveness (B) prominence (C) reputation (D) obscurit

434. He is **encumbered** with numerous obligations.
(A) enmeshed (B) burdened (C) hampered (D) disburden

435. His arrogant behaviour **infuriated** me.
(A) incensed (B) pacified (C) fired (D) provoked

436. Social system has still **enslaved** womenfolk.
(A) bonded (B) imprisomed (C) emancipated (D) suppressed

437. Toys of childhood are **ephemeral**.
(A) temporary (B) permanent (C) shortlived (D) long lasting

438. **Epicurean** leaders of present time are in sharp contrast of Gandhian leaders.
(A) indulgent in luxury (B) sensuous (C) ascetic (D) licentious

439. We **esteem** him for his honesty.
(A) commend (B) respect (C) disdain (D) support

440. The universe is **eternal**.
(A) unchanging (B) perpetual (C) enduring (D) transitory

441. Griffing with patients' treatment is against the professional **ethics**.
(A) beliefs (B) honesty (C) immorality (D) principles of morality

442. The minister tried to **evade** reporter's questions.
(A) dodge (B) confront (C) escape (D) elude

443. Adversaries always tend to **exaggerate** one's weakness.
(A) extenuate (B) magnify (C) overstate (D) extend

444. He was **exzalted** to venerable position by the people.
(A) elevated (B) depreciated (C) downgraded (D) praisesd

445. The boy is endowed with **exceptional** intellect.
(A) special (B) peculiar (C) average (D) outstanding

446. He is reputed to be easily **excitable**.
(A) stimulated (B) placid (C) infuriated (D) provoked

447. The old woman began to **execrate** all those who were teasing.
(A) denounce (B) imprecate (C) damn (D) bless

448. Cool breeze **exhilarated** the morning walkers.
(A) inspired (B) exhorted (C) cheered up (D) depressed

449. Moneylenders charge **exorbitant** interests on loans.
(A) prevailing (B) usurious (C) fair (D) unusual

450. He ordered his staff to **expedite** the work.
(A) hasten (B) move (C) procrastinate (D) ensnare

451. He is an **expert** in this field.
(A) experienced (B) greenhorn (C) knowledgeable (D) connoiss

452. He expressed his **explicit** opinion.
(A) open (B) unequivocal (C) confused (D) ambiguous

453. His remark was **extraneous** to the topic at hand.
(A) extrinsic (B) extra (C) impertinent (D) rare

454. He is an **extravagant** person.
(A) expensive (B) spendthrift (C) immoderate (D) thrifty

455. This the story of **fabulous** exploits of an adventure.
(A) marvellous (B) fictitious (C) factual (D) historical

456. The hall is adorned with **factitious** flowers.
(A) fictional (B) artificial (C) real (D) factual

457. Fiction writer needs a fecund mind.
(A) prolific (B) fruitful (C) effete (D) lazy

458. He made a **fervent** appeal for support.
(A) feverish (B) fiery (C) burning (D) dispassionate

459. He is a person of exteremely **fickle** mind.
(A) capricious (B) stable (C) capacious (D) fictitious

460. The servant's **fidelity** towards his master is perfect.
(A) fealty (B) belief (C) disloyalty (D) confidence

461. He extended a **flimsy** excuse for his failure.
(A) thin (B) shoddy (C) loose (D) convincing

462. He is my bitter **foe**.
(A) adversary (B) feud (C) friend (D) fiend

463. Lack of generosity is his notable **foible**.
(A) failing (B) character (C) forte (D) flaw

464. Speeches shall be **followed** by dinner.
(A) accompanied (B) succeeded (C) preceded (D) ensued

465. He is feeling **forlorn** of own people in this distant city.
(A) sad (B) in company of (C) desolate (D) hopeless

466. The **former** of the two suggestions was acceptable.
(A) prior (B) past (C) latter (D) ancient

467. A **fortuitous** incident changed his life.
(A) fortunate (B) incidental (C) accidental (D) deliberate

468. He is a man of **frail** body constitution.
(A) fragile (B) brittle (C) delicate (D) robust

469. Fresh vegetables are available in abundance.
(A) new (B) raw (C) unfaded (D) stale

470. She is worried about her **froward** daughter.
(A) contrary (B) arrogant (C) tractable (D) frowing

471. He is very **frugal** in spending money.
(A) miser (B) prudent (C) penurious (D) lavish

472. He made a **futile** attempt to appease his foe.
(A) vain (B) fruitless (C) effectual (D) frivolous

473. **Gallant** soldier captured the enemy post singlehanded.
(A) galloping (B) chivalrous (C) valorous (D) cowardly

474. Clouds are **gathering** in the sky indicating rainfall.
(A) accumulating (B) collecting (C) dispersing (D) fritteri

475. **Gaudy** decor looks vulgar.
(A) showy (B) garish (C) immodest (D) sober

476. Kids were frolicking in **gay** spirit.
(A) miserable (B) jolly (C) wanton (D) showy

477. **Germane** facts were collected to reach the conclusion.
(A) genuine (B) relevant (C) inept (D) inapt

478. **Giant** stature of a woman makes her unattractive.
(A) great (B) monstrous (C) huge (D) petite

479. His carrer prospect seems to be gloomy.
(A) shady (B) dark (C) bright (D) hopeless

480. He is sitting with **glum** face.
(A) morose (B) dark (C) sorrowful (D) cheerful

481. His social service brought **glory** to her.
(A) wonder (B) fame (C) grace (D) obloquy

482. Human beings are generally **gregarious** people.
(A) reclusive (B) seclusive (C) social (D) unsocial

483. He **grieves** over the loss in business.
(A) laments (B) weeps (C) rejoices (D) keens

484. Ordinary people **hallow** the saints.
(A) honour (B) venerate (C) consecrate (D) desecrate

485. Bad weather **hampered** the progress of the work.
(A) hindered (B) furthered (C) interfered (D) delayed

486. The group, though looked cohesive, lacked **harmony**.
(A) symmetry (B) melody (C) concord (D) discord

487. A **hasty** decision usually makes one repentant.
(A) precipitate (B) testy (C) deliberate (D) quick

488. He never **heeds** sane advice.
(A) listens (B) cares (C) worries (D) ignores

489. He was punished for his **heinous** offence.
(A) sinful (B) feral (C) irreprehensible (D) admirable

490. He is **humble** despite high rank.
(A) arrogant (B) polite (C) meek (D) submissive

491. He is **ignorant** of what is happening around him.
(A) oblivious (B) unknown (C) aware (D) illiterate

492. He was censured for his **ignoble** conduct.
(A) honuorable (B) ignominious (C) inferior (D) infamous

493. Breaking out of war with hostile country is **imminent**.
(A) impending (B) possible (C) remote (D) impossible

494. Innoculation renders a child **immune** from diseases.
(A) impune (B) exempt (C) resistant to (D) susceptible

495. His **impassionate** appeal moved people.
(A) emotional (B) impassive (C) tranquil (D) inflamed

496. An **impecunious** person was unable to procure basic needs.
(A) penniless (B) poor (C) wealthy (D) indigent

497. He was feared due to his **imperious** behaviour.
(A) unnecessary (B) perilous (C) overbearing (D) submissive

498. His **impertinent** behaviour annoyed me.
(A) irrelevant (B) brazen (C) insane (D) polite

499. He is known to always take **impetuous** decisions.
(A) rash (B) emotional (C) careful (D) studied

500. A country is left **impoverished** by war it fights.
(A) reduced to poverty (B) bereft (C) enriched (D) poor

501. The boy got punishment for his **impudent** behaviour.
(A) bold (B) arrogant (C) brazen (D) courteous

502. His habit of lying is **acquired** since childhood.
(A) inherent (B) natural (C) cultivated (D) congenital

503. Dissatisfaction **incites** anger.
(A) stimulates (B) instigates (C) subsides (D) encourages

504. The crowd was **instigated** by inflammatory speech to resort to violence.
(A) provoked (B) exhorted (C) deterred (D) urged

505. The police **inculpated** him with unlawful activity.
(A) exonerated (B) incriminated (C) ensnared (D) indicted

506. He is **indifferent** towards politics.
(A) attracted (B) unconcerned (C) concerned (D) similar

507. This plant is **indigenous** to India.
(A) autochthonous (B) aboriginal (C) alien (D) natural

508. The **implacable** creditor refused to give more time to return money despite entreaties.
(A) cruel (B) inexorable (C) merciful (D) flexible

509. He **improvised** his act directly on the stage.
(A) extemporize (B) rehearsed (C) provided (D) prepared

510. Rain water **ingressed** into the houses in the low-lying areas.
(A) immersed (B) entered (C) egressed (D) progressed

511. People somehow got rid of **iniquitous** despot.
(A) unjust (B) cruel (C) hostile (D) righteous

512. **Inordinate** delay in the train's arrivals irked the passengers.
(A) disorderly (B) excessive (C) unreasonable(D) moderate

513. **Inquisitive** mind keeps on asking why.
(A) prying (B) peeking (C) curious (D) uninterested

514. An **intrepid** person des not hesitate to venture.
(A) anxious (B) fearless (C) shaky (D) timid

515. The **irascible** old man was easily provoked to anger.
(A) testy (B) irritating (C) calm (D) rash

516. The spy was in **jeopardy** of being discovered.
(A) danger (B) hazard (C) chance (D) safety

517. He is in **jolly** mood.
(A) sportive (B) jovial (C) melancholy (D) playful

518. She **ravelled** the knot like a Gordian knot.
(A) tangled (B) unravelled (C) revolved (D) complicated

519. They pursued their goal in a **lackadaisical** manner.
(A) lacking (B) listless (C) unconcerned (D) lively

520. Spectators **lauded** their home team for winning the game.
(A) extolled (B) celebrated (C) lamented (D) shouted

521. She **lavished** praise on him.
(A) lashed (B) heaped (C) grudged (D) reserved

522. **Lax** laws engenders a sense of impunity in the offenders.
(A) rigid (B) strict (C) lenient (D) loose

523. He **leeched** his friend until the entire fortune was exhausted.
(A) sucked (B) sponged on (C) treated (D) befooled

524. A **libertine** person is despicable.
(A) free (B) licentious (C) prudish (D) pure

525. It was **lifeless** performance.
(A) dead (B) animate (C) dull (D) living

526. Gymnast's daily practice keeps his muscles **limber**.
(A) stiff (B) lithe (C) bending (D) loose

527. His body was **limp** with exhaustion.
(A) loose (B) drooping (C) tired (D) erect

528. One can see the bottom of the **limpid** pool.
(A) pellucid (B) lucid (C) calm (D) opaque

529. **Lineage** of a race horse determines its worth.
(A) age (B) pedigree (C) posterity (D) performance

530. In the absence of meaningful engagements, time **lingers**.
(A) fleets (B) lengthens (C) tarries (D) stays

531. An incompetent person becomes **malevolent** towards successful people.
(A) injurious (B) malicious (C) benevolent (D) selfish

532. **Malign** people in high position without substance.
(A) vilify (B) abuse (C) praise (D) despise

533. He is suffering from **malignant** tumour.
(A) malevolent (B) malicious (C) pernicious (D) benign

534. The holiday was **marred** by bad weather.
(A) damaged (B) impaired (C) spoilt (D) enhanced

535. The lawyer **marshalled** facts before arguing the case in the court.
(A) ordered for (B) arranged in order (C) combined (D) scattered

536. He is a **mendacious** person.
(A) false (B) veracious (C) lying (D) untrue

537. Mostly the non-government organizations, though they profess to work for poor people, yet are **mercenary**.
(A) profit-seeking (B) venal (C) voluntary (D) dishonest

538. He is **meticulous** about his physical appearance.
(A) finical (B) fearful (C) methodical (D) careless

539. A **moderate** change in the existing law is required.
(A) mild (B) excessive (C) radical (D) harsh

540. He leads a **modest** life.
(A) modern (B) moderate (C) pretentious (D) unassuming

541. Need to take tough stand against corruption is a **moot** point.
(A) doubtful (B) debatable (C) indisputable (D) major

542. **Morbid** condition of the economy is a cause of concern.
(A) deadly (B) bad (C) sick (D) healthy

543. Rejected by voters in the election, many small parties are in **moribund** state.
(A) discarded (B) dying (C) vivacious (D) closure

544. His death was **mourned** by his colleagues.
(A) deplored (B) lamented (C) remembered (D) rejoiced

545. He **mumbled** his views on the subject of discussion.
(A) articulated (B) muted (C) muttered (D) uttered

546. She is so **naive** as to believe in anyone.
(A) novice (B) simpleton (C) crafty (D) non-sense

547. His wife keep on **nagging** at him all day.
(A) pricking (B) hectoring (C) comforting (D) complaining

548. He **nibbled** at the apple he was eating.
(A) bite (B) gorged (C) gulped (D) scratched

549. He gave the restaurant waiter a **niggardly** tip.
(A) poor (B) stingy (C) miser (D) generous

550. The accused was pronounced guilty, defence lawyer's brilliant arguments **notwithstanding**.
(A) failure (B) despite (C) due to (D) without

551. He is a **novice** in politics.
(A) tyro (B) experienced (C) fool (D) new

552. **Obnoxious** smell forced us to cover our nose.
(A) annoying (B) odious (C) offensive (D) delightful

553. New models of cars become **obsolete** in a few years.
(A) old (B) outdated (C) in vogue (D) antique

554. **Ominous** dark clouds look **ominous**.
(A) portentous (B) threatening (C) propitious (D) harmful

555. Public anger against price-rise of petrol is **palpable**.
(A) obvious (B) evident (C) perceptible (D) imperceptible

556. An amount of one rupee is a **paltry** sum these days.
(A) petty (B) contemptible (C) significant (D) inconsiderable

557. He **paraded** his medal and prizes proudly.
(A) marched (B) flaunted (C) concealed (D) promenaded

558. Checking corruption in the country is **paramount**.
(A) supreme (B) most important (C) unimportant (D) superior

559. Grief is **patent** on her face.
(A) unconcealed (B) latent (C) dim (D) obscure

560. The old man was sitting in **pensive** mood.
(A) sorry (B) grieving (C) thinking (D) thoughtless

561. It is a **perennial** fruit bearing plant.
(A) throughout the year (B) seasonal (C) perpetual (D) eternal

562. His **perfidious** friend ditched him.
(A) faithful (B) disloyal (C) perfect (D) false

563. He does his job in **perfunctory** manner.
(A) professional (B) functional (C) indifferent (D) diligent

564. Mountaineering is a **perilous** adventure.
(A) injurious (B) risky (C) safe (D) disadvantageous

565. The building **perished** in the earthquake.
(A) ruined (B) survived (C) decayed (D) disappeared

566. The shrine witnesses **perpetual** stream of pilgrims.
(A) unending (B) discontinuous (C) permanent (D) temporary

567. **Persistent** incidents of violence in the city make people afraid of moving out freely.
(A) insistent (B) steady (C) sporadic (D) tenacious

568. A **perspicacious** person does not easily get befooled.
(A) astute (B) transparent (C) imperceptive (D) dim

569. The import of what he said in his speech was **perspicuous**.
(A) indistinct (B) lucid (C) opaque (D) bright

570. He was **persuaded** to perjure in the court.
(A) agreed (B) induced (C) dissuaded (D) coaxed

571. Do not try to **pervert** my statement.
(A) distort (B) correct (C) mislead (D) misuse

572. A hypochondriac in suffering from **phantom** feeling of pain in the abdomen.
(A) real (B) imaginary (C) ghost (D) illusory

573. He is a man of **phlegmatic** disposition.
(A) humorous (B) placid (C) passionate (D) passive

574. The devotee leads a life full of **piety**.
(A) pain (B) devotion (C) veneration (D) irreverence

575. His **piteous** cry for help moved us.
(A) reverent (B) pathetic (C) delightful (D) pious

576. The political leaders **pillory** each other in public fora.
(A) push (B) ridicule publicly (C) approbate (D) laugh at

577. His slogans are full of **platitudes**.
(A) cliche (B) novelty (C) repetitions (D) trivial

578. He gave a **plausible** explanation of his failure to accomplish the assigned task.
(A) applaudable (B) truthful (C) specious (D) untrue

579. People of **plebeian** taste can't appreciate abstract art works.
(A) sophisticated (B) vulgar (C) popular (D) trite

580. The power breakdown **plunged** the whole city into darkness.
(A) stooped (B) submerged (C) emerged (D) soared

581. His **poignant** remorse was cathartic.
(A) severe (B) pricking (C) sincere (D) mild

582. She was walking carefully **poising** a water jug on her head.
(A) balancing (B) controlling (C) disbalancing (D) stabilizing

583. **Polemical** views of bigots are a threat to social harmony.
(A) uncompromising (B) controversial
(C) eirenic (D) argumentative

584. To joust with a potent person is not a **politic** act.
(A) shrewd (B) expedient (C) tactless (D) clever

585. People's outrage over rising hardships due to high inflation **portends** doom for the government.
(A) augurs (B) forebodes (C) threatens (D) foretells

586. Judgment of this age should be left to **posterity**.
(A) descendants (B) ancestry (C) priority (D) future

587. Several **potent** arguments were put forward to prove the point.
(A) weak (B) powerful (C) cogent (D) useful

588. His plan was unacceptable because it was not **practicable**.
(A) practical (B) feasible (C) unattainable (D) worth

589. He is a **practical** politician.
(A) sensible (B) unwise (C) practising (D) practicable

590. Job tenure in private companies is **precarious**.
(A) secure (B) unsure because of depending on other's mercy
(C) unsteady (D) dangerous

591. Many a tribal society is still mired in **primitive** traditions.
(A) primary (B) pristine (C) old (D) modern

592. He is highly regarded because of his impeccable **probity**.
(A) venality (B) rectitude (C) obediency (D) sincerity

593. A **prodigal** person is likely to be impoverished in due course of time.
(A) improvident (B) frugal (C) proud (D) extraordinary

594. A precocious child possesses **prodigious** talent.
(A) extra-ordinarily marvellous
(B) commonplace (C) proven (D) progressing

595. Harsh retort by the son **ruffled** his father.
(A) upset (B) untidied (C) smoothed (D) soothed

596. Tyrants are **ruthless**.
(A) compassionate (B) cruel (C) adamant (D) ferocious

597. Holy shrines are **sacred** to the devotees.
(A) pious (B) blasphemous (C) pure (D) venerable

598. **Sagacious** patriarch is a source of prudent advice.
(A) sapient (B) practical (C) illustrious (D) foolish

599. **Salient** features of a machine determine its price.
(A) solid (B) outstanding (C) basic (D) unimportant

600. The chief organizer delivered his **salutatory** speech.
(A) valedictory (B) welcoming (C) favourable (D) beneficial

601. The criminals committed the crime with complete **sangfroid**.
(A) composure (B) discomfiture (C) confusion (D) easiness

602. The boy passed **scurrilous** remarks on the girls passing by.
(A) obscene (B) jocular (C) decent (D) crude

603. He has **queer** notion about life in U.S.A.
(A) different (B) odd (C) usual (D) questionable

604. **Radical** change in polity is needed to check rampant corruption.
(A) root (B) basic (C) superficial (D) drastic

605. He failed to **redeem** his pawned watch due to want of money.
(A) reclaim (B) ransom (C) forfeit (D) abandon

606. It is very difficult to handle a **refractory** child.
(A) hard (B) obstinate (C) obedient (D) rude

607. The party refused the return of the **renegades** into party fold.
(A) apostates (B) adherents (C) sticklers (D) traitors

608. **Repentance** cleanses the sinner's soul.
(A) remorse (B) sorrow (C) impenitence (D) regret

609. He **repudiated** the charges made against him.
(A) disowned (B) enforced (C) accepted (D) contradicted

610. Dispersal of clouds **revealed** the sun in the sky.
(A) shrouded (B) divulged (C) unveiled (D) concealed

611. The river takes a **sinuous** path through the valley.
(A) side (B) straight (C) flexuous (D) circuitious

612. People are **skeptical** about government's sincerity to curb corruption.
(A) shaky (B) confident (C) doubtful (D) cynic

613. A **somber** passage way led to the large hall.
(A) gloomy (B) doleful (C) dusky (D) bright

614. The **voluble** spokesman kept on speaking to the chagrin of the listeners.
(A) succinct (B) verbose (C) strident (D) loud

615. Only a few lucky ones could **survive** in the disaster.
(A) succour (B) remain alive (C) succumb (D) win

616. It is not wise to **squander** the precious resources.
(A) spend (B) preserve (C) dissipate (D) splurge

617. He is **steadfast** in his faith.
(A) staunch (B) firm (C) wavering (D) constant

618. He unleashed a vicious campaign to **tarnish** my reputation.
(A) blacken (B) blemish (C) brighten (D) exalt

619. His position in the team is **tenuous**.
(A) slender (B) strong (C) attenuated (D) tender

620. She took out frozen stuff from the refrigerator and kept on the table to let it **thaw**.
(A) warm (B) deliquesce (C) melt (D) freeze

621. It is not good to **traduce** someone's character.
(A) malign (B) abuse (C) praise (D) expose

622. **Treason** is an unforgivable crime.
(A) loyalty (B) sedition (C) treachery (D) patriotism

623. He was forgiven for **venial** offence.
(A) vicious (B) pardonable (C) felonious (D) serious

624. His **wanton** disregard of others' sentiments is not appreciable.
(A) willful (B) reckless (C) lewd (D) unintentional

625. This town has **warm** climate throughout the year.
(A) hot (B) moderately hot (C) cold (D) cool

626. The wet log got **warped** on getting dried up.
(A) bent (B) straightened (C) twisted (D) flat

627. His **wayward** son has become incorrigible.
(A) willful (B) obedient (C) astray (D) capricious

628. He looked **weary** after long hours of work.
(A) tired (B) interested (C) energetic (D) sad

ANSWERS

1. (D)	**2.** (B)	**3.** (D)	**4.** (A)	**5.** (A)	**6.** (C)	**7.** (A)	**8.** (A)
9. (A)	**10.** (A)	**11.** (A)	**12.** (C)	**13.** (B)	**14.** (A)	**15.** (C)	**16.** (C)
17. (C)	**18.** (A)	**19.** (C)	**20.** (B)	**21.** (C)	**22.** (D)	**23.** (A)	**24.** (B)
25. (A)	**26.** (D)	**27.** (C)	**28.** (C)	**29.** (A)	**30.** (B)	**31.** (B)	**32.** (A)
33. (B)	**34.** (B)	**35.** (B)	**36.** (C)	**37.** (A)	**38.** (B)	**39.** (B)	**40.** (C)
41. (C)	**42.** (D)	**43.** (C)	**44.** (D)	**45.** (C)	**46.** (C)	**47.** (A)	**48.** (C)
49. (A)	**50.** (A)	**51.** (B)	**52.** (B)	**53.** (C)	**54.** (D)	**55.** (A)	**56.** (C)
57. (B)	**58.** (B)	**59.** (D)	**60.** (D)	**61.** (A)	**62.** (B)	**63.** (A)	**64.** (D)
65. (A)	**66.** (B)	**67.** (A)	**68.** (A)	**69.** (D)	**70.** (B)	**71.** (B)	**72.** (A)
73. (D)	**74.** (A)	**75.** (B)	**76.** (B)	**77.** (B)	**78.** (B)	**79.** (A)	**80.** (C)
81. (B)	**82.** (B)	**83.** (B)	**84.** (A)	**85.** (A)	**86.** (C)	**87.** (D)	**88.** (A)
89. (C)	**90.** (C)	**91.** (B)	**92.** (C)	**93.** (B)	**94.** (A)	**95.** (C)	**96.** (B)
97. (D)	**98.** (B)	**99.** (D)	**100.** (C)	**101.** (C)	**102.** (A)	**103.** (C)	**104.** (B)
105. (D)	**106.** (D)	**107.** (B)	**108.** (D)	**109.** (B)	**110.** (B)	**111.** (A)	**112.** (A)
113. (C)	**114.** (D)	**115.** (D)	**116.** (B)	**117.** (A)	**118.** (B)	**119.** (B)	**120.** (C)
121. (C)	**122.** (B)	**123.** (A)	**124.** (C)	**125.** (A)	**126.** (B)	**127.** (A)	**128.** (A)
129. (C)	**130.** (C)	**131.** (A)	**132.** (C)	**133.** (A)	**134.** (B)	**135.** (B)	**136.** (B)
137. (B)	**138.** (B)	**139.** (A)	**140.** (B)	**141.** (A)	**142.** (C)	**143.** (A)	**144.** (C)
145. (B)	**146.** (C)	**147.** (D)	**148.** (C)	**149.** (A)	**150.** (A)	**151.** (B)	**152.** (B)
153. (A)	**154.** (B)	**155.** (D)	**156.** (A)	**157.** (C)	**158.** (B)	**159.** (B)	**160.** (A)
161. (B)	**162.** (A)	**163.** (B)	**164.** (A)	**165.** (B)	**166.** (D)	**167.** (C)	**168.** (B)
169. (C)	**170.** (A)	**171.** (B)	**172.** (B)	**173.** (D)	**174.** (B)	**175.** (B)	**176.** (A)
177. (A)	**178.** (D)	**179.** (A)	**180.** (C)	**181.** (D)	**182.** (B)	**183.** (C)	**184.** (A)
185. (B)	**186.** (B)	**187.** (B)	**188.** (C)	**189.** (B)	**190.** (D)	**191.** (C)	**192.** (A)
193. (B)	**194.** (C)	**195.** (C)	**196.** (D)	**197.** (B)	**198.** (A)	**199.** (D)	**200.** (A)
201. (B)	**202.** (C)	**203.** (C)	**204.** (C)	**205.** (D)	**206.** (B)	**207.** (D)	**208.** (B)
209. (C)	**210.** (A)	**211.** (B)	**212.** (C)	**213.** (B)	**214.** (B)	**215.** (B)	**216.** (B)
217. (A)	**218.** (C)	**219.** (A)	**220.** (D)	**221.** (B)	**222.** (A)	**223.** (C)	**224.** (D)
225. (D)	**226.** (D)	**227.** (B)	**228.** (B)	**229.** (B)	**230.** (B)	**231.** (D)	**232.** (A)
233. (B)	**234.** (A)	**235.** (C)	**236.** (A)	**237.** (B)	**238.** (A)	**239.** (C)	**240.** (D)
241. (B)	**242.** (A)	**243.** (B)	**244.** (B)	**245.** (A)	**246.** (C)	**247.** (C)	**248.** (B)
249. (B)	**250.** (C)	**251.** (D)	**252.** (A)	**253.** (B)	**254.** (C)	**255.** (A)	**256.** (D)

257. (A) **258.** (B) **259.** (C) **260.** (C) **261.** (C) **262.** (B) **263.** (B) **264.** (A)
265. (A) **266.** (B) **267.** (D) **268.** (C) **269.** (D) **270.** (C) **271.** (C) **272.** (D)
273. (B) **274.** (A) **275.** (B) **276.** (A) **277.** (B) **278.** (A) **279.** (C) **280.** (D)
281. (A) **282.** (D) **283.** (D) **284.** (C) **285.** (C) **286.** (A) **287.** (C) **288.** (B)
289. (D) **290.** (B) **291.** (C) **292.** (C) **293.** (D) **294.** (C) **295.** (C) **296.** (D)
297. (B) **298.** (B) **299.** (A) **300.** (C) **301.** (A) **302.** (B) **303.** (C) **304.** (D)
305. (B) **306.** (D) **307.** (C) **308.** (B) **309.** (A) **310.** (D) **311.** (A) **312.** (B)
313. (C) **314.** (C) **315.** (C) **316.** (C) **317.** (D) **318.** (D) **319.** (A) **320.** (B)
321. (A) **322.** (A) **323.** (A) **324.** (D) **325.** (D) **326.** (B) **327.** (C) **328.** (C)
329. (B) **330.** (C) **331.** (D) **332.** (B) **333.** (A) **334.** (B) **335.** (D) **336.** (A)
337. (C) **338.** (D) **339.** (D) **340.** (C) **341.** (C) **342.** (A) **343.** (D) **344.** (B)
345. (A) **346.** (B) **347.** (A) **348.** (C) **349.** (B) **350.** (C) **351.** (D) **352.** (A)
353. (B) **354.** (B) **355.** (A) **356.** (A) **357.** (A) **358.** (C) **359.** (A) **360.** (D)
361. (B) **362.** (A) **363.** (B) **364.** (C) **365.** (B) **366.** (B) **367.** (A) **368.** (A)
369. (B) **370.** (B) **371.** (C) **372.** (B) **373.** (B) **374.** (C) **375.** (C) **376.** (A)
377. (B) **378.** (B) **379.** (B) **380.** (B) **381.** (B) **382.** (B) **383.** (A) **384.** (C)
385. (A) **386.** (A) **387.** (A) **388.** (B) **389.** (B) **390.** (B) **391.** (C) **392.** (B)
393. (A) **394.** (C) **395.** (A) **396.** (B) **397.** (C) **398.** (A) **399.** (A) **400.** (B)
401. (B) **402.** (B) **403.** (B) **404.** (B) **405.** (D) **406.** (B) **407.** (C) **408.** (A)
409. (B) **410.** (B) **411.** (B) **412.** (A) **413.** (A) **414.** (A) **415.** (B) **416.** (B)
417. (B) **418.** (C) **419.** (C) **420.** (A) **421.** (B) **422.** (B) **423.** (A) **424.** (B)
425. (B) **426.** (A) **427.** (A) **428.** (C) **429.** (B) **430.** (B) **431.** (A) **432.** (A)
433. (B) **434.** (B) **435.** (A) **436.** (A) **437.** (C) **438.** (A) **439.** (B) **440.** (B)
441. (D) **442.** (A) **443.** (C) **444.** (A) **445.** (D) **446.** (A) **447.** (B) **448.** (C)
449. (B) **450.** (A) **451.** (D) **452.** (B) **453.** (A) **454.** (B) **455.** (A) **456.** (B)
457. (A) **458.** (B) **459.** (A) **460.** (A) **461.** (B) **462.** (A) **463.** (A) **464.** (B)
465. (C) **466.** (A) **467.** (B) **468.** (C) **469.** (A) **470.** (A) **471.** (B) **472.** (A)
473. (C) **474.** (A) **475.** (B) **476.** (B) **477.** (B) **478.** (C) **479.** (B) **480.** (A)
481. (B) **482.** (C) **483.** (A) **484.** (B) **485.** (A) **486.** (C) **487.** (A) **488.** (B)
489. (C) **490.** (C) **491.** (A) **492.** (B) **493.** (A) **494.** (C) **495.** (A) **496.** (A)
497. (C) **498.** (B) **499.** (A) **500.** (A) **501.** (C) **502.** (C) **503.** (A) **504.** (A)
505. (B) **506.** (B) **507.** (A) **508.** (B) **509.** (A) **510.** (B) **511.** (A) **512.** (B)
513. (C) **514.** (B) **515.** (A) **516.** (B) **517.** (B) **518.** (A) **519.** (B) **520.** (A)
521. (B) **522.** (C) **523.** (B) **524.** (B) **525.** (A) **526.** (B) **527.** (B) **528.** (A)
529. (B) **530.** (C) **531.** (B) **532.** (A) **533.** (C) **534.** (C) **535.** (B) **536.** (C)
537. (A) **538.** (A) **539.** (A) **540.** (D) **541.** (B) **542.** (C) **543.** (B) **544.** (B)
545. (C) **546.** (B) **547.** (B) **548.** (A) **549.** (B) **550.** (B) **551.** (A) **552.** (C)
553. (B) **554.** (A) **555.** (C) **556.** (D) **557.** (B) **558.** (B) **559.** (A) **560.** (C)
561. (A) **562.** (B) **563.** (C) **564.** (B) **565.** (A) **566.** (A) **567.** (B) **568.** (A)
569. (B) **570.** (B) **571.** (A) **572.** (B) **573.** (B) **574.** (C) **575.** (B) **576.** (B)
577. (A) **578.** (C) **579.** (B) **580.** (B) **581.** (B) **582.** (A) **583.** (B) **584.** (B)
585. (B) **586.** (A) **587.** (B) **588.** (B) **589.** (A) **590.** (B) **591.** (B) **592.** (B)
593. (A) **594.** (A) **595.** (A) **596.** (B) **597.** (D) **598.** (A) **599.** (B) **600.** (B)
601. (A) **602.** (A) **603.** (B) **604.** (A) **605.** (A) **606.** (B) **607.** (A) **608.** (A)
609. (A) **610.** (C) **611.** (C) **612.** (C) **613.** (C) **614.** (B) **615.** (B) **616.** (C)
617. (A) **618.** (B) **619.** (C) **620.** (C) **621.** (A) **622.** (B) **623.** (B) **624.** (A)
625. (B) **626.** (A) **627.** (A) **628.** (A)

❑❑❑

Exercises On

SYNONYMS

TEST 1

Use the most appropriate meaning of the words out of the given options:

1. Archaic
   (A) Archive (B) Abysmal (C) Antiquated (D) Pristine
2. Assignation
   (A) Tryst (B) Assignment (C) Secret meeting (D) Secrecy
3. Assent
   (A) Accede (B) Acquiesce (C) Subscribe (D) Disagree
4. Aborigine
   (A) Indigenous (B) Native (C) Original (D) Imported
5. Abandon
   (A) Desert (B) Forsake (C) Abjure (D) Renounce
6. Abate
   (A) Alleviate (B) Mitigate (C) Stop (D) Assuage
7. Abstain
   (A) Refrain (B) Abscond (C) Elude (D) Assert
8. Confess
   (A) Admit (B) Surrender (C) Affirm (D) Approve
9. Apposite
   (A) Opposite (B) Appropriate (C) Germane (D) Opposing
10. Appraise
    (A) Apprise (B) Evaluate (C) Appease (D) Approve
11. Exhort
    (A) Criticize (B) Urge (C) Abuse (D) Rebuke
12. Conspicuous
    (A) Manifest (B) Secret (C) Conspiring (D) Clear
13. Anthem
    (A) Praise (B) Requiem (C) Admiration (D) Alleluia
14. Aroma
    (A) Bouquet (B) Flavour (B) Arrogance (D) Malodour
15. Obstinate
    (A) Audacious (B) Obscure (C) Obvious (D) Austere
16. Avert
    (A) Convert (B) Revert (C) Advert (D) Evade

17. Indict
(A) Impeach (B) Indicate (C) Infuriate (D) Dictate
18. Abject
(A) Ignoble (B) Objectionable (C) Abominable (D) None of these
19. Usurp
(A) Arrogate (B) Soak (C) Use up (D) Unusual
20. Aquit
(A) Quit (B) Exple (C) Exonerate (D) Remove
21. Levitate
(A) Float in air (B) Soar (C) Ascend (D) Make lavish
22. Franchise
(A) Delegate (B) Emancipate (C) Incriminate (D) Chafe
23. Abscond
(A) Skive (B) Abstain (C) Discard (D) Forfeit
24. Vitriolic
(A) Virtuous (B) Verify (C) Mordant (D) Habituated
25. Deft
(A) Skilled (B) Deaf (C) Dumb (D) Very fast
26. Hug
(A) Defile (B) Cling (C) Humiliate (D) Honour
27. Adjourn
(A) Prorogue (B) Resume (C) Applaud (D) Inflict
28. Distraught
(A) Disturbed (B) Disconcerted (C) Startled (D) Amazed
29. Fealty
(A) Allegiance (B) Dirty (C) Befitting (D) Augur
30. Minatory
(A) Minaret (B) Menacing (C) Mean-minded (D) Minimal

Choose the word pairs out of the given options which resemble in meanings:

31. (A) Chafe (B) Ignoble (C) Clumsy (D) Excoriate
32. (A) Impeach (B) Arraign (C) Obviate (D) Indicate
33. (A) Ancestor (B) Progeny (C) Offspring (D) Forebears
34. (A) Despot (B) Tyrant (C) Dreadful (D) Dreaded
35. (A) Bizarre (B) Blizzard (C) Plethora (D) Preposterous
36. (A) Galore (B) Glare (C) Abundant (D) Grotesque
37. (A) Autochthon (B) Aborigine (C) Automatic (D) Automation
38. (A) Discard (B) Dispose (C) Desert (D) Forsake
39. (A) Abysmal (B) Fathomless (C) Zenith (D) Shun
40. (A) Dextrous (B) Doomed (C) Deft (D) Lazy

41. (A) Avow (B) Avid (C) Avouch (D) Devout
42. (A) Dilettante (B) Gourmet (C) Dissatisfied (D) Alienated
43. (A) Atone (B) Petrify (C) Expiate (D) Intrepid
44. (A) Herald (B) Harbinger (C) Exasperate (D) Outrage
45. (A) Cogent (B) Condign (C) Pristine (D) Tough
46. (A) Audacious (B) Audible (C) Obstinate (D) Harsh
47. (A) Facet (B) Ramification (C) Facade (D) Feature
48. (A) Imbibe (B) Assimilate (C) Reject (D) Avert
49. (A) Feign (B) Malinger (C) Defunct (D) Defend
50. (A) Maladroit (B) Malignant (C) Clumsy (D) Malodorant

Choose the odd one out from the options in each set of 4 words:

51. (A) Aficionado (B) Fan (C) Kindred (D) Dilettante
52. (A) Cling (B) Inflict (C) Affix (D) Adhere
53. (A) Cognate (B) Rattle (C) Faze (D) Agitate
54. (A) Bunk (B) Elope (C) Elude (D) Outrage
55. (A) Commend (B) Fealty (C) Hail (D) Acclaim
56. (A) Esprit d' corps (B) Fidelity (C) Devotion (D) Auspicious
57. (A) Parry (B) Imbibe (C) Obviate (D) Stave off
58. (A) Deserted (B) Solitary (C) Lonely (D) Forlorn
59. (A) Surfeit (B) Legion (C) Host (D) Cloy
60. (A) Toddle (B) Taint (C) Tinge (D) Contaminate
61. (A) Teem (B) Swarm (C) Glut (D) Taint
62. (A) Chomp (B) Eschew (C) Shun (D) Refrain
63. (A) Inure (B) Accustom (C) Aver (D) Habituate
64. (A) Alibi (B) Plea (C) Pretext (D) Plead
65. (A) Chagrin (B) Charge (C) Exasperate (D) Annoy
66. (A) Rage (B) Fury (C) Outrage (D) Demolish
67. (A) Arrogant (B) Paragon (C) Nonpareil (D) Epitome
68. (A) Harsh (B) Severe (C) Austere (D) Fret
69. (A) Menacing (B) Benign (C) Awesome (D) Formidable
70. (A) Severe (B) Melancholic (C) Atrabilious (D) Hypochondriac

ANSWERS

1. (C) See Archaic **2.** (C) See Assignation **3.** (C) See Assent
4. (B) See Aborigine **5.** (A) See Abandon **6.** (B) See Abate
7. (A) See Abstain **8.** (A) See Confess **9.** (B) See Apposite
10. (B) See Apraise **11.** (B) See Exhort
12. (A) See Conspicuous
13. (D) See Anthem (it means song of praise for country, institution, etc. Requiem means song of lamentation for the dead person)
14. (B) See Aroma **15.** (A) See Obstinate **16.** (D) See Avert

17. (A) See Indict	**18.** (A) See Abject	**19.** (A) See Usurp
20. (C) See Aquit	**21.** (A) See Levitate	**22.** (A) See Franchise
23. (A) See Abscond	**24.** (C) See Vitriolic	**25.** (A) See Deft
26. (B) See Hug	**27.** (A) See Adjourn	**28.** (B) See Distraught
29. (A) See Allegiance	**30.** (B) See Awesome	**31.** A-D See Abrade
32. A-B See Accuse	**33.** A-D See Ancestor	**34.** A-B See Autocrat
35. A-D See Absurd	**36.** A-C See Ancestor	**37.** A-B See Aborigine
38. A-B See Discard	**39.** A-B See Abysmal	**40.** A-C See Adroit
41. A-C See Affirm	**42.** A-B See Admirer	**43.** A-C See Amends
44. A-B See Announcer	**45.** A-B See Appropriate	46. A-C See Arrogant
47. A-B See Aspect	**48.** A-B See Absorb	49. A-B See Affect
50. A-C See Awkward	**51.** (C) See Admirer	52. (B) See Affix
53. (A) See Agitate	**54.** (D) See Abscond	55. (B) See Admire
56. (D) See Allegiance	**57.** (B) See Avert	58. (A) See Alone
59. (D) See Abundant	**60.** (A) See Adulterate	61. (D) See Abound
62. (A) See Abstain	**63.** (C) See Acclimatise	64. (D) See Alibi
65. (B) See Annoy	**66.** (D) See Anger	67. (A) See Apotheosis
68. (D) See Austere	**69.** (B) See Awesome	70. (A) See Atrabilious

TEST 2

Select Synonyms of the given words out of the options mentioned:

1. Bequeath
   (A) Benumb (B) Bludgeon (C) Demise (D) Bemuse
2. Box
   (A) Cuff (B) Bait (C) Faint (D) Clog
3. Ersatz
   (A) Zealot (B) Ennui (C) Sham (D) Placebo
4. Scald
   (A) Berate (B) Chide (C) Scorch (D) Brat
5. Prolapse
   (A) Progress (B) Proceed (C) Sag (D) Bump
6. Swag
   (A) Boast (B) Bundle (C) Wad (D) Faggot
7. Dash
   (A) Bump (B) Breach (C) Bale (D) Tuft
8. Parapet
   (A) Moat (B) Stein (C) Rampart (D) Doldrums
9. Pandemonium
   (A) Credence (B) Demeanour (C) Uproar (D) Tedium

10. Retract
    (A) Recant (B) Retrogress (C) Extradite (D) Stun
11. Fetid
    (A) Placebo (B) Musty (C) Blend (D) Cloy
12. Doldrums
    (A) Unsteady (B) Obstruction (C) Tedium (D) Tuft
13. Clog
    (A) Jam (B) Stop (C) Cluster (D) Crash
14. Braggart
    (A) Bigot (B) Fanatic (C) Brat (D) Batter
15. Stun
    (A) Petrify (B) Beat (C) Pound (D) Thress
16. Peel
    (A) Rind (B) Slog (C) Perplex (D) Stupefy
17. Ruse
    (A) Rancid (B) Rot (C) Faint (D) Faith
18. Exile
    (A) Expel (B) Excommunicate (C) Extradite (D) Ban
19. Slog
    (A) Smite (B) Flay (C) Slobber (D) Thress
20. Importune
    (A) Fate (B) Beseech (C) Supplicate (D) Bias

Choose a pair of words having similarity in meanings out of the four given options:

21. (A) Comportment (B) Deportment (C) Credit (D) Faith
22. (A) Credit (B) Entreat (C) Conduct (D) Implore
23. (A) Forswear (B) Forgo (C) Welsh (D) Abuse
24. (A) Commotion (B) Bedlam (C) Bias (D) Demise
25. (A) Demeanour (B) Behaviour (C) Mean-ness (D) Meaningless
26. (A) Predilection (B) Predisposition (C) Credence (D) Brouhaha
27. (A) Chauvinist (B) Sham (C) Braggart (D) Fanatic
28. (A) Tassel (B) Tuft (C) Skein (D) Faggot
29. (A) Rancid (B) Ruse (C) Putrid (D) Retrograde
30. (A) Bait (B) Baffle (C) Banish (D) Befuddle

Choose the odd one out from the following options:

31. (A) Melee (B) Rumpus (C) Malignant (D) Babel
32. (A) Wad (B) Bale (C) Sheaf (D) Fad
33. (A) Boycott (B) Ostracize (C) Buckle (D) Outcaste
34. (A) Bounce (B) Collide (C) Rebound (D) Reverberate

35.	(A) Tedium	(B) Ennui	(C) Boredom	(D) Ostracize
36.	(A) Contaminate	(B) Adulterate	(C) Taint	(D) Clog
37.	(A) Stance	(B) Trait	(C) Tendency	(D) Stare
38.	(A) Thrash	(B) Thress	(C) Trash	(D) Pound
39.	(A) Magnate	(B) Magnet	(C) Baron	(D) Tycoon
40.	(A) Prohibit	(B) Inhibit	(C) Forbid	(D) Protest

ANSWERS

1. (C) See Bequeath	**2.** (A) See Beat	**3.** (C) See Bogus
4. (C) See Burn	**5.** (C) See Buckle	**6.** (B) See Bundle
7. (A) See Bump	**8.** (C) See Boundary	**9.** (C) See Babel
10. (A) See Backtrack	11. (B) See Bad Smelling	**12.** (C) See Boredom
13. (A) See Block	**14.** (C) See Brat	**15.** (A) See Benumb
16. (A) See Bark	**17.** (C) See Bait	**18.** (C) See Banish
19. (A) See Beat	**20.** (B) See Beg	**25.** (A) and (B)
21. A-B See Behaviour	**22.** B-D See Beg	**26.** (A) and (B)
23. A-C See Backtrack	**24.** A-B See Bias	**27.** A-D See Bigot
28. A-B See Bundle	**29.** A-C See Bad Smelling	**30.** B-D See Baffle
31. (C) See Bable	**32.** (D) See Bundle	**33.** (C) See Boycott
34. (B) See Bounce	**35.** (D) See Bundle	36. (D) See Adulterate
37. (D) See Bias	38. (C) See Beat	**39.** (B) See Baron
40. (D) See Forbid		

TEST 3

Choose the synonymous words for the given words out of the following options:

1. Anathematise
   (A) Hate (B) Dislike (C) Imprecate (D) Criticize
2. Preen
   (A) Caress (B) Praise (C) Pinch (D) Ruminate
3. Compensate
   (A) Compare (B) Complete (C) Rebate (D) Indemnify
4. Haggard
   (A) Haggler (B) Careworn (C) Vagary (D) Drivel
5. Universal
   (A) Catholic (B) Christian (C) Omnipresent (D) Worldly
6. Wory
   (A) Weary (B) Sorrowful (C) Chary (D) Cliche
7. Prattle
   (A) Practise (B) Avoid (C) Blabber (D) Condemn

8. Keen
(A) Interested (B) Anxious (C) Care (D) Wail

9. Cant
(A) Lingo (B) Limbo (C) Catch (D) Caper

10. Disdain
(A) Fearless (B) Spite (C) Diatribe (D) Decry

11. Placid
(A) Lazy (B) Dupe (C) Tranquil (D) Complacent

12. Cull
(A) Gather (B) Muster (C) Accumulate (D) Waste

13. Invective
(A) Investment (B) Curse (C) Philippic (D) Impute

14. Vicissitude
(A) Vacillate (B) Adventure (C) Vagary (D) Luck

15. Chant
(A) Recite (B) Shout (C) Call (D) Chatter

16. Cringe
(A) Prostrate (B) Tremble (C) Crowl (D) Cower

17. Hoodwink
(A) Huddle (B) Dupe (C) Drivel (D) Excoriate

18. Clique
(A) Panel (B) Troupe (C) Crook (D) Claque

19. Creep
(A) Sip (B) Impound (C) Pleat (D) Slither

20. Yearn
(A) Craze (B) Fad (C) Long (D) Gape

21. Impute
(A) Insert (B) Condemn (C) Attribute (D) Insult

22. Nab
(A) Wink (B) Sleep (C) Apprehend (D) Frolick

23. Cavort
(A) Jump (B) Hold (C) Gambol (D) Grab

24. Imposter
(A) Prosper (B) Chant (C) Fret (D) Con

25. Ruminate
(A) Rue (B) Row (C) Chew (D) Rumble

26. Reprehend
(A) Comprehend (B) Apprehend (C) Castigate (D) Munch

27. Circadian
(A) Actor (B) Diurnal (C) Approximate (D) Colossal

28. Bliss
(A) Trance (B) Bless (C) Beautiful (D) Chasm

29. Savage
(A) Ruin (B) Ferocious (C) Tyrant (D) Curse

30. Hiatus
(A) Sorrow (B) Disaster (C) Depression (D) Chasm

31. Lustrate
(A) Cleanse (B) Mop (C) Scour (D) Wash

32. Flush
(A) Flood (B) Swill (C) Emunge (D) Sort

33. Sort
(A) Category (B) Sport (C) Assort (D) Reduce

34. Sagacious
(A) Shrewd (B) Smug (C) Congenital (D) Timid

35. Vicinity
(A) Vainglory (B) Vanity (C) Propinquity (D) Venture

36. Congeal
(A) Hide (B) Concoct (C) Curdle (D) Solidify

37. Mall
(A) Smear (B) Clot (C) Entrust (D) Meditate

38. Incarcerate
(A) Exempt (B) Confiscate (C) Immure (D) Refute

39. Distrain
(A) Detatch (B) Separate (C) Escheat (D) Confiscate

40. Parley
(A) Parlay (B) Confer (C) Cooperate (D) Collude

Choose the pair of given words with similar meanings out of the four in each set:

41. (A) Continuously (B) Perpetually (C) Continually (D) Constantly
42. (A) Contemporary (B) Coeval (C) Coetaneous (D) Pristine
43. (A) Coward (B) Crazy (C) Timorous (D) Courageous
44. (A) Grovel (B) Truckle (C) Breed (D) Long
45. (A) Worn (B) Torn (C) Pinched (D) Tranquil
46. (A) Jargon (B) Janket (C) Lingo (D) Frolick
47. (A) Fondle (B) Like (C) Reject (D) Pet
48. (A) Blow (B) Babble (C) Curse (D) Blabber
49. (A) Generate (B) Engender (C) Spoil (D) Ruin
50. (A) Generated (B) Congenital (C) Progenitor (D) Innate

Choose the odd one out from the four options given in each set:

51. (A) Crevice (B) Rent (C) Fissure (D) Craze

52. (A) Vituperate (B) Vilify (C) Inveigh (D) Objurgate

53. (A) Twaddle (B) Prattle (C) Drivel (D) Wail

54. (A) Cavort (B) Grasp (C) Nab (D) Grab

55. (A) Swindle (B) Grab (C) Defraud (D) Dupe

56. (A) Claque (B) Choir (C) Troupe (D) Criticize

57. (A) Segregate (B) Secede (C) Sort (D) Assort

58. (A) Nomination (B) Denomination (C) Genre (D) Genus

59. (A) Astute (B) Sagacious (C) Thrifty (D) Perspicacious

60. (A) Summon (B) Marshall (C) Muster (D) Order

ANSWERS

1. (C) See Curse	**2.** (A) See Caress	3. (D) See Compensate
4. (B) See Cadaverous	**5.** (A) See Catholic	**6.** (C) See Cautious
7. (C) See Chatter	**8.** (D) See Cry	**9.** (A) See Cant
10. (B) See Contempt	**11.** (C) See Calm	**12.** (A) See Collect
13. (C) See Contempt	**14.** (C) See Caprice	**15.** (A) See Chant
16. (D) See Cringe	**17.** (B) See Cheat (v)	**18.** (A) See Clique
19. (D) See Crawl	**20.** (C) See Crave	**21.** (C) See Credit
22. (C) See Catch	**23.** (C) See Caper	**24.** (D) See Cheat
25. (C) See Chew	**26.** (C) See Chide	**27.** (B) See Circadian
28. (A) See Climax	**29.** (B) See Cruel	**30.** (D) See Hiatus
31. (A) See Clean	**32.** (B) See Clean	**33.** (C) See Classify
34. (A) See Clever	**35.** (C) See Closeness	**36.** (C) See Clot
37. (D) See Cogitate	**38.** (C) See Confine	
39. (C) See Confiscate	**40.** (B) See Consult	
41. A-B See Continuously	42. B-C See Contemporary	
43. A-C See Coward	44. A-B See Cringe	**45.** A-C See Cadaverous
46. A-C See Cant	**47.** A-D See Caress	**48.** B-D See Chatter
49. A-B See Create	**50.** B-D See Congenital	**51.** (D) See Crack
52. (B) See Criticize	**53.** (D) See Chatter	**54.** (A) See Catch
55. (B) See Cheat	**56.** (D) See Clique	**57.** (B) See Classfiy
58. (A) See Class	**59.** (C) See Clever	**60.** See Collect

TEST 4

Choose the most suitable synonym of the given word out of the four suggested options :

1. Fabricate
   (A) Fashion (B) Imagine (C) Figment (D) Repair
2. Raven
   (A) Shout (B) Rout (C) Devour (D) Shatter

3. Pedestrian
(A) Walker (B) Pedlar (C) Humdrum (D) Hawker

4. Impair
(A) Damage (B) Imply (C) Pare (D) Risk

5. Lacklustre
(A) Shine (B) Monotonous (C) Sticky (D) Darkness

6. Jeopardy
(A) Risk (B) Calamity (C) Distrust (D) Vanish

7. Guzzle
(A) Dazzle (B) Dribble (C) Quaff (D) Adorn

8. Cadaver
(A) Greedy (B) Garnish (C) Debris (D) Carcass

9. Wilt
(A) Sag (B) Droop (C) Crumple (D) Slump

10. Coruscate
(A) Crash (B) Guzzle (C) Glitter (D) Crack

11. Confer
(A) Talk (B) Discuss (C) Endue (D) Denounce

12. Grope
(A) Gap (B) Dark (C) Fizzle (D) Frisk

13. Debris
(A) Stone (B) Scum (C) Fragment (D) Rubble

14. Dominance
(A) Dormancy (B) Hegemony (C) Jurisdiction (D) Courage

15. Proclaim
(A) Decide (B) Deny (C) Herald (D) Support

16. Embellish
(A) Garnish (B) Delude (C) Garner (D) Embolden

17. Dilapidated
(A) Damaged (B) Loose (C) Ruined (D) Rickety

18. Lees
(A) Clout (B) Weeds (C) Dregs (D) Forge

19. Vilify
(A) Defile (B) Asperse (C) Vanquish (D) Validate

20. Turncoat
(A) Deceive (B) Overhaul (C) Proselyte (D) Rectify

21. Handicap
(A) Lacuna (B) Disabled (C) Weakness (D) Delicate

22. Impoverish
(A) Improper (B) Degenerate (C) Impair (D) Dull

23. Hibernating
(A) Dormant (B) Domineering (C) Swaying (D) Revealing

24. Predicament
(A) Importance (B) Prediction (C) Dilemma (D) Dispute

25. Exhume
(A) Burry (B) Resume (C) Confiscate (D) Disinter

26. Discrepancy
(A) Discredit (B) Disparity (C) Demerit (D) Discord

27. Dunk
(A) Immerse (B) Prick (C) Drone (D) Murmur

28. Procrastinate
(A) Crush (B) Swat (C) Dawdle (D) Accuse

29. Apocalypse
(A) Divulge (B) Eucalyptus (C) Calamity (D) Dispair

30. Cynicism
(A) Foolishness (B) Patriotism (C) Mistrust (D) Dejection

Choose pairs of words with similar meanings out of the given options:

31. (A) Masquerade (B) Lampoon (C) Disguise (D) Eructate

32. (A) Jib (B) Balk (C) Split (D) Reek

33. (A) Disgorge (B) Ooze (C) Coruscate (D) Dazzle

34. (A) Jettison (B) Jetsam (C) Jilt (D) Absolve

35. (A) Betray (B) Cheat (C) Hoodwink (D) Divulge

36. (A) Dault (B) Deter (C) Threaten (D) Challenge

37. (A) Recusant (B) Rude (C) Cruel (D) Froward

38. (A) Unkempt (B) Disgruntled (C) Dishevelled (D) Shed

39. (A) Parry (B) Duck (C) Secede (D) Drool

40. (A) Costume (B) Custom (C) Trousseau (D) Garnish

Choose the odd one out from the given options:

41. (A) Gleam (B) Sparkle (C) Coruscate (D) Impair

42. (A) Lackadaisical (B) Dreary (C) Dull (D) Glittering

43. (A) Ken (B) Province (C) Realm (D) Dominance

44. (A) Execrate (B) Manifest (C) Decry (D) Deprecate

45. (A) Invoke (B) Evince (C) Flaunt (D) Parade

46. (A) Scoff (B) Sneer (C) Pillory (D) Repudiate

47. (A) Curse (B) Conation (C) Volition (D) Wish

48. (A) Grit (B) Mettle (C) Fret (D) Resolve

49. (A) Moult (B) Mould (C) Shed (D) Slough

50. (A) Despair (B) Despondence (C) Dejection (D) Disaster

ANSWERS

1. (A) See Devise	2. (C) See Devour	3. (C) See Dull
4. (A) See Damage	5. (B) See Dull	6. (A) See Danger
7. (C) See Drink	8. (D) See Deadbody	9. (B) See Droop
10. (C) See Dazzle	11. (C) See Demise	12. (D) See Delve
13. (D) See Debris	14. (B) See Dominance	15. (C) See Declare
16. (A) See Decorate	17. (D) See Decrepit	18. (C) See Dregs
19. (B) See Defame	20. (C) See Defector	21. (A) See Defect
22. (B) See Degenerate	23. (A) See Dormant	24. (C) See Dilemma
25. (D) See Digout	26. (B) See Difference	27. (A) See Dip
28. (C) See Dilly-dally	**29.** (C) See Disaster	**30.** (C) See Disbelief
31. A-C See Disguise	**32.** A-B See Disobey	**33.** A-B See Disgorge
34. A-C See Discard	**35.** A-D See Disclose	**36.** A-B See Discourage
37. A-D See Disobedient	38. A-C See Disorderly	**39.** A-B See Dodge
40. A-C See Dress	41. (D) See Dazzle	**42.** (D) See Dull
43. (D) See Domain	44. (B) See Denounce	**45.** (A) See Demonstrate
46. (D) See Deride	**47.** (A) See Desire	
48. (C) See Determination	**49.** (B) See Discard	
50. (D) See Disappointment		

TEST 5

Choose the most appropriate synonym of the given words out of the suggested options:

1. Instance
   (A) Occurrence (B) Example (C) Accident (D) Event
2. Inquisitive
   (A) Curious (B) Enquiring (C) Careful (D) Investigating
3. Gloze
   (A) Shining (B) Glaze (C) Mitigate (D) Glare
4. Protract
   (A) Prolong (B) Lengthen (C) Elongate (D) Lengthy
5. Spout
   (A) Fat (B) Rotund (C) Spit (D) Spurt
6. Prodigal
   (A) Outstanding (B) Talented (C) Spendthrift (D) Marvellous
7. Efficacious
   (A) Efficient (B) Effective (C) Effluent (D) Affluent
8. Fervour
   (A) Passion (B) Flow (C) Raging (D) Fire

9. Expatiate
   (A) Spotless (B) Praise (C) Expound (D) Partition
10. Indispensable
   (A) Essential (B) Disposable (C) Likable (D) Acceptable
11. Equivalence
   (A) Balanced (B) Equilibruim (C) Valid (D) Parity
12. Snuff (out)
   (A) Sniffle (B) Snuffle (C) Extinguish (D) Snore
13. Puppet
   (A) Marionette (B) Doll (C) Mannequin (D) Statue
14. Scarecrow
   (A) Effigy (B) Scaring object to frighten crows/birds
   (C) Ugly (D) Crow
15. Flagrant
   (A) Flag bearer (B) Flagitious (C) Outrageous (D) Flowing
16. Phenomenal
   (A) Universal (B) Egregious (C) Phantom (D) Prodigious
17. Vet
   (A) Veteran (B) Validate (C) Scrutinize (D) Virtue
18. Indispensable
   (A) Essential (B) Rejectable (C) Intolerable (D) Useless
19. Parity
   (A) Pare (B) Pruning (C) Purity (D) Equality
20. Transitory
   (A) Transit (B) Touring (C) Ephemeral (D) Eternal
21. Educe
   (A) Deduce (B) Provoke (C) Produce (D) Evoke
22. Heave
   (A) Sigh (B) Swing (C) Hoist (D) Cry
23. Exude
   (A) Fart (B) Belch (C) Ooze out (sweat) (D) Expel
24. Stress
   (A) Accentuate (B) Strain (C) Press (D) Defy
25. Ape
   (A) Ancestor (B) Forebears (C) Imitate (D) Infringe
26. Mime
   (A) Mimic (B) Deride (C) Amuse (D) Entertain
27. Transgress
   (A) Translate (B) Tranfer (C) Encroach (D) Travel

28. Infiltrate
   (A) Filter through/into (permeate) (B) Purify (C) Intrude
   (D) Invade

29. Eradicate
   (A) Radicalise (B) Extirpate (C) Suffocate (D) Remove

30. Extempore
   (A) Impromptu (B) Expire (C) Extra (D) Timely

Choose pair of words out of the given options, which are similar in meaning:

31. (A)Keen (B) Cry (C) Sharp (D) Agog
32. (A)Fleecing (B) Fluent (C) Fleeting (D) Transient
33. (A)Elope (B) Beguile (C) Benign (D) Inveigle
34. (A)Lift (B) Crane (C) Escalator (D) Boost
35. (A)Belch (B) Fart (C) Eructate (D) Expel
36. (A)Enshrine (B) Holy (C) Reverence (D) Consecrate
37. (A)Paradigm (B) Example (C) Parable (D) Comparison
38. (A)Weary (B) Bleary (C) Weird (D) Languid
39. (A)Quail (B) Quack (C) Quell (D) Tremble
40. (A)Blatant (B) Clamourous (C) Flagrant (D) Arrogant

Choose the odd one out from the given options:

41. (A)Extravagant (B) Prodigal (C) Spendthrift (D) Thrift
42. (A)Artificial (B) Mannequin (C) Effigy (D) Toy
43. (A)Query (B) Audit (C) Vet (D) Check
44. (A)Hoist (B) Elicit (C) Rear (D) Elevate
45. (A)Clash (B) Encounter (C) Confrontation (D) Encroachment
46. (A)Entwine (B) Ensnare (C) Entangle (D) Intrude
47. (A)Deduce (B) Seduce (C) Suborn (D) Beguile
48. (A)Indispensable (B) Compulsory (C) Disposable (D) Necessary
49. (A)Morale (B) Morality (C) Ethics (D) Morals
50. (A)Effect (B) Consequence (C) Results (D) Affect

ANSWERS

1. (B) See Example **2.** (A) See Eager **3.** (C) See Extenuate
4. (A) See Protract **5.** (D) See Eject **6.** (C) See Extravagant
7. (B) See Effective **8.** (A) See Enthusiasm **9.** (C) See Explain
10. (A) See Essential **11.** (D) See Equality **12.** (C) See Extinquish
13. (A) **14.** (B) See Scarecrow **15.** (C) See Flagrant
16. (D) See Extraordinary **17.** (C) See Examine **18.** (A) See Essential
19. (D) See Equality **20.** (C) See Ephemeral **21.** (D) See Educe
22. (C) See Heave **23.** (C) See Exude **24.** (A) See Emphasize
25. (C) See Ape **26.** (A) See Mime **27.** (C) See Transgress

28. (C) See Infiltrate	**29.** (B) See Eradicate	**30.** (A) See Extempore
31. A-C See Keen	**32.** C-D See Ephemeral	**33.** B-D See Inveigle
34. A-D See Boost	**35.** A-C See Belch	**36.** A-D See Enshrine
37. A-B See Paradigm	**38.** A-D	**39.** A-D
40. A-C	**41.** (D)	**42.** (A)
43. (A)	**44.** (B) See Elevate	**45.** (D) See Encounter
46. (D)	**47.** (A)	**48.** (C) See Essential
49. (A)	**50.** (D)	

TEST 6

Choose the closest synonym of the given words below:

1. Triffling
   (A) Joking (B) Terrorising (C) Frivolous (D) Flitting
2. Augur
   (A) Portend (B) Omen (C) Forecast (D) Accuse
3. Facade
   (A) Main door (B) Main front (C) Physiognomy (D) Fraud
4. Rattle
   (A) Shake (B) Scare (C) Panic (D) Shout
5. Muzzle
   (A) Gun (B) Face (C) Pipe (D) Suffocate
6. Autonomous
   (A) Automatic (B) Sovereign (C) Authority (D) Authorised
7. Prophesy
   (A) Prophet (B) Oracle (C) Rare (D) Predict
8. Chum
   (A) Crony (B) Sycophant (C) Spoon (D) Slave
9. Counterfeit
   (A) Illegal (B) Contrary (C) Fake (D) Encounter
10. Cherish
    (A) Charge (B) Accuse (C) Vivid (D) Nurture
11. Proscribe
    (A) Prescribe (B) Describe (C) Forbid (D) Write
12. Sinuous
    (A) Meandering (B) Sensitive (C) Serious (D) Soaring
13. Sham
    (A) Shameful (B) Spurious (C) Shy (D) Superior
14. Stagger
    (A) Spread (B) Stump (C) Flounder (D) Stay

15. Fare

(A) Charge (B) Fee (C) Tariff (D) Freight

16. Henchmen

(A) Cohort (B) Follower (C) Criminals (D) Today

17. Debacle

(A) Debate (B) Difference (C) Miscarriage (D) Downfall

18. Fussy

(A) Noisy (B) Leaking (C) Fused (D) Finnicky

19. Fawn

(A) Deer (B) Today (C) Lick (D) Favour

20. Standard

(A) Upright (B) Quality (C) Colours (D) Banner

21. Fisticuff

(A) Fists (B) Scuffle (C) Fright (D) Horror

22. Eminent

(A) Exceptional (B) Arrogant (C) Renowned (D) Great

23. Lethal

(A) Lazy (B) Late (C) Languid (D) Fatal

24. Vision

(A) Foresight (B) Clarity (C) Visuals (D) Eyes

Choose the pair of words, out of given options, which bear the same meaning:

25. (A) Muzzle (B) Visage (C) Face (D) Countenance

26. (A) Freight (B) Tariff (C) Fee (D) Rent

27. (A) Frighten (B) Intimidate (C) Horrify (D) Fawn

28. (A) Portend (B) Portly (C) Round (D) Prognosticate

29. (A) Facet (B) Facetious (C) Factitious (D) Frivolous

30. (A) Rear (B) Nurture (C) Posterior (D) Nullify

31. (A) Autarky (B) Autonomy (C) Autocracy (D) Automatic

32. (A) Alter ego (B) Alternative (C) Friend (D) Egocentric

33. (A) Torturous (B) Tortuous (C) Painful (D) Sinuous

Choose the odd one out from the given options:

34. (A) Colours (B) Standard (C) Banner (D) Flag

35. (A) Winding (B) Sinuous (C) Flexuous (D) Torturous

36. (A) Flatter (B) Inhibit (C) Prohibit (D) Forbid

37. (A) Renowned (B) Famous (C) Popular (D) Nominated

38. (A) Stumble (B) Flounder (C) Fumble (D) Falter

39. (A) Sham (B) Humiliating (C) Ersatz (D) Fake

40. (A) Fitful (B) Fisticuff (C) Scuffle (D) Fight

ANSWERS

1. (C) See Facetious	2. (A) See Foretell	3. (B) See Face
4. (B) See Frighten	5. (B) See Face	6. (B) See Free
7. (D) See Foretell	8. (A) See Friend	9. (C) See Fake
10. (D) See Foster	11. (C) See Forbid	12. (A) See Flexuous
13. (B) See Fake	14. (C) See Falter	15. (D) See Fare

16. (A) See Follower (Henchmen is plural of Henchman, Cohort is plural)

17. (C) See Failure	18. (D) See Fastidious	19. See Flatter
20. (C) See Flag	21. (B) See Fight	22. (C) See Famous
23. (D) See Fatal	24. (A) See Foresight	25. A-C See Face
26. B-C See Fare	27. A-B See Frighten	28. A-D See Foretell
29. B-D See Facetious	30. A-B See Foster	31. A-B See Free
32. A-C See Friend	33. B-D See Fluxuous	34. (C) See Flag
35. (D) See Flexuous	36. (A) See Forbid	37. (D) See Famous
38. (A) See Falter	39. (B) See Fake	40. (A) See Fight

TEST 7

Choose the appropriate word to be filled in the blank space of the sentence out of the four suggested options in the following:

1. The .... from every household is to be thrown at a specified place, from where municipal trucks collect it for disposal.
   (A) Refuse (B) Sullage (C) Rubbish (D) Garbage
2. Getting annoyed, he .... at me in anger.
   (A) Looked (B) Stared (C) Glared (D) Peered
3. A large number of sikhs were .... in the wake of the assassination of Indira Gandhi.
   (A) Massacred (B) Butchered (C) Killed (D) Murdered
4. A large number of sikhs lost their lives in .... post Indira Gandhi's assassination.
   (A) Pogrom (B) Genocide (C) Carnage (D) Revenge
5. The drainage was choked with ....
   (A) Refuse (B) Trash (C) Sullage (D) Rubbish
6. The plastic tea cups are .... after use.
   (A) Dispensed with (B) Got rid of (C) Disposed of (D) Thrown
7. He .... himself with sweets in the party until felt aversion.
   (A) Surfeited (B) Sated (C) Satiated (D) Gorged
8. He earned the fame as .... of research in cancer treatments.
   (A) Guide (B) Trailblazer (C) Usher (D) Pioneer

9. An atheist does not hesitate to .... religion in speech.
(A) Blaspheme (B) Profane (C) Insult (D) Criticize

10. An expressionless countenance of a .... person does not betray his emotions.
(A) Impassive (B) Phlegmatic (C) Stolid (D) Stoic

11. A person of .... courage is called a brave person.
(A) Indomitable (B) Unconquerable
(C) Invincible (D) Unwavering

12. He was cautious in speaking to women to avoid being blamed of .... behaviour.
(A) Indecent (B) Scurrilous (C) Risque (D) Vulgar

13. The boys standing on the road-side .... at the girls passing by furtively.
(A) Stared (B) Gazed (C) Peered (D) Glanced

14. Festering grievances against the government ...... people to revolt.
(A) Instigate (B) Arouse (C) Foment (D) Incite

15. It is very difficult to distinguish the .... of synonymous words.
(A) Nuances (B) Differences (C) Gradation (D) Shades

16. A boy .... himself through the crowd to the frontline near the dais.
(A) Inserted (B) Pushed (C) Insinuated (D) Penetrated

17. Teeth .... food in the mouth before being swallowed.
(A) Grind (B) Triturate (C) Comminute (D) Pulverise

18. The .... at the insulting remark hurt him deeply.
(A) Resentment (B) Pique (C) Dudgeon (D) Annoyance

19. A student .... a question in the class much to the annoyance of the lecturer.
(A) Intervened (B) Interceded (C) Interjected (D) Asked

20. The cat .... at me when I tried to chase it.
(A) Grumbled (B) Snarled (C) Purred (D) Growled

21. The patient's condition worsened because he ignored doctor's .... to desist from taking oily food.
(A) Injunction (B) Directive (C) Instruction (D) Prescription

22. He .... the boy by showing a chocolate but not giving him.
(A) Persecuted (B) Tormented (C) Tantalised (D) Harried

23. He has no .... of where his friend has gone without informing him.
(A) Intuition (B) Anticipation(C) Hunch (D) Inkling

24. He was upset with the .... of ghost's apparitions in the darkness of night.
(A) Apprehension (B) Premonition
(C) Presentiment (D) Prescience

25. An old model car was .... so to look like a new model.
(A) Innovated (B) Renovated (C) Revamped (D) Retrofitted

26. Unhygienic condition is .... to our health.
(A) Injurious (B) Disastrous (C) Deleterious (D) Inimical

27. Kids would do good to themselves by heeding to .... advices of their elders.
(A) Salutary (B) Salubrious (C) Sanitary (D) Wholesome

28. .... of bees invaded the person who stoked their beehive.
(A) Shoal (B) Drove (C) Swarm (D) Flock

29. He.......... his malevolence behind his affected geniality towards me.
(A) Dissembled (B) Disguised (C) Ensconced (D) Masked

30. I have no .... as to how to solve this problem.
(A) Cue (B) Hint (C) Clue (D) Allusion

31. The horse suddenly .... at dragging the cart, despite goading.
(A) Hesitated (B) Jibbed (C) Balked (D) Dithered

32. A temple is .... for the devotees.
(A) Holy (B) Divine (C) Sacrosanct (D) Sacred

33. The mob .... stones on policemen.
(A) Lobbed (B) Hurled (C) Pelted (D) Tossed

34. We have strange .... about aliens.
(A) Notion (B) Idea (C) Perception (D) Concept

35. He is in the habit of giving unsolicited .... advice to others.
(A) Officious (B) Meddlesome (C) Obtrusive (D) Intrusive

36. His new shoes .... on his toes.
(A) Pricked (B) Prickled (C) Impinged (D) Hurt

37. A nail .... his finger.
(A) Impinged (B) Prickled (C) Punctured (D) Pricked

38. Wrongly parked vehicles were towed to be .... by traffic police.
(A) Intered (B) Imprisoned (C) Interned (D) Impounded

39. Patriotism makes us .... to feel happy over our national team's victory in international games.
(A) Biased (B) Inclined (C) Pre-disposed (D) Tend

40. His hobnobbing with an opposition leader was .... to be an act of disloyalty to the party.
(A) Inferred (B) Deduced (C) Interpreted (D) Construed

41. The rich man adequately .... the person who saved his life from an assailant.
(A) Indemnified (B) Compensated (C) Recompensed (D) Repaid

42. A gunman fired shots ....
(A) Haphazardly (B) Randomly
(C) All around (D) Indiscriminately

43. Propaganda .... doubt about someone's probity in people's mind.
(A) Inculcates (B) Instils (C) Infuses (D) Insinuates

44. Investors were .... of the risks involved in investing in stocks.
(A) Informed (B) Acquainted (C) Advised (D) Aprised

45. Arrogance is .... in him.
(A) Immanent (B) Inherent (C) Innate (D) Intrinsic

46. A chemical factory's chimney spewed .... fumes.
(A) Obnoxious (B) Noxious (C) Poisonous (D) Injurious

47. Politicians are infamous for being .... in shady deals with criminals.
(A) Involved (B) Indulged (C) Engrossed (D) Complicit

48. The host himself .... each guest to his seat in the hall.
(A) Led (B) Guided (C) Ushered (D) Accompanied

49. The tigers .... at the circus ringmaster even as they meekly followed his command.
(A) Purred (B) Grumbled (C) Snarled (D) Growled

50. Beggars in streets .... him for alms.
(A) Harassed (B) Tormented (C) Badgered (D) Bothered

ANSWERS

1. (D) See Garbage for explanation
2. (C) See Gaze
3. (A) See Genocide
4. (B) See Genocide
5. (C) See Garbage
6. (C) See Get rid of
7. (A) See Gorge
8. (D) See Guide
9. (A) See Impious
10. (C) See Impassive
11. (A) See Invincible
12. (C) See Indecent
13. (D) See Gaze
14. (D) See Instigate
15. (A) See Gradation
16. (C) See Inserted
17. (C) See Grind
18. (B) See Irritation
19. (C) See Interject
20. (C) See Growl
21. (C) See Instruction
22. (C) See Harass
23. (D) See Inkling
24. (C) See Inkling
25. (D) See Innovate
26. (C) See Injurious
27. (A) See Healthful
28. (C) See Herd
29. (A) See Hide
30. (C) See Hint
31. (B) See Hesitate
32. (C) See Holy
33. (C) See Hurl
34. (A) See Idea
35. (A) See Intrusive
36. (C) See Impinge
37. (D) See Impinge
38. (D) See Imprison
39. (C) See Inclination
40. (D) See Infer
41. (C) See Indemnify
42. (D) See Indiscriminate
43. (D) See Insert
44. (C) See Inform
45. (B) See Inherent
46. (B) See Injurious
47. (D) See Involved
48. (C) See Guide
49. (D) See Growl
50. (C) See Harass

TEST 8

Choose the correct word out of the given options, which would fit in the blank.

1. He is a person of .... character.
   (A) Impeccable (B) Immaculate (C) Consummate (D) Divine
2. His action is not .... with requirement.
   (A) Congruous (B) Compatible (C) Consistent (D) Consonant
3. .... kids are frolicking joyously.
   (A) Animate (B) Vivacious (C) Active (D) Energetic
4. The accused was finally .... by the enquiry committee.
   (A) Exonerated (B) Exculpated (C) Acquited (D) Released
5. He was .... in a case of bribery.
   (A) Accused (B) Indicted (C) Arraigned (D) Incriminated
6. He has .... enormous wealth.
   (A) Amassed (B) Acquired (C) Gained (D) Gathered
7. One has to overcome .... in one's life.
   (A) Adversity (B) Affliction (C) Ordeal (D) Disaster
8. A .... deliberately parades his knowledge.
   (A) Quack (B) Charlatan (C) Pedant (D) Hypocrite
9. He .... his ignorance in this matter.
   (A) Vouched (B) Avouched (C) Avowed (D) Averred
10. He played a hoax of bomb scare for a ....
    (A) Lark (B) Amusement (C) Racreation (D) Entertainment
11. The police earned .... for timely recovery of a bomb planted in the marketplace by a terrorist.
    (A) Kudos (B) Approbation (C) Admiration (D) Appreciation
12. Ice hockey is played on a ....
    (A) Turf (B) Playground (C) Rink (D) Gymnasium
13. Police .... the criminal's hideout to apprehend.
    (A) Raided (B) Invaded (C) Attacked (D) Assaulted
14. His aggressive nature is .... to his upbringing.
    (A) Ascribed (B) Imputed (C) Attributed (D) Assigned
15. He was .... to the criminal activity of corruption by the lure of lucre.
    (A) Seduced (B) Enticed (C) Allured (D) Attracted
16. America's .... over weaker nations enables it to cast its influence to further its interests.
    (A) Preponderance (B) Hegemony (C) Dominance (D) Command

17. The boy is wont to .... illness to avoid going to school.
(A) Malinger (B) Feign (C) Pretend (D) Affect

18. Chimney of chemical factory spews .... fumes.
(A) Noisome (B) Noxious (C) Abnoxious (D) Foul

19. An elderly person, who wishes well of others, is a ....
(A) Benevolent person (B) Benefactor
(C) Samaritan (D) Altruist

20. Devotees .... their hands and feet with holy water before entering sanctum sanctorum of holy place.
(A) Clean (B) Cleanse (C) Lustrate (D) Anoint

21. He reached the .... of his career in a short span of time.
(A) Climax (B) Peak (C) Zenith (D) Pinnacle

22. The doctor .... the patient to follow the regimen of treatment.
(A) Ordered (B) Decreed (C) Ordained (D) Enjoined

23. His conscience .... him to confess his crime.
(A) Coerced (B) Constrained (C) Restrained (D) Exacted

24. He .... his hatred against me by pretending to be friendly.
(A) Dissembled (B) Concealed (C) Cloaked (D) Camouflaged

25. She .... my offer of help by ignoring it.
(A) Snubbed (B) Scoffed (C) Sneered (D) Scorned

26. He earned fame as a .... of research in cancer treatment.
(A) Guide (B) Trailblazer (C) Usher (D) Pioneer

27. He is a person of .... courage.
(A) Indomitable (B) Unconquerable
(C) Invincible (D) Unwavering

28. He was upset with the .... of ghost's apparitions.
(A) Premonition (B) Presentiment
(C) Apprehension (D) Prescience

29. Unhygienic conditions are .... to our health.
(A) Injurious (B) Disastrous (C) Deleterious (D) Inimical

30. I have no .... as to how to solve this problem.
(A) Cue (B) Clue (C) Hint (D) Allusion

31. Beggars in streets .... people for alms.
(A) Harass (B) Badger (C) Bother (D) Torment

32. The rich man adequately .... the person who saved his life.
(A) Indemnified (B) Compensated (C) Recompensed (D) Repayed

33. The circus tigers .... at the ringmaster even as they meekly follwed his command.
(A) Purred (B) Grumbled (C) Snarled (D) Growled

34. The host himself .... each guest to his seat in the reception hall.
(A) Led (B) Guided (C) Ushered (D) Accompanied

35. The horse suddenly .... at dragging the cart despite goading.
(A) Hesitated (B) Balked (C) Jibbed (D) Dithered

36. He is in the habit of giving unsolicited .... advice to others.
(A) Officious (B) Meddlesome (C) Obtrusive (D) Intrusive

37. Patriotism makes us .... to feel happy over the victory of our cricket team.
(A) Pre-disposed (B) Inclined (C) Biased (D) Disposed

38. His hobonobbing with the opposition leaders was .... to be an act of disloyalty to his own party.
(A) Inferred (B) Deduced (C) Interpreted (D) Construed

39. It is good to heed .... advice of elders.
(A) Salubrious (B) Sanitary (C) Wholesome (D) Salutary

40. .... of bees invaded the person who stoked the beehive.
(A) Shoal (B) Drove (C) Swarm (D) Flock

41. He has no .... of where has his friend has gone.
(A) Intuition (B) Anticipation (C) Hunch (D) Inkling

42. He .... the boy by showing a chocolate but not giving it to him.
(A) Harried (B) Tormented (C) Annoyed (D) Tantalised

43. The boy .... himself through the crowd to the front line near the dais.
(A) Pushed (B) Penetrated (C) Insinuated (D) Inserted

44. Festering grievances against the government .... people to revolt.
(A) Instigate (B) Incite (C) Arouse (D) Foment

45. An expressionless countenance of a ....person does not betray his emotions.
(A) Impassive (B) Phlegmatic (C) Stolid (D) Stoic

46. Plastic tea cups are .... after use.
(A) Dispensed with (B) Disposed of (C) Got rid of (D) Discarded

47. The drainage was choked with ....
(A) Refuse (B) Trash (C) Sullage (D) Rubbish

48. A large number of sikhs lost life in ....post Indira Gandhi's assassination.
(A) Pogrom (B) Genocide (C) Carnage (D) Killings

49. The boys standing on the roadside .... at the girls passing by furtively.
(A) Stared (B) Gazed (C) Peered (D) Glanced

50. Teeth .... food in the mouth before being swallowed.
(A) Grind (B) Triturate (C) Comminute (D) Pulverise

ANSWERS

1. (A) Immaculate is used for spotless, clean dress, consummate means perfect, Divine means sacred.

2. (C) Compatible means capable of existing together, congruous means resembling in shape of parts, consonant means being in harmony of sound.

3. (B) Vivacious means full of vigour.

4. (A) Exonerate means declare free from charges, Exculpate means declare free from criminal offence, Acquit means declare free by a court, Release means set free from captivity.

5. (D) Indict means accuse of wrong doing. Means call to court for answering indictment, Incriminate means charge of involvement in an act of crime.

6. (A) Acquire means come to possess as property, assets; Gain profit, etc. Gather means to collect by picking up as flowers.

7. (A) Affiction means to cause pain by diseases, injury, ordeal means trial to prove innocence as an ordeal by fire, Disaster means natural calamity, viz., flood, earthquake.

8. (C) Quack is an unqualified practitioner, charlatan is a pretender to have knowledge, Hypocrite is a person who professes to have qualification which he does not possess himself. Pedant is a person who makes excessive show of his knowledge.

9. (C) Aver means to assert with confidence, Avouch means to assert with full responsibility, Avow means to declare openly, Vouch means to confirm something to be true.

10. (A) Lark means to have fun.

11. (B) Kudos means praise, Admire means to praise for wonderful job, Appreciate means to praise in high estimation of person.

12. (C) Playground on ice is called Rink.

13. (A) Invade means attack enemy's territory, Assault means to attack to injure, harm.

14. (C) Ascribe is to give credit, Impute is used for questionable intention, Assign is to allot duty, reason.

15. (A) Seduce means to lead away on wrong path. All other words are related to the meaning of 'get attracted towards'.

16. (B)

17. (C) Malinger means pretend illness to bunk classes etc.

18. (B) Poisonously harmful is noxious. Abnoxious means having offending smell as is Noisome & Foul.

19. (A) Benefactor helps with money to the needy, samaritan helps people in distress, Attruist keeps others' interests above his own interest.

20. (C) Clean is to wash or remove dirt, cleanse is to purify from the guilt of sin, Anoint is to wash with oil for consecration of deity.

21. (D) Climax is used for interest, Peak for mountain, Zenith for planet's orbit of movement.

22. (D) Order is official, Decree is court's order, ordain is holy or divine order, Enjoin is order with emphasis on compliance.

23. (B) Constrain means to compel to do something. Coerce means compel by threatening, Restrain means compel someone not to do something, and Exact means compel to comply with as repayment of loan, payment of fine, etc.

24. (A) Dissemble means to hide one's emotional feelings, Conceal means to hide from others' view, Cloak means to hide by putting under cover, Camouflage means to hide by painting in colour of surroundings so that detection is diffcult.

25. (A) Show contempt by ignoring or dismissing something means to snub, scoff is to laugh at disdainfully, Sneer is to smile disdainfully, Scorn means to treat someone contemptuously.

26. (D) Pioneer is one who is first in a field of enterprise.

27. (A) Indomitable is what can't be subdued, Invincible is what can't be defeated, Unwavering means not flickering.

28. (C) Premonition means feeling anxiety over future event, Presentiment means feeling of something bad to happen, Prescience is foreknowledge of what will happen. Apprehension mens fear of coming evil.

29. (C) Deleterious is injurious to health.

30. (B)

31. (B) Badger means annoy with persistent nagging.

32. (C) Indemnify means to ensure to make up for possible loss caused by one's action, compensate means make up for the loss, Recompense means to pay as reward for services or help rendered.

33. (C) Snarl means to growl in anger, Purr means to make sound as by a cat, Grumble is to make indistinct guttural voice as in discontent.

34. (C)

35. (B) Balk means hesitate or refuse to move forward due to some problem ahead, Jib means to move backward instead of forward, Dither means hesitate due to fear or threat.

36. (A) **37.** (A)

38. (D) Interpret means explain the meaning of, Infer means to derive by reasoning, Deduce means to conclude from something else, Construe means to assign a particular interpretation.

39. (D) Salutary means causing beneficial effect, Salubrious means health promoting climate, Sanitary means health promoting cleanliness, Wholesome means conducive to general well-being.

40. (C) **41.** (D) **42.** (D) **43.** (C)

44. (B) Incite is used for provoking to do something unlawful as by one's internal urge, Instigate is used when someone provokes, Arouse means stir someone to action, Foment means to promote the growth of or to allow the development of something undesirable, viz., to foment dissatisfaction.

45. (C) **46.** (B) **47.** (C)

48. (B) Carnage means killings of a great number of people, Genocide means killing deliberately of people belonging to particular racial group, Pogrom means organised killings.

49. (D)

50. (C) Grind means to reduce to fine particles, Comminute means to break into small particles, Pulverise means to reduce to powder, Triturate means to reduce to powder by rubbing.

TEST 9

Choose the most appropriate synonym of the words out of given options:

1. Abandon
   (A) Desert (B) Jilt (C) Abundant (D) Decontrol
2. Rate
   (A) Evaluate (B) Value (C) Run (D) Repeat
3. Fashion
   (A) Blase (B) Dandy (C) Vogue (D) Beauty
4. Look
   (A) Pore (B) Pour (C) Askance (D) Browse
5. Gaze
   (A) Peer (B) Glare (C) Gloat (D) Glower
6. Behaviour
   (A) Demeanour (B) Mien (C) Action (D) Delinquency
7. Complacent
   (A) Calm (B) Cool (C) Smug (D) Compliment
8. Acclimatise
   (A) Inure (B) Adapt (C) Adopt (D) Satisfy

9. Order
   (A) Judgement (B) Diktat (C) Arrange (D) Serialise
10. Refuse
   (A) Baulk (B) Denial (C) Disorder (D) Admit
11. Disobedient
   (A) Rude (B) Recusant (C) Docile (D) Dormant
12. Native
   (A) Autochthon (B) Birthplace (C) Resident (D) Endemic
13. Protest
   (A) Avoid (B) Contest
   (C) Declaration (expressing disagreement, disapproval or opposition)
   (D) Contravene
14. Calamity
   (A) Apocalypse (B) Earthquake (C) Enemity (D) Flood
15. Disaster
   (A) Monster (B) Accident (C) Catastrophe (D) Contest
16. Premonition
   (A) Foreboding (B) Admonition (C) Denomination (D) Guess
17. Lazy
   (A) Languorous (B) Slow (C) Inactive (D) Dormant
18. Criticism
   (A) Critical judgement (B) Inveigh (C) Vituperate (D) Excoriate
19. Earmark
   (A) Assign (B) Necessary (C) Spot (D) Point out
20. Surprise
   (A) Wonder (B) Annoy (C) Astound (D) Apprehend
21. Compulsory
   (A) Compelling (B) Optional (C) Sine qua non(D) Composite
22. Deny
   (A) Repudiate (B) Surrender (C) Refuse (D) Negate
23. Hint
   (A) Refer (B) Allude (C) Remark (D) Indication
24. Insinuation
   (A) Insult (B) Accuse (C) Innuendo (D) Reference
25. Desire
   (A) Conation (B) Pray (C) Lust (D) Greed
26. Anthologize
   (A) Apologize (B) Cull (C) Amass
   (D) Gathering selected literary works and poems

27. Accumulate
(A) Accommodate (B) Fill (C) Amass (D) Overflow

28. Vomit
(A) Throw out (B) Disgorge (C) Ooze out (D) Expel

29. Ascend
(A) Levitate (B) Soar (C) Lift (D) Heave

30. Boost
(A) Stoop (B) Condescend (C) Raise (D) Burst

31. Rear
(A) Back (B) Lift (C) Forward (D) Retreat

32. Surfeited
(A) Surplus (B) Blase (C) Glut (D) Overflow

33. Maverick
(A) Trick (B) Transient (C) Docile (D) Intractable

34. Dive
(A) Swoop (B) Jump (C) Fall (D) Swim

35. Plunge
(A) Flight (B) Soar (C) Plummet (D) Dip

36. Justify
(A) Explain (B) Decide (C) Rationalise (D) Adjudicate

37. Toss
(A) Throw (B) Project (C) Roll (D) Lob

38. Zeal
(A) Jealousy (B) Envy (C) Fervour (D) Vagary

39. Vicissitude
(A) Luck (B) Vagrant (C) Vagary (D) Sway

40. Foment
(A) Froth (B) Incite (C) Impel (D) Goad

41. Provoke
(A) Goad (B) Poke (C) Prick (D) Promote

42. Inquisitive
(A) Curious (B) Enquiring (C) Insisting (D) Questioning

43. Topsy-Turvy
(A) Top heavy (B) Topple (C) Turmoil (D) Turning around

44. Impolite
(A) Hard (B) Impertinent (C) Unpolished (D) Angry

45. Herald
(A) Fore runner (B) Shining (C) Hamper (D) Impudent

46. Instance
(A) Insistence (B) Precedent (C) Incident (D) Attempt

47. Sadist
(A) Gloomy (B) Unhappy (C) Cruel (D) Depressed

48. Forlorn
(A) Sad (B) Ebulient (C) Upset (D) Agitated

49. Disinterested
(A) Uninterested (B) Indifferent (C) Distraught (D) Gloomy

50. Upset
(A) Unhappy (B) Discomfited (C) Annoyed (D) Unconcerned

51. Breach
(A) Void (B) Boost (C) Coast (D) Violation

52. Sobriquet
(A) Sober (B) Epithet (C) Nom de plume (D) Denomination

53. Designation
(A) Design (B) Post (C) Denomination (D) Nomenclature

54. Boredom
(A) Doldrums (B) Cloyness (C) Blase (D) Sadness

55. Ennui
(A) Unique (B) Disinclined (C) Tedium (D) Gloom

56. Adamant
(A) Rude (B) Insolent (C) Resolute (D) Reckless

57. Wonderful
(A) Exceptional (B) Superb (C) Phenomenal (D) Magnificent

58. Transgress
(A) Transpire (B) Transit (C) Infringe (D) Transport

59. Glut
(A) Plethora (B) Rot (C) Dearth (D) Transport

60. Authorise
(A) Empower (B) Allow (C) Franchise (D) Entitle

61. Baron
(A) Prince (B) Don (C) Tycoon (D) Laity

62. Realm
(A) Reality (B) Truth (C) Domain (D) Cosmos

63. Construe
(A) Interpret (B) Construct (C) Restrain (D) Constrain

64. Exude
(A) Expel (B) Emit (C) Transmit (D) Intrude

65. Inherent
(A) Innate (B) Immanent (C) Congenital (D) Inherited

66. Intrude
(A) Trespass (B) Invade (C) Insert (D) Penetrate

67. Conjecture
(A) Wonder (B) Guess (C) Imagine (D) Fluke

68. Compatible
(A) Compact (B) Commensurate (C) Conforming (D) Compressible

69. Solicit
(A) Beseech (B) Solitary (C) Affirm (D) Lament

70. Assert
(A) Consent (B) Agree (C) Profess (D) Advise

71. Affront
(A) Afraid (B) Push (C) Umbrage (D) Regret

72. Repent
(A) Rue (B) Curse (C) Damn (D) Reject

73. Disparage
(A) Discourage (B) Insinuate (C) Disperse (D) Lampoon

74. Discard
(A) Remove (B) Garbage (C) Molt (D) Dampen

75. Segregate
(A) Degrade (B) Congregate (C) Quarantine (D) Dissociate

76. Relic
(A) Antique (B) Remains (C) Extant (D) Obsolete

77. Cynicism
(A) Madness (B) Distrust (C) Unreliability (D) Arrogance

78. Pride
(A) Ego (B) Hubris (C) Egoism (D) Egotism

79. Controvert
(A) Contravene (B) Decline (C) Refuse (D) Dismiss

80. Enervate
(A) Debilitate (B) Nervous (C) De-energize (D) Castrate

81. Miser
(A) Thrifty (B) Frugal (C) Parsimonious (D) Austere

82. Chauvinist
(A) Zealous (B) Patriot (C) Jealous (D) Tough

83. Predicament
(A) Pre-decided (B) Prediction (C) Quandary (D) Addiction

84. Vitriolic
(A) Bitter (B) Blue (C) Shining (D) Rotten

85. Slaughter
(A) Decimate (B) Kill (C) Murder (D) Assassinate

86. Pogrom
(A) Decorum (B) Fury (C) Carnage (D) Atrocity

87. Emaciate
(A) Attenuate (B) Extenuate (C) Weaken (D) Discourage

88. Dwindle
(A) Exhaust (B) Deplete (C) Wane (D) Deficit

89. Shudder
(A) Hudle (B) Shut down (C) Quake (D) Shiver

90. Demean
(A) Draw meaning (B) Devalue (C) Debase (D) Abase

91. Sullage
(A) Garbage (B) Refuse (C) Rubbish (D) Sewage

92. Incarcerate
(A) Curse (B) Immure (C) Enclose (D) Arrest

93. Coax
(A) Cajole (B) Cogitate (C) Enrage (D) Contemplate

94. Strident
(A) Cacophonous (B) Stringent (C) Striving (D) Studious

95. Bolland
(A) Pylon (B) Pole (C) Prop (D) Stake

96. Defile
(A) Scrape (B) Defalcate (C) Ruin (D) Desecrate

97. Flexuous
(A) Flexible (B) Flowing (C) Sinuous (D) Rigid

98. Crafty
(A) Artist (B) Expert (C) Cunning (D) Clever

99. Grind
(A) Chew (B) Ruminate (C) Triturate (D) Crush

100. Sycophant
(A) Obsequious (B) Survivor (C) Obedient (D) Toady

101. Ploy
(A) Plight (B) Bait (C) Decoy (D) Ruse

102. Retrench
(A) Reduce (Staff/workers for economising)
(B) Dig (C) Punish (D) Cashier

103. Comouflage
(A) Subterfuge (B) Cover (C) Dissemble (D) Deprive

104. Veneer
(A) Ensconce (B) Vent (C) Mask (D) Paint

105. Bark
(A) Rind (B) Cuticle (C) Scurf (D) Hide

106. Truncate
(A) Trim (B) Turn away (C) Relinquish (D) Concise

107. Itinerate
(A) Iterate (B) Scour (C) Intimidate (D) Sojourn

108. Rickety
(A) Decrepit (B) Thin (C) Emaciated (D) Dislocated

109. Cache
(A) Catch (B) Care (C) Store (D) Conceal

110. Reprimand
(A) Resent (B) Irritate (C) Censure (D) Quarrel

111. Pugnacious
(A) Pug marked (B) Quarrelsome (C) Cruel (D) Huffy

112. Scrap
(A) Fracas (B) Waste (C) Litters (D) Tear

113. Prolapse
(A) Prolong (B) Elongate (C) Relapse (D) Sag

114. Disposition
(A) Displacement (B) Dispersal (C) Tendency (D) Scattering

115. Brood
(A) Drove (B) Clutch (C) Flock (D) Litters

116. Singe
(A) Charm (B) Soothe (C) Scald (D) Languish

117. Ricochet
(A) Rebound (B) Crook (C) Curved (D) Collide

118. Delve
(A) Dip (B) Insert (C) Grope (D) Bounce

119. Drool
(A) Devil (B) Fool (C) Dump (D) Drivel

120. Obviate
(A) Observe (B) Avert (C) Disobey (D) Rebound

121. Dilly-dally
(A) Dandle (B) Hurry (C) Dawdle (D) Hamper

122. Contort
(A) Retort (B) Distort (C) Fraud (D) Diffuse

123. Imposter
(A) Defraud (B) Swindle (C) Cheat (D) Timid

124. Stagnate
(A) Rot (B) Stink (C) Linger (D) Swindle

125. Swat
(A) Perspirate (B) Slog (C) Satiate (D) Bat

126. Eerie
(A) Calm (B) Macabre (C) Timid (D) Tranquil

127. Hector
(A) Berate (B) Heckle (C) Bully (D) Hamper

128. Dunk
(A) Dubious (B) Scold (C) Drown (D) Slug

129. Congeal
(A) Curdle (B) Thaw (C) Freeze (D) Melt

130. Haggard
(A) Tired (B) Careworn (C) Torn (D) Unhappy

131. Smother
(A) Asphyxiate (B) Smoothen (C) Sway (D) Clean

132. Turncoat
(A) Paint (B) Torn (C) Apostate (D) Refund

133. Abject
(A) Ignoble (B) Absurd (C) Abominate (D) Benign

134. Hiatus
(A) Plateau (B) Peak (C) Cleavage (D) Charm

135. Grit
(A) Scrape (B) Scrap (C) Mettle (D) Grated

136. Confine
(A) Refined (B) Contain (C) Incarcerate (D) Arrest

137. Ersatz
(A) Razzmatazz (B) Sham (C) Coruscate (D) Polish

138. Daze
(A) Bewilder (B) Dazzle (C) Faze (D) Polish

139. Inculcate
(A) Calculate (B) Calcify (C) Instil (D) Insert

140. Stink
(A) Rancid (B) Fetid (C) Rankle (D) Rot

141. Treat
(A) Regale (B) Behave (C) Punish (D) Threaten

142. Officious
(A) Officiating (B) Rude (C) Meddlesome (D) Hard-working

143. Nepharious
(A) Nephrological (B) Obnoxious (C) Naive (D) Wicked

144. Behold
(A) Catch (B) Look (C) Oblige (D) Accuse

145. Exonerate
(A) Acquit (B) Exaggerate (C) Feign (D) Treat

146. Raze
(A) Anger (B) Chide (C) Wreck (D) Ruin

147. Debris
(A) Rubble (B) Ruin (C) Raze (D) Damage

148. Tarnish
(A) Tear (B) Frazzle (C) Tatter (D) Besmirch

149. Pound
(A) Sterling (B) Surround (C) Thrash (D) Ditch

150. Opulent
(A) Fatty (B) Rotund (C) Rich (D) Opaque

151. Vicinity
(A) Propinquity (B) Visual (C) Vices (D) Cauge

152. Retrofit
(A) Retreat (B) Revamp (C) Counterfeit (D) Misfit

153. Greenhorn
(A) Immature (B) Tyro (C) Greenery (D) Revoke

154. Fathom
(A) Depth (B) Bottom (C) Measure the depth (D) Froth

155. Extirpate
(A) Annihilate (B) Uproot (C) Eradicate (D) Terrorize

156. Deprave
(A) Dissolute (B) Deprived (C) Snatch (D) Denounce

157. Raven
(A) Voracious (B) Greedy (C) Devour (D) Rude

158. Injunction
(A) Diktat (B) Order (C) Directive (D) Advice

159. Latent
(A) Dormant (B) Live (C) Active (D) Dull

160. Humdrum
(A) Doldrums (B) Noise (C) Hollow (D) Dreary

161. Excommunicate
(A) Banish (B) Extradite (C) Exile (D) Contact

162. Fealty
(A) Fidelity (B) Patriotism (C) Morality (D) Mimicry

163. Trail
(A) Pursue (B) Follow (C) Contrail (D) Trim

164. Apprehend
(A) Comprehend (B) Reprehend (C) Nab (D) Refuge

165. Riposte
(A) Repose (B) Resume (C) Repartee (D) Relax

166. Sanctum sanctorum
(A) Shrine (B) Sanctify (C) Sanctity (D) Sanctimonious

167. Continence
(A) Abstinence (B) Self-restraint (in sexual urge)
(C) Abstention (D) Control

168. Conundrum
(A) Doldrum (B) Connivance (C) Puzzle (D) Trick

169. Prolific
(A) Copious (B) Lavish (C) Profuse (D) Fecund

170. Vendetta
(A) Revenge (B) Vend (C) Venality (D) Revolt

171. Demise
(A) Bestow (B) Endow (C) Bequeath (D) Confer

172. Evince
(A) Convince (B) Manifest (C) Evict (D) Influence

173. Corroborate
(A) Prove (B) Substantiate (C) Correspond (D) Relate

174. Applaud
(A) Commend (B) Clap (C) Uproar (D) Shout

175. Nurture
(A) Tender (B) Rear (C) Rupture (D) Nurse

176. Atone
(A) Tone down (B) Tend (C) Expiate (D) Amend

177. Redeem
(A) Restore (B) Recuperate (C) Rejuvenate (D) Retrieve

178. Largesse
(A) Largeness (B) Bounty (C) Bonus (D) Incentive

179. Recede
(A) Concede (B) Retreat (C) Secede (D) Proceed

180. Recant
(A) Chant (B) Repeat (C) Revert (D) Renege

181. Vintage
(A) Distillary (B) Viticulture (C) Vignette (D) Primitive

182. Rend
(A) Rent out (B) Rendition (C) Split (D) Hire

183. Distend
(A) Extend (B) Bulge (C) Attenuate (D) Project

184. Prorogue
(A) Inveigle (B) Provoke (C) Protract (D) Adjourn

185. Rampant
(A) Scatter (B) Disseminate (C) Wanton (D) Unkempt

186. Quail
(A) Quake (B) Quiver (C) Gore (D) Quell

187. Divagate
(A) Wander (B) Gad (C) Digress (D) Diffuse

188. Execrate
(A) Exculpate (B) Denounce (C) Dread (D) Excuse

189. Skive
(A) Bunk (B) Elope (C) Skuttle (D) Scoot

190. Faux pas
(A) Failure (B) Mistake (C) Gaffe (D) Awe

191. Betray
(A) Cheat (B) Deceive (C) Befool (D) Hamper

192. Philippic
(A) Philander (B) Philanthrope (C) Philately (D) Tirade

193. Wring
(A) Crush (B) Mash (C) Twist (D) Squash

194. Concoct
(A) Blend (B) Brew (C) Taint (D) Tinge

195. Jaunt
(A) Expedition (B) Cruise (C) Junket (D) Junk

196. Stymie
(A) Stem (B) Arrest (C) Curb (D) Stanch

197. Squirm
(A) Wallow (B) Writhe (C) Squirt (D) Welter

198. Preposterous
(A) Grotesque (B) Fantastic (C) Antic (D) Strange

199. Malice
(A) Malign (B) Spite (C) Malignant (D) Malediction

200. Pandemonium
(A) Uproar (B) Harmony (C) Panic (D) Distrust

Choose the odd word out of the set given below:

201. (A) Brat (B) Braggart (C) Braggidocio (D) Bereft
202. (A) Bedlam (B) Babble (C) Brouhaha (D) Malee
203. (A) Indemnify (B) Recompense (C) Subsidize (D) Compensate
204. (A) Stubborn (B) Astute (C) Audacious (D) Obstinate
205. (A) Arrogate (B) Usurp (C) Supplant (D) Urge
206. (A) Lynch (B) Slay (C) Flay (D) Assassinate
207. (A) Deter (B) Dissuade (C) Discourage (D) Desperate
208. (A) Defeat (B) Rout (C) Route (D) Vanquish
209. (A) Brandish (B) Flaunt (C) Flounder (D) Flourish
210. (A) Intrude (B) Meddle (C) Obtrude (D) Ingress
211. (A) Laugh (B) Guffaw (C) Leer (D) Fleer
212. (A) Deleterious (B) Delectable (C) Detrimental (D) Insidious
213. (A) Prone (B) Liable (C) Susceptible (D) Disposed
214. (A) Impair (B) Damage (C) Weaken (D) Improve
215. (A) Capitulate (B) Concede (C) Capture (D) Succumb
216. (A) Domination (B) Hegemony (C) Supremacy (D) Bully
217. (A) Demur (B) Jib (C) Dim (D) Baulk
218. (A) Teeter (B) Totter (C) Sway (D) Temper
219. (A) Harry (B) Tantalise (C) Hamper (D) Badger
220. (A) Adorn (B) Garnish (C) Embellish (D) Cartel
221. (A) Patent (B) Manifest (C) Latent (D) Conspicuous
222. (A) Mop (B) Swill (C) Flush (D) Expunge
223. (A) Jargon (B) Lingo (C) Limbo (D) Argot
224. (A) Prudent (B) Prurient (C) Pragmatic (D) Politic
225. (A) Parity (B) Analogy (C) Plurality (D) Correspondence
226. (A) Acquiesce (B) Acquit (C) Assent (D) Consent
227. (A) Sympathy (B) Ruth (C) Commiseration (D) Apathy
228. (A) Doctrine (B) Dogma (C) Nurture (D) Tenet
229. (A) Bouquet (B) Fragrance (C) Buffet (D) Redolence
230. (A) Introspect (B) Cogitate (C) Retrospect (D) Prospect
231. (A) Commit (B) Demit (C) Confide (D) Entrust
232. (A) Shy (B) Coy (C) Demure (D) Brash
233. (A) Haven (B) Harbour (C) Hovel (D) Refuge
234. (A) Serene (B) Tranquil (C) Serenade (D) Placid

	(A)	(B)	(C)	(D)
235.	(A) Zenith	(B) Pinnacle	(C) Apex	(D) Peek
236.	(A) Propitious	(B) Proprietary	(C) Auspicious	(D) Benign
237.	(A) Requiem	(B) Elegy	(C) Dirge	(D) Encomium
238.	(A) Transient	(B) Transitory	(C) Ephemeral	(D) Eternal
239.	(A) Pedant	(B) Charlatan	(C) Erudite	(D) Omniscient
240.	(A) Malinger	(B) Malignant	(C) Feign	(D) Pretend
241.	(A) Clairvoyance	(B) Foresight	(C) Foresee	(D) Vision
242.	(A) Apostate	(B) Proselyte	(C) Renegade	(D) Appease
243.	(A) Finicky	(B) Feverish	(C) Fussy	(D) Fastidious
244.	(A) Lackadaisical	(B) Pedestrian	(C) Lacklustre	(D) Lampoon
245.	(A) Cringe	(B) Cram	(C) Cower	(D) Crunch
246.	(A) Flounder	(B) Fumble	(C) Falter	(D) Flunk
247.	(A) Swag	(B) Booty	(C) Spoils	(D) Sag
248.	(A) Vocation	(B) Avocation	(C) Avouch	(D) Metier
249.	(A) Stupendous	(B) Enormous	(C) Immense	(D) Immeasurable
250.	(A) Distraught	(B) Dismantle	(C) Disconcerted	(D) Disconsolate
251.	(A) Mammoth	(B) Monster	(C) Monolith	(D) Colossal
252.	(A) Germane	(B) Cogent	(C) Absurd	(D) Apropos
253.	(A) Credence	(B) Credibility	(C) Credit	(D) Debit
254.	(A) Teem	(B) Abound	(C) Tamper	(D) Swarm
255.	(A) Predict	(B) Prophesy	(C) Prophecy	(D) Augur
256.	(A) Redoubtable	(B) Formidable	(C) Dubious	(D) Menacing
257.	(A) Reveal	(B) Betray	(C) Divulge	(D) Dissemble
258.	(A) Eke	(B) Stint	(C) Conserve	(D) Compensate
259.	(A) Odium	(B) Oddity	(C) Opprobrium	(D) Ignominy

For explanations, go to the synonyms of the chosen option as mentioned in comprehensive list synonymous words.

ANSWERS

1. (A)	**2.** (A)	**3.** (C)	**4.** (A)	**5.** (A)	**6.** (A)	**7.** (C)	**8.** (A)
9. (B)	**10.** (A)	**11.** (B)	**12.** (A)	**13.** (C)	**14.** (A)	**15.** (C)	**16.** (A)
17. (A)	**18.** (A)	**19.** (A)	**20.** (C)	**21.** (C)	**22.** (A)	**23.** (B)	**24.** (C)
25. (A)	**26.** (D)	**27.** (C)	**28.** (B)	**29.** (B)	**30.** (C)	**31.** (A)	**32.** (C)
33. (D)	**34.** (A)	**35.** (C)	**36.** (C)	**37.** (D)	**38.** (C)	**39.** (C)	**40.** (B)
41. (A)	**42.** (A)	**43.** (B)	**44.** (B)	**45.** (A)	**46.** (B)	**47.** (C)	**48.** (A)
49. (B)	**50.** (B)	**51.** (D)	**52.** (B)	**53.** (C)	**54.** (A)	**55.** (C)	**56.** (C)
57. (C)	**58.** (C)	**59.** (A)	**60.** (C)	**61.** (C)	**62.** (C)	**63.** (A)	**64.** (B)
65. (B)	**66.** (A)	**67.** (B)	**68.** (C)	**69.** (A)	**70.** (C)	**71.** (C)	**72.** (A)
73. (D)	**74.** (C)	**75.** (C)	**76.** (B)	**77.** (B)	**78.** (B)	**79.** (A)	**80.** (A)
81. (C)	**82.** (A)	**83.** (C)	**84.** (A)	**85.** (A)	**86.** (C)	**87.** (C)	**88.** (B)
89. (C)	**90.** (D)	**91.** (D)	**92.** (B)	**93.** (A)	**94.** (A)	**95.** (D)	**96.** (D)

97. (C) **98.** (C) **99.** (C) **100.** (D) **101.** (D) **102.** (A) **103.** (C) **104.** (C)
105. (A) **106.** (A) **107.** (B) **108.** (A) **109.** (D) **110.** (C) **111.** (B) **112.** (A)
113. (D) **114.** (C) **115.** (B) **116.** (C) **117.** (A) **118.** (C) **119.** (D) **120.** (B)
121. (C) **122.** (B) **123.** (C) **124.** (C) **125.** (B) **126.** (C) **127.** (C) **128.** (C)
129. (A) **130.** (B) **131.** (A) **132.** (C) **133.** (A) **134.** (C) **135.** (C) **136.** (C)
137. (B) **138.** (A) **139.** (C) **140.** (C) **141.** (A) **142.** (C) **143.** (D) **144.** (B)
145. (A) **146.** (C) **147.** (A) **148.** (D) **149.** (C) **150.** (C) **151.** (A) **152.** (B)
153. (B) **154.** (C) **155.** (A) **156.** (A) **157.** (C) **158.** (C) **159.** (A) **160.** (D)
161. (A) **162.** (A) **163.** (C) **164.** (C) **165.** (C) **166.** (A) **167.** (B) **168.** (C)
169. (D) **170.** (A) **171.** (C) **172.** (B) **173.** (B) **174.** (B) **175.** (B) **176.** (C)
177. (A) **178.** (B) **179.** (B) **180.** (D) **181.** (D) **182.** (C) **183.** (B) **184.** (D)
185. (C) **186.** (D) **187.** (C) **188.** (B) **189.** (A) **190.** (C) **191.** (B) **192.** (D)
193. (C) **194.** (A) **195.** (C) **196.** (D) **197.** (B) **198.** (A) **199.** (B) **200.** (A)
201. (D) **202.** (B) **203.** (C) **204.** (B) **205.** (D) **206.** (C) **207.** (D) **208.** (C)
209. (C) **210.** (D) **211.** (C) **212.** (B) **213.** (D) **214.** (D) **215.** (C) **216.** (D)
217. (C) **218.** (D) **219.** (C) **220.** (D) **221.** (C) **222.** (D) **223.** (C) **224.** (B)
225. (C) **226.** (B) **227.** (D) **228.** (C) **229.** (C) **230.** (D) **231.** (B) **232.** (D)
233. (C) **234.** (C) **235.** (D) **236.** (B) **237.** (D) **238.** (D) **239.** (B) **240.** (B)
241. (C) **242.** (D) **243.** (B) **244.** (D) **245.** (B) **246.** (D) **247.** (D) **248.** (C)
249. (B) **250.** (B) **251.** (B) **252.** (C) **253.** (D) **254.** (C) **255.** (C) **256.** (C)
257. (D) **258.** (D) **259.** (B)

TEST 10

Choose the word which is the closest in meaning to the given word:

1. Junket
   (A) Junk (B) Jaunt (C) Worthless (D) Rusted
2. Ruse
   (A) Gimmick (B) Red (C) Insolent (D) Jeer
3. Benevolent
   (A) Violent (B) Well-wisher (C) Benign (D) Magnanimous
4. Lewd
   (A) Greed (B) Irritating (C) Lascivious (D) Listless
5. Impertinent
   (A) Impatient (B) Unsuitable (C) Imprudent (D) Insolent
6. Jut out
   (A) Protuberate (B) Lob (C) Throw (D) Remove
7. Peril
   (A) Push (B) Pre-empt (C) Jeopardy (D) Protrude
8. Decimate
   (A) Decimal (B) Droll (C) Pillory (D) Recant

9. Lampoon
(A) Laugh (B) Declare (C) Laughter (scornful) (D) Decant

10. Bemoan
(A) Grieve (B) Cry (C) Grumble (D) Groan

11. Chortle
(A) Guffaw (B) Ogle (C) Pore (D) Flirt

12. Vengeance
(A) Retribution (B) Vindication (C) Contrary (D) Threat

13. Jurist
(A) Lawyer (B) Juror (C) Judge (D) Journalist

14. Lassitude
(A) Disinclination (B) Listlessness
(C) Lasciviousness (D) Desolate

15. Reciprocate
(A) Rationalise (B) Retaliate (C) Requite (D) Revive

16. Flabby
(A) Sluggish (B) Limp (C) Wilted (D) Lewd

17. Opulent
(A) Fluffy (B) Swollen (C) Affluent (D) Rude

18. Leer
(A) Ogle (B) Lecher (C) Lewd (D) Lascivious

19. Cashier
(A) Castrate (B) Count (C) Retrench (D) Restore

20. Stentorian
(A) Musty (B) Shrill (C) Rank (D) Tempting

21. Mend
(A) Criticize (B) Remind (C) Retrench (D) Rectify

22. Allegiance
(A) Allegation (B) Criticism (C) Fealty (D) Alleviation

23. Reprove
(A) Reproach (B) Prove (C) Repent (D) Repay

24. Rancour
(A) Pain (B) Repentance (C) Spleen (D) Stink

25. Remains
(A) Remainder (B) Dividend (C) Relic (D) Dead body

26. Rut
(A) Spoor (B) Rot (C) Rancid (D) Putrid

27. Rehabilitation
(A) Relocation (B) Re-instatement (C) Return (D) Relapse

28. Phenomenon
(A) Marvel (B) Trailblazer (C) Fundamental (D) Essence

29. Expostulate
(A) Propose (B) Expound (C) Remonstrate(D) Expatiate

30. Carnage
(A) Carnality (B) Corporal (C) Incarnate (D) Pogrom

31. Quagmire
(A) Quaint (B) Quid (C) Bog (D) Quilt

32. Pugnacious
(A) Potent (B) Bellicose (C) Belligerent (D) Bully

33. Gaffe
(A) Hook (B) Gobble (C) Faux pas (D) Gap

34. Quack
(A) Cheat (B) Novice (C) Charlatan (D) Pedant

35. Afflatus
(A) Affairs (B) Suborn (C) Flatulence (D) Inspiration

36. Riddle
(A) Puncture (B) Hole (C) Conundrum (D) Fracture

37. Gobble dygook
(A) Gambling (B) Poppycock (C) Ogle (D) Inchoate

38. Greenhorn
(A) Unicorn (B) Tyro (C) Impugn (D) Montage

39. Gore
(A) Bloody (B) Impale (C) Coax (D) Stake

40. Overture
(A) Overboard (B) Overwhelm (C) Tender (D) Ordain

41. Inchoate
(A) Coax (B) Incipient (C) Innocent (D) Intent

42. Impugn
(A) Spin (B) Fight (C) Dispute (D) Decide

43. Happenstance
(A) Chance (B) Instantly (C) Incidence (D) Omen

44. Portent
(A) Augury (B) Bad omen (C) Archaic (D) Outdated

45. Antiquated
(A) Ante-diluvian (B) Antic (C) Antique (D) Neophyte

46. Unpropitious
(A) Improper (B) Unlucky (C) Portentous (D) Unimportant

47. Antithesis
(A) Opposite (B) Synthesis (C) Synchronous (D) Annex

48. Edict
    (A) Edit (B) Adopt (C) Diktat (D) Bid

49. Pragmatic
    (A) Provident (B) Indigent (C) Potent (D) Contrary

50. Zenith
    (A) Zeal (B) Zest (C) Sky (D) Pinnacle

Choose the pair of words out of the given options which resembles in meanings:

51. (A) Pilgrimage (B) Excursion (C) Devotion (D) Caravan
52. (A) Deem (B) Trim (C) Recon (D) Recant
53. (A) Humane (B) Humid (C) Kind (D) Human-being
54. (A) Lascivious (B) Sticky (C) Greedy (D) Libidinous
55. (A) Churlish (B) Churning (C) Brash (D) Creaking
56. (A) Vindicate (B) Vent (C) Justify (D) Vend
57. (A) Risible (B) Risque (C) Drill (D) Ludicrous
58. (A) Kowtow (B) Cower (C) Decimate (D) Stickout
59. (A) Jeer (B) Scoff (C) Jaunt (D) Deny
60. (A) Mourn (B) Maim (C) Mount (D) Condole
61. (A) Laugh (B) Ridicule (C) Mute (D) Cachinnate
62. (A) Renege (B) Revenge (C) Recant (D) Ridicule
63. (A) Indolent (B) Pedant (C) Languid (D) Lustful
64. (A) Languid (B) Sluggish (C) Lonely (D) Desolate
65. (A) Revive (B) Resuscitate (C) Redeem (D) Recuperate
66. (A) Venal (B) Desolate (C) Deserted (D) Strident
67. (A) Mutiny (B) Musty (C) Opulent (D) Uprising
68. (A) Spy (B) Espy (C) Peer (D) Intent
69. (A) Solicit (B) Request (C) Suite (D) Dismiss
70. (A) Glance (B) Glee (C) Gaze (D) Pour
71. (A) Supersede (B) Overlay (C) Substitute (D) Obsolete
72. (A) Pillage (B) Despoil (C) Profit (D) Protrude
73. (A) Assuage (B) Assure (C) Mitigate (D) Reject
74. (A) Spite (B) Despite (C) Spit (D) Alternative
75. (A) Regret (B) Sorry (C) Deny (D) Rue
76. (A) Tail (B) Contrail (C) Tally (D) Trail
77. (A) Retaliate (B) Recede (C) Retreat (D) Secede
78. (A) Miracle (B) Prodigy (C) Pogrom (D) Mystic
79. (A) Snub (B) Snore (C) Spurn (D) Snuff
80. (A) Mercenary (B) Mariner (C) Venal (D) Arbiter
81. (A) Souvenir (B) Remembrance (C) Reminder (D) Showbiz
82. (A) Quibble (B) Quiz (C) Queer (D) Pettifog
83. (A) Abject (B) Ignoble (C) Object (D) Abstract
84. (A) Extol (B) Enigma (C) Fervour (D) Approbate

85. (A) Absurd (B) Abstruse (C) Recondite (D) Neophyte
86. (A) Realty (B) Personalty (C) Profession (D) Metier
87. (A) Hubris (B) Horror (C) Vainglory (D) Fib
88. (A) Impediment (B) Hurdle (C) Manacle (D) Eminent
89. (A) Penury (B) Palter (C) Privation (D) Secrecy
90. (A) Rattle (B) Faze (C) Rout (D) Defunct
91. (A) Pry (B) Prick (C) Voyeur (D) Peer
92. (A) Discomfit (B) Disconcert (C) Doubt (D) Dubious
93. (A) Conman (B) Canon (C) Cannon (D) Injunction
94. (A) Mast (B) Pylon (C) Bolard (D) Obelisk
95. (A) Poverty (B) Pot pourri (C) Medley (D) Palter
96. (A) Puissant (B) Potent (C) Privation (D) Collage
97. (A) Prayer (B) Song (C) Anthem (D) Paternoster
98. (A) Precedence (B) Priority (C) Preceding (D) Prior
99. (A) Palter (B) Patter (C) Equivocate (D) Prefer
100. (A) Fortune (B) Wealth (C) Incentive (D) Prize

Choose the odd one out from the given options:

101. (A) Journey (B) Voyage (C) Expedition (D) Erand
102. (A) Ploy (B) Subterfuse (C) Pillory (D) Feint
103. (A) Benign (B) Benevolent (C) Magnanimous (D) Mourn
104. (A) Erudite (B) Pedant (C) Scholar (D) Charlatan
105. (A) Insolent (B) Intolerant (C) Impertinent (D) Impudent
106. (A) Dirge (B) Elegy (C) Requiem (D) Downcast
107. (A) Hazard (B) Hamper (C) Risk (D) Jeopardy
108. (A) Kneel (B) Genuflect (C) Bend (D) Kowtow
109. (A) Fleer (B) Sneer (C) Flail (D) Jeer
110. (A) Lament (B) Laugh (C) Bemoan (D) Grieve
111. (A) Giggle (B) Titter (C) Snigger (D) Totter
112. (A) Reverence (B) Veneration (C) Obeisance (D) Repentance
113. (A) Advocate (B) Attorney (C) Arbitrator (D) Solicitor
114. (A) Languor (B) Lassitude (C) Listlessness (D) Lewd
115. (A) Retrieve (B) Restore (C) Restitute (D) Destitute
116. (A) Limp (B) Flaccid (C) Levity (D) Flabby
117. (A) Sedition (B) Pillory (C) Putsch (D) Insurgency
118. (A) Hold (B) Behold (C) Peer (D) Pore
119. (A) Supplicate (B) Entreat (C) Importune (D) Curtsy
120. (A) Raucus (B) Strident (C) Arrogant (D) Stertorous
121. (A) Vanity (B) Penitence (C) Remorse (D) Contrition
122. (A) Entice (B) Inveigle (C) Lure (D) Attract
123. (A) Apposite (B) Opposite (C) Germane (D) Pertinent
124. (A) Noisome (B) Fetid (C) Foul (D) Rancid
125. (A) Repartee (B) Riposte (C) Retort (D) Retrench
126. (A) Pogrom (B) Aftermath (C) Trail (D) Contrail

127.	(A) Retract	(B) Repercuss	(C) Boomerang	(D) Recochet
128.	(A) Mash	(B) Squash	(C) Powder	(D) Crumple
129.	(A) Admonish	(B) Objurgate	(C) Upbraid	(D) Punish
130.	(A) Memento	(B) Mentality	(C) Memorabilia	(D) Token
131.	(A) Cenotaph	(B) Mousoleum	(C) Tomb	(D) Sensitive
132.	(A) Fracas	(B) Fracture	(C) Scrap	(D) Melee
133.	(A) Frugal	(B) Parisimonious	(C) Stingy	(D) Prudent
134.	(A) Panegyrise	(B) Eulogize	(C) Laud	(D) Euphoria
135.	(A) Induce	(B) Encourage	(C) Poke	(D) Suborn
136.	(A) Wage	(B) Largesse	(C) Reward	(D) Bounty
137.	(A) Doctrine	(B) Dogma	(C) Tenet	(D) Reward
138.	(A) Profess	(B) Malinger	(C) Fein	(D) Malign
139.	(A) Prevaricate	(B) Fabricate	(C) Palter	(D) Fib
140.	(A) Caper	(B) Cajole	(C) Wheedle	(D) Inveigle

ANSWERS

1. (B) See Journey	**2.** (A) See Ruse	**3.** (C) See Kind
4. (C) See Lewd	**5.** (D) See Rude	**6.** (A) See Jut out
7. (C) See Risk	**8.** (C) See Kill	**9.** (C) See Ridicule
10. (A) See Lament	**11.** (A) See Laugh	**12.** (A) See Revenge
13. (A) See Lawyer	**14.** (B) See Laziness	**15.** (C) See Retaliate
16. (B) See Limp	**17.** (C) See Rich	**18.** (A) See Look
19. (C) See Retrench	**20.** (B) See Loud	**21.** (D) See Repair
22. (C) See Loyalty	**23.** (A) See Reprimand	**24.** (C) See Malice
25. (C) See Relic	**26.** (A) See Mark	**27.** (B) See Rehabilitation
28. (A) See Marvel	**29.** (C) See Reason	**30.** (D) See Masacre
31. (C) See Mire	**32.** (B) See Quarrelsome	**33.** (C) See Mistake
34. (C) See Quack	**35.** (D) See Motive	**36.** (C)
37. (B) See Nonsense	**38.** (B) See Novice	**39.** (B) See Pierce
40. (C) See Overture	**41.** (B) See Nascent	**42.** (C) See Object
43. (C) See Occurrence	**44.** (B) See Omen	45. (A) See Outdated
46. (C) See Ominous	**47.** (A) See Opposite	48. (C) See Order
49. (A) See Politic	**50.** (D) See Peak	**51.** A-B See Journey
52. A-C See Regard	**53.** A-C See Kind	**54.** A-D See Lewd
55. A-C See Rude	**56.** A-C See Justify	**57.** A-D See Ridiculous
58. A-B See Kneel	**59.** A-B See Ridicule	**60.** A-D See Lament
61. A-D See Laugh	**62.** A-C See Retract	**63.** A-C See Lazy
64. A-B See Lazy	65. A-B See Resurrect	**66.** B-C See Lonely
67. A-D See Revolt	68. B-C See Look	**69.** A-B See Request
70. A-C See Look	71. A-C See Replace	**72.** A-B See Loot
73. A-C See Relieve	74. A-B See Malice	**75.** A-D See Regret
76. B-D See Mark	77. B-C See Recede	**78.** A-B See Marvel

79. A-C See Rebuff	80. A-C See Mercenary	**81.** A-B See Memento
82. (D) See Quibble	**83.** A-B See Miserable	**84.** A-D See Praise
85. B-C See Mysterious	**86.** A-B See Property	**87.** A-C See Pride
88. A-B See Obstacle	**89.** A-C See Poverty	**90.** A-B See Perplex
91. A-C See Peep	**92.** A-B See Perplex	**93.** B-D See Order
94. A-B See Pillar	**95.** B-C See Potpourri	**96.** A-B See Powerful
97. A-D See Prayer	**98.** A-B See Precedence	**99.** A-C See Prevaricate
100. A-B See Property	**101.** (D) See Journey	**102.** (C) See Ploy
103. (D) See Kind	**104.** (D) See Learned	**105.** (B) See Rude
106. (D) See Lamentation		**107.** (B) See Risk
108. (C) See Kneel	**109.** (C) See Ridicule	**110.** (B) See Lament
111. (D) See Laugh	**112.** (D) See Reverence	**113.** (C) See Lawyer
114. (D) See Laziness	**115.** (D) See Restore	**116.** (C) See Limp
117. (B) See Revolt	**118.** (A) See Look	**119.** (D) See Request
120. (C) See Loud	**121.** (A) See Repentance	**122.** (D) See Lure
123. (B) See Relevant	**124.** (C) See Malodoraous	
125. (D) See Recrimination		**126.** (A) See Mark
127. (A) See Rebound	**128.** (C) See Mash	**129.** (D) See Rebuke
130. (B) See Memento	**131.** (D) See Memento	**132.** (B) See Quarrel
133. (D) See Miser	**134.** (D) See Praise	**135.** (C) See Motivate
136. (A) See Prize	**137.** (D) See Principle	**138.** (D) See Pretend
139. (B) See Prevaricate	**140.** (A) See Persuade	

TEST 11

Choose the closest word out of the given options, which has the same meaning as the word suggested:

1. Heresy
   (A) Hearsay (B) Hermit (C) Blasphemy (D) Hermetic
2. Writhe
   (A) Wrest (B) Wring (C) Squirm (D) Twist
3. Forlorn
   (A) Sarcastic (B) Doleful (C) Crazy (D) Solemn
4. Flotsam
   (A) Levitate (B) Flat (C) Prostrate (D) Jetsam
5. Sardonic
   (A) Satirical (B) Bitter (C) Caustic (D) Sardine
6. Iniquitous
   (A) Unequal (B) Flagitious (C) Ubiquitous (D) Unkempt
7. Skit
   (A) Slip (B) Squat (C) Squib (D) Irony
8. Caveat
   (A) Cavern (B) Callous (C) Caution (D) Cater

9. Segregate
(A) Assemble (B) Sort (C) Aggregate (D) Sway

10. Vagabond
(A) Vagary (B) Tramp (C) Vacuous (D) Stray

11. Somber
(A) Amber (B) Ember (C) Soar (D) Staid

12. Wanton
(A) Upheaval (B) Arrogant (C) Rampant (D) Upset

13. Shimmer
(A) Simmer (B) Incense (C) Glimmer (D) Glean

14. Ubiquitous
(A) Unique (B) Omnipresent (C) Reticent (D) Untidy

15. Wizen
(A) Shrivel (B) Wizard (C) Conform (D) Aroma

16. Wrench
(A) Turn (B) Mangle (C) Wring (D) Nexus

17. Coy
(A) Cozy (B) Caring (C) Demure (D) Gyrate

18. Watershed
(A) Flow (B) Epoch (C) Water colour (D) Spill over

19. Parity
(A) Paring (B) Peer (C) Analogy (D) Semblance

20. Dock
(A) Lop (B) Detour (C) Dais (D) Tumble

21. Homily
(A) Humility (B) Humanity (C) Sermon (D) Honour

22. Purloin
(A) Pilfer (B) Pruriance (C) Besiege (D) Besmirch

23. Coercion
(A) Coarse (B) Cruelty (C) Duress (D) Crude

24. Goad
(A) Impel (B) Trot (C) Burgle (D) Choke

25. Stub
(A) Stab (B) Stamp (C) Stomp (D) Stubble

Choose the pair of words out of the given options, which have the same meanings:

26. (A) Conation (B) Cheating (C) Volition (D) Reconning

27. (A) Welter (B) Swelter (C) Sweat (D) Wriggle

28. (A) Lugabrious (B) Melancholic (C) Laborious (D) Mournful

29. (A) Loll (B) Lull (C) Lounge (D) Lug

30. (A) Profuse (B) Dissipate (C) Diffuse (D) Defer

31. (A) Weird (B) Wind (C) Wound (D) Macabre

32. (A) Sharp (B) Shred (C) Shrapnel (D) Fragment

33. (A) Turmoil (B) Trouble (C) Topsyturvy (D) Distress

34. (A) Objectionable (B) Obsequious (C) Staid (D) Slavish

35. (A) Licentious (B) Dissolute (C) Turbulent (D) Eerie

36. (A) Simper (B) Pilfer (C) Teeter (D) Totter

37. (A) Upset (B) Distraught (C) Terrible (D) Sully

38. (A) Commensuration (B) Correspondence (C) Commendation (D) Condemnation

39. (A) Drown (B) Dowse (C) Douse (D) Dunk

40. (A) Nefarious (B) Nexus (C) Nascent (D) Coordination

41. (A) Train (B) Box (C) Cuff (D) Trigger

42. (A) Frolick (B) Fraud (C) Fisc (D) Coffer

43. (A) Buffet (B) Bouquet (C) Redolence (D) Buffer

44. (A) Legate (B) Ligate (C) Lever (D) Tether

45. (A) Philippic (B) Tirade (C) Gyrate (D) Tamper

46. (A) Imprompt (B) Extempore (C) Instant (D) Instense

47. (A) Long (B) Linger (C) Tarry (D) Tract

48. (A) Hoist (B) Heist (C) Gird (D) Larceny

49. (A) Besmirch (B) Sully (C) Besot (D) Bespecle

50. (A) Rend (B) Rent (C) Sunder (D) Thrash

Choose the odd one out form the given options in each set of words:

51. (A) Desolate (B) Disconsolate (C) Doleful (D) Doubtful

52. (A) Waver (B) Waiver (C) Vacillate (D) Dither

53. (A) Scatter (B) Scare (C) Disseminate (D) Disperse

54. (A) Gallivant (B) Gad (C) Fad (D) Loaf

55. (A) Graze (B) Grate (C) Scrape (D) Grunt

56. (A) Prove (B) Attest (C) Authenticate (D) Vouch

57. (A) Shrill (B) Shriek (C) Screech (D) Sharp

58. (A) Toddle (B) Wobble (C) Totter (D) Trip

59. (A) Unnerve (B) Uncanny (C) Eerie (D) Weird

60. (A) Brazen (B) Brash (C) Impudent (D) Redolent

61. (A) Slatternly (B) Slovenly (C) Slum (D) Dishevelled

62. (A) Port (B) Harbour (C) Haven (D) Refuge

63. (A) Educe (B) Strive (C) Endeavour (D) Persevere

64. (A) Immerse (B) Emerge (C) Inundate (D) Submerge

65. (A) Laconic (B) Reticent (C) Lacuna (D) Taciturn

66. (A) Trip (B) Truncate (C) Prune (D) Clip
67. (A) Quirk (B) Smirk (C) Simper (D) Grin
68. (A) Quiver (B) Shiver (C) Shudder (D) Tether
69. (A) Whirl (B) Whine (C) Whorl (D) Twirl
70. (A) Brook (B) Tolerate (C) Bear (D) Cataract
71. (A) Spoil (B) Spoils (C) Booty (D) Swag
72. (A) Toss (B) Pelt (C) Lob (D) Gird
73. (A) Cleave (B) Rive (C) Rend (D) Bulge
74. (A) Loquacious (B) Garrulous (C) Glib (D) Blemish
75. (A) Slug (B) Lug (C) Slog (D) Swat

ANSWERS

1. (C) See Sacrilege
2. (C) See Writhe
3. (B) See Sad/Alone
4. (D) See Wreckage
5. (A) See Sarcastic
6. (B) See Wicked
7. (C) See Satire
8. (C) See Warning
9. (B) See Seclude
10. (B) See Vagabond
11. (D) See Serious
12. (C) See Unrestrained
13. (C) See Shine
14. (B) See Ubiquitous
15. (A) See Shrink
16. (C) See Twist
17. (C) See Shy
18. (B) See Turning Point
19. (C) See Similarity
20. (A) See Trim
21. (C) See Speech
22. (A) See Steal
23. (C) See Threat
24. (A) See Stimulate
25. (D) See Stub
26. A-C See Will
27. A-D See Writhe
28. A-B See Sad
29. A-C See While away
30. B-C See Scatter
31. A-D See Weird
32. C-D See Scrap
33. A-C See Upheaval
34. B-D See Servile
35. A-B See Unrestrained
36. C-D See Shake
37. A-B See Upset
38. A-B See Similarity
39. A-D See Sink
40. B-D See Understanding
41. B-C See Slap
42. C-D See Treasury
43. B-C See Smell
44. B-D See Tie
45. A-B See Speech
46. A-B See Spontaneous
47. B-C See Stay
48. B-D See Theft
49. A-B See Tarnish
50. A-C See Tear
51. (D) See Sad
52. (B) See Waver
53. (B) See Scatter
54. (C) See Wander
55. (D) See Scrape
56. (A) See Verify
57. (D) See Scream
58. (D) See Shake
59. (A) See Weird
60. (D) See Shameless
61. (C) See Untidy
62. (A) See Shelter
63. (A) See Try
64. (B) See Sink
65. (C) See Uncommunicative
66. (A) See Trim
67. (A) See Smile
68. (D) See Tremble
69. (B) See Spin
70. (D) See Tolerate
71. (A) See Spoils
72. (D) See Throw
73. (D) See Tear
74. (D) See Talkative
75. (B) See Strike

Part B

ANTONYMS

- **Words Beginning with A to Z**
- **Multiple Choice Questions-Answers**
- **Exercises on Antonyms (with Answers)**

ANTONYMS

Words beginning with ———— A ————

Abandon = *leave alone*	: Adopt = *to take up on one's own*
Abashed = *ashamed*	: Honoured = *highly respected, esteemed*
Abate = *lose intensity*	: Intensity = *the quality of being intense*
Aberration = *unwelcome deviation from right course*	: Rectitude = *right path as of morality*
Abet = *help in wrong doing*	: Deter = *discourage from wrong doing*
Ability = *skill of doing*	: Inability = *absence of skill to do something*
Abhor = *hate*	: Adore = *like*
Abject = *degrading*	: Honourable = *respectful, exalted*
Abjure = *swear not to do*	: Indulge = *involve in doing; keep on doing*
Abolish = *scrap a rule/act*	: Implement = *to enforce a rule or a project*
Abominate = *hate*	: Like
Aboriginal = *belonging to a place from beginning*	: Exogenous, Alien = *coming from outside*
Abridge = *make short*	: Expand, Enlarge = *make large*
Abrogate = *do away with rule*	: Promulgate = *enforce rule with official proclamation*
Abrupt = *suddenly*	: Gradual = *slowly*
Abscond = *flee away from custody/ justice; hide away*	: Surrender = *to submit*
Absence = *being away from a place*	: Presence = *be in a place*
Absolute = *not subject to limitation*	: Qualified = *subject to conditions*
Absolve = *free from charge*	: Incriminate = *put charge against*
Abstain = *keep away from indulgence*	: Indulge = *get oneself involved in undesirable activity*
Abstemious = *keep away from excessive eating*	: Gluttonous = *eating without restraint*
Absurd = *not sensible, illogical*	: Logical = *sensible*

Abundance = *excessiveness* : Scarcity, Dearth = *insufficient availability*

Abundant = *excessive in amount* : Scarce = *not sufficient*

Accede = *to agree* : Reject = refuse to agree

Accelerate = *increase speed* : Decelerate = *reduce speed*

Accept = *agree to receive* : Decline = *refuse to accept*

Acclaim = *praise* : Denounce = *criticize*

Accomplish = *to complete task* : Abort = *terminate before completion*

Accord = *agreement* : Discord = *disagreement*

Accumulate = *to store* : Deplete, Dissipate = *to exhaust*

Accusation = *blame* : Approbation = *praise*

Acerbic = *bitter; sour* : Meltiferous = *sweet like honey*

Acknowledge = *accept to have knowledge of responsibility* : Deny = *refuse to, repudiate responsibility on a claim*

Acquiesce = *keep quiet instead of protesting* : Protest = *to raise voice*

Acquit = *declare not guilty* : Convict = *declare guilty*

Acrimony = *bitter feeling* : Harmony = *concord*

Active = *capable to act* : Passive = *not active*

Acute = *severe* : Mild = *not severe*

Adamant = *refusing to yield; unrelenting* : Relenting = *yield*

Adequate = *sufficient* : Inadequate = *not sufficient*

Adjourn = *postpone a meeting* : Convene = *to call a meeting*

Admire = *to praise* : Censure = *criticize*

Adroit = *skillful* : Unskilled, Clumsy

Advance = *move forward* : Retreat = *move backward*

Avenge = *punish in return for a wrong act* : Forgive = *excuse for offence*

Adverse = *unfavourable* : Favourable

Aeons = *very long period of time* : Trice = *a moment, very short period*

Affectation = *pretentious behaviour*: Sincerity = *unpretentious behaviour*

Affection = *fond feeling* : Disaffection = *loss of affection*

Affinity = *spontaneous liking* : Aversion = *spontaneous disliking*

Affirm, Affirmative, Afford = *provide* : Deprive = *deny to provide, negate, deny negative*

Affluence = *floor of wealth*	: Penury = *lacking in wealth, poverty*
Affluent = *wealthy*	: Indigent = *poor*
Agitated = *disturbed*	: Quiescent = *Calm, Tranquil*
Agnostic = *unknowledgeable person*	: Gnostic = *knowlegeable person*
Agoraphobia = *morbid fear of open space*	: Claustrophobia = *morbid fear of closed space*
Aggresive = *attacking without provocation*	: Defensive = *protecting oneself from attack*
Aggravate = *to make a situation worse*	: Alleviate = *Assuage, Mitigate*
Albino = *person with white skin and hair*	: Brunette = *woman with dark skin and hairs*
Alert = *attention directed to pick up danger*	: Distracted = *attention diverted; mentally drawn in different directions*
Alien = *belonging to another place & hence unknown*	: Familiar, Native = *well known*
Alight = *to dismount from a horse's back or a vehicle*	: Board = *to ride on a vehicle*
Alike = *having likeness*	: Unlike = *not alike*
Alleviate = *to lessen intensity of pain, problem*	: Aggravate = *make intensity of pain*
Allow = *permit*	: Disallow = *not allow*
Allure = *entice, attract*	: Repulse, Disinterest = *to keep away*
Alto = *highest pitch of male voice*	: Soprano = *highest pitch of female voice*
Altruism = *selfless concern for*	: Egoism = *concern for self others; self-cntredness; self-opinionatedness*
Amateur = *inexperienced in art*	: Connoisseur = *experience knowledgeable person in art*
Ambiguous = *not clearly understood*	: Obvious, clear = *clearly understood*
Ameliorate = *make better*	: Exacerbate = *make worse*
Ancestor = *a person more remote than a grandparent*	: Descendant = *progeny*
Analogy = *similarity between two things*	: Anomaly = *deviation from one another; irregularity of condition or behaviour*
Ancestry = *generation of ancestors*	: Posterity = *generation of progenies, succeeding generation*

Word	Opposite
Annex = *to add something else to something*	Cede = *to separate something to give to someone else*
Anorexia = *loss of appetite*	Bulimia = *increase in appetite; ravenous hunger*
Antagonist = *opposite to lead pole in cinema*	Protagonisι = *lead actor in cinema*
Antagonize = *cause to become hostile*	Appease = *to please, make one to be pleased*
Anterior = *frontal part of something*	Exterior, Posterior = *back part*
Antipathy = *hostile feeling*	Sympathy = *compassionate feeling*
Applaud = *praise by clapping*	Heckle, Hoot, Denounce = *disapprove by hooting*
Appreciate = *recognize the value of*	Depreciate = *make something lose value*
Approbation = *praise in approval*	Disapproval = *disapprove by expressing it*
Apt = *suitable*	Inapt = *not suitable*
Armaggedon = *fierce war*	Skirmish = *minor scuffle*
Aristocracy = *upper class of society*	Plebeian = *lower class of society*
Arouse = *excite emotion*	Pacify = *calm the passion/emotion*
Arranged = *ordered*	Haphazard = *disordered*
Arrive = *to come to destination*	Depart = *to leave for arriving a place*
Arrogant = *exaggerated sense of self-importance*	Modest = *moderate sense of self importance*
Arrogate = *usurp other's credit*	Credit = *give someone his due credit*
Articulate = *speak clearly*	Babble = *speak incomprehensively*
Artificial = *not genuine*	Genuine
Ascend = *to go up*	Descend = *to come down*
Ascetic = *one who lives simple life*	Epicure = *one who lives luxurious enjoyable life*
Ashamed	Proud
Assemble = *to gather in a place*	Disperse = *get scattered from a place*
Ashore	Adrift
Assent = *express approval*	Dissent = *express disapproval*
Asset = *something which is usable with positive value*	Liability = *something which is burdensome and with negative value if not invested properly*

Assuage = *lessen unpleasant feelings*	: Aggravate = *worsen*
Atonement = *make amends for sins*	: Impenitent = *unregretful for sins committed*
Atrabilious = *ill tempered*	: Genial = *pleasantly warm tempered; pertaining to natural disposition*
Attention	: Distraction
Attentive	: Inattentive
Attract	: Repel, Distract
Attraction	: Repulsion
Audacity = *arrogance*	: Humility = *devoid of arrogance*
Audible = *which can be heard*	: Inaudible = *which cannot be heard*
Auspicious = *indicating favourable chance*	: Ominous = *indicating harmful results*
Austere = *strict in manners*	: Lax = *lenient*
Authentic = *genuinely true*	: Dubious = *doubtful*
Avant garde = *front runner in a field, trailblazer*	: Follower = *running behind; laggard*
Avarice = *greed*	: Lustless = *devoid of greed*
Avenge = *punish in return for a wrong act*	: Forgive = *excuse for offence*
Averse = *not inclined*	: Disposed = *inclined*
Aversion	: Affinity, predilection
Avert = *turn away*	: Confront = *to face headlong*
Avoid = *to ignore*	: Indulge = *to become involved*
Awake = *get up from sleep*	: Asleep = *in state of sleep*
Aware = *be alert*	: Unaware = *not alert*
Awkward = *clumsy; predicament*	: Elegant = *graceful*

Words beginning with —— B ——

Babble	: Articulate
Backwards = *towards back*	: Forward = *towards ahead*
Bait = *something used to allure, towards the trap*	: Spy = *secret agent; one who attract works covertly to distract attention from the trap laid by the authorities*
Balkanise = *to separate people into hostile groups*	: Confederate = *to bring together separate people*

Ban = *to prohibit*	: Permit = *to allow*
Banal = *uninteresting*	: Stimulating = *inciting interest*
Bane = *cause of distress, curse*	: Boon = *cause of gain, blessings to people*
Benevolence = *well-wishing for others*	: Malevolence = *malignant towards others*
Bankrupt = *go without money by way of losing it in business*	: Prosperous, Flourishing = *be wealthy*
Barbaric = *uncivilized as brabarians*	: Civilized
Barren = *unable to produce yields*	Fertile = *able to produce yields*
Basement = *area of a building ground floor*	: Pent-house = *area/floor at the before top of a building*
Bass = *lowest pitch of male voice*	: Contalto = *lowest pitch of female voice*
Belie = *fail to achieve as hoped*	: Realise = *achieve as hoped*
Belief = *firmly held opinion*	: Disbelief = *firmly rejected opinion*
Benediction = *speaking good to others, belessings*	: Malediction = *speaking evil for others, curse*
Benefaction = *doing good to others*	: Malefaction
Benevolence	: Malevolence
Benignant = *not harmful in effect; favourable; kind*	: Malignant = *harmful in effect*
Bequeath = *to hand over property to descendant*	: Inherit = *to get properly left by an ancestor*
Bete noire = *one who is hated most by someone*	: Cynosure = *one who is the star attraction of all*
Betray = *to disclose internal feelings as by facial expressions*	: Dissemble = *to hide internal emotions*
Bias = *unjust inclination*	: Impartial, Disinterested
Bibliophile = *book lover; collector of books*	: Bibliophobe
Bigot = *intolerant to contrary opinion of others*	: Broad-minded, Secular
Bland, Insipid = *state, tasteless*	: Delectable = *tasty*
Blaspheme = *speak irreverently*	: Revere = *to show profound respect*
Blend = *mix with something else*	: Separate = *remove from a mix*
Bless	: Curse, Anathematise
Blessed	: Damned, Cursed

Bliss = *highest level of pleasure* : Melancholy = *profound sadness*

Blithe = *cheerful* : Dejected = *disheartened*

Blunt = *without sharpness* : Sharp

Blunt, Rude = *harsh* : Humble, Polite = *not harsh*

Bold = *daring* : Timid, Timorous, Coward = *lacking courage*

Bonafide = *sincere intention* : Malafide = *bad intention*

Boost = *to enhance* : Depress = *to lower*

Board = *enter into vehicle* : Alight = *come out of a vehicle*

Boon : Bane

Brave, Intrepid : Pusillanimous

Brazen = *shameless* : Shy

Brief = *concise, short* : Lengthy

Bright = *shining* : Dull = *lacking shine*

Brilliant = *brightly colourful* : Lacklustre = *lacking lustre/shine*

Brisk = *energetic* : Lethargic = *sluggish, lacking energy*

Broad = *wide* : Narrow = *not wide*

Brook = *tolerate opposition* : Resent = *not tolerate opposition or such behaviour*

Brunette : Albino

Brutal = *cruel* : Dainty = *small and delicate body, merciful*

Build = *to construct* : Demolish = *pull down*

Bury = *to put underground* : Disinter, Exhume = *to dig out of ground*

Bulimia : Anorexia

Bustle = *move around excitedly* : Quiet, Unhurried = *move around quietly*

Words beginning with —— C ——

Cacophony = *bitter and harsh sound to ears* : Symphony = *pleasant sound to hear*

Cadaverous = *like deadbody* : Vivacious = *like full of life*

Callow = *inexperienced* : Expert

Calm = *undisturbed* : Agitated = *disturbed*

Candour = *open and honest* : Duplicity = *not open and showing double character*

Capacitate = *make capable* : Incapacitate = *make incapable*

Capitulate = *surrender under pressure* : Resist, challenge = *fight to overcome release*

Caprice = *sudden change of mood without reason* : Stoicism = *remain without change of mood in pleasure of pain*

Capture = *catch hold of* : Release

Careful : Careless

Cascade = *fall down in stages* : Precipitate = *fall down steeply headlong*

Casual = *not according to norms, relaxed* : Formal = *according to accepted norms*

Catholic = *of wide attitude/outlook* : Parochial = *of narrow attitude*

Caustic = *causing burn* : Soothing = *causing comfortable feeling*

Cautious = *alert from danger/ situation* : Reckless = *not caring for dangerous effects*

Celebrity = *celebrated person, famous* : Neophyte, Tyro = *newcomer in a field*

Celibate = *abstaining from sex* : Lecher = *excessively indulging in sex*

Censure = *criticize* : Admire

Central = *near centre* : Peripheral, Fringe = *near outer limit*

Centrifugal = *moving away from centre* : Centripetal = *moving towards centre*

Chary = *cautious* : Negligent, Careless

Cheerful : Doleful, Sad, Depressed

Claim : Forego

Clairvoyance = *ability to see distant objects or actions beyond the power of natural viewing; sagacious* : Myopia = *near sightedness*

Clamorous = *shouting* : Quiet = *making no noise*

Clarity = *state of being clear* : Obscurity = *state of being unclear*

Classic = *of high quality* : Kitsch = *of cheap quality; inferior*

Claustrophobia = *abnormal fear of or narrow places* : Agoraphobia = *an abnormal enclosed fear of being in an open space*

Cleanse = *to clean* : Defile = *to make dirty*

Clement = *kind (weather); merciful; kind* : Inclement = *stormy (weather); severe; harsh*

Clinche = *stale due to repeating* : Novel = *new*

Climax = *highest point of excitement* : Anticlimax = *sudden end of excitement*

Cogniscenti = *knowledgeable group*: Ignoramous = *ignorant group*

Coherent = *logically consistent* : Incoherent = *logically inconsistent*

Collosal = *huge in size; gigantic* : Tiny = *very small in size*

Comfort = *feeling of ease* : Discomfort = *feeling of unease*

Comfortable = *in state of comfort* : Uncomfortable

Commence = *to begin a meeting* : Conclude = *to end meeting after completing deliberations*

Commend = *to praise for good work;* entrust : Criticize

Commit = *send a case to higher court of judicature* : Remit = *send a case to lower court*

Commodious = *Comfortably spacious* : Incommodious = *not spacious causing discomfort*

Commonplace = *usual, not extraordinary* : Outstanding = *extraordinary*

Commensurate = *equal in measure or expert; in due proportion* : Incommensurate

Compassionate = *showing pity* : Cruel = *causing pain or torture*

Competent = *able to succeed* : Incompetent = *not able to succeed; unfit*

Complexity : Simplicity

Comply = *act according to the command or complete the requirements* : Defy = *refuse to act according to the command*

Conceal = *to hide something* : Reveal = *to remove veil on something*

Concern = *worry* : Indifference = *without concern, aloof*

Conclude = *come to end* : Commence = *start*

Condemn = *to denounce* : Commend, Approbate = *to praise; laud*

Confess = *to accept one's wrong deed* : Refute = *to deny accusation*

Confidence = *feeling of trust* : Mistrust = *lack of trust*

(Self) Confidence : Diffidence = *lack of self-confidence*

Confident = *to be sure of achieving something* : Diffident = *lacking in confidence*

Conflict = *lack of aggreement in opinion* : Accord = *agreement in opinion*

Conformist = *one who acts according to norms* : Iconoclast, Non-conformist

Confront : Skip, Avert

Congeal = *to coagulate; curdle* : Thaw = *to melt or transform into liquid*

Congenial = *pleasant* : Hostile = *showing dislike*

Congested = *crowded so as to hinder movement* : Spacious = *having free space*

Congregate = *to assemble in a place* : Segregate = *to remove apart*

Congruent = *identical in form* : Incongruent

Connoisseur = *expert in intricacies of art* : Dilettante = *lover of art without having expert knowledge*

Consensual : Contentious, Dissentious

Consent = *give approval* : Dissent = *express disapproval*

Consecrate = *to treat as sacred* : Desecrate = *to violate sacredness; to defile*

Conservative = *averse to change* : Liberal = *open to change*

Conserve = *to avoid misuse of resources* : Squander = *waste recklessly*

Considerate = *careful about other's interests* : Inconsiderate = *not caring for other's interests*

Consistent = *not changing over time* : Inconsistent = *changing over time*

Constrain = *compel someone to do something* : Restrain = *compel someone not to do something*

Constrict = *make narrow* : Dilate = *make wider*

Contemptible = *deserving contempt*: Admirable = *deserving praise*

Contemptuous = *showing hatred* : Respectful = *showing respect*

Contest = *challenge* : Surrender = *submit*

Continent = *able to self-control* : Incontinent = *unable to exercise control over desires*

Continuous = *continuing without break*: Sporadic = *resuming or happening at periodic intervals*

Contradict = *oppose mother's viewpoint* : Corroborate = *to confirm statement*

Conventional = *meeting norms* : Unconventional = *deviating from norms*

Contentious = *causing controversy* : Uncontentious = *not causing controversy*

Controversy = *disagreement* : Unanimity = *one opinion*

Converge = *meet at a point* : Diverge = *go away in different directions from a point*

Convict = *declare guilty* : Exonerate = *declare not guilty*

Copse = *small bunch of trees forming jungle*	: Glade = *small space without trees in jungle*
Corporeal = *related to body*	: Spiritual = *related to spirit, non-physical*
Corpulent = *of hefty body; obese*	: Emaciated = *of thin (without flesh) body = a state of body health caused by either flesh-water or lack of nutrition*
Corrigible = *that can be corrected or reformed*	: Incorrigible = *that cannot be corrected*
Corroborate	: Contradict
Cosmopolitan = *belonging to all places*	: Provincial = *concerned with locality cowardice, timidity*
Counterfeit = *forged to cheat*	: Genuine = *truly real*
Couth = *well mannered*	: Uncouth = *ill-mannered*
Covert	: Overt
Covet = *long to possess*	: Renounce = *give up; abandon*
Coward = *lacking courage*	: Brave, Intrepid
Cowardice	: Courage
Crafty, Cunning	: Ingenuous = *simpleton*
Credible = *believable*	: Incredible = *unbelievable*
Credit (v)	: Arrogate
Credit (n) = *trust in someone*	: Discredit = *distrust*
Credulous = *inclined to believe*	: Sceptic, Incredulous
Cressendo = *gradually increasing music*	: Diminuendo
Crest = *top of a wave*	: Trough = *lower part between two crests*
Criticize	: Commend = *praise*
Critical = *of decisive importance*	: Uncritical
Crude = *unrefined*	: Refined
Cruel	: Compassionate
Cunning	: Simpleton, Ingenuous
Curious = *eager to know*	: Indifferent = *unconcerned*
Curse	: Bless
Curtail = *cut short*	: Prolong, Protract
Cynic, Sceptic	: Credulous
Cynosure	: Bete noire

Dainty	:	Burly
Damned = *cursed or sentenced to eternal punishment*	:	Blessed = *a person upon whom divine powers/favours are invoked*
Dandy = *excessively fashionable; keeping oneself in vogue to a degree*	:	Sloven = *person who is habitually untidy or dirtily remarkable dressed*
Dawn = *sunrise period*	:	Dusk = *sunset period*
Debit	:	Credit
Deciduous = *(plant) which sheds its leaves once every year*	:	Perrenial, Evergreen = *tree which does not annually shed its leaves*
Decipher = *to uncode a coded language or message*	:	Encrypt = *write into code*
Decline = *fail to be inclined to do something; disinclined*	:	Incline = *to lean towards; to dispose; to land*
Decry = *publicly denounce*	:	Laud = *publicly praise*
Deep	:	Shallow
De facto = *by the fact itself; rightful*	:	De jure = *by dirt of law; actually*
Defensive	:	Aggresive, offensive
Deficient = *lacking sufficiency*	:	Sufficient
Deficit = *amount by which falling short*	:	Surplus = *amount in excess*
Defile = *befoul; pollute*	:	Cleanse = *purify*
Deflate = *make flat by taking out air*	:	Inflate = *distend or swell by filling with air*
Deft = *skilled in doing something; clever*	:	Inept = *unskilled; unfit*
Defy = *challenge; resist*	:	Comply = *yield or defer to the wishes of another*
Degenerate = *decay*	:	Flourish = *grow*
Dejected = *depressed in spirits; disheartened; low spirited*	:	Blithe = *joyous; merry or gay in disposition*
Deleterious = *injurious*	:	Salutary = *beneficial*
Delete = *remove something from written*	:	Insert, Enter = *incorporate*
Delectable = *pleasing; delightful; tasty; dainty*	:	Insipid = *tasteless* Insipid person = *dull; devoid of intelligence*

Delegate = *transfer power to someone in authority* : Usurp = *to arrogate to oneself an individual or authority*

Deliberate = *intentionally (do something); by design* : Inadvertent = *unintentionally*

Deliver = *to hand over* : Receive

Demean = *to lose dignity* : Dignify = *to gain dignity*

Demise = *hand over by will* : Inherit = *receive from ancestor*

Demure = *shy and modest (woman)*: Coy = *pretend to be shy*

Denounce : Acclaim = applaud; to solute with shouts or sounds of joy and approval

Denouement = *end part of a film* : Exordium = *beginning part; introduction*

Dense = *thick* : Sparse = *thinly dispersed*

Deny : Acknowledge

Depreciate = *become less in value* : Appreciate = *increase in value*

Depressed = *feel dejected* : Cheerful

Desecrate : Consecrate

Desist = *abstain from doing something* : Insist = *persistently try to do something (upon)*

Deplete (adj.) = *reduced stock* : Replete = *filled with stock*

Deplete (v) = *reduce quantity of stock* : Replenish = *restore the reduced stock*

Deprive = *take away from someone* : Afford, Provide

Descend = *come down from a height* : Ascend = *go up*

Descendant = *progeny* : Ancestor = *forefathers*

Desecrate : Consecrate

Despair = *be without hope* : Hope

Despairing = *without hope; despondent* : Sanguine = *cheerfully optimistic; hopeful; confident*

Despondent = *in state of losing hope* : Euphoric = *in state of happy feeling*

Desultory = *not serious in intent about* : Fastidious = *serious in intent doing work in perfect manner*

Deteriorate = *worsen* : Improve = *get better*

Deter = *discourage from doing wrong*: Abet = *help in doing wrong*

Dextrous = *skilled in doing work with hands* : Maladroit = *inefficient in doing work*

Devolve = *roll down; transmit* : Evolve = *develop in succesion of processes*

Diatribe = *bitter verbal attack*	: Encomium = *verbal praise*
Difficulty	: Facility
Diffident = *wanting in confidence*	: Confident
Dignify	: Demean
Dignity	: Indignity
Dilate = *enlarge*	: Constrict
Dilettante = *one who loves the fine in a superficial way and without serious purpose*	: Connoisseur = *well informed arts but judge in the arts*
Diminish = *reduce*	: Enhance = *increase*
Dirigisme = *policy of government control over economic and social spheres*	: Laissez faire = *policy of granting freedom/non-interference*
Disaffection = *loss of affection*	: Affection = *fondness for, or devotion to, a person or thing; emotion; sentiment; love*
Disclose = *reveal*	: Conceal = *hide a secret*
Discord = *disagreement; strife*	: Accord
Discredit	: Credit
Discreet = *carefully considered (action)*	: Indiscreet, Rash = *hasty (action)*
Discrete = *distinctly separate from each other*	: Indiscrete = *homogeneous; not separated or distinguishable in parts*
Discretion = *prudence*	: Indiscretion = *want of discretion; rashness*
Disdainful = *undeserving respect*	: Respectful
Disenfranchise = *take away voting rights*	: Enfranchise = *grant voting rights*
Disgorge = *to expel from mouth (food)*	: Gorge = *to eat greedily*
Dishevelled = *disorderly*	: Spruced = *neatly arranged*
Disinter = *digout*	: Bury = *put in ground*
Disinterest = *impartiality; bias*	: Bias = *unjustly inclined in free from favour of another/others*
Disparity = *inequality in comparison*	: Parity = *equality in comparison*
Dispensable = *which can be disposed*	: Indispensable = *which is required and can't be disposed*

Disperse = *scatter*	: Assemble
Disrepute = *loss of repute*	: Repute
Dissatisfy = *not satisfy*	: Satisfy
Dissemble = *hide*	: Betray
Disseminate = *spread widely*	: Garner = *collect*
Dissent	: Consent
Dissuade = *discourage from doing by convincing*	: Persuade = *encourage to do something by convincing*
Distract = *divert attention*	: Attract = *full attention*
Diurnal = *of day time (activity)*	: Nocturnal = *of night time (activity)*
Diverge = *spread in different directions from a point*	: Converge = *to come from different directions to a point*
Divest = *dispossess someone of power, authority*	: Invest (with) = *put power or authority in someone*
Divine = *devoted to God, spiritual*	: Mundane = *of earthly matters*
Docile = *who can be taught to do*	: Maverick, Intractable = *minded independent as desired*
Dogmatic = *asserting a thing as were a dogma*	: Pragmatic = *practical in doing if it*
Doleful	: Cheerful
Doyen = *seniormost person of a family*	: Scion = *youngest person of a family*
Drooping = *hanging down*	: Erect
Dubitable = *doubtful*	: Indubitable = *incapable of being doubted*
Duffer = *stupid*	: Genius = *exceptionally intelligent*
Dull = *lacking brightness or energy*	: Ebulient = *full of enthusiasm*
Duplicity = *double behaviour by way of being dishonest*	: Candour = *honest & open behaviour*
Dusk = *sunset time*	: Dawn = *sunrise time*

***Words beginning with* ——— E ———**

Eager = *Interested to know*	: Indifferent = *not interested*
Early	: Late
Earthly, Mundane = *worldly*	: Divine, Spiritual = *godly*
Ebullient = *enthusiastic*	: Dull
Ecstasy = *feeling of great happiness*	: Dolefulness

Effectual = *effective in accomplishing desired purpose*	: Ineffectual
Effeminate = *having womanly characteristics*	: Virile = *having manly characteristics*
Effete = *no longer capable of producing offspring or being effective*	: Fecund = *capable of producing many offsprings*
Efficacious = *effective in producing good results*	: Inefficacious
Effluent = *flowing out*	: Influent = *flowing in*
Egoism	: Altruism
Egotism = *quality or habit of being excessively conceited and talks only about oneself*	: Modesty = *quality of being self-effacing or unassuming*
Egress = *go out of a place*	: Ingress
Eirenic/Irenic = *promoting peace*	: Polemic = *controversial*
Eject = *throw out*	: Inject = *push in*
Elaborate = *detail*	: Sketchy = *imperfect/inadequate*
Elastic = *resilient*	: Inelastic
Eligible = *satisfying required conditions for something*	: Ineligible = *not fulfilling the* : *required conditions*
Elder = *of more age than someone else*	: Younger = *of lower age than someone's*
Elevation = *height above surface*	: Depression = *depth below surface*
Elicit = *draw out response from someone*	: Insinuate = *insert a suggestion or hint or remark, etc. in speech*
Elite, Aristocrat	: Plebeian
Eliminate = *remove from consideration*	: Incorporate = *include in something as its part*
Eloquent = *speaking fluently*	: Taciturn = *uncommunicative; reticent*
Emaciated	: Corpulent
Emancipate = *free from bondage*	: Enthrall, Enslave
Embark = *go on board a ship or aircraft for voyage or travel*	: Dis-embark = *alight from a ship/flight*
Embarrass = *disconcert awkward or ashamed*	: Plim = *cause to swell with pride*
Emerge = *come out of a place*	: Immerge = *to go in*
Emerse = *emerge; standing out of surface of a liquid*	: Immerse = *dip under the water*

Emigrate = *to leave or go out of one's own country to migrate to another country*	: Immigrate = *to come into another (foreign) country*
Eminent = *outstanding*	: Unknown
Empty (adj.) = *unoccupied place by: usual contents*	Full = *occupied fully*
Empty (v) = *to remove usual contents from a place or container*	: Fill = *to make it full by pouring into container*
Enchant = *to charm, bewitch*	: Disenchant
Encomium = *praise*	: Diatribe = *a continued discourse or disputation*
Encrypt = *to put electronic information in a code form which can only be interpreted with a special purpose equipment*	: Decipher = *to discover the meaning of something written badly or in a difficult or hidden way; interpret the code word*
Endogamy = *practice of marrying within the same community*	: Exogamy = *marrying out of own community*
Endogenous = *growing from within*	: Exogenous = *growing by successive additions to the outside*
Enervate = *cause to lose vigour*	: Invigorate = *to give vigour; to strengthen*
Enfranchise = *give political freedom*	: Subjugate, Enslave
Enhance = *increase, improve, raise to higher degree*	: Reduce, Diminish
Enmity = *hatred*	: Amity = *friendship*
Enormous = *vast*	: Normal = *usual; common*
Enrage = *make one angry, infuriate*	: Pacify = *to calm; to appease*
Enrich = *make rich*	: Impoverish = *make poor*
Enthrall = *enslave*	: Emancipate = *set free*
Enthusiastic = *filled with zeal or interest; zealous*	: Reluctant = *devoid of zeal,interest; hesitant*
Entitle = *give someone a claim*	: Forfeit = *make one lose claim*
Entrance = *way to enter*	: Exit = *way to come out*
Envigorate = *fill with vigour*	: Enervate = *cause to lose vigour*
Ephemeral = *shortlived*	: Eternal = *lasting forever*
Equitable = *just, fair*	: Inequitable = *unfair*
Equity = *fairness & just*	: Inequity = *lack of fairness & just*
Erect = *tightly straight*	: Prostrate, Drooping = *bending downward*

Erratum = *list of errors in print*	: Corrigendum = *list of amendments made in print*
Escalate = *increase to higher level*	: De-escalate = *drop to lower level*
Esoteric = *not openly admitted; private knowledgeable persons*	: Exoteric = *understood by all*
Esteem = *respect*	: Disdain = *contempt; scorn*
Eternal = *everlasting; without beginning or end*	: Ephemeral = *lasting for a very short time*
Euphoria = *feeling of well-being*	: Despondence, Dysphoria
Evade = *to escape from doing or happening something*	: Pursue = *to follow, chase*
Evitable = *that can be avoided*	: Inevitable = *that cannot be avoided; something bound to happen*
Evince = *show indirectly, manifest by indication*	: Hide = *conceal*
Evolve = *develop (e.g. policy*	: Devolve (upon) = *to pass on; plan) transmit*
Exacerbate = *make bitter or worse*	: Ameliorate = *make less painful, better*
Exaggerate = *to make something excessively described*	: Underestimate = *to underplay*
Excision = *Act of cutting out/off, as in a surgical operation; extirpation*	: Incision = *A slit or opening mode with a cutting instrument as in an operation*
Exclude = *keep out of consideration*	: Include = *take into consideration*
Exculpate = *to declare free from accusation/blame; prove innocent*	: Inculpate = *frame charges/ accusation*
Exempt = *free from liability*	: Liable = *be under obligation*
Exhale = *breathe out*	: Inhale = *breathe in*
Exhaust = *to consume something completely*	: Replenish = *to fill again what has been exhausted*
Exhume = *dig out what is burried*	: Bury
Exist = *be in living condition*	: Disappear = *cease to be in existence*
Existent = *be present in living state*	: Extinct = *cease to be present in living state*
Exit	: Entrance
Exogenous	: Endogenous
Exonerate = *set free from charges*	: Convict
Exorable = *that/who can be made to yield by entreaty*	: Inexorable

Expedient = *desirable step under the circumstance*	: Inexpedient = *foolish step in a given situation*
Expedite = *to speed up a process progress*	: Delay, Impede = *to hinder of a process = defer*
Expel = *remove out of a place*	: Admit = *allow to come in a place*
Expert = *very skillful*	: Callow, Greenhorn = *unskilled*
Explicable = *capable of being explained by unfolding facts*	: Inexplicable = *not capable of being explained*
Explicate = *to unfold*	: Implicate = *to involve/ensnare within fold of something*
Explicit = *clearly expressed*	: Implicit = *implied – not directly expressed*
Explode = *to burst suddenly*	: Implode = *to burst internally*
Expropriate = *take possession of land/money for public use*	: Impropriate = *take possession for own private use*
Exterior = *external part of something*	: Interior = *internal part of something*
Extinct	: Existent
Extinguish = *put out fire*	: Kidle = *start a fire, make something burn*
Extraneous = *not related to topic*	: Relevant, Pertinent = *related to a topic*
Extravagant = *of expressively wasteful spending*	: Thrifty, Frugal = *of spending judiciously*
Extrinsic	: Intrinsic
Extrovert	: Intrinsic
Extrovert = *expressing one's mind freely*	: Introvert = *not expressing one's thoughts*
Extrude = *to force out which has entered somewhere unwantedly*	: Intrude = *to enter somewhere unwelcomed*
Extrusive = *tending to extrude*	: Intrusive = *tending to intrude*
Exuberant = *effusive*	: Subdued = *repressed, quiet*

Words beginning with — F

Facilitate = *to make easy*	: Hinder = *to make difficult*
Factious = *tending to encourage factions*	: Unanimous = *without diversity of opinions*
Fascination = *attraction*	: Revulsion = *a sudden change of feeling; complete disgust or aversion*

Fictitious = *imaginary; feigned*	: Genuine = *original, pure & real*
Fade = *to become dull*	: Brighten = *to make shining*
Fallible = *liable to error or mistake; liable to be erroneous or false in judgment or action*	: Infallible = *incapable of fallacy or error; reliable; certain*
Familiar = *well known*	: Unfamiliar
Famous = *renowned for good deeds; renowned*	: Infamous, Notorious = *for bad reasons*
Fanatic = *intolerant to one who differs, zealot*	: Liberal
Fastidious = *aweful/intolerant to deficiency; hard to please in matters of taste; overly delicate or sensitive*	: Slipshod, Desultory = *slovenly; sloppy; untidy and careless in appearance; imperfect in work habits*
Faux pas = *blunder in etiquette; breach of tact or manners*	: Savoir faire = *conduct suitable to etiquette*
Facility	: Difficulty
Fecund = *faithful; fertile*	: Efette = *incapable of further production; barren*
Felicitate = *to congratulate for good deed*	: Loath = *to hate for misdeeds, abhor*
Felony = *serious crime (punishable with forfeiture of lauds or chattels)*	: Peccadillo = *trifling fault*
Ferocious = *violently, cruel, savage*	: Innocuous = *unharming*
Fidelity = *trustfulness, faithfulness*	: Infidelity = *unfaithfulness*
Finale = *final part of performance*	: Premiere = *first performance*
Flaccid = *not rigid, loose*	: Tight = *close fitting*
Flatterer = *one who pleases by praising*	: Detractor = *one who belittles another; diminish reputation defame*
Fledgling = *immature like a bird which is yet to learn flying; inexperienced person*	: Mature; fully developed
Flexible = *capable of bending*	: Rigid = *not bending due to stiffness*
Flippant = *frivolous, lacking seriousness*	: Meticulous = *careful to the minute details in working*
Foe = *enemy*	: Friend
Forbid = *order not to do*	: Permit = *allow to do*

Foresight = *ability to see ahead*	Hind-sight = *ability to see in the back*
Forfeit	Entitle
Forgo	Claim
Formal	Informal, Casual
Former = *first of the two*	Latter = *second of the two*
Forte = *strong point of someone's ability*	Handicap = *weak point of someone's ability*
Fortify = *to make strong by providing strength*	Undermine, Subvert = *to make weak by digging at the root*
Fortuitous = *happening by chance*	Pre-meditated = *happening as a sequel to after careful considerations*
Fractions = *irritable*	Calm
Fragile = *capable of breaking*	Unbreakable
Franchise = *empower with voting rights*	Disenfranchise = *take away voting rights*
Frank = *open-minded*	Cunning, Wily = *crafy*
Fraternal twins	Identical twins
Frantic = *wild with panic*	Patient = *calm in diffcult time*
Freedom	Subjection
Frequent = *too often at regular intervals*	Infrequent, Sporadic = *not often*
Fresh	Stale = *not fresh*
Friend	Foe
Fringe = *outer border*	Mainstream = *main part*
Frivolous = *lacking seriousness, one frivols*	Solemn = *serious as warranted who by the occasion*
Front = *foremost part*	Rear = *back portion*
Froward = *doing against suggestion; self-willed*	Docile = *submissive; easily managed*
Fructuous = *producing results*	Infructuous = *not producing expected results*
Frugal, Thrifty	Extravagant, Spendthrift
Fulminate = *to appear or come upon suddenly as sudden explosion*	Evanesce = *to disappear suddenly*
Funereal = *mournful, gloomy as on the occasion of a funeral*	Sanguine = *cheerful*

Furl = *to fold by rolling up* : Unfurl = *to spread open a rolled up length of cloth or sheet*

Futile = *producing no result* : Fruitful = *producing result*

Futility = *quality or state of being useless as an effort* : Utility = *quality of being useful*

Words beginning with ——— G ———

Gain = *advantage* : Loss = *disadvantage*

Gall = *irritate* : Soothe = *give comfort feeling*

Garner = *to collect* : Disseminate = *to scatter, spread widely*

Garrulous = *excessively speaking as habit, using too many words* : Laconic = *expressing in too few words*

Gather = *collect* : Disperse, Scatter

General = *not particular* : Specific = *particular*

Generalize = *make general; common* : Specify = *particularise*

Genius = *superbly intelligent* : Duffer = *lacking intelligence; dull*

Generous = *munificent, liberal in giving* : Niggardly = *stingy, miserly*

Genial = *of cordial nature* : Querulous, Sullen = *of complaining nature*

Genuine : Artificial, Sham

Gigantic = *very large in size* : Tiny = *very small in size*

Glade = *an open space in a wood* : Copse = *a small wood; coppice*

Glance = *to look briefly* : Stare = *to look fixedly*

Glare = *to shine intensely* : Gleam = *to shine softly*

Glitter = *shine brilliantly* : Glimmer = *to shine faintly*

Gloomy = *sad* : Cheerful

Glory = *exalted fame disgrace,* : Ignominy = *abject insult/obloquy*

Glean = *to gather by picking up bit* : Scatter *by bit*

Glut = *excessive, abundance of, supply* : Scarcity = *acute/inordinate shortage*

Gnostic = *one who is having knowledge about something* : Agnostic = *one who is not knowledgeable about something*

Gobble = *to eat in large morsels* : Nibble = *to eat by biting small pieces*

Gradual = *in slow pace or steps* : Abrupt = *suddenly*

Gluttonous = *one who eats voraciously* : Abstemious = *abstain from much eating and drinking*

Grace = *politeness in behaviour* : Disgrace = *Insulting behaviour*

Grateful = *obliged* : Ungrateful, Ingrate

Gravameu (of changes) : Quintescence (of firhus)

Gravitate = *fall down to the lowest level* : Levitate = *to rise up to float in air*

Gregarious = *living in flocks or herd* : Recluse = *living in solitude; secluded*

Grieve = *lament* : Rejoice = *to feel delight*

Groan = *make low sound as in pain* : Moan = *make low sound as in intense pleasure*

Guilt = *act of sin crime* : Innocence = *fact of free from guilt*

***Words beginning with* — H —**

Hallow = *show deep respect* : Denigrate = *ruin respect unfairly*

Harmony = *state of pleasant understanding with others* : Disharmony = *absence of harmony*

Haphazard = *disorderly* : Orderly

Hasten = *to quicken* : Retard = *to slow down*

Heaven : Hell

Heckle = *to hoot* : Applaud = *to praise, approbate*

Heed = *to pay attention to advice* : Ignore = *to disregard advice*

Hegemony = *state of predominating in influence on others* : Subservience = *state of being subordination*

Heinous = *reprehensive (act)* : Venial = *pardonable (act)*

Hell : Heaven

Heresy = *action/opinion contrary to conforming religious beliefs* : Conformism = *act of to accepted belief*

Heterodoxy = *holding unorthodox doctrine* : Orthodoxy = *holding accepted doctrine*

Heterogeneous = *not uniform* : Homogeneous = *uniform*

Hinder = *put obstacle in progress* : Facilitate

Hindsight : Foresight

Hide : Display

Honorable = *worthy of honour* : Abject = *cast away; mean; worthless*

Honoured : Abashed; dishonoured

Hostile = *not favourable* : Favourable

Hubris = *extreme arrogance; insolence* : Humility = *humbleness*

Humble = *not proud*	: Rude, Proud
Humility	: Hubris, Pride
Hypocrisy = *not practising what one preaches*	: Sincerity = *honesty in practising what one preaches*
Hygienic	: Unhygienic

Words beginning with —— I

Iconoclast = *breaker of accepted norms or beliefs*	: Conformist = *follower of accepted norms or beliefs*
Identical twins = *twins having identical gender and resembling appearance*	: Fraternal twins = *twins of different or same gender but not having resemblance in appearance*
Ignoble = *dishonourable*	: Honourable = *noble; illustrious*
Ignominy = *public disgrace; infamy*	: Glory = *renown; exalted; triumphant honour*
Ignorant = *without knowledge*	: Knowledgeable = *possessing knowledge; intelligent*
Ignore = *disregard; set aside*	: Heed = *to attend to; to observe*
Illegible = *writing which cannot be clearly read*	: Legible = *which can be clearly read*
Illegitimate = *unlawful*	: Legitimate = *lawful; having the legal status of those born in wedlock*
Illicit = *not permitted; unlawful; unlicensed*	: Licit = *permitted*
Immaculate = *spotlessly clean*	: Maculate = *spotted by stains; flemished*
Immense = *too large to measure*	: Limited, Measurable
Immerge	: Emerge
Immerse	: Emerse
Immigrant	: Emigrant
Imminent = *impending*	: Remote (chance) = *distant*
Immune = *protected from harm*	: Susceptible = *prone to harm*
Impair = *damage the condition of something, e.g., health*	: Improve, Repair
Impartial	: Biased
Impassioned = *filled with passion*	: Impassive = *devoid of passion*
Impede = *to retard progress*	: Expedite = *to increase the pace of progress*

Impenitence = *not regretting*	Atonement = *regretting for sins*
Impertinent = *rude*	Polite = not rude
Impotent	Potent
Improvident = *not taking care for future needs*	Provident = *taking care for future needs*
Impertinent = *intrusive; interfering*	Pertinent = *relevant; appropriate*
Imprudent = *wanting foresight or discretion*	Prudent = *discreet*
Inadvertently = *failing to turning attention to something; unintentionally*	Deliberately = *intentionally*
Implicate = *to ensnare in accusation*	Explicate = *to lay open or explain the meaning of*
Implicit = *implied*	Explicit = *conclusion; distinctly stated*
Implore = *beg for something tearfully*	Spurn = *reject to accept scornfully*
Impoverish = *make poor*	Enrich = *make rich*
Improvement	Deterioration
Impulsive = *impetuous, hasty*	Thoughtful, Considered
Inapt = *inappropriate*	Apt = *appropriate, suited to situation*
Inclement = *unkind, unfavourable, troublesome*	Clement
Include = *enclose; to reckon as a part*	Exclude = *to shutout; to except; to thrust out*
Incorporate = *to embody*	Eliminate = *remove; cancel; got rid of*
Incriminate = *to charge with crime*	Absolve = *to set free; pardon*
Indifferent = *without importance*	Curious = *inquisitive*
Indigent = *poor*	Wealthy; rich
Inept = *unfit; irritant; futile*	Deft = *handy; clever*
Indigenous = *native*	Exogenous = *derived externally*
Indulge = *to yield to the wishes of*	Abstain, Refrain, Abjure
Inexorable = *not able to be made to yield*	Exorable = *who can be made to yield*
Inferior = *of low quality*	Superior = *higher in place, rank or excellence*
Inflate = *to make swell by introducing air inside*	Deflate = *to make flat by removing air from its within*

Influx = *flow into something* : Efflux = *flowing out*

Influent = *inflowing; exerting influence* : Effluent = *flowing; liquid industrial waste*

Infuriate = *enrage, anger* : Pacify = *to calm*

Ingress = *come in* : Egress = *go out*

Ingenuous = *simpleton* : Cunning, Wily

Inhale = *breathe in* : Exhale = *breathe forth*

Inherit : Bequeath, Demise

Iniquitous = *wicked, perverse; unjust* : Righteous = *morally upright; unjust*

Innocuous = *harmless* : Ferrocious = *ravage;*

Insane = *of unsound mind* : Sane = *of sound mind*

Insipid = *tasteless* : Delectable = *delightful*

Insist (upon) = *to speak emphatically; persist in pressing for an act or confiscation* : Desist = *refrain*

Intelligible = *able to be understood* : Un-intelligible; *not comprehensible*

Inferior = *lower in any respect; quality* : Superior = *higher in status; poor in rank or excellence*

Insinuate = *to hint; to enter gently* : Elicit = *to draw forth; to ....*

Integrate = *to bring together in a whole* : Dis-integrate = *to break up*

Intensity = *to make intense* : Abate = *to lessen intensity*

Interested = *be curious in something* : Un-interested = *not interested*

Interest = *concern for self-gain concern* : Dis-interest = *having no intention/ scheme for self-gain; free from bias*

Interior = *inner* : Exterior = *outer*

Intimacy = *close relationship* : Alienation, Estrangement = *break up of relationship*

Intrepid = *undaunted; without fear* : Pusillanimous = *cowardly*

Intrinsic = *inward* : Extrinsic = *external; foreign*

Introvert = *a person interested mainly in his own inner states and processes* : Extrovert = *a person interested mainly in the world external to himself*

Intrude = *to enter uninvited or welcome* : Protrude, Extrude = *to project; to thrust or push out or forward; to expel*

Invest = *insuperable*	: Divest = *disinvest*
Invincible = *who cannot be to lay out for profit*	: Vincible = *capable of being subdued; conquered*
Invoke = *call a rule in application*	: Revoke = *cancel a rule in operation*
Irenic, Eirenic = *which promotes peace; tending to create peace*	: Polemic = *given to disputing controversial*
Irritate	: Pacify

Words beginning with — J —

Jabber = *chatter; indistinct or idle talk*	: Breviloguy = *speak in short*
Jaded, Blase = *bored with over-eating*	: Insatiated = *not fully satisfied or satiated*
Jealous = *one who feels resentment over other's success*	: Magnanimous = *long/kind-hearted*
Jeer = *to shout derisively*	: Extol = *to praise*
Jinx = *that brings bad luck*	: Mascot = *that brings good luck*
Jitter = *nervousness*	: Elation = *feeling of high spirit*
Jolt = *shake roughly*	: Lull = *to quiet down*
Jovial = *pleasantly humorous*	: Splenetic, Mirthless = *joyless; cheerless*
Jubilant = *exultant, rejoice; triumph*	: Depressed = *dispirited*
Judicious = *showing judgement*	: Injudicious Iniquitous = *wicked; unjust; unreasonable*
Jumble = *mixed in unravelling mass*	: Unravel = *to disentangle*
Just = *justified*	: Unjust

Words beginning with — K —

Keen = *very curious; eager*	: Indifferent = *apathetic*
Kempt = *combed (hairs)*	: Unkempt = *uncombed*
Kindle = *to light up; to arouse passions; to provoke*	: Extinguish; to put out fire
Kitsch = *cheap quality of art/literature*	: Classic = *superb quality of art/literature*
Knave = *crooked person deceitful fellow*	: Simpleton = *a weak or foolish person*
Knowledge = *information; instruction*	: Ignorance = *want of knowledge*

Laconic = *expressing in few words*	: Garrulous, Prolix = *talkative*
Laity = *layman*	: Cogniscenti = *a group of people who have a great knowledge and understanding of a particular subject, especially one of the arts*
Lament = *to express sorrow*	: Rejoice; *show jubilant attitude*
Languid = *lacking in vigour*	: Vigorous = *full of spirit, liveliness*
Latent = *not openly visible*	: Patent = *lying open*
Later = *after the usual time*	: Sooner = *before the usual time*
Latter	: Former
Lax = *loose/not strict in observance*	: Strict, Astere
Laxity = *state of carelessness; inattention or going beyond control*	: Control = *order; rule*
Laud = *to praise publicly*	: Decry = *to lament*
Lavish = *spending in great amount*	: Parsimoniously = *miserly spending*
Legible	: Illegible
Legitimate	: Illegitimate
Lenient = *not strict*	: Strict, Rigid
Lithe = *supple, flexible*	: Rigid, Stiff
Lessee = *one who takes on lease*	: Lessor = *one giving on lease*
Lethargic = *sluggish*	: Vivacious = *lively active*
Levitate = *raise in air*	: Gravitate = *to be attracted; move by force of gravitation*
Levity = *absence of seriousness in behaviour*	: Solemnity, Earnestness
Liability	: Assets
Liable = *subject to suffer/obligation to be fulfilled for avoiding financial loss*	: Exempt = *free from obligation*
Liberal = *generous; noble-minded*	: Conservative = *averse to change*
Liberate = *to set free*	: Enslave = *to reduce to slavery*
Libertine = *who behaves in lewd manner*	: Prude = *who is shocked by what is in lewd*
Liberty = *freedom to act, not binding*	: Compulsion = *state of being compulsory*
Licit = *lawful; permissible*	: Illicit = *unlawful*
Likely = *possible to occur*	: Unlikely = *not likely*

Word	Antonym
Limber = *flexible*	: Stiff = *rigid*
Limited	: Unlimited, Immense
Limp = *lacking stiffness*	: Stiff
Link = *to connect*	: Delink
Lively = *full of life*	: Torpid = *lacking energy*
Loath = *hate, dislike*	: Felicitate
Lofty = *sublime, high-sounding in contents*	: Base = *low in quality*
Logical = *in accordance with reasonability*	: Absurd, Illogical = *improper*
Loquacious = *talkative*	: Taciturn = *brief in speaking*
Loud = *making great sound*	: Muted = *suppressed loudness*
Loyal = *faithful to allegiance*	: Storm, Agitate, Jolt
Ludicrous = *laughably absurd*	: Solemn = *deeply sincere*
Lustre = *shine*	: Dullness = *faintness*

Words beginning with —— M ——

Word	Antonym
Maculate = *spotted*	: Immaculate = *spotlessly clean; unblemished*
Magnanimous = *large hearted*	: Parvanimous = *small hearted in showing kindness*
Magnify = *to make large*	: Reduce, Diminish = *to make small*
Majority = *larger than half of total*	: Minority = *less than half of total*
Make	: Mar = *spoil*
Maladroit	: Dextrous
Malafide	: Bonafide
Malevolent	: Benevolent
Malfeasance	: Beneficence
Malignant	: Benignant
Manifest = *clearly obvious*	: Obscure = *not visible*
Masochist = *one who takes pleasure in pain or humiliation inflicted on him or her*	: Sadist = *one who takes pleasure by inflicting pain or humiliation on others*
Mandatory = *ordered by authority to obey*	: Optional = *given **choice** to act on others*
Marooned = *left on desolate island*	: Stranded = *left aground on sea shore, unable to go ahead*

Mascot = *bringer of good luck*	: Jinx = *bringer of bad luck*
Mature	: Immature, Fledgeling
Maverick = *independent minded in taking decision*	: Docile = *who can be taught to do as desired*
Meagre = *much less in quantity*	: Plentiful = *abundance*
Malancholy	: Bliss
Meliorate = *make better*	: Exacerbate = *make condition even more worse*
Melliferous = *carrying honey and hence sweet*	: Acerbic = *bitter; astringent*
Mellifluous = *sweet as honey*	: Discordant, Cacophonous
Mercenary = *motivated by gain/ profit earning*	: Voluntary = *motivated by self-desire*
Merit	: Demerit
Messy, Sloppy = *disordered*	: Tidiness = *neatly arranged*
Metamorphosis = *change in physical form*	: Stasis = *no change in state*
Meticulous	: Flippant
Mild = *gentle, not harsh*	: Severe = *harsh*
Minnow = *small fish like insignificant person*	: Triton = *very large size, very influential person among minnows; resourceful*
Miraculous = *strange as act of god*	: Mundane = *ordinary*
Misanthrope = *one who hates mankind*	: Philanthrope = *one who likes mankind*
Miser = *one who hates spending money*	: Generous = *one who lavishly spends money*
Misogynest = *one who hates women folk*	: Philogynist = *one who likes womenfolk*
Mitigate = *to lessen the gravity of something*	: Aggravate = *one who makes the gravity worse*
Moan = *lament; complaint*	: Groan = *utter in distress or disapprobation*
Modest = *humble about one's own importance*	: Immodest, Egotist
Modesty	: Egotism
Mollify = *to appear the anger*	: Enrage = *to provoke one's anger*

Mondaine = *fashionable woman*	: Slut = *woman who is untidy, dirty in habits and appearance (slut = woman who is untidy; dirty in habits and appearance)*
Monopoly = *control over market by seller*	: Monopsony = *control over market by purchaser*
Monotheism = *belief in one god*	: Pantheism = *belief in all religions gods*
Morose = *bad mood*	: Cheerful = *spirited mood*
Mortal = *liable to die*	: Immortal
Motivate = *stimulate someone to do*	: Demotivate *something*
Mourn = *to lament*	: Rejoice
Mundane = *worldly*	: Spiritual = *transcending worldly matters; metaphysical*
Munificent = *generous*	: Stingy
Murky (water)	: Pellucid, limpid (water)
Mute = *silent*	: Vociferous = *shouting*
Myopic = *short-sighted*	: Clairvoyant = *far-sighted*

Words beginning with —— N ——

Nadir = *the lowest position in a path of sphere*	: Zenith = *the highest point*
Native = *one who belongs to a place by birth*	: Alien = *one who belongs to another place*
Negate = *to deny, nullify*	: Affirm = *firmly accept or declare*
Negative	: Positive, Affirmative
Negligent = *careless*	: Chary, Careful
Novice = *inexperienced*	: Expert, Veteran
Nepotism = *favouritism granted to relatives*	: Fairness = *justice done in decisions*
Nibble = *to bite gently or by small bites*	: Gobble = *devour; to swallow in lumps*
Niggardly	: Generous
Nightmare = *frightening experience or dream*	: Nostalgia = *longing to experience or remembering happy moments of past life*
Nocturnal = *active by night*	: Diurnal = *active by the day-time*
Noisy	: Quiet
Non-conformist	: Conformist

Normal = *usual in extent normal* : Enormous = *out or beyond extent in size, cruelty, loss, etc.*

Novel : Trite = *cliche*

Words beginning with —— O ——

Object = *express dissent* : Subscribe (to) = *express consent to a program by signing in its favour*

Objective = *free from personal opinion* : Subjective = *based on personal opinion*

Obnoxious = *unpleasant, annoying* : Pleasant

Obscene = *indecent* : Decent

Obverse = *front side of coin* : Reverse = *back side*

Obvious = *clearly visible* : Obscure, Vague = *hazy*

Occident = *countries of the west* : Orient = *countries of the east*

Occupy = *take possession of a place* : Vacate

Offensive = *attacking, disagreeable*: Inoffensive, Defensive

Ominous = *of frightening omen* : Auspicious = *indicating favourable omen*

Omnipotent = *all powerful* : Impotent = *devoid of power*

Opaque = *not transparent* : Translucent, Transparent = *see able through*

Optimist = *one who hopes for the best* : Pessimist = *one who does not have hopes for something good to happen*

Orthodox : Heterodox

Orderly : Haphazard

Outlandish = *belonging to another land & so unfamiliar* : Familiar

Outrageous = *grossly unpleasant* : Flattering = *which pleases*

Outstanding = *extraordinary in nature* : Commonplace = *that which is found everywhere*

Overt = *openly* : Covert = *in a concealed manner*

Own = *to accept as belonging to oneself* : Disown = *not accept as one's own*

Words beginning with —— P ——

Pacify = *make calm* : Provoke, Infuriate, Irritate, Enrage

Palliate = *alleviate* : Aggravate

Word	Antonym
Pantheon = *a memorial for all the illustrious persons, temple of all Gods*	Monotheon
Parity	Disparity
Parochial	Catholic
Parsimonious	Lavish
Partial = *biased to someone*	Impartial = *not biased*
Patriot = *one who is loyal to his or her own country*	Traitor = *one who is disloyal to his/her own country*
Passionate = *moved by passion*	Impassive = *imperturbable*
Passive	Active
Peccadillo = *minor offence*	Felony = *serious offence*
Patience	Impatience
Peevish = *querulous, fretful*	Jovial, Genial
Penury = *extreme poverty*	Affluence = *wealthiness, Richness*
Perdition = *state of ruination of soul*	Salvation = *deliverance of soul*
Perennial = *perpetual*	Deciduous = *shedding all the leaves together at a certain period*
Perfidious = *unfaithful; treacherous*	Faithful = *loyal*
Perfunctory = *(work) done in trivial manner*	Meticulous = *careful about perfection in work*
Perpetual = *lasting forever*	Transitory, Temporary = *lasting for a short period*
Persuade = *make one agree to do something as desired; prevail upon*	Dissuade = *discourage*
Pertinent = *relevant to the subject*	Impertinent = *irrelevant*
Petty = *lacking importance*	Important
Phantom = *ghost, unreal in existence*	Real
Placid = *undisturbed*	Agitated, Ebulient
Plebeian = *undisturbed strata*	Elite = *people of the highest strata society*
Plentiful	Meagre
Plausible = *seemingly credible*	Dubious = *doubtful*
Polite = *humble*	Rude, Insolent, Impertinent
Polemic	Irenic
Politic = *prudent, expedient sagacious*	Impolitic = *inexpedient, imprudent*
Posterior	Anterior

Posterity = *succeeding generation*	: Ancestry = *prceding generation*
Postpone = *defer to a later time*	: Prepone = *advance to earlier time period*
Potent	: Impotent
Pour = *to make liquid flow down in stream*	: Trickle = *to flow down (liquid) in drops*
Pragmatic = *based on practicality*	: Dogmatic = *based on rules/ principles; disapproving*
Praise	: Criticize
Predator = *an animal which preys on another*	: Prey = *an animal which is killed by another animal for food*
Predecessor = *one who has preceded instituter by someone*	: Successor = *one who other in office/ another*
Premiere	: Finale
Premium = *price to be paid over and above the normal price*	: Discount = *deduction in price to be paid by a customer*
Prescribe = *recommend*	: Proscribe = *prohibit as outlaw*
Preserve = *to save stock*	: Squander = *waste away*
Prey	: Predator
Privilege = *special advantage*	: Disadvantage = *lacking advantage*
Proactive = *act forward*	: Retroactive = *act later in response*
Probity = *upright honesty*	: Improbity = *dishonesty*
Proud	: Ashamed
Profane = *irreverent*	: Sacred, Holy = *reverent*
Profound = *having depth*	: Superficial, Shallow = *of no depth*
Profuse = *pouring abundantly*	: Scanty
Progenitor = *who gives birth*	: Progeny = *who is produced/born*
Progress = *move ahead*	: Regress = *go back to early state*
Prolix = *lengthy in duration of speech*	: Succinct
Prolong	: Curtail
Promiscuous = *unselective*	: Selective, Discriminating
Promulgate = *to bring into effect*	: Abrogate = *repeal, revoke*
Propriety = *state of being proper/ appropriate*	: Impropriety
Propitiate, Appease = *to make pleased*	: Antagonize = *to displease*

Prospective = *effective from a future date*	: Retrospective = *effective from back date*
Prostrate	: Erect, Upright
Protract = *lengthen in duration*	: Curtail
Protector = *one who protects*	: Protege = *one who is protected*
Protrude = *to enter forward*	: Intrude = *to enter inside*
Proud	: Humble
Provide = *to give, supply*	: Deprive = *to take away from possessing, deny possession*
Provident = *careful for providing future needs*	: Improvident
Provoke = *instigate*	: Pacify = *calm down*
Provincial	: Cosmopolitan
Pursue = *chase to catch*	: Evade = *to avoid from being caught*
Prudent = *wise to be practical in approach*	: Imprudent, Unwise
Pungent = *sharp in smell or taste*	: Bland = *lacking taste*
Pull = *drag towards oneself*	: Push = *drag away from oneself*
Punctilious = *meticulous*	: Flippant
Pusillanimous = *faint-hearted, fearful*	: Intrepid, Brave = *who is not lacking courage*

Words beginning with — Q —

Quaint = *pleasantly unusual due to being old fashioned*	: Modern; *one who keep in rogue*
Qualified = *restrict with a condition*	: Unqualified, Absolute = *unconditional*
Quash = *to declare illegal or invalid*	: Uphold = *to declare valid*
Quell = *to suppress*	: Fan, Provoke = *to instigate*
Querulous = *complaining*	: Genial = *cordial in nature*
Quiet = *silent*	: Clamorous, Clamant = *shouting*
Quixotic = *impractical*	: Practical

Words beginning with — R —

Radical = *having roots*	: Superficial = *being on surface*
Rapacious = *greedy*	Generous = *not greedy*
Rarely	: Frequently

Rash	: Discreet, Cautious
Rear	: Front
Rearguard = *guard standing in the back*	: Vanguard = *guard standing in front*
Receive = *take what is given*	: Deliver = *to give something to someone*
Reciprocal = *mutual in exchanging; give something in return*	: Unilateral = *one-sided*
Recluse = *one who lives in solitude*	: Gregarious = *living in group/flock*
Rectitude = *moral uprightness*	: Turpitude = *morally depraved*
Reduce	: Magnify
Refrain = *abstain from doing something*	: Indulge = *involve in doing something*
Refined	: Crude
Regressive = *going back in reducing or to the statue quo ante*	: Progressive = *going forward in quantity increasing quantity or improving condition*
Regret = *feel sorrow*	: Rejoice = *feel joy*
Relenting	: Adamant
Recluse = *secluded*	: Gregarious = *fond of the company of others*
Regular = *bound by religious rules*	: Secular = *not following religious rules*
Rejoice = *take delight*	: Grieve, Lament, Mourn = *to express sorrow*
Religious	: Profane
Relinquish = *to give up*	: Retain = *to hold in possession*
Reluctant = *unwilling*	: Enthusiastic = *filled with zeal*
Replenish	: Exhaust
Replete = *fill up with*	: Deplete = *diminish/reduce e.g. stock*
Resilient = *flexible; elastic*	: Rigid = *stiff; unfeasible*
Resist = *oppose pressure*	: Yield = *surrender to pressure*
Repulsion = *driving away*	: Attraction = *drawing to wards*
Rescind = *repeal a law in force*	: Promulgate = *proclaim*
Resolute = *firm in opinion*	: Wavering = *fluctuating in opinion; vacillating*
Restrain = *mandating not to do things*	: Constrain = *compelled by certain circumstances*

Retain = *hold back* : Relinquish = abandon; give up cease to hold an office

Retard = *to slow down* : Hasten

Reticent = *keeping oneself silent* : Loquacious, Talkative

Retract = *to draw back* : Stretch = *to draw out*

Retreat = *move back* : Advance = *move ahead*

Retroactive = *acting fact ward* : Proactive = *acting forward*

Retrospective = *taking backward effect* : Prospective = *effective from a future date*

Retrogress = *move back to inferior condition* : Progress = *move forward to better condition*

Reveal = *to remove veil from; disclose* : Conceal = *to hide (e.g a secret)*

Revoke = *to cancel, nullify* : Invoke, Promulagate

Revulsion = *repugnance* : Fascination = *attraction*

Righteous = *just; upright* : Iniquitous = *unjust*

Rigid = *stiff; inflexible* : Resilient, Flexible

Rude = *impertinent* : Polite = *city life*

Ruffle = *to disturb smoothness* : Spruce, Preen = *to set in smooth manner*

Rural = *of village life; rustic* : Urban = *of town life; city life*

Rustic = *uncouth in manner* : Urbane, Sophisticated

Remote, Distant : Imminent

Remote = *far away situated* : Vicinal = *nearby; in close proximity*

Words beginning with —— S ——

Sad = *regretful* : *Mirthful, Cheerful*

Sacred = *pure* : Profane = *desecrate*

Sadist = *sexual perversion with passion* : Masochist = *sexual perversion with pleasure in being dominated or treated cruelly by the other sex*

Sagacious = *practically wise* : Impractical/unwise = *foolish in being practical as per situation*

Salient = *raised up so to be above* : Inconspicuous = *not visible else*

Salutary = *giving healthy effect* : Deleterious = *giving harmful effect*

Salvation = *saving of man from the penalty* : Perdition = *utter loss of power and happiness*

Sane = *of sound mind* : Insane = *of unsound mind*

Sanguine = *cheerful; hopeful* : Funereal = *mournful*

Scarcity : Abundance, Glut; over supply

Scanty : Profuse

Scatter = *spread* : Glean, Gather

Sceptic, Skeptic : Credulous

Scion : Doyen

Scrupulous = *careful about right or wrong in action* : Unscrupulous, Trifling = *not careful about right or wrong*

Scurrilous = *insultingly bad* : Decent = *nice*

Secluded = *removed apart from others* : Incorporated

Secular : Regular

Sediment = *matter settled on the bottom of liquid* : Scum = *matter forming layer on liquid surface*

Segregate = *separate from flock* : Congregate

Seize = *catch hold of* : Release = *set free*

Selfish : Unselfish, Altruist

Severe = *harsh* : Mild = *not harsh, gentle*

Shallow = *without depth* : Deep, Profound

Sham = *spurious* : Genuine = authentic

Sharp = pointed : Blunt = *not sharp*

Shove = *move something by pushing* : Tow = *drag (vehicle) by tying to a rope from backside*

Shrink = *make smaller in size* : Stretch = *make large in size; enlarge; expand*

Simplicity : Complexity

Sinistral = *on the left side, left-handed* : Dextral = *right-handed*

Skilful = *showing skill* : Clumsy = *not skilful*

Skirt = *move around a problem, avoiding it* : Confront = *to meet a problem headlong*

Skirmish = *scuffle, minor fight* •: Armaggedon = *score of the final struggle between the powers of good and evil; a great war or battle of nations*

Slender = *thin* : Plump = *rounded in shape*

Sling = *hang loosely by a strip*	: Cling = *hang tightly adhered to something*
Slipshod = *careless manner*	: Fastidious
Sloven = *one who is habitually untidy in appearance*	: Dandy = *one who is habitually careful about tidy appearance*
Sluggish = *slow in action*	: Active = *fast in action*
Slut = *habitually untidy woman,*	: *fashionable woman slattern*
Soar = *rise up vertically upward in speed*	: Swoop = *come down in speed*
Solemn	: Frivolous
Somber = *dull in colour*	: Bright, Mirthful
Soothe = *give comfort*	: Upset = *disturb*
Sororate = *marriage with wife's sister*	: Levirate = *marriage with husband's brother an ancient custom, in conformity with the Biblical times required in warranting circumstances*
Sorority = *sisterhood*	: Fraternity = *brotherhood*
Spartan = *living a life devoid of luxury*	: Voluptuary = *living a life full of luxury*
Spendthrift = *extravagant person*	: Thrift = *frugal person*
Specific = *of particular kind*	: Generalised = *of general kind*
Spirited = *lively*	: Dispirited, Dejected
Spiritual	: Mundane, Corporeal
Spontaneous = *occurring without pre-meditation*	: Pre-meditated = *happening with much deliberation beforehand*
Sporadic = *occurring at irregular intervals*	: Frequent = *occurring at regular intervals*
Spruced = *well groomed; fastidious*	: Dishevelled, Ruffled; keeping loose hair
Spurious = *counterfeit*	: Authentic = *genuine*
Sincere	: Affected, Pretended
Squander	: Conserve
Static = *in stationary state*	: Dynamic = *in moving state*
Stationary	: Moving
Steady = *in stable state*	: Unsteady = *in unstable state*
Stiff = *rigid*	: Lithe, Supple = *flexible*

Stingy, Niggard = *miser*	: Generous = *liberal in spending*
Stoic = *unmoved even in adverse circumstances*	: Capricious = *changing mood without any plausible reason*
Straight = *not bent*	: Crooked = *bent*
Strange = *unfamiliar*	: Familiar
Stretch = *extend outward*	: Retract = *to draw back*
Strict	: Lenient
Stringent = *strict; harsh*	: Mild, Liberal
Stubborn = *haughty*	: Tractable = *controllable*
Stupendous = *causing amazement,*	: Un-impressive *stounding*
Subdued = *suppressed*	: Exuberant = *effusive; luxuriant; over flowing*
Subjection	: Freedom
Subjective = *subject to personal opinion*	: Objective = *not subject to personal opinion, based on objectivity*
Subjugate = *enslave*	: En-franchise
Subvert, Undermine = *damage*	: Fortify = *to make strong*
Susceptible (to)	: Immune (from)
Superior	: Inferior
Sublime	: Ludicrous
Submerge	: Emerge
Supple	: Stiff
Successor	: Predecessor
Succinct = *concise*	: Loquacious, Prolix = *in detail; elaborate*
Surrender, appear	: Abscond = *flee away*
Swoop = *sudden onslaught to come down with a sweeping rush*	: Soar = *to rise to a great height*
Succumb = *to get defeated to pressure, injury or disease*	: Survive = *to remain alive after an accident, or after someone else's death*
Symphony = *melodious sound*	: Cacophony = *noisy sound*
Sufficient = *adequate*	: Deficient = *shortfall*
Sullen = *sulky*	: Cheerful = *joyous*
Superior = *higher in status*	: Inferior = *lower in status*
Superficial = *occurring on the Periphery only*	: Deep, Radical, Profound

Supple = *flexible*	: Rigid = *stiff*
Surfeit = *excessive in amount*	: Deficient = *lacking in amount*
Surplus	: Deficit
Survive = *outlive someone*	: Succumb = *to yield to something and die*

***Words beginning with* —— T ——**

Tawdry = *cheap in quality; showy without taste or worth*	: Elegant = *refined or luxurious*
Terminate = *end a process*	: Originate = *start a process*
Terrestrial = *living on earth*	: Celestial = *belonging to heaven*
Terrible = *frightening*	: Delightful = *joyful*
Testate = *having made a will to property*	: Intestate = *having not made a demise will (before death)*
Timid, Timorous	: Courageous, Bold
Thaw = *to melt by warmth*	: Congeal = *to frost by cold to semisolid state*
Thrifty	: Extravagant, Spendthrift
Thrive = *grow vigorously*	: Languish = *lie in bad condition*
Traduce = *ridicule*	: Praise
Traitor	: Patriot
Transient = *of short duration*	: Perpetual = *incessant; permanent*
Transparent	: Opaque
Trice	: Aeons
Trickle	: Pour
Trifling, Flippant	: Scrupulous, Punctilious
Trite	: Novel
Triumph = *victory*	: Defeat
Trivial = *having no importance*	: Serious
Trough	: Crest
Trust	: Distrust
Turmoil	: Tranquil
Turpitude	: Rectitude
Tyron = *novice*	: Celebrity
Tiny	: Gigantic

Words beginning with — U

Ultra = *extreme*	: Infra = *below*
Un-animous	: Factious
Un-animity	: Controversy
Uncouth	: Couth
Underestimate	: Exaggerate
Undermine	: Fortify
Unfurl (a flag)	: Furl
Unhygienic	: Hygienic
Unilateral	: Reciprocal
Unkempt	: Kempt
Unwavering	: Resolute
Upright	: Erect, Prostrate
Usurp	: Delegate
Utility	: Futility

Words beginning with — V

Vacant = *empty*	: Occupied = *filled; captured; held*
Vacate = *to make or leave empty*	: Occupy = *to held; to fill*
Vague = *indefinite; unclear*	: Obvious, Clear
Vainglory = *too much pride*	: Humility = *Humble*
Valedictory = *on the occasion of closing ceremony*	: Inaugural, Salutatory = *on the ocasion of opening ceremony*
Valour = *courage*	: Cowardice = *lacking courage*
Vanguard	: Rearguard
Variable = *changing*	: Fixed, Constant
Veil = *cover to hide*	: Unveil = *uncover to expose*
Venial = *pardonable*	: Heinous = *wicked in a high degree*
Veracious = *truthful*	: Mendacious = *untruthful, lying*
Vertical = *standing upward*	: Horizontal
Veteran = *person of long experience*	: Tyro = *novice*
Viable = *capable of succeeding*	: Unviable = *incapable of being successful*
Vigilant = *careful*	: Careless
Vigorous = *full of strength*	: Dull = *lacking viguor*
Vice = *bad habit*	: Virtue = *good habit*
Vincible	: Invincible

Vindictive = *revengeful*	: Forgiving = *being able to forgive*
Virgin = *being near in close proximity with*	: Remote = *being distant*
Virgin = *not defiled*	: Defiled = *polluted; corrupted*
Virile = *of manly characteristics*	: Effeminate = *having unmanly characteristics*
Virtue = *moral excellence*	: Vice = *moral depravity*
Virtuous = *having good quality*	: Vicious = *having bad quality*
Vis-á-vis = *face to face*	: Dos-á-dos = *back-to-back*
Vivacious = Cheerful	: Cadaverous = *looking like corpse*
Vociferous = *shouting; noisy*	: Mute = *silent*
Voluble = *speaking much*	: Taciturn = silent
Voluntary = *on one's own will volition*	: Compulsory, Involuntary
Voluptuary = *sensual*	: Spartan = *rigorous; frugal*
Vulgar = *indecent*	: Refined = *sophisticated*
Vulnerable = *exposed to harm*	: Protected = *safe from harm*

Words beginning with —— W ——

Wallow = *to lie in a comfortable place and enjoy it*	: Welter = *to lie writhing in trouble/ suffering*
Wane = *gradually decrease in size*	: Wax = *gradually increase in the size of moon*
Wanton = *unrestrained in something bad*	: Restrained
Warm	: Cool
Wary (of) = *alert as to avoid danger*	: Unwary = *not watchful against danger*
Wavering = *vacillating, changing mind*	: Resolute = *firm in opinion/ decision*
Weal = *well-being*	: Woe = *distress*
Weary = *tired*	: Energetic = *full of energy*
Wild = *untamed*	: Tame
Wily = *cunning*	: Ingenuous, Straightforward = *artless, not crafty*
Wont = *accustomed (to)*	: Unaccustomed *(to)*

Words beginning with —— Z ——

Zenith = *the highest point of career, path*	: Nadir = *the lowest point*

❑❑❑

MULTIPLE CHOICE QUESTION ANSWERS

Choose the opposite words (out of the options given hereunder) for:

1. Abet
   (A) Reduce (B) Deter (C) Alleviate (D) Abscond
2. Abstemious
   (A) Absentism (B) Absolute (C) Gluttonous (D) Absurd
3. Acerbic
   (A) Bitter (B) Sweet (C) Melliferous (D) Cruel
4. Absolve
   (A) Disperse (B) Dissolve (C) Distribute (D) Incriminate
5. Zenith
   (A) Nadir (B) Abysmal (C) Wonder (D) Scintillating
6. Vice
   (A) Deputy (B) Virtue (C) Vicious (D) Crook
7. Valedictory
   (A) Valuable (B) Virtuous (C) Inaugural (D) Departing
8. Wane
   (A) Wax (B) Alleviate (C) Abate (D) Welter
9. Abject
   (A) Humiliating (B) Despicable (C) Honourable (D) Wax
10. Acclaim
    (A) Claim (B) Assert (C) Denounce (D) Curse
11. Arrogant
    (A) Mild (B) Absolute (C) Modest (D) Curse
12. Ameliorate
    (A) Better (B) Worse (C) Sweeten (D) Exacerbate
13. Analogy
    (A) Similarity (B) Difference (C) Anomaly (D) Absurdity
14. Arrogate
    (A) Arrogant (B) Credit (C) Usurp (D) Appreciate
15. Ascetic
    (A) Miser (B) Thrifty (C) Spendthrift (D) Epicure
16. Bequeath
    (A) Donate (B) Demise (C) Inherit (D) Bestow
17. Bete noire
    (A) Beloved (B) Likable (C) Hated (D) Cynosure

18. Classic
    (A) Kitsch (B) Novel (C) Superb (D) Classified
19. Curious
    (A) Agog (B) Anxious (C) Indifferent (D) Inquisitive
20. Elite
    (A) Plebeian (B) Shining (C) Aristocrat (D) Lighted
21. Affluent
    (A) Flowing (B) Static (C) Indigent (D) Prosperous
22. Effluent
    (A) Indigent (B) Clotted (C) Influent (D) Stagnant
23. Eloquent
    (A) Loquacious (B) Fluent (C) Dumb (D) Taciturn
24. Emerse
    (A) Dip (B) Inundate (C) Immerse (D) Merge
25. Profound
    (A) Deep (B) Superb (C) Shallow (D) Sallow
26. Provide
    (A) Supply (B) Give (C) Arrange (D) Deprive
27. Resilient
    (A) Elastic (B) Flexible (C) Rigid (D) Arrogant
28. Segregate
    (A) Separate (B) Congregate (C) Gregarious (D) Grave
29. Sadism
    (A) Masochism (B) Sad (C) Sorrow (D) Cruelty
30. Symphony
    (A) Harmony (B) Melody (C) Cacophony (D) Strident
31. Weal
    (A) Woe (B) Sympathy (C) Welfare (D) Wilful
32. Provoke
    (A) Irritate (B) Stimulate (C) Pacify (D) Punish
33. Adamant
    (A) Arrogant (B) Relenting (C) Sympathetic (D) Vicious
34. Albino
    (A) Brunette (B) White (C) Black (D) Dark
35. Cleanse
    (A) Emunge (B) Scour (C) Wash (D) Defile
36. Mundane
    (A) Bland (B) Bald (C) Spiritual (D) Worldly

37. Novel
(A) Story (B) New (C) Trite (D) Novice

38. Dandy
(A) Sloven (B) Slattern (C) Slut (D) Dirty

39. Biased
(A) Disinterested (B) Prejudiced (C) Belligerent (D) Bullied

40. Catholic
(A) Christian (B) European (C) Parochial (D) Pantheism

41. Agoraphobia
(A) Fear of darkness (B) Fear of daylight
(C) Xenophobia (D) Claustrophobia

42. Myopia
(A) Blindness (B) Clairvoyance (C) Meteropia (D) Alopecia

43. Outstanding
(A) Egregious (B) Blatant (C) Flagrant (D) Commonplace

44. Garner
(A) Collect (B) Scatter (C) Disseminate (D) Gather

45. Squander
(A) Waste (B) Spend (C) Conserve (D) Throw

46. Soar
(A) Levitate (B) Ascend (C) Swoop (D) Descend

47. Generous
(A) Kind (B) Stingy (C) Generating (D) Gracious

48. Ruffle
(A) Spouce (B) Uncomb (C) Wet (D) Wilt

49. Perennial
(A) Annual (B) Daily (C) Deciduous (D) Monthly

50. Transient
(A) Temporary (B) Transitory (C) Perpetual (D) Evanescent

51. Benevolent
(A) Banal (B) Benign (C) Malevolent (D) Tyrant

52. Dissemble
(A) Pretend (B) Hide (C) Betray (D) Disclose

53. Intrepid
(A) Pusillanimous (B) Brave (C) Adventurous (D) Courageous

54. Auspicious
(A) Gracious (B) Merciful (C) Ominous (D) Kind

55. Blaspheme
(A) Blast (B) Reputable (C) Insulting (D) Revere

56. Cadaverous
(A) Vivacious (B) Corpulent (C) Deadly (D) Lifeless

57. Deliberate
(A) Intentional (B) Knowingly (C) Pre-meditated (D) Inadvertent

58. Dilettante
(A) Novice (B) Connoisseur (C) Cad (D) Novice

59. Scion
(A) Shoot (B) Young (C) Offspring (D) Doyen

60. Corpulent
(A) Fatty (B) Rotund (C) Emaciated (D) Cadaverous

61. Hubris
(A) Fatty (B) Rotund (C) Emaciated (D) Cadaverous

62. Inept
(A) Expert (B) Foolish (C) Skilled (D) Deft

63. Eirenic
(A) Ironic (B) Polemic (C) Syncretic (D) Peaceful

64. Judicious
(A) Honest (B) Mediator (C) Judging (D) Iniquitous

65. Latent
(A) Dormant (B) Hibernating (C) Patent (D) Hidden

66. Parsimonious
(A) Lavish (B) Poor (C) Miserly (D) Cautious

67. Laud
(A) Hail (B) Applaud (C) Shout (D) Decry

68. Exacerbate
(A) Acerbate (B) Meliorate (C) Annoy (D) Offend

69. Misogynist
(A) Philanthrope (B) Philander (C) Philogynist (D) Cynic

70. Nocturnal
(A) Diurnal (B) Naughty (C) Dreadful (D) Daily

71. Protege
(A) Supporter (B) Disciple (C) Subordinate (D) Protector

72. Succumb
(A) Surrender (B) Yield (C) Survive (D) Resist

73. Slipshod
(A) Fastidious (B) Haphazard (C) Loose (D) Dirty

74. Promulgate
(A) Pronounce (B) Declare (C) Abrogate (D) Defy

75. Monopoly
(A) Control (B) Superiority (C) Monopsony (D) Monarchy

ANSWERS

1. (B)	**2.** (C)	**3.** (C)	**4.** (D)	**5.** (A)	**6.** (B)	**7.** (C)	8. (A)
9. (C)	**10.** (C)	**11.** (C)	**12.** (D)	**13.** (C)	**14.** (B)	15. (D)	**16.** (C)
17. (D)	**18.** (A)	**19.** (C)	**20.** (A)	**21.** (C)	22. (C)	**23.** (D)	**24.** (C)
25. (C)	**26.** (D)	**27.** (C)	**28.** (B)	29. (A)	**30.** (C)	**31.** (A)	**32.** (C)
33. (B)	**34.** (A)	**35.** (D)	36. (C)	**37.** (C)	**38.** (A)	**39.** (A)	**40.** (C)
41. (D)	**42.** (B)	43. (D)	**44.** (C)	**45.** (C)	**46.** (C)	**47.** (B)	**48.** (A)
49. (C)	50. (C)	**51.** (C)	**52.** (C)	**53.** (A)	**54.** (C)	**55.** (D)	**56.** (A)
57. (D)	**58.** (B)	**59.** (D)	**60.** (C)	**61.** (A)	**62.** (D)	**63.** (B)	64. (D)
65. (C)	**66.** (A)	**67.** (D)	**68.** (B)	**69.** (C)	**70.** (A)	71. (D)	**72.** (C)
73. (A)	**74.** (C)	**75.** (C)					

EXPLANATIONS

1. Abet = help someone to commit crime
   Deter = discourage someone from doing something by threatening reprisal; so, Help is opposite of Discourage
2. Abstemious = not indulging in over-eating
   Gluttonous = devouring everything in excessive amount
3. Acerbic = bitter
   Melliferous = carrying honey, sweet
4. Absolve = set free from charges
   Incriminate = set charges against someone
5. Zenith = highest point in sky above our head
   Nadir = lowest point
6. Vice = evil habits
   Virtue = righteous conduct
7. Valedictory = related to saying goodbye
   Inaugural = making the beginning of an event
8. Wax = gradual increase in size of moon every night
   Wane = gradual decrease in size
9. Abject = utterly humiliating
   Honourable = causing honour
10. Acclaim = praise openly
    Denounce = condemn publicly
11. Arrogant = one who makes unwarranted claims, superiority
    Modest = one showing humble estimation of oneself
12. Ameliorate = make the condition better
    Exacerbate = make the condition bitter, *i.e.,* worse

13. Analogy = comparison of similar features of two things
    Anomaly = deviation from usual feature
14. Arrogate = usurp credit which belongs to someone else
    Credit = recognize credit of someone
15. Ascetic = person who practises self-denial to pleasures of life
    Epicure = person who believes in enjoying pleasurable things in life
16. Bequeath = to hand down property to someone by an act of will
    Inherit = to get property of one's ancestor as a right to heir
17. Bete noir = an object of intense hate
    Cynosure = an object of utmost attraction
18. Classic = (something, especially art, literature) of highest class
    Kitsch = (art, literature) having little value
19. Curious = be eager to know about something
    Indifferent = have to interest about something
20. Elite = people belonging to highest class of society
    Plebeian = people belonging to comon class of society
21. Affluent = prosperous, wealthy person
    Indigent = poor person
22. Effluent = (water, etc.) flowing out (prefix Ex to fluent)
    Influent = flowing in a place
23. Eloquent = speaking out fluently and forcefully
    viz. He gave an eloquent speech
    Taciturn = reserve in speech
24. Emerse = to come out (Ex + merge)
    Immerse = to go in (In + merge)
25. Profound=ofgreatdepth;*viz.* Hehasaprofoundknowledge;aprofoundgrief
    Shallow = of little depth
26. Provide = make available to someone
    Deprive = deny the privilege of having something
27. Resilient = returning to earlier position, flexible
    Rigid = refusing to shift, bend
28. Segregate = separate things into groups, separate something from others of a group
    Congregate = to come together, assemble
29. Sadism = enjoy one's act of cruelty on others
    Masochism = enjoy sufferings inflicted on oneself by others
30. Symphony = harmonious combination of different sounds
    Cacophony = harsh discordant combination

31. Weal = well-being, prosperity, and happiness *viz.* A work for people's weal
    Woe = distress, trouble; Indescribable woe
32. Provoke = incite
    Pacify = to make calm
33. Adamant = refusing to yield
    Relenting = soften one's temper
34. Albino = a person whose skin lacks in melanin, causing white skin, hairs, eyebrows, etc.
    Brunette = person with dark hairs, eyes and skin
35. Cleanse = to clean for religious, spiritual purpose; cleanse one's soul of sins
    Defile = to make a sacred place dirty
36. Mundane = belonging to worldly things
    Spiritual = belonging to soul, not physical or worldly things
37. Novel = having newness
    Trite = boring due to being repeated many times
38. Dandy = a person who is very careful about his physical appearance, neat dress, caressed hairs etc
    Sloven = a person who is habitually negligent of his appearance, dress, cleanliness
39. Biased = prejudiced
    Disinterested = unbiased due to having no personal interest
40. Catholic = wideness of one's attitude
    Parochial = narrow in attitude
41. Agoraphobia = morbid dread of open space, marketplace
    Claustrophobia = morbid dread of closed, congested place
42. Myopia = lacking the power to see in distant future, lacking foresight
    Clairvoyance = having super-power to see in distance
43. Outstanding = standing above others in good quality
    Commonplace = having nothing special to mention
44. Garner = to pick up grains and collect
    Disseminate = scatter
45. Squander = spend extravagantly
    Conserve = to save by spending judiciously
46. Soar = rise up straight in sky at great speed
    Swoop = to come down at great speed to attack on prey
47. Generous = giving out something with open hand
    Stingy = reluctant to give or spend, niggardly

48. Ruffle = disturb smoothness, neatness
Spruce/Preen = arrange neatly
49. Perennial = (plants) covered with green leaves throughout the year (per + ennial)
Deciduous = (plants) shedding leaves in a season every year, so as to take on new leaves afresh
50. Transient = staying for short duration
Perpetual = continuing forever
51. Benevolent = bene + volent = wishing well of others
Malevolent = male + volent = wishing evil of others
52. Dissemble = to hide inner emotion, attitude
Betray = to reveal inner emotion, attitude inadvertently through external facial or behavioural expression
53. Intrepid = one who is fearless (In + trepid)
Pusillanimous = one who is faint hearted (pisillus = petty +anium = spirited)
54. Auspicious = favourable due to propitious luck
Ominous = inauspicious
55. Blaspheme = speak irreverentially against
Revere = show respect
56. Cadaverous = like a corpse, looking pale and lifeless
Vivacious = full of life and zeal
57. Deliberate = carefully thought about, intentional
Inadvertent = unintentional
58. Dilettante = a person who enjoys art, music for having interest in it
Connoisseur = a person who is conversant with intricate knowledge of art, music and so he enjoys it
59. Scion = young shoot of a tree, young person of a well-known family or group
Doyen = senior person of family or group
60. Corpulent = of bulky body
Emaciated = of lean and thin body
61. Hubris = full of arrogant pride
Humility = full of humbleness
62. Inept = without aptitude for a particular task, lacking skill
Deft = skillful
63. Eirenic or Irenic = (activity) promoting peace and harmony
Polemic = promoting controversy
64. Judicious = doing justice
Iniquitous = characterised by gross injustice

65. Latent = hidden from sight
    Patent = openly visible
66. Parsimonious = stingy, showing miserliness
    Lavish = spending or living luxuriously
67. Laud = praise someone for doing good
    Decry = to speak disparagingly, denounce
68. Exacerbate = make condition worse
    Meliorate = Ameliorate
69. Misogynist = Miso = hate, gyny = female
    Philoginist = Philo = like, gyny = female
70. Nocturnal = (activity) done during night
    Diurnal = done during day time
71. Protege = a person who is under protection of someone powerful
    Protector = a person who protects
72. Succumb = to yield to disease, injury, etc., *i.e.,* to die
    Survive = remain alive after an accident, injury
73. Slipshod = untidy, sloppy
    Fastidious = critical to untidiness, sloppiness
74. Promulgate = put a law into operation
    Abrogate = to repeal a law
75. Monopoly = control of seller on market
    Monopsony = control of buyer on market

+++

Exercises On

ANTONYMS

TEST 1

Choose the most appropriate antonym out of the given options for the word (in bold) in the sentences:

1. He is **crazy** about cricket game.
   (A) mad (B) cool (C) sane (D) shaky
2. He is temperamentally a **cedulous** person.
   (A) suspicious (B) creditable (C) unsuspecting (D) crude
3. It is a very **critical** moment in his life.
   (A) hazardous (B) crucial (C) precarious (D) unimportant
4. He was censured for his **culpable** act.
   (A) criminal (B) heinous (C) blameworthy (D) praiseworthy
5. He is trying to **cultivate** friendship with me.
   (A) till (B) grow (C) neglect (D) improve
6. He is crazy about **accumulating** wealth.
   (A) amassing (B) gathering (C) filling (D) squandering
7. Police used force to **curb** violence.
   (A) quell (B) check (C) block (D) encourage
8. He is very **curious** about his neighbours.
   (A) desirous (B) inquisitive (C) indifferent (D) excited
9. **Current** practice of endogamous marriages is crumbling now.
   (A) prevalent (B) running (C) obsolete (D) modern
10. He gave a very **curt** reply to my query.
    (A) rude (B) brief (C) abrupt (D) polished
11. He followed **customary** practice of visiting neighbours occasionally.
    (A) habitual (B) conventional (C) uncommon (D) regular
12. He is **cynical** about his colleague's motives.
    (A) insane (B) contemptuous (C) distrustful (D) trusting
13. He deliberately **dallies** with his duties.
    (A) procrastinates (B) fondles (C) hastens (D) loiters
14. There is a **dearth** of doctors in hospitals.
    (A) famine (B) abundance (C) plethora (D) scarcity
15. Health gradually **decays** in old age.
    (A) rots (B) degenerates (C) decomposes (D) flourishes

16. She has acquired reputation for **deceit**.
(A) deception (B) fraud (C) honesty (D) distortion

17. **Deciduous** trees take on new leaves annually.
(A) permanent (B) shedding (C) evergreen (D) eternal

18. He is a man of **decisive** actions.
(A) determining (B) determined
(C) conclusive (D) prevaricating

19. He **affirmed** his intention to resign his job.
(A) offended (B) averred (C) denied (D) assented

20. A **decrepit** old man could hardly walk.
(A) weak (B) infirm (C) emaciated (D) vigorous

21. **Dedicated** workers are assets of a company.
(A) devoted (B) sacrificing (C) dallying (D) triffling

22. He is a scholar of **deep** knowledge.
(A) profound (B) abysmal (C) shallow (D) drowning

23. **Defective** machine hampered the progress of work.
(A) imperfect (B) faulty (C) flawless (D) abnormal

24. The meeting was **deferred** due to lack of quorum.
(A) postponed (B) put off (C) held on schedule (D) yielded

25. He was in **defiant** mood.
(A) defeating (B) obedient (C) rebellious (D) decorous

26. **Deficit** in money withheld the work on the project.
(A) flaw (B) shortage (C) want (D) surplus

27. The **defiled** house was stinking.
(A) impure (B) sullied (C) impure (D) immaculate

28. He felt **degraded** with their remark.
(A) disgraced (B) deprived (C) reduced (D) exalted

29. The defeated team members wore a **dejected** expression.
(A) rejected (B) sad (C) despirited (D) elated

30. The guests were treated with **delectable** dinner.
(A) delightful (B) tasteful (C) charming (D) disagreeable

31. Factory chimney spewed **delectable** dinner.
(A) lamless (B) pernicious (C) stinking (D) unpleasant

32. It was a **deliberate** action.
(A) careful (B) intentional (C) premeditated (D) impulsive

33. He has a **delicate** sense of smell.
(A) crude (B) exquisite (C) fragile (D) delightful

34. She takes great **delight** in teasing me.
(A) charm (B) joy (C) satisfaction (D) distress

35. Oh! God, **deliver** me from these boring people.
(A) throw (B) liberate (C) enthrall (D) save

36. He **demurred** to accept the post offered to him.
(A) wavered (B) hesitated (C) refused (D) agreed

37. The **demure** girl sat aloof.
(A) sober (B) hesitant (C) indecorous (D) arrogant

38. People **denounce** politicians as morally corrupt.
(A) declare (B) announce (C) condemn (D) commend

39. He **denied** me what was my due.
(A) refuse (B) withheld (C) allowed (D) repudiated

40. We all should **deplore** the present state of morality.
(A) bemoan (B) denounce (C) rejoice (D) applaud

41. One earnestly **desires** to join family get-together in festivals.
(A) yearns (B) craves (C) solicits (D) loathes

42. Polar regions are **desolate** place.
(A) sad (B) uninhabited (C) populous (D) barren

43. Rescuers made a final **desperate** attempt to save the child.
(A) reckless (B) hopeless (C) hopeful (D) intolerable

44. He has become **despondent** about his failing health.
(A) dependent (B) despairing (C) happy (D) encouraged

45. He is now **destitute** of resources due to reckless squandering.
(A) deprived (B) needy (C) impoverished(D) affluent

46. He could not get a job yet, due to his **desultory** attempts.
(A) distressing (B) fitful (C) consistent (D) pertinent

47. He **detected** a thief lurking behind the house in dark.
(A) descried (B) discovered (C) overlooked (D) missed

48. He is a devout Hindu.
(A) sincere (B) holy (C) pious (D) irreverent

49. He is a **dextrous** artist.
(A) deft (B) clever (C) inept (D) right-handed

50. This creeper is **dextrorse**.
(A) right-handed (B) climbing from right to left
(C) climbing straight up (D) sinistrorse right

51. **Diffident** person shirks from taking responsibility.
(A) confused (B) defiant (C) unconfident (D) self-confident

52. Narrow arteries are **dilated** to all blood flow.
(A) expanded (B) expatiated (C) spread (D) constricted

53. The government adopts **dilatory** tactics in taking unpalatable decisions.
(A) procrastinating (B) deferring (C) prompt (D) widening

54. He **discarded** old hat.
(A) rejected (B) cast aside (C) threw (D) retained

55. Hooting by audience **disconcerted** the orator.
(A) ruffled (B) discomfitted (C) calmed (D) confused

56. Bereaved of elder brother, he was **disconsolate**.
(A) unhappy (B) inconsolable (C) soothed (D) sad

57. There is stark **discrepancy** in what you preach and what you practise.
(A) gap (B) contrariness (C) consistency (D) discreetness

58. He brought **disgrace** on his family with his misdeeds.
(A) insult (B) ignominy (C) respect (D) honour

59. His petty quibblings **disgusted** me.
(A) delighted (B) relished (C) offended (D) annoyed

60. A gust of wind **dishevelled** his hairs.
(A) tidied (B) disarrayed (C) hanged (D) loosened

61. Stashed pot of valuables was **disintered** from the courtyard's underground.
(A) burried (B) exhumed (C) dug out (D) extracted

62. He is **disinterested** in their dispute.
(A) impartial (B) un-interested
(C) having selfish motive (D) indifferent

63. He was in **dismal** mood.
(A) sinister (B) melancholic (C) gay (D) annoyed

64. He **dismantled** machine's parts for packing.
(A) broke (B) knocked down (C) separated (D) assembled

65. Deadlock in negotiation **dismayed** both sides.
(A) grieved (B) disheartened (C) encouraged (D) pained

66. Wind **dispersed** the cloud in the sky.
(A) dispelled (B) gathered (C) blew (D) drove away

67. His disposition towards meticulousness in work is appreciable.
(A) liking (B) proclivity (C) unwillingness (D) mentality

68. He **disregarded** my advice.
(A) ignored (B) heeded (C) disrespected (D) mistreated

69. She **dissembled** crookedness with ingenuous pretentions.
(A) betrayed (B) concealed (C) dispersed (D) dismantled

70. I **dissuated** him from leaving the job.
(A) persuaded (B) deterred (C) discouraged (D) dissipated

71. His stomach **distended** with flatulence.
(A) extended (B) protruded (C) bloated (D) shrunk

72. **Distinction** in height helps us identify the twins.
(A) clarity (B) confusion (C) difference (D) resemblance

73. The boy was reading the story of a damsel in **distress**.
(A) agony (B) comfort (C) danger (D) safety

74. **Diurnal** cacophony on city roads subsides in late evening.
(A) daytime (B) nocturnal (C) daily (D) morning

75. Social and cultural **diversity** is the uniqueness of our country.
(A) divergence (B) dis-similarity (C) difference (D) uniformity

76. Compassion is **divine** virtue in a person.
(A) supreme (B) sacred (C) mundane (D) religious

77. **Docile** workers readily follow the instructions.
(A) submissive (B) meek (C) intractable (D) stubborn

78. Pet is a **domesticated** animal.
(A) domestic (B) tamed (C) household (D) wild

79. He is sitting with **dreary** face.
(A) fearful (B) gloomy (C) dreaded (D) cheerful

80. He is a **droll** person.
(A) comically humorous (B) serious (C) boring (D) whimsical

81. He is a person with **dusky** complexion.
(A) shadowy (B) swarthy (C) blond (D) twilight

82. He made an **earnest** appeal to people to help him.
(A) urgent (B) arrogant (C) fervent (D) triffling

83. It is our weakness to run after **earthly pleasures**.
(A) divine (B) mundane (C) ordinary (D) worthless

84. His **egotism** has alienated all his friends.
(A) egoism (B) self-conceit (C) humility (D) selfishness

85. The sun **emerged** from behind the clouds.
(A) came out (B) emanated (C) immerged (D) mixed up

86. Hordes of technocrats **emigrate** to U.S.A. every year.
(A) leave own country to settle in foreign countries
(B) immigrate (C) move (D) flee

87. He soon rose to **eminence** in his field of expertise.
(A) exclusiveness (B) prominence (C) reputation (D) obscurity

88. He is **encumbered** with numerous obligations.
(A) enmeshed (B) burdened (C) hampered (D) disburdened

89. His arrogant behaviour **infuriated** me.
(A) incensed (B) pacified (C) fired (D) provoked

90. Social system has still **enslaved** womenfolk.
(A) bonded (B) imprisoned (C) emancipated (D) suppressed

91. Joys of childhood are **ephemeral**.
(A) temporary (B) permanent
(C) shortlived (D) long lasting

92. **Epicurean** leaders of present time are in sharp contrast to Gandhian leaders.
(A) indulgent in luxury (B) sensuous (C) ascetic (D) licentious

93. I **esteem** him for his honesty.
(A) commend (B) respect (C) disdain (D) support

94. The universe is **eternal**.
(A) unchanging (B) perpetual (C) enduring (D) transitory

95. Triffling with patients' treatment is against the professional **ethics**.
(A) beliefs (B) honesty (C) immorality (D) principles of morality

96. The minister tried to **evade** reporter's questions.
(A) dodge (B) confront (C) escape (D) elude

97. Adversaries always tend to **exaggerate** one's weaknesses.
(A) extenuate (B) magnify (C) overstate (D) extend

98. He was **exalted** to venerable position by the people.
(A) elevated (B) depreciated (C) downgraded (D) praised

99. The boy is endowed with **exceptional** intellect.
(A) special (B) peculiar (C) average (D) outstanding

100. He is reputed to be easily **excitable**.
(A) stimulated (B) placid (C) infuriated (D) provoked

101. The old woman began to **execrate** all those who were teasing her.
(A) denounce (B) imprecate (C) damn (D) bless

102. Cool breeze **exhilarated** that morning walkers.
(A) inspired (B) exhorted (C) cheered up (D) depressed

103. Moneylenders charge **exorbitant** interests on loans.
(A) prevailing (B) usurious (C) fair (D) unusual

104. He ordered his staff to **expedite** the work.
(A) hasten (B) move (C) procrastinate (D) ensnare

105. He is an **expert** in this field.
(A) experienced (B) greenhorn
(C) knowledgeable (D) connoisseur

106. He expressed his **explicit** opinion.
(A) open (B) unequivocal (C) confused (D) ambiguous

107. His remark was **extraneous** to the topic at hand.
(A) extrinsic (B) extra (C) intrinsic/pertinent (D) rare

108. He is an **extravagant** person.
(A) expensive (B) spendthrift
(C) immoderate (D) thrifty

109. This is the story of **fabulous** exploits of an adventurer.
(A) marvellous (B) fictitious (C) factual (D) historical

110. The hall is adorned with **factitious** flowers.
(A) fictional (B) artificial (C) real (D) factual

111. Fiction writer needs a **fecund** mind.
(A) prolific (B) fruitful (C) effete (D) lazy

112. He made a **fervent** appeal for support.
(A) feverish (B) fiery (C) burning (D) dispassionate

113. He is a person of extremely **fickle** mind.
(A) capricious (B) stable (C) capacious (D) fictitious

114. The servant's **fidelity** towards his master is perfect.
(A) fealty (B) belief (C) disloyalty (D) confidence

115. He extended a **flimsy** excuse for his failure.
(A) thin (B) shoddy (C) loose (D) convincing

116. He is my bitter **foe**.
(A) adversary (B) feud (C) friend (D) fiend

117. Lack of generosity is his notable **foible**.
(A) failing (B) character (C) forte (D) flaw

118. Speeches shall be **followed** by dinner.
(A) accompanied (B) succeeded (C) preceded (D) ensued

119. He is feeling **forlorn** of own people in this distant city.
(A) sad (B) in company of (C) desolate (D) hopeless

120. The **former** of the two suggestions was acceptable.
(A) prior (B) past (C) latter (D) ancient

121. A **fortuitous** incident changed his life.
(A) fortunate (B) incidental (C) accidental (D) deliberate

122. He is a man of **frail** body constitution.
(A) fragile (B) brittle (C) delicate (D) robust

123. **Fresh** vegetables are available in abundance.
(A) new (B) raw (C) unfaded (D) stale

124. She is worried about her **forward** daughter.
(A) contrary (B) arrogant (C) tractable (D) frowning

125. He is very **frugal** in spending money.
(A) miser (B) prudent (C) penurious (D) lavish

126. He made a **futile** attempt to appease his foe.
(A) vain (B) fruitless (C) effectual (D) frivolous

127. **Gallant** soldier captured enemy post single handed.
(A) galloping (B) chivalrous (C) valorous (D) cowardly

128. Clouds are **gathering** in the sky indicating rainfall.
(A) accumulating (B) collecting (C) dispersing (D) frittering

129. **Gaudy** decoy looks vulgar.
(A) showy (B) garish (C) immodest (D) sober

130. Kids were frolicking in **gay** spirit.
(A) miserable (B) jolly (C) wanton (D) showy

131. **Germane** facts were collected to reach the conclusion.
(A) genuine (B) relevant (C) inept (D) inapt

132. **Giant** stature of a woman makes her unattractive.
(A) great (B) monstrous (C) huge (D) petite

133. His career prospect seems to be **gloomy**.
(A) shady (B) dark (C) bright (D) hopeless

134. He is sitting with **glum** face.
(A) morose (B) dark (C) sorrowful (D) cheerful

135. His social service brought **glory** to her.
(A) wonder (B) fame (C) grace (D) obloquy

136. Human-beings are generally **gregarious** people.
(A) reclusive (B) seclusive (C) social (D) un-social

137. He **grieves** over the loss in business.
(A) laments (B) weeps (C) rejoices (D) desecrate

138. Ordinary people **hallow** saints.
(A) honour (B) venerate (C) consecrate (D) desecrate

139. Bad weather **hampered** progress of the work.
(A) hindered (B) furthered (C) interferred (D) delayed

140. The group, though looked cohesive, lacked **harmony**.
(A) symmetry (B) melody (C) concord (D) discord

141. A **hasty** decision usually makes one repentant.
(A) precipitate (B) testy (C) deliberated (D) quick

142. He never **heeds** sane advice.
(A) listens (B) cares (C) worries (D) ignores

143. He was punished for his **heinous** offence.
(A) sinful (B) feral (C) reprehensible (D) admirable

144. He is **humble**, despite his high rank.
(A) arrogant (B) polite (C) meek (D) submissive

145. He is **ignorant** of what is happening around him.
(A) oblivious (B) unknown (C) aware (D) illiterate

146. He was censured for his **ignoble** conduct.
(A) honourable (B) ignominious (C) inferior (D) infamous

147. Breaking out of war with hostile country is **imminent**.
(A) impending (B) possible (C) remote (D) impossible

148. Innoculation renders a child **immune** to diseases.
(A) impunity (B) exempt (C) resistant (D) susceptible

149. His **impassionate** appeal moved people.
(A) emotional (B) impassive (C) tranquil (D) inflamed

150. An **impecunious** person was unable to procure basic needs.
(A) penniless (B) poor (C) wealthy (D) indigent

151. He was feared due to his **imperious** behaviour.
(A) unnecessary (B) perilous (C) overbearing (D) submissive

152. His **impertinent** behaviour annoyed me.
(A) irrelevant (B) brazen (C) insane (D) polite

153. He is known always to take **impetuous** decisions.
(A) rash (B) emotional (C) careful (D) studied

154. A country is left **impoverished** by war it fights.
(A) reduced to poverty (B) bereft (C) enriched (D) poor

155. The boy got punishment for his **impudent** behaviour.
(A) bold (B) arrogant (C) brazen (D) courteous

156. His habit of lying is **acquired** since childhood.
(A) inherent (B) natural (C) cultivated (D) congenital

157. Dissatisfaction **incites** anger.
(A) stimulates (B) instigates (C) subsides (D) encourage

158. The crowd was **instigated** by inflammatory speech to resort to violence.
(A) provoked (B) exhorted (C) deterred (D) urged

159. The police **inculpated** him with unlawful activity.
(A) exonerated (B) incriminated (C) ensnared (D) indicted

160. He is **indif ferent** towards politics.
(A) attracted (B) unconcerned (C) concerned (D) similar

161. This plant is **indigenous** to India.
(A) autochthonous (B) aboriginal (C) alien (D) natural

162. The **implacable** creditor refused to give more time to return money, despite entreaties.
(A) cruel (B) inexorable (C) merciful (D) flexible

163. He **improvised** his act directly on the stage.
(A) extemporize (B) rehearsed (C) provided (D) prepared

164. Rain water **ingressed** into houses in low-lying areas.
(A) immersed (B) entered (C) egressed (D) progressed

165. People somehow got rid of **iniquitous** despot.
(A) unjust (B) cruel (C) hostile (D) righteous

166. **Inordinate** delay in the train's arrival irked the passengers.
(A) disorderly (B) excessive (C) unreasonable (D) moderate

167. **Inquisitive** mind keeps on asking why.
(A) prying (B) peeking (C) curious (D) uninterested

168. An **intrepid** person does not hesitate to venture.
(A) anxious (B) fearless (C) shaky (D) timid

169. The **irascible** old man was easily provoked to anger.
(A) testy (B) irritating (C) calm (D) rash

170. The spy was in **jeopardy** of being discovered.
(A) danger (B) hazard (C) chance (D) safety

171. He is in **jolly** mood.
(A) sportive (B) jovial (C) melancholy (D) playful

172. She **ravelled** the knot like a Gordian knot.
(A) tangled (B) unravelled (C) revolved (D) complicated

173. They pursued their goal in **lackadaisical** manner.
(A) lacking (B) listless (C) unconcerned (D) lively

174. Spectators **lauded** their home team for winning the game.
(A) extolled (B) celebrated (C) lamented (D) shouted

175. She **lavished** praise on him.
(A) lashed (B) heaped (C) grudged (D) reserved

176. **Lax** laws engenders sense of impunity in offenders.
(A) rigid (B) strict (C) lenient (D) loose

177. He ...... his friend until entire fortune was exhausted.
(A) sucked (B) sponged on (C) treated (D) befooled

178. A **libertine** person is despicable.
(A) free (B) licentious (C) prudish (D) pure

179. It was a **lifeless** performance.
(A) dead (B) animate (C) dull (D) living

180. Gymnast's daily practice keeps his muscles **limber**.
(A) stiff (B) lithe (C) bending (D) loose

181. His body was **limp** with exhaustion.
(A) loose (B) drooping (C) tired (D) erect

182. One can see the bottom of the **limpid** pool.
(A) pellucid (B) lucid (C) calm (D) opaque

183. **Lineage** of a race horse determines its worth.
(A) age (B) pedigree (C) posterity (D) performance

184. In the absence of meaningful engagements, time **lingers**.
(A) fleets (B) lengthens (C) tarries (D) stays

185. An incompetent person becomes **malevolent** towards successful people.
(A) injurious (B) malicious (C) benevolent (D) selfish

186. **Malign** people in high position without substance.
(A) vilify (B) abuse (C) praise (D) despise

187. He is suffering from **malignant** tumour.
(A) malevolent (B) malicious (C) pernicious (D) benignant

188. The holiday was **marred** by bad weather.
(A) damaged (B) impaired (C) spoilt (D) enhanced

189. The lawyer **marshalled** facts before arguing the case in the court.
(A) ordered for (B) arranged in order (C) combined (D) scattered

190. He is a **mendacious** person.
(A) false (B) veracious (C) lying (D) untrue

191. Mostly the non-government organizations, though profess to work for poor people, are **mercenary**.
(A) profit-seeking (B) venal (C) voluntary (D) dishonest

192. He is **meticulous** about his physical appearance.
(A) finical (B) fearful (C) methodical (D) careless

193. A **moderate** change in the existing law is required.
(A) mild (B) excessive (C) radical (D) harsh

194. He leads a **modest** life.
(A) modern (B) moderate (C) pretentious (D) unassuming

195. The need to take tough stand against corruption is a **moot** point.
(A) doubtful (B) debatable (C) indisputable (D) major

196. **Morbid** condition of economy is the cause of concern.
(A) deadly (B) bad (C) sick (D) healthy

197. Rejected by voters in election, many small parties are in **moribund** state.
(A) discarded (B) dying (C) vivacious (D) closure

198. His death was **mourned** by his colleagues.
(A) deplored (B) lamented (C) remembered (D) rejoiced

199. He **mumbled** his views on the subject of discussion.
(A) articulated (B) muted (C) muttered (D) uttered

200. She is so **naive** as to believe in anyone.
(A) novice (B) simpleton (C) crafty (D) nonsense

201. His wife keeps on **nagging** at him all day.
(A) pricking (B) hectoring (C) comforting (D) complaining

202. He **nibbled** at the apple he was eating.
(A) bite (B) gorged (C) gulped (D) scratched

203. He gave the restaurant waiter a **niggardly** tip.
(A) poor (B) stingy (C) miser (D) generous

204. The accused was pronounced guilty, defence lawyer's brilliant arguments **notwithstanding**.
(A) failure (B) despite (C) due to (D) without

205. He is a **novice** in politics.
(A) tyro (B) experienced (C) fool (D) new

206. **Obnoxious** smell forced us to cover our nose.
(A) annoying (B) odious (C) offensive (D) delightful

207. New models of cars become **obsolete** in a few years.
(A) old (B) outdated (C) in vogue (D) antique

208. Dark clouds look **ominous**.
(A) portentous (B) threatening (C) propitious (D) harmful

209. Public anger against price-rise of petrol is **palpable**.
(A) obvious (B) evident (C) perceptible (D) mperceptible

210. An amount of one rupee is a **paltry** sum these days.
(A) petty (B) contemptible
(C) significant (D) inconsiderable

211. He **paraded** his medal and prizes proudly.
(A) marched (B) flaunted (C) concealed (D) promenaded

212. Checking corruption in the country is **paramount**.
(A) supreme (B) most important
(C) unimportant (D) superior

213. Grief is **patent** on her face.
(A) unconcealed (B) latent (C) dim (D) obscure

214. The old man was sitting in a **pensive** mood.
(A) sorry (B) grieving (C) thinking (D) thoughtless

215. It is a **perennial** fruit-bearing plant.
(A) throughout the year (B) seasonal (C) perpetual (D) eternal

216. His **perfidious** friend ditched him.
(A) faithful (B) disloyal (C) perfect (D) false

217. He does his job in **perfunctory** manner.
(A) professional (B) functional (C) indifferent (D) diligent

218. Mountaineering is a **perilous** adventure.
(A) injurious (B) risky (C) safe (D) disadvantageous

219. The building **perished** in the earthquake.
(A) ruined (B) survived (C) decayed (D) disappeared

220. The shrine witnesses **perpetual** stream of pilgrims.
(A) unending (B) discontinuous (C) permanent (D) temporary

221. **Persistent** incidents of violence in the city make people afraid of moving out freely.
(A) insistent (B) steady (C) sporadic (D) tenacious

222. A **perspicacious** person does not easily get befooled.
(A) astute (B) transparent (C) imperceptive (D) dim

223. The import of what he said in his speech was **perspicuous**.
(A) indistinct (B) lucid (C) paque (D) bright

224. He was **persuaded** to perjure in the court.
(A) agreed (B) induced (C) dissuaded (D) coaxed

225. Do not try to **pervert** my statement.
(A) distort (B) correct (C) mislead (D) misuse

226. A hypochondriac is suffering from **phantom** feeling of pain in abdomen.
(A) real (B) imaginary (C) ghost (D) illusory

227. He is a man of **phlegmatic** disposition.
(A) humorous (B) placid (C) passionate (D) passive

228. The devotee leads a life full of **piety**.
(A) pain (B) devotion (C) veneration (D) irreverence

229. His **piteous** cry for help moved us.
(A) reverent (B) pathetic (C) delightful (D) pious

230. The political leaders **pillory** each other in public fora.
(A) push (B) ridicule publicly (C) approbate (D) laugh at

231. His slogans are full of **platitudes**.
(A) cliche (B) novelty (C) repetitions (D) trivial

232. He gave a **plausible** explanation of his failure to accomplish the assigned task.
(A) applaudable (B) truthful (C) specious (D) untrue

233. People of **plebeian** taste can't appreciate abstract art works.
(A) sophisticated (B) vulgar (C) popular (D) trite

234. The power breakdown **plunged** the whole city into darkness.
(A) stooped (B) submerged (C) emerged (D) soared

235. His **poignant** remorse was cathartic.
(A) severe (B) pricking (C) sincere (D) mild

236. She was walking carefully **poising** a water jug on her head.
(A) balancing (B) controlling (C) disbalancing (D) stabilizing

237. **Polemical** views of bigots are threat to social harmony.
(A) uncompromising (B) controversial
(C) eirenic (D) argumentative

238. To joust with a potent person is not a **politic** act.
(A) shrewd (B) expedient (C) tactless (D) clever

239. People's outrage over rising hardships due to high inflation **portends** doom for the government.
(A) augurs (B) forebodes (C) threatens (D) foretells

240. Judgement of this age should be left to **posterity**.
(A) descendants (B) ancestry (C) priority (D) future

241. Several **potent** arguments were put forward to prove the point.
(A) weak (B) powerful (C) cogent (D) useful

242. His plan was unacceptable because it was not **practicable**.
(A) practical (B) feasible (C) unattainable (D) worth

243. He is a **practical** politician.
(A) sensible (B) unwise (C) practising (D) practicable

244. Job tenure in private companies is **precarious**.
(A) secure
(B) unsure because of depending on other's mercy
(C) unsteady (D) dangerous

245. Many a tribal society is still mired in **primitive** traditions.
(A) primany (B) pristine (C) old (D) modern

246. He is highly regarded because of his impeccable **probity**.
(A) venality (B) rectitude (C) obediency (D) sincerity

247. A **prodigal** person is likely to be impoverished in due course of time.
(A) improvident (B) frugal (C) proud (D) extraordinary

248. A precocious child possesses **prodigious** talent.
(A) extraordinarily marvellous (B) commonplace
(C) proven (D) progressing

249. Harsh retort by the son **ruffled** his father.
(A) upset (B) untidied (C) smoothed (D) soothed

250. Tyrants are **ruthless**.
(A) compassionate (B) cruel (C) adamant (D) ferocious

251. Holy shrines are **sacred** to the devotees.
(A) pious (B) blasphemous (C) pure (D) venerable

252. **Sagacious** patriarch is a source of prudent advice.
(A) sapient (B) practical (C) illustrious (D) foolish

253. **Salient** features of a machine determine its price.

(A) solid (B) outstanding (C) basic (D) unimportant

254. The chief organizer delivered his **salutatory** speech.

(A) valedictory (B) welcoming (C) favourable (D) beneficial

255. The criminals committed the crime with complete **sangfroid**.

(A) composure (B) discomfiture (C) confusion (D) easiness

256. The boy passed **scurrilous** remark on girls passing-by.

(A) obscene (B) jocular (C) decent (D) crude

257. He has a **queer** notion about life in U.S.A.

(A) different (B) odd (C) usual (D) questionable

258. **Radical** change in polity is needed to check rampant corruption.

(A) root (B) basic (C) superficial (D) drastic

259. He failed to **redeem** his pawned watch due to want of money.

(A) reclaim (B) ransom (C) forfeit (D) abandon

260. It is very difficult to handle a **refractory** child.

(A) hard (B) obstinate (C) obedient (D) rude

261. The party refused the return of the **renegades** into party fold.

(A) apostates (B) adherents (C) sticklers (D) traitors

262. **Repentance** cleanses the sinner's soul.

(A) remorse (B) sorrow (C) impenitence (D) regret

263. He **repudiated** charges made against him.

(A) disowned (B) enforced (C) accepted (D) contradicted

264. Dispersal of clouds **revealed** the sun in the sky.

(A) shrouded (B) divulged (C) unveiled (D) concealed

265. The river takes a **sinuous** path through the valley.

(A) side (B) straight (C) flexuous (D) circuitous

266. People are **skeptical** about government's sincerity to curb corruption.

(A) shaky (B) confident (C) doubtful (D) cynic

267. A **somber** passage way led to the large hall.

(A) gloomy (B) doleful (C) dusky (D) bright

268. The **volube** spokesman kept on speaking to the chagrin of the listeners.

(A) succinct (B) verbose (C) strident (D) loud

269. Only a few lucky ones could **survive** in the disaster.

(A) succour (B) remain alive (C) succumb (D) win

270. It is not wise to **squander** precious resources.

(A) spend (B) preserve (C) dissipate (D) splurge

271. He is **steadfast** in his faith.

(A) staunch (B) firm (C) wavering (D) constant

272. He unleashed vicious compaign to **tarnish** my reputation.
(A) blacken (B) blemish (C) brighten (D) exalt

273. His position in the team is **tenuous**.
(A) slender (B) strong (C) attenuated (D) tender

274. She took out frozen stuff from refrigerator and kept on the table to let it **thaw**.
(A) warm (B) deliquesce (C) melt (D) freeze

275. It is not good to **traduce** someone's character.
(A) malign (B) abuse (C) praise (D) expose

276. **Treason** is an unforgivable crime.
(A) loyalty (B) sedition (C) treachery (D) patriotism

277. He was forgiven for **venial** offence.
(A) vicious (B) pardonable (C) felonious (D) serious

278. His **wanton** disregard of others' sentiments is not appreciable.
(A) willful (B) reckless (C) lewd (D) unintentional

279. This town has **warm** climate throughout the year.
(A) hot (B) moderately hot (C) cold (D) cool

280. The wet log got **warped** on getting dried up.
(A) bent (B) straightened (C) twisted (D) flat

281. His **wayward** son has become incorrigible.
(A) willful (B) obedient (C) astray (D) capricious

282. He looked weary after long hours of work.
(A) tired (B) interested (C) energetic (D) sad

ANSWERS

1. (B)	**2.** (A)	**3.** (D)	**4.** (D)	**5.** (C)	**6.** (D)	**7.** (D)	**8.** (C)
9. (C)	**10.** (D)	**11.** (C)	**12.** (D)	**13.** (C)	**14.** (B)	**15.** (D)	**16.** (C)
17. (C)	**18.** (D)	**19.** (C)	**20.** (D)	**21.** (D)	**22.** (C)	**23.** (C)	**24.** (C)
25. (B)	**26.** (D)	**27.** (D)	**28.** (D)	**29.** (D)	**30.** (D)	**31.** (A)	**32.** (D)
33. (A)	**34.** (D)	**35.** (C)	**36.** (D)	**37.** (C)	**38.** (D)	**39.** (C)	**40.** (C)
41. (D)	**42.** (C)	**43.** (C)	**44.** (C)	**45.** (D)	**46.** (C)	**47.** (C)	**48.** (D)
49. (C)	**50.** (D)	**51.** (D)	**52.** (D)	**53.** (C)	**54.** (D)	**55.** (C)	**56.** (C)
57. (C)	**58.** (D)	**59.** (A)	**60.** (A)	**61.** (A)	**62.** (C)	**63.** (C)	**64.** (D)
65. (C)	**66.** (B)	**67.** (C)	**68.** (B)	**69.** (A)	**70.** (A)	**71.** (D)	**72.** (D)
73. (D)	**74.** (B)	**75.** (D)	**76.** (C)	**77.** (C)	**78.** (D)	**79.** (D)	**80.** (B)
81. (C)	**82.** (D)	**83.** (A)	**84.** (C)	**85.** (C)	**86.** (B)	**87.** (D)	**88.** (D)
89. (B)	**90.** (C)	**91.** (D)	**92.** (C)	**93.** (C)	**94.** (D)	**95.** (C)	**96.** (B)
97. (A)	**98.** (C)	**99.** (C)	**100.** (B)	**101.** (D)	**102.** (D)	**103.** (C)	**104.** (C)
105. (B)	**106.** (D)	**107.** (C)	**108.** (D)	**109.** (C)	**110.** (C)	**111.** (C)	**112.** (D)

113. (B)	**114.** (C)	**115.** (D)	**116.** (C)	**117.** (C)	**118.** (C)	**119.** (B)	**120.** (C)
121. (D)	**122.** (D)	**123.** (D)	**124.** (C)	**125.** (D)	**126.** (C)	**127.** (D)	**128.** (C)
129. (D)	**130.** (A)	**131.** (D)	**132.** (D)	**133.** (C)	**134.** (D)	**135.** (D)	**136.** (B)
137. (C)	**138.** (D)	**139.** (B)	**140.** (D)	**141.** (C)	**142.** (D)	**143.** (D)	**144.** (A)
145. (C)	**146.** (A)	**147.** (C)	**148.** (D)	**149.** (B)	**150.** (C)	**151.** (D)	**152.** (D)
153. (D)	**154.** (C)	**155.** (D)	**156.** (A)	**157.** (C)	**158.** (C)	**159.** (A)	**160.** (C)
161. (C)	**162.** (C)	**163.** (B)	**164.** (C)	**165.** (D)	**166.** (D)	**167.** (D)	**168.** (D)
169. (C)	**170.** (D)	**171.** (C)	**172.** (B)	**173.** (D)	**174.** (C)	**175.** (C)	**176.** (B)
177. (C)	**178.** (C)	**179.** (B)	**180.** (A)	**181.** (D)	**182.** (D)	**183.** (C)	**184.** (A)
185. (C)	**186.** (C)	**187.** (D)	**188.** (D)	**189.** (D)	**190.** (B)	**191.** (C)	**192.** (D)
193. (C)	**194.** (C)	**195.** (C)	**196.** (D)	**197.** (C)	**198.** (D)	**199.** (A)	**200.** (C)
201. (C)	**202.** (B)	**203.** (D)	**204.** (C)	**205.** (B)	**206.** (D)	**207.** (C)	**208.** (C)
209. (D)	**210.** (C)	**211.** (C)	**212.** (C)	**213.** (B)	**214.** (C)	**215.** (B)	**216.** (A)
217. (D)	**218.** (C)	**219.** (B)	**220.** (B)	**221.** (C)	**222.** (C)	**223.** (A)	**224.** (C)
225. (B)	**226.** (A)	**227.** (C)	**228.** (D)	**229.** (C)	**230.** (C)	**231.** (B)	**232.** (B)
233. (A)	**234.** (C)	**235.** (D)	**236.** (C)	**237.** (C)	**238.** (C)	**239.** (A)	**240.** (B)
241. (A)	**242.** (C)	**243.** (B)	**244.** (A)	**245.** (D)	**246.** (A)	**247.** (B)	**248.** (B)
249. (D)	**250.** (A)	**251.** (B)	**252.** (D)	**253.** (D)	**254.** (A)	**255.** (B)	**256.** (C)
257. (C)	**258.** (C)	**259.** (C)	**260.** (C)	**261.** (B)	**262.** (C)	**263.** (C)	**264.** (A)
265. (B)	**266.** (B)	**267.** (D)	**268.** (A)	**269.** (C)	**270.** (B)	**271.** (C)	**272.** (D)
273. (B)	**274.** (D)	**275.** (C)	**276.** (D)	**277.** (C)	**278.** (D)	**279.** (D)	**280.** (B)
281. (B)	**282.** (C)						

TEST 2

Choose the correct option for antonyms of the given words:

1. Impeccability
   (A) Faultlessness (B) Sin (C) Wrongfulness (D) Rightness
2. Immaculate
   (A) Clean (B) Spotless (C) Tainted (D) Defective
3. Vivacious
   (A) Lively (B) Energetic (C) Animated (D) Inanimated
4. Exonarate
   (A) Aquit (B) Exculpate (C) Punish (D) Release
5. Amass
   (A) Gather (B) Exhaust (C) Fritter (D) Collect
6. Pedant
   (A) Learned (B) Charlatan (C) Attach (D) Fool
7. Kudos
   (A) Criticism (B) Approbation (C) Applause (D) Appreciation

8. Entice
(A) Allure (B) Attract (C) Repulse (D) Feign

9. Noisome
(A) Pleasant (B) Noxious (C) Distasteful (D) Foul

10. Benevolence
(A) Beneficence (B) Charity (C) Malevolence (D) Arrogance

11. Annoint
(A) Consecrate (B) Desecrate (C) Purify (D) Paint

12. Zenith
(A) Nadir (B) Depth (C) Acme (D) Pinnacle

13. Zealous
(A) Apathetic (B) Enthusiastic (C) Passionate (D) Dull

14. Youthful
(A) Young (B) Senile (C) Aged (D) Dotard

15. Yield
(A) Surrender (B) Repent (C) Submit (D) Resist

16. Compliant
(A) Obedient (B) Submissive (C) Intractable (D) Dutiful

17. Yearn
(A) Loathe (B) Crave (C) Long (D) Wish

18. Adore
(A) Worship (B) Revere (C) Scorn (D) Venerate

19. Worldly
(A) Mundane (B) Temporal (C) Spiritual (D) Base

20. Womanly
(A) Virile (B) Effeminate (C) Feminine (D) Masculine

21. Wither
(A) Shrivel (B) Decay (C) Refresh (D) Fade

22. Interest
(A) Indifference (B) Liking (C) Choice (D) Attraction

23. Thrive
(A) Flourish (B) Prosper (C) Decay (D) Grow

24. Wilful
(A) Intentional (B) Fortuitous (C) Meditated (D) Desired

25. Contemplate
(A) Pender (B) Reflect (C) Ignore (D) Cogitate

26. Wax
(A) Wane (B) Enlarge (C) Amplify (D) Reduce

27. Waver
(A) Flicker (B) Vacillate (C) Fickle (D) Stay firm

28. Want
(A) Abundance (B) Paucity (C) Privation (D) Penury

29. Wander
(A) Rove (B) Linger (C) Traipse (D) Ramble

30. Vulgar
(A) Unrefined (B) Refined (C) Of common people (D) Crude

31. Vivid
(A) Vague (B) Lively (C) Bright (D) Animated

32. Virulent
(A) Malevolent (B) Benign (C) Spiteful (D) Wicked

33. Vengeance
(A) Retribution (B) Forgiveness (C) Revenge (D) Reprisal

34. Venal
(A) Mercenary (B) Corrupt (C) Upright (D) Saleable

35. Veil
(A) Conceal (B) Cloak (C) Mask (D) Bare

36. Vapid
(A) Stale (B) Insipid (C) Stimulating (D) Banal

37. Vanish
(A) Evanesce (B) Appear (C) Disappear (D) Dissolve

38. Vainglory
(A) Humility (B) Conceit (C) Vanity (D) Arrogance

39. Erect
(A) Crooked (B) Upright (C) Straight (D) Unbent

40. Unkempt
(A) Untidy (B) Rumpled (C) Preened (D) Ruffled

41. Unintelligible
(A) Lucid (B) Vague (C) Ambiguous (D) Indistinct

42. Unfold
(A) Furl (B) Spread (C) Open up (D) Unwrap

43. Ultimate
(A) Final (B) Last (C) Latest (D) Foremost

44. Triumph
(A) Victory (B) Conquest (C) Defeat (D) Win

45. Trifling
(A) Frivolous (B) Trivial (C) Petty (D) Serious

46. Trite
(A) Novel (B) Commonplace (C) Hackneyed (D) Stale

47. Trepidation
(A) Boldness (B) Fearlessness (C) Fright (D) Dread

48. Traduce
(A) Extol (B) Malign (C) Vilify (D) Revile

49. Touchy
(A) Snappish (B) Testy (C) Stolid (D) Peevish

50. Thaw
(A) Solidify (B) Melt (C) Liquefy (D) Dissolve

51. Thankful
(A) Grateful (B) Obliged (C) Obligated (D) Ungrateful

52. Testify
(A) Refute (B) Attest (C) Endorse (D) Witness

53. Terrify
(A) Embolden (B) Intimidate (C) Horrify (D) Appal

54. Tenacious
(A) Lax (B) Steadfast (C) Pertinent (D) Persistent

55. Temperate
(A) Extreme (B) Moderate (C) Restrained (D) Controlled

56. Temerity
(A) Audacity (B) Timidity (C) Hardihoodness (D) Recklessness

57. Tardy
(A) Punctual (B) Sloth (C) Slow (D) Delayed

58. Tangible
(A) Palpable (B) Tactile (C) Perceptible (D) Untouchable

59. Deft
(A) Adroit (B) Dextrous (C) Inept (D) Proficient

60. Survive
(A) Live (B) Continue (C) Continued (D) Succumb

61. Succinct
(A) Garrulous (B) Curt (C) Terse (D) Brief

62. Subtle
(A) Subliminal (B) Obvious (C) Imperceptible (D) Indirect

63. Subside
(A) Relent (B) Aggravate (C) Decline (D) Decrease

64. Submissive
(A) Deferential (B) Yielding (C) Compliant (D) Intractable

65. Stop
(A) Start (B) Begin (C) End (D) Commence

66. Speak
(A) Talk (B) Utter (C) Hush (D) Tell

67. Corporal
(A) Somatic (B) Corporeal (C) Physical (D) Spiritual

68. Solemn
(A) Grave (B) Sedate (C) Cheerful (D) Staid

69. Indigent
(A) Impoverished (B) Impecunious (C) Destitute (D) Affluent

70. Stern
(A) Strict (B) Stringent (C) Lenient (D) Harsh

71. Scanty
(A) Meagre (B) Plentiful (C) Sparse (D) Scarce

72. Savage
(A) Wild (B) Ferocious (C) Kind (D) Cruel

73. Sagacious
(A) Prudent (B) Reckless (C) Judicious (D) Foresighted

74. Sag
(A) Raise (B) Bend (C) Prolapse (D) Buckle

75. Sacred
(A) Holy (B) Divine (C) Profane (D) Pious

76. Rigid
(A) Stiff (B) Supple (C) Inflexible (D) Unbending

77. Libertine
(A) Licentious (B) Profligate (C) Righteous (D) Immoral

78. Preposterous
(A) Sound (B) Ridiculous (C) Farcial (D) Absurd

79. Reward
(A) Recompense (B) Wages (C) Prize (D) Award

80. Revile
(A) Honour (B) Traduce (C) Asperse (D) Malign

81. Retreat
(A) Recede (B) Retract (C) Withdraw (D) Advance

82. Retard
(A) Impede (B) Accelerate (C) Decelerate (D) Slow down

83. Restraint
(A) Liberty (B) Constraint (C) Check (D) Regulate

84. Reluctant
(A) Averse (B) Loath (C) Disinclined (D) Disposed

85. Regal
(A) Royal (B) Imperial (C) Plebeian (D) Majestic

86. Sham
(A) Real (B) Counterfeit (C) Fictitious (D) False

87. Readable
(A) Legible (B) Illegible (C) Distinct (D) Clear

88. Raze
(A) Construct (B) Demolish (C) Wreck (D) Refined

89. Raw
(A) Coarse (B) Crude (C) Rough (D) Refined

90. Ravage
(A) Protect (B) Pillage (C) Sack (D) Plunder

91. Raucus
(A) Strident (B) Hoarse (C) Harmonious (D) Discordant

92. Rapture
(A) Bliss (B) Exaltation (C) Delight (D) Woe

93. Rankle
(A) Redolence (B) Stink (C) Stench (D) Reck

94. Rancour
(A) Ill-will (B) Spite (C) Malice (D) Benevolence

95. Raging
(A) Fierce (B) Mild (C) Intense (D) Acute

96. Radical
(A) Root (B) Fundamental (C) Shallow (D) Ouintessential

97. Rabid
(A) Sober (B) Frenzied (C) Violent (D) Raving

98. Quell
(A) Crush (B) Suppress (C) Stiffle (D) Foment

99. Queer
(A) Odd (B) Strange (C) Familiar (D) Outlandish

100. Quash
(A) Validate (B) Nullify (C) Annul (D) Cancel

101. Quandary
(A) Plight (B) Predicament (C) Dilemma (D) Certainty

102. Provident
(A) Frugal (B) Prodigal (C) Thrifty (D) Sparing

103. Provide
(A) Deprive (B) Endow (C) Bestow (D) Afford

104. Supercilious
(A) Meek (B) Overbearing (C) Haughty (D) Disdainful

105. Protract
(A) Retract (B) Spread (C) Expand (D) Elongate

106. Propensity
(A) Proclivity (B) Predisposition (C) Aversion (D) Tendency

107. Propel
(A) Halt (B) Actuate (C) Impel (D) Drive

108. Propagate
(A) Transmit (B) Relay (C) Spread (D) Hold back

109. Prolific
(A) Fecund (B) Effete (C) Productive (D) Fertile

110. Prodigious
(A) Usual (B) Marvellous (C) Remarkable (D) Astonishing

111. Primordial
(A) Modern (B) Pristine (C) Quaint (D) Primitive

112. Pretend
(A) Be honest (B) Profess (C) Feign (D) Affect

113. Precarious
(A) Dependent on mercy (B) Unsafe (C) Perilous (D) Secured

114. Postpone
(A) Defer (B) Prepone (C) Delay (D) Adjourn

115. Phlegmatic
(A) Passionate (B) Impassive (C) Sluggish (D) Lazy

116. Philanthrope
(A) Benevolent (B) Humane (C) Altruist (D) Misanthrope

117. Petty
(A) Significant (B) Pattry (C) Trivial (D) Trifling

118. Pester
(A) Chafe (B) Annoy (C) Bother (D) Console

119. Pertinent
(A) Relevant (B) Extraneous (C) Germane (D) Apropos

120. Perspicacious
(A) Discerning (B) Understanding (C) Unknowing (D) Wise

121. Perspicuous
(A) Transparent (B) Limpid (C) Opaque (D) Visible

122. Persist
(A) Cease (B) Persevere (C) Endure (D) Continue

123. Persecute
(A) Harass (B) Torment (C) Harry (D) Help

124. Perpetual
(A) Ephemeral (B) Eternal (C) Unceasing (D) Everlasting

125. Penitent
(A) Remorseful (B) Contrite (C) Repentant (D) Remorseless

126. Parsimonious
(A) Miser (B) Generous (C) Stingy (D) Niggardly

127. Pacify
(A) Agitate (B) Lull (C) Calm (D) Compose

128. Overbearing
(A) Humble (B) Domineering (C) Imperious (D) Dominant

129. Outdated
(A) Obsolete (B) Old-fashioned (C) Haute couture (D) Outmoded

130. Ostracize
(A) Banish (B) Excommunicate (C) Admit (D) Exile

131. Onerous
(A) Facile (B) Arduous (C) Sisypheous (D) Taxing

132. Offer
(A) Proffer (B) Tender (C) Deny (D) Propose

133. Offend
(A) Outrage (B) Flatter (C) Provoke (D) Irritate

134. Obvious
(A) Obscure (B) Patent (C) Manifest (D) Apparent

135. Obtain
(A) Acquire (B) Possess (C) Attain (D) Forfeit

136. Obdurate
(A) Callous (B) Stubborn (C) Tender (D) Tough

137. Nurture
(A) Cherish (B) Rear (C) Cheer (D) Neglect

138. Novice
(A) Expert (B) Greenhorn (C) Caddie (D) Neophyte

139. Novel
(A) New (B) Unique (C) Original (D) Trite

140. Nervous
(A) Upset (B) Rattled (C) Flustered (D) Tranquil

141. Friendly
(A) Amicable (B) Congenial (C) Amiable (D) Hostile

142. Negligent
(A) Lax (B) Indifferent (C) Meticulous (D) Remiss

143. Nebulous
(A) Hazy (B) Fuzzy (C) Clouded (D) Distinct

144. Spruced
(A) Unkempt (B) Tidy (C) Preened (D) Elegant

145. Sloppy
(A) Slovenly (B) Slut (C) Dirty (D) Smart

146. Native
(A) Alien (B) Aborigine (C) Indigenous (D) Autochthon

147. Narrow-minded
(A) Cosmopolitan (B) Provincial (C) Parochialism (D) Catholic

148. Murky
(A) Gloomy (B) Obscure (C) Dark (D) Clear

149. Muster
(A) Garner (B) Collect (C) Scatter (D) Marshall

150. Mumble
(A) Mutter (B) Whisper (C) Stammer (D) Shout

151. Monotonous
(A) Humdrum (B) Tedious (C) Boring (D) Exciting

152. Mar
(A) Spoil (B) Impair (C) Make (D) Damage

153. Mad
(A) Sane (B) Insane (C) Crazy (D) Demented

154. Luscious
(A) Delicious (B) Delectable (C) Tasteless (D) Tasty

155. Loathsome
(A) Delightful (B) Abominable (C) Odious (D) Unpleasant

156. Linger
(A) Tarry (B) Flit (C) Stay (D) Delay

157. Limber
(A) Supple (B) Flexible (C) Loose (D) Stiff

158. Liberate
(A) Emancipate (B) Deliver (C) Enthral (D) Enfranchise

159. Liable
(A) Answerable (B) Amenable (C) Likely (D) Exempt

160. Lethargic
(A) Active (B) Sluggish (C) Lazy (D) Dull

161. Legitimate
(A) Rightful (B) Lawful (C) Illicit (D) Licit

162. Learned
(A) Erudite (B) Scholarly (C) Pedantic (D) Ignorant

163. Laud
(A) Praise (B) Commend (C) Extol (D) Criticise

164. Lament
(A) Laud (B) Deplore (C) Regret (D) Keen

165. Knack
(A) Ineptitude (B) Talent (C) Aptitude (D) Propensity

166. Kindle
(A) Ignite (B) Inflame (C) Arouse (D) Extinguish

167. Keen
(A) Astute (B) Blunt (C) Acute (D) Sharp

168. Joyous
(A) Melancholy (B) Mirthful (C) Blithe (D) Jovial

169. Jeer
(A) Scoff (B) Sneer (C) Fleer (D) Laud

170. Intrinsic
(A) Extrinsic (B) Inherent (C) Innate (D) Inborn

171. Intentional
(A) Deliberate (B) Contemplated (C) Pre-meditated (D) Accidental

172. Insult
(A) Honour (B) Affront (C) Outrage (D) Indignity

173. Inquisitive
(A) Uninterested (B) Prying (C) Curious (D) Inquiring

174. Innate
(A) Inborn (B) Congenital (C) Natural (D) Acquired

175. Detrimental
(A) Deleterious (B) Harmful (C) Injurious (D) Salutary

176. Inhibit
(A) Contain (B) Restrain (C) Bridle (D) Encourage

177. Inflate
(A) Distend (B) Dilate (C) Swell (D) Deflate

178. Just
(A) Iniquitous (B) Fair (C) Impartial (D) Proper

179. Frail
(A) Decrepit (B) Vulnerable (C) Robust (D) Weak

180. Indolent
(A) Slothful (B) Sluggish (C) Torpid (D) Zestful

181. Indebted
(A) Un-obligated (B) Obliged (C) Beholden (D) Grateful

182. Imply
(A) Connote (B) Denote (C) Mean (D) Assert

183. Implore
(A) Solicit (B) Entreat (C) Bestow (D) Importune

184. Impertinent
(A) Polite (B) Brazen (C) Impudent (D) Rude

185. Impair
(A) Improve (B) Mar (C) Spoil (D) Damage

186. Immerse
(A) Dunk (B) Sink (C) Submerge (D) Emerge

187. Immense
(A) Minuscule (B) Enormous (C) Humongous (D) Vast

188. Immaculate
(A) Spotless (B) Tainted (C) Unblemished (D) Clean

189. Imitation
(A) Replica (B) Simile (C) Prototype (D) Magnette

190. Imitate
(A) Mimic (B) Ape (C) Simulate (D) Pioneer

191. Imbibe
(A) Exude (B) Drink (C) Assimilate (D) Eat

192. Imbecile
(A) Dullhead (B) Nincompoop (C) Idiot (D) Clever

193. Imaginative
(A) Prosaic (B) Inventive (C) Visionary (D) Clairvoyant

194. Illusive
(A) Real (B) Misleading (C) False (D) Unreal

195. Elusive
(A) Escaping (B) Unrealising (C) Slipping (D) Apprehensive

196. Allusive
(A) Direct (B) Indirect (C) Hinting (D) Indicating

197. Ignorant
(A) Unaware (B) Familiar (C) Oblivious (D) Un-informed

198. Ignominious
(A) Exalted (B) Abject (C) Despicable (D) Ignoble

199. Ideal
(A) Fantastic (B) Utopian (C) Impractical (D) Practical

200. Idea
(A) Notion (B) Impression (C) Knowledge (D) Concept

201. Honesty
(A) Dishonesty (B) Sincerity (C) Integrity (D) Uprightness

202. Hideous
(A) Attractive (B) Ugly (C) Unattractive (D) Repulsive

203. Holy
(A) Divine (B) Pious (C) Hallowed (D) Impious

204. Hobby
(A) Pastime (B) Vocation (C) Avocation (D) Occupation

205. Hire
(A) Employ (B) Enlist (C) Engage (D) Fire

206. Hide
(A) Dissemble (B) Betray (C) Disguise (D) Cloak

207. Latent
(A) Dormant (B) Inactive (C) Invisible (D) Patent

208. Hesitation
(A) Conviction (B) Scruple (C) Suspense (D) Doubt

209. Hesitate
(A) Demur (B) Waver (C) Falter (D) Resolve

210. Abet
(A) Connive (B) Assist (C) Thwart (D) Collude

211. Acme
(A) Apex (B) Pinnacle (C) Vertex (D) Base

212. Hearty
(A) Cordial (B) Earnest (C) Warm (D) Cool

213. Cheerful
(A) Dispirited (B) Animated (C) Exhilarated (D) Elated

214. Forlorn
(A) Sad (B) Desolate (C) Disconsolate (D) Exulted

215. Healthy
(A) Wholesome (B) Salutary (C) Salubrious (D) Noxious

216. Hatred
(A) Dislike (B) Ill-will (C) Loathing (D) Affection

217. Hate
(A) Loathe (B) Abominate (C) Admire (D) Abhor

218. Scurry
(A) Scamper (B) Scoot (C) Sprint (D) Lurch

219. Expedite
(A) Hasten (B) Accelerate (C) Dawdle (D) Quicken

220. Harmony
(A) Accord (B) Concord (C) Discord (D) Unison

221. Hamper
(A) Hinder (B) Obstruct (C) Thwart (D) Expedite

222. Hallow
(A) Dishonour (B) Exalt (C) Glorify (D) Consecrate

223. Guile
(A) Wile (B) Craftiness (C) Chicanery (D) Innocence

224. Grow
(A) Bloom (B) Snowball (C) Shrink (D) Burgeon

225. Grief
(A) Joy (B) Woe (C) Distress (D) Anguish

226. Govern
(A) Rule (B) Submit (C) Reign (D) Command

227. Gorgeous
(A) Ugly (B) Grand (C) Dazzling (D) Magnificent

228. Fade
(A) Wither (B) Shrivel (C) Decay (D) Enliven

229. Glut
(A) Teen (B) Swarm (C) Overflow (D) Deplete

230. Dismal
(A) Sullen (B) Sad (C) Gay (D) Dreary

231. Confer
(A) Deny (B) Bestow (C) Award (D) Grant

232. Fuzzy
(A) Hazy (B) Blurred (C) Obscure (D) Lucid

233. Imminent
(A) Impending (B) On the anvil (C) Ulterior (D) In the offing

234. Futile
(A) Fruitful (B) Vain (C) Worthless (D) Useless

235. Fury
(A) Wrath (B) Rage (C) Fierveness (D) Calmness

236. Furtive
(A) Clandestine (B) Surreptitious (C) Unhidden (D) Secret
237. Brawl
(A) Melee (B) Skirmish (C) Strife (D) Peace
238. Frail
(A) Fragile (B) Delicate (C) Sturdy (D) Dainty
239. Formidable
(A) Unimpressive (B) Imposing (C) Forbidding (D) Awesome
240. Formal
(A) Conventional (B) Ceremonious (C) Proper (D) Informal
241. Forbid
(A) Permit (B) Ban (C) Prohibit (D) Disallow
242. Foe
(A) Friend (B) Enemy (C) Adversary (D) Antagonist
243. Capricious
(A) Fitful (B) Fickle (C) Unstable (D) Steady
244. Drooping
(A) Sagging (B) Limp (C) Prolapsing (D) Stiff
245. Ferocious
(A) Savage (B) Wild (C) Brutal (D) Innocuous
246. Famous
(A) Renowned (B) Infamous (C) Unknown (D) Eminent
247. Familiar
(A) Intimate (B) Acquainted (C) Conversant (D) Unfamiliar
248. Feign
(A) Fake (B) Pretend (C) Malinger (D) Be honest
249. Foible
(A) Fraility (B) Strength (C) Peccadillo (D) Defect
250. Front
(A) Face (B) Facade (C) Visage (D) Rear
251. Extend
(A) Protrude (B) Project (C) Manhandle (D) Retract
252. Exhaust
(A) Replenish (B) Drain (C) Empty (D) Deplete
253. Excite
(A) Arouse (B) Incite (C) Stimulate (D) Lull
254. Eternal
(A) Everlasting (B) Perpetual (C) Transient (D) Endless
255. Evade
(A) Confront (B) Avert (C) Avoid (D) Parry

256. Erroneous
(A) Fallacious (B) Mistaken (C) Wrong (D) Accurate

257. Colossal
(A) Gargantuan (B) Gigantic (C) Humongous (D) Tiny

258. Involve
(A) Engross (B) Engage (C) Occupy (D) Keep away

259. Elegant
(A) Unrefined (B) Polished (C) Refined (D) Cultured

260. Dissipate
(A) Conserve (B) Squander (C) Diffuse (D) Dwindle

261. Disperse
(A) Scatter (B) Collect (C) Disseminate (D) Sprinkle

262. Disgrace
(A) Odium (B) Dignity (C) Obloquy (D) Disrepute

263. Disdainful
(A) Regardful (B) Contemptuous (C) Scornful (D) Disgraceful

264. Disavow
(A) Repudiate (B) Acknowledge (C) Reject (D) Disown

265. Disaster
(A) Fortune (B) Calamity (C) Catastrophe (D) Misfortune

266. Din
(A) Hush (B) Voice (C) Hum (D) Clamour

267. Dextrous
(A) Deft (B) Adroit (C) Proficient (D) Clumsy

268. Deprive
(A) Restitute (B) Bereave (C) Strip (D) Snatch

269. Deliver
(A) Enslave (B) Emancipate (C) Liberate (D) Rescue

270. Delicious
(A) Delectable (B) Savoury (C) Unpalatable (D) Tasty

271. Decrepit
(A) Strong (B) Infirm (C) Rickety (D) Dilapidated

272. Decorate
(A) Garnish (B) Adorn (C) Deface (D) Beautify

273. Decent
(A) Comely (B) Seemly (C) Decorous (D) Vulgar

274. Daunt
(A) Deter (B) Intimidate (C) Dishearten (D) Encourage

275. Daring
(A) Timorous (B) Intrepid (C) Bold (D) Brave

276. Dandy
(A) Fop (B) Coxcomb (C) Sloven (D) Fashionable

277. Damnable
(A) Commendable (B) Execrable (C) Outrageous (D) Evil

278. Zig-zag
(A) Meandering (B) Curved (C) Straight (D) Flexuous

279. Crave
(A) Hanker (B) Long (C) Desire (D) Dislike

280. Contrary
(A) Obedient (B) Stubborn (C) Wilful (D) Perverse

281. Contemplate
(A) Ponder (B) Disregard (C) Reflect (D) Think

282. Confess
(A) Confute (B) Refute (C) Admit (D) Accept

283. Compassionate
(A) Cruel (B) Benign (C) Kind (D) Merciful

284. Commendation
(A) Applause (B) Praise (C) Condemnation (D) Approbation

285. Circumspect
(A) Vigilant (B) Wary (C) Provident (D) Heedless

286. Exhume
(A) Disinter (B) Excavate (C) Digout (D) Bury

287. Brag
(A) Vaunt (B) Swagger (C) Boast (D) Be modest

288. Banish
(A) Harbour (B) Exile (C) Deport (D) Oust

289. Banal
(A) Hackneyed (B) Trite (C) Humdrum (D) Stimulating

290. Austere
(A) Lenient (B) Stern (C) Harsh (D) Strict

291. Abandon
(A) Desert (B) Discard (C) Relinquish (D) Acquire

292. Assemble
(A) Gather (B) Congregate (C) Disperse (D) Collect

293. Ascend
(A) Soar (B) Rise (C) Climb (D) Descend

294. Anxiety
(A) Nonchalance (B) Concern (C) Apprehension (D) Disquiet

295. Board
(A) Embark (B) Alight (C) Mount (D) Ride

ANSWERS

1. (B)	**2.** (C)	**3.** (D)	**4.** (C)	**5.** (C)	**6.** (B)	**7.** (A)	**8.** (C)
9. (A)	**10.** (C)	**11.** (B)	**12.** (A)	**13.** (D)	**14.** (C)	**15.** (D)	**16.** (C)
17. (A)	**18.** (C)	**19.** (C)	**20.** (A)	**21.** (C)	**22.** (A)	**23.** (C)	**24.** (B)
25. (C)	**26.** (A)	**27.** (D)	**28.** (A)	**29.** (B)	**30.** (B)	**31.** (A)	**32.** (B)
33. (B)	**34.** (C)	**35.** (D)	**36.** (C)	**37.** (B)	**38.** (A)	**39.** (A)	**40.** (C)
41. (A)	**42.** (A)	**43.** (D)	**44.** (C)	**45.** (D)	**46.** (A)	**47.** (B)	**48.** (A)
49. (C)	**50.** (A)	**51.** (D)	**52.** (A)	**53.** (A)	**54.** (A)	**55.** (A)	**56.** (B)
57. (A)	**58.** (D)	**59.** (C)	**60.** (D)	**61.** (A)	**62.** (B)	**63.** (B)	**64.** (D)
65. (A)	**66.** (C)	**67.** (D)	**68.** (C)	**69.** (D)	**70.** (C)	**71.** (B)	**72.** (C)
73. (B)	**74.** (A)	**75.** (C)	**76.** (B)	**77.** (C)	**78.** (A)	**79.** (B)	**80.** (A)
81. (D)	**82.** (B)	**83.** (A)	**84.** (D)	**85.** (C)	**86.** (A)	**87.** (B)	**88.** (A)
89. (D)	**90.** (A)	**91.** (C)	**92.** (D)	**93.** (A)	**94.** (D)	**95.** (B)	**96.** (C)
97. (A)	**98.** (D)	**99.** (C)	**100.** (A)	**101.** (D)	**102.** (B)	**103.** (A)	**104.** (A)
105. (A)	**106.** (C)	**107.** (A)	**108.** (D)	**109.** (B)	**110.** (A)	**111.** (A)	**112.** (A)
113. (D)	**114.** (B)	**115.** (A)	**116.** (D)	**117.** (A)	**118.** (D)	**119.** (B)	**120.** (C)
121. (C)	**122.** (A)	**123.** (D)	**124.** (A)	**125.** (D)	**126.** (B)	**127.** (A)	**128.** (A)
129. (C)	**130.** (C)	**131.** (A)	**132.** (C)	**133.** (B)	**134.** (A)	**135.** (D)	**136.** (C)
137. (D)	**138.** (A)	**139.** (D)	**140.** (D)	**141.** (D)	**142.** (C)	**143.** (D)	**144.** (A)
145. (D)	**146.** (A)	**147.** (D)	**148.** (D)	**149.** (C)	**150.** (D)	**151.** (D)	**152.** (C)
153. (A)	**154.** (C)	**155.** (A)	**156.** (B)	**157.** (D)	**158.** (C)	**159.** (D)	**160.** (A)
161. (C)	**162.** (D)	**163.** (D)	**164.** (A)	**165.** (A)	**166.** (D)	**167.** (B)	**168.** (A)
169. (D)	**170.** (A)	**171.** (D)	**172.** (A)	**173.** (A)	**174.** (D)	**175.** (D)	**176.** (D)
177. (D)	**178.** (A)	**179.** (C)	**180.** (D)	**181.** (A)	**182.** (D)	**183.** (C)	**184.** (A)
185. (A)	**186.** (D)	**187.** (A)	**188.** (B)	**189.** (C)	**190.** (D)	**191.** (A)	**192.** (D)
193. (A)	**194.** (A)	**195.** (D)	**196.** (A)	**197.** (B)	**198.** (A)	**199.** (D)	**200.** (C)
201. (A)	**202.** (A)	**203.** (D)	**204.** (B)	**205.** (D)	**206.** (B)	**207.** (D)	**208.** (A)
209. (D)	**210.** (C)	**211.** (D)	**212.** (D)	**213.** (A)	**214.** (D)	**215.** (D)	**216.** (D)
217. (C)	**218.** (D)	**219.** (C)	**220.** (C)	**221.** (D)	**222.** (A)	**223.** (D)	**224.** (C)
225. (A)	**226.** (B)	**227.** (A)	**228.** (D)	**229.** (D)	**230.** (C)	**231.** (A)	**232.** (D)
233. (C)	**234.** (A)	**235.** (D)	**236.** (C)	**237.** (D)	**238.** (C)	**239.** (D)	**240.** (D)
241. (A)	**242.** (A)	**243.** (D)	**244.** (D)	**245.** (D)	**246.** (C)	**247.** (D)	**248.** (D)
249. (B)	**250.** (D)	**251.** (D)	**252.** (A)	**253.** (D)	**254.** (C)	**255.** (A)	**256.** (D)
257. (D)	**258.** (D)	**259.** (A)	**260.** (A)	**261.** (B)	**262.** (B)	**263.** (A)	**264.** (B)
265. (A)	**266.** (A)	**267.** (D)	**268.** (A)	**269.** (A)	**270.** (C)	**271.** (A)	**272.** (C)
273. (D)	**274.** (D)	**275.** (A)	**276.** (C)	**277.** (A)	**278.** (C)	**279.** (D)	**280.** (A)
281. (B)	**282.** (B)	**283.** (A)	**284.** (C)	**285.** (D)	**286.** (D)	**287.** (D)	**288.** (A)
289. (D)	**290.** (A)	**291.** (D)	**292.** (C)	**293.** (D)	**294.** (A)	**295.** (B)	

❑❑❑

Comprehensive List of Synonymous Words

For Synonyms of	*See*
A	
Abandon	- Relinquish; give up
Abandoned	- Relinquished
Abase	- Devalue
Abash	- Shame
Abate	- Abate
Abdicate	- Abandon
Abject	- Abject, Miserable
Abjure	- Abandon
Aborigine	- Original inhabitants
Abound	- Full
Abrade	- Abrade
Abrogate	- Annul
Abscond	- Flee
Absolve	- Aquit, Discharge
Absorb	- Absorb
Abstain	- Refrain
Abstemious	- Abstemiousness
Abstinence	- Abstemiousness
Abtruse	- Mysterious
Absurd	- Strange, Absurd
Abundant	- Abundant
Abysmal	- Abysmal
Accede	- Assent
Accentuate	- Emphasize
Accept	- Accept
Accidental	- Casual
Acclaim	- Admire
Acclimatise	- Acclimatise
Accredit	- Authorise

For Synonyms of	*See*
Accumulate	- Collect
Accursed	- Accursed
Accuse	- Accuse
Accustom	- Acclimatise
Acerbic	- Acerbic
Acknowledge	- Accept
Acquaint	- Inform
Acquit	- Discharge, Acquit
Acquiesce	- Assent
Acrid	- Acerbic
Actuate	- Stimulate
Adamant	- Adamant
Address	- Speech
Adept	- Adroit
Adhere	- Affix
Adjourn	- Adjourn
Admire	- Admire
Admit	- Accept
Admonish	- Rebuke
Ado	- Ado
Adorn	- Decorate
Adroit	- Adroit
Adulterate	- Adulterate
Advances	- Overture
Advent	- Advent
Advise	- Consult, Inform
Advocate	- Lawyer
Aesthete	- Admirer
Activated	- Dormant
Affect	- Affect
Affirm	- Affirm
Affix	- Affix

For Synonyms of	See
Afflatus	- Motive
Affluent	- Rich
Afflict	- Afflict
Affront	- Insult
Aficionado	- Admirer
Aftermath	- Mark
Aggravate	- Aggravate
Agitate	- Agitate, Perplex
Agitated	- Agitated
Agnate	- Agnate
Agnate	- Ignoramus
Agog	- Eager
Aid	- Aid
Alibi	- Alibi
Alienation	- Alienation
Allay	- Abate; quell
Allegiance	- Allegiance
Alleluia	- Anthem
Alleviate	- Abate
Allocate	- Allot
Allot	- Allot; earmark
Allusion	- Hint
Alone	- Quarrel
Alter ego	- Friend
Amaze	- Amaze, Surprise
Amend	- Amend
Amends	- Amends
Anathema	- Anathema
Ancestor	- Ancestor
Anger	- Anger
Angst	- Anxiety
Annihilate	- Destroy
Announce	- Announce, Declare

For Synonyms of	See
Announcer	- Annuncer
Annoy	- Annoy
Annoyance	- Annoyance
Annul	- Annul; cancel
Anomaly	- Paradox
Antecedent	- Precedence
Antediluvian	- Outdated
Anthem	- Anthem
Antic	- Strange
Anticipation	- Inkling
Antimony	- Paradox
Antiquated	- Outdated, Archaic
Antithesis	- Opposite
Anxiety	- Anxiety, Distress
Ape	- Emulate
Apex	- Peak
Apocalypse	- Disaster
Apostate	- Defector
Apotheosis	- Apotheosis
Appalling	- Terrifying
Apparent	- Apparent
Appeal	- Appeal
Appease	- Appease
Appellation	- Epithet
Applaud	- Admire
Apportion	- Allot
Apposite	- Apposite, Apt, Relevant
Appraise	- Appraise
Apprehend	- Catch
Apprehension	- Apprehension, Inkling
Apprentice	- Novice
Apprise	- Inform

For Synonyms of	See
Approach	- Overture
Approbate	- Praise
Appropriate	- Appropriate
Approve	- Approve
Apropos	- Apposite
Arbiter	- Mediator
Arbitrator	- Mediator
Arcane	- Mysterious
Archaic	- Outdated, Archaic
Ardour	- Passion, Enthusiasm
Argot	- Cant
Aroma	- Aroma, Smell
Arouse	- Stimulate
Arraign	- Accuse
Arrest	- Stop
Arrival	- Advent
Arrogance	- Arrogance
Arrogant	- Arrogant
Arrogate	- Arrogate
Ascend	- Ascend
Aspect	- Aspect
Asperse	- Defame
Asphyxiate	- Suffocate
Assail	- Denounce
Assassinate	- Kill
Assent	- Assent
Assert	- Affirm
Assess	- Appraise
Asset	- Property
Assiduous	- Assiduous
Assign	- Allot, Credit
Assignation	- Assignation
Assimilate	- Absorb

For Synonyms of	See
Assort	- Seclude Classify
Assuage	- Relieve, Appease, Abate
Astonish	- Amaze, Surprise
Astound	- Surprise, Amaze
Astute	- Clever
Asylum	- Shelter
Atone	- Amends
Atrabilious	- Atrabilious
Attack	- Fit
Attempt	- Attempt
Attest	- Verify
Attitude	- Inclination
Attorney	- Lawyer
Attribute	- Credit
Attrition	- Attrition
Audacious	- Arrogant
Audacity	- Arrogance
Audit	- Examine
Augur	- Augur, Foretell
Augury	- Omen
Auspicious	- Auspicious
Austere	- Austere, Strict
Autarky	- Free
Authenticate	- Verify
Authorise	- Authorise
Autocrat	- Autocrat
Autonomous	- Free
Avenge	- Avenge
Aver	- Affirm
Avert	- Avoid, Avert
Avocation	- Profession
Avoid	- Avoid
Avouch	- Affirm; declare
Avow	- Affirm

For Synonyms of	See
Award	- Prize
Aware	- Cautious
Awe	- Fear
Awesome	- Terrifying, Awesome
Awful	- Terrible
Awkward	- Awkward; predicament

B

For Synonyms of	See
Babble	- Chatter
Babel	- Babel
Backtrack	- Backtrack, Retreat, Retract
Backward	- Backward
Badger	- Harass
Bad smelling	- Bad smelling; odour
Baffle	- Baffle
Bailiwick	- Domain
Bait	- Bait
Bale	- Bundle
Balk	- Disobey, Hesitate
Ban	- Ban; embargo
Banish	- Banish; excommunicate
Banner	- Flag
Barbarian	- Cruel
Bark	- Bark
Baron	- Baron
Barrier	- Obstacle
Barrister	- Lawyer
Bash	- Beat
Batter	- Beat
Beam	- Pillar
Bear	- Tolerate
Bedlam	- Babel
Beat	- Beat
Befitting	- Appropriate
Befuddle	- Baffle
Beg	- Beg
Beget	- Create
Beguile	- While away, Deceive, Entice
Behaviour	- Behaviour
Behest	- Order
Behold	- Look
Beleaguer	- Surround
Belch	- Emit
Belief	- Belief
Belittle	- Devalue
Bellicose	- Quarrelsome
Belligerent	- Quarrelsome
Bemoan	- Lament
Bemuse	- Baffle
Beneficent	- Kind
Benevolent	- Auspicious, Kind
Benign	- Auspicious, Kind
Benumb	- Benumb
Bequeath	- Demise, Bequeath
Berate	- Chide
Beseech	- Beg, Request
Besiege	- Surround
Besmear	- Tarnish
Besmirch	- Tarnish
Bestow	- Demise
Bete noire	- Anathema
Betray	- Deceive, Disclose
Bevy	- Herd
Bewilder	- Baffle

For Synonyms of	See
Bias	- Bias, Inclination
Bid	- Overture
Bigot	- Bigot
Bizarre	- Absurd, Strange
Blabber	- Chatter
Blasphemous	- Impious
Blasphemy	- Sacrilege
Blatant	- Egregious
Blemish	- Tarnish
Blench	- Flinch
Blend	- Blend
Bliss	- Climax
Bloat	- Swell
Block	- Block
Blockade	- Obstacle
Blockage	- Obstacle
Bludgeon	- Beat
Blunder	- Mistake
Board	- Climb
Bog	- Mire
Bogus	- Bogus
Bonus	- Prize
Boomerang	- Rebound
Boost	- Elevate
Booty	- Spoils
Boredom	- Boredom
Bother	- Harass
Bounce	- Bounce
Boundary	- Boundary
Bounty	- Prize
Bouquet	- Aroma, Smell
Box	- Beat, Slap
Boycott	- Boycott
Braggart	- Brat

For Synonyms of	See
Braggadocio	- Brat
Brash	- Rude, Shameless
Brat	- Brat
Brawl	- Quarrel
Brazen	- Shameless
Breach	- Breach
Breed	- Create
Brew	- Blend
Bristled	- Erect
Broil	- Quarrel
Bromide	- Cliche
Brood	- Herd; incubation
Brook	- Tolerate
Brouhaha	- Babel
Buckle	- Buckle
Bulge	- Swell
Bump	- Bump
Bunch	- Bunch
Bundle	- Bundle
Bunk	- Abscond
Burgle	- Steal
Burglary	- Theft
Business	- Profession
Bustle	- Ado
Butcher	- Massacre
Butchery	- Genocide

C

For Synonyms of	See
Cache	- Hide
Cachinnate	- Laugh
Cad	- Ignoramus
Cadaver	- Deadbody
Cadaverous	- Cadaverous
Cajole	- Persuade
Calamity	- Disaster
Calm	- Calm

For Synonyms of	See
Calumniate	- Defame
Camouflage	- Hide
Canon	- Order
Cant	- Cant
Cantankerous	- Irritable
Caper	- Caper
Capitulate	- Surrender
Caprice	- Caprice
Captivate	- Hold
Carcass	- Deadbody
Caress	- Caress
Careworn	- Cadaverous
Carnage	- Genocide, Slaughter
Carp	- Complain
Carrion	- Deadbody
Cashier	- Retrench
Castigate	- Chide
Casual	- Casual
Cataclysm	- Disaster
Catastrophe	- Disaster
Catch	- Catch
Categorise	- Classify
Category	- Class
Catholic	- Catholic
Catnap	- Nap
Caution	- Warning
Cautious	- Cautious
Caveat	- Warning
Cavil	- Complain
Cavort	- Caper
Cede	- Cede
Celebration	- Celebration
Cenotaph	- Memorial
Ceremony	- Celebration

For Synonyms of	See
Certify	- Verify
Chafe	- Abrade
Chagrin	- Annoy, Annoyance
Chant	- Chant
Chaos	- Babel
Charge	- Accuse, Fare
Charlatan	- Quack
Chary	- Cautious
Chasm	- Crack
Chasten	- Chide
Chastise	- Chide
Chattel	- Property
Chatter	- Chatter
Chauvinist	- Bigot
Cheat	- Cheat
Check	- Examine, Stop
Checkmate	- Surround
Cherish	- Foster
Chew	- Chew
Chide	- Chide, Rebuke
Chimeral	- Fanciful
Choir	- Clique
Choke	- Suffocate
Choletic	- Irritable
Chomp	- Chew
Chortle	- Laugh
Chuckle	- Laugh
Chum	- Friend
Churlish	- Rude
Circadian	- Circadian
Circumspect	- Cautious
Clairvoyance	- Foresight
Clamber	- Climb
Clamour	- Babel

For Synonyms of	See
Claque	- Clique
Class	- Class
Classify	- Classify
Clean	- Clean
Cleanse	- Clean
Cleavage	- Crack
Cleave	- Tear
Clever	- Clever
Cliche	- Cliche
Climacteric	- Turning Point
Climax	- Climax
Climb	- Climb
Cling	- Affix
Clip	- Trim
Clique	- Clique
Clobber	- Beat
Clog	- Block
Closeness	- Closeness
Clot	- Clot
Clout	- Beat, Dominance, Influence, Strike
Cloyness	- Boredom
Clue	- Hint
Clumsy	- Awkward
Cluster	- Bunch
Clutch	- Herd
Coagulate	- Clot
Coax	- Persuade
Coercion	- Threat
Coetaneous	- Contemporary
Coffer	- Treasury
Cogent	- Appropriate, Apposite
Cogitate	- Cogitate
Cognate	- Agnate

For Synonyms of	See
Cogniscenti	- Learned
Cohort	- Follower
Collaborate	- Cooperate
Collage	- Pot pourie
Collect	- Collect
Colossal	- Colossal
Colours	- Flag
Command	- Order
Commend	- Admire, praise; entrust
Commensuration	- Equality, Similarity
Commiseration	- Sympathy
Commit	- Commit
Commotion	- Babel
Companion	- Companion
Compare	- Compare
Compassion	- Sympathy
Compensate	- Indemnify, Compensate
Complacent	- Complacent
Complain	- Complain
Complicit	- Involved
Compliment	- Admire
Comportment	- Behaviour
Compulsory	- Essential
Compunction	- Pricking of conscience
Con	- Cheat
Conation	- Will, Desire
Conceal	- Hide
Concede	- Surrender; admit
Conceit	- Pride
Concept	- Idea
Concession	- Concession

For Synonyms of	See
Conclude	- Infer
Concoct	- Devise, Blend
Condescend	- Stoop
Condign	- Appropriate
Condole	- Lament
Condolence	- Sympathy, Lamentation
Conduct	- Behaviour
Confer	- Consult, Demise
Confess	- Accept
Confide	- Commit; trust
Confine	- Confine
Confiscate	- Confiscate
Conformity	- Similarity
Confute	- Confute
Confrontation	- Encounter
Congeal	- Clot
Congenital	- Congenital
Conjecture	- Guess
Consanguinous	- Agnate
Consecrate	- Enshrine
Consent	- Assent
Consequence	- Effect
Consign	- Commit
Consort	- Companion
Conspicuous	- Apparent
Construe	- Infer
Conserve	- Conserve
Constantly	- Continuously
Consult	- Consult
Contaminate	- Adulterate, Defile
Contemporary	- Contemporary
Contend	- Struggle
Contemporaneous	- Contemporary
Contentious	- Controversial

For Synonyms of	See
Contempt	- Contempt
Contiguity	- Closeness
Contingent	- Contingent
Continually	- Continuously
Continence	- Abstemiousness
Continuously	- Continuously
Contort	- Twist
Contrail	- Mark
Contradictory	- Opposite
Contrary	- Disobedient, Opposite
Contrast	- Compare
Contravene	- Breach
Contravention	- Violation
Contrition	- Attrition, Repentance
Contrive	- Devise
Controversial	- Controversial
Conundrum	- Puzzle
Convulse	- Shake
Convulsion	- Fit (epillepsy)
Cooperate	- Cooperate
Coordination	- Understanding
Cope	- Struggle
Cordon	- Surround
Correspondence	- Similarity
Corruscate	- Dazzle
Cosmic	- Catholic
Cosmopolitan	- Catholic
Costume	- Dress
Countenance	- Face
Counterfeit	- Fake
Countermand	- Annul
Coupd'etat	- Revolt
Courage	- Courage

For Synonyms of	See
Covet	- Crave
Coward	- Coward
Cower	- Cringe, Kneel
Coy	- Shy
Crack	- Crack
Crafty	- Clever
Crash	- Bump
Crave	- Crave
Crawl	- Crawl
Craze	- Craze
Create	- Create
Credence	- Belief
Credit	- Credit, Belief
Creep	- Crawl
Crevice	- Crack
Cringe	- Cringe
Criticize	- Criticize
Criticism	- Criticism
Crony	- Friend
Crop	- Trim
Crouch	- Cringe
Cruel	- Cruel
Cruise	- Journey
Crumple	- Mash
Cry	- Cry
Cue	- Hint
Cuff	- Slap, Beat
Cull	- Collect, Kill
Culminate	- Climax
Curb	- Stop
Curdle	- Clot
Curious	- Eager
Curse	- Curse
Custom	- Tradition
Cynicism	- Disbelief

For Synonyms of	See

D

For Synonyms of	See
Dainty	- Exquisite
Dally	- Trifle
Damage	- Damage
Dammed	- Accursed
Danger	- Danger
Dash	- Bump
Daunt	- Discourage
Dawdle	- Dilly-dally
Daze	- Baffle
Dazzle	- Dazzle, Shine
Deadbody	- Deadbody; cadaver
Deadlock	- Deadlock
Deadly	- Fatal
Dearth	- Dearth
Debacle	- Failure
Debase	- Devalue
Debris	- Debris
Deceive	- Deceive
Decimate	- Massacre, Kill
Declaim	- Affirm
Declare	- Announce, Declare
Decline	- Deny, Reject
Decorate	- Decorate
Decoy	- Bait
Decrease	- Deplete
Decree	- Order
Decrepit	- Decrepit
Decry	- Denounce
Deduce	- Infer
Deem	- Regard
Defalcate	- Defalcate
Defame	- Defame

For Synonyms of	See
Defeat	- Defeat
Defect	- Defect
Defector	- Defector
Defer	- Adjourn, Surrender
Deference	- Reverence
Deficiency	- Defect
Defile	- Defile, Tarnish
Defraud	- Cheat
Defray	- Demise
Deft	- Disobey
Degenerate	- Degenerate
Degrade	- Abash, Devalue
Deign	- Stoop
Dejection	- Disappointment
Delectable	- Tasty
Delegate	- Authorise
Deleterious	- Injurious
Delicate	- Delicate
Delicious	- Tasty
Deliver	- Discharge
Deliverence	- Deliverence
Delude	- Deceive
Delve	- Delve
Demean	- Devalue
Demeanour	- Behaviour
Demise	- Bequeath, Cede
Demit	- Cede
Demolish	- Demolish
Demonstrate	- Demonstrate
Demur	- Hesitate
Demure	- Shy
Denomination	- Class
Denounce	- Denounce
Deny	- Deny, Deprive, Reject

For Synonyms of	See
Deplete	- Deplete
Deplore	- Denounce
Deportment	- Behaviour
Deprave	- Abash
Deprecate	- Denounce
Depreciate	- Degenerate
Deprive	- Deprive
Deride	- Deride, Ridicule
Derogate	- Insult
Derogatory	- Insulting
Descend	- Descend
Descendant	- Descendant
Desecrate	- Defile
Desert	- Abandon
Deserted	- Lonely
Desire	- Desire
Desist	- Abstain
Desolate	- Lonely, Sad, Alone
Despair	- Disappointment
Despite	- Malice
Despoil	- Loot
Despondence	- Disappointment
Despot	- Autocrat
Destitute	- Poor
Destitution	- Poverty
Destroy	- Destroy, Demolish
Detain	- Stop
Deter	- Discourage
Deteriorate	- Degenerate
Determination	- Determination
Detrimental	- Injurious
Devalue	- Devalue
Devastate	- Destory

For Synonyms of	See
Deviate	- Deviate; aborrate
Devise	- Devise
Devotion	- Allegiance, Loyalty
Devour	- Devour
Dextrous	- Adroit
Diatribe	- Criticism
Differ	- Disagree
Difference	- Difference
Differences	- Differences; dissentions
Diffuse	- Disperse, Scatter
Digout	- Digout
Digress	- Deviate
Diktat	- Order
Dilapidated	- Decrepit
Dilate	- Swell
Dilemma	- Dilemma
Dilettante	- Admirer
Diligent	- Assiduous
Dilly-dally	- Dilly-dally
Dimension	- Aspect
Diminish	- Deplete
Din	- Din
Dip	- Dip, Sink
Directive	- Instruction
Dirge	- Lamentation
Disaffection	- Alienation
Disagree	- Disagree
Disappear	- Disappear
Disappointment	- Disappointment
Disapprove	- Disagree
Disaster	- Disaster
Disastrous	- Injurious
Disavow	- Deny

For Synonyms of	See
Disbelief	- Disbelief
Discard	- Discard
Discarded	- Abandoned
Discharge	- Discharge, Emit
Disclose	- Disclose
Discomfit	- Perplex, Agitate
Disconcert	- Perplex, Agitate
Disconcerted	- Upset, Agitated
Disconsolate	- Agitated, Sad, Upset
Discontented	- Dissatisfied
Discord	- Differences
Discount	- Concession
Discourage	- Discourage
Discourse	- Speech
Discrepancy	- Difference
Distain	- Contempt
Disenfranchise	- Deprive
Disgorge	- Disgorge
Disgress	- Insult
Disgruntled	- Dis-satisfied
Disguise	- Hide, Disguise
Dishevelled	- Disorderly, Untidy
Dishonour	- Insult
Disinter	- Digout
Disintegrate	- Disintegrate
Dismay	- Distress
Dismiss	- Retrench
Disobey	- Disobey
Disobedient	- Disobedient
Disorderly	- Disorderly
Disparage	- Insult
Disparaging	- Insulting
Disparaging	- Difference

For Synonyms of	See
Dispense	- Get rid of
Disperse	- Disperse, Scatter
Display	- Demonstrate
Dispose of	- Discard, Get rid of
Disposition	- Inclination, Bias
Disprove	- Confute
Dispute	- Object, Differences
Disregard	- Ignore
Disruption	- Deadlock
Dissatisfied	- Dissatisfied
Dissemble	- Hide
Disseminate	- Scatter
Dissent	- Disagree, Differences
Dissipate	- Scatter, Disperse
Dissociate	- Dissociate
Dissolute	- Unrestrained
Dissuade	- Discourage
Distend	- Swell
Distinct	- Apparent; Clear
Distinction	- Difference
Distort	- Twist
Distrain	- Confiscate
Distraught	- Agitated, Upset
Distress	- Distress
Distrust	- Disbelief
Ditch	- Deceive
Dither	- Hesitate, Waver
Dithyramb	- Chant
Diurnal	- Nocturnal
Divagate	- Deviate
Dive	- Descend
Diverge	- Deviate
Divine	- Holy

For Synonyms of	See
Divulge	- Disclose
Dock	- Trim
Doctrine	- Principle
Dodge	- Dodge
Dogma	- Principle
Doldrums	- Boredom
Doleful	- Sad
Doll	- Effigy
Domain	- Domain
Dominance	- Dominance
Dominate	- Dominate
Domineer	- Dominate
Doomed	- Accursed
Dormant	- Dormant
Drawback	- Defect
Dread	- Fear
Dreadful	- Terrifying
Dreary	- Dull
Dregs	- Dregs
Dress	- Dress
Dribble	- Dribble
Drink	- Drink
Drip	- Dribble
Drivel	- Chant, Chatter, Dribble, Nonsense
Droll	- Ridiculous
Drone	- Din
Drool	- Dribble
Droop	- Droop
Drove	- Herd
Drown	- Drown, Sink
Duck	- Dodge
Dudgeon	- Irritation
Dull	- Dull
Dunk	- Sink, Dip

For Synonyms of	See
Dupe	- Cheat
Duress	- Threat
Dwarf	- Dwarf
Dwindle	- Deplete

E

For Synonyms of	See
Eager	- Eager
Ecumenical	- Catholic
Edict	- Order
Educe	- Elicit
Eerie	- Weird
Effect	- Effect
Effective	- Effective
Effectual	- Effective
Efficacious	- Effective
Effigy	- Effigy
Egregious	- Egregious
Ejaculate	- Eject
Eject	- Eject
Eke out	- Conserve
Elegant	- Equisite
Elegy	- Lamentation
Elevate	- Elevate
Elicit	- Elicit
Elongate	- Elongate
Elope	- Abscond
Elucidate	- Explain
Elude	- Abscord
Emanate	- Emit
Embark	- Climb
Embellish	- Decorate
Embezzle	- Defalcate
Embrace	- Embrace, Affix
Embroiled	- Involved; mired
Emend	- Amend

For Synonyms of	See
Eminent	- Eminent
Emit	- Emit
Empathy	- Sympathy
Emphasize	- Emphasize
Empty	- Vacant
Emulate	- Emulate
Emunge	- Clean
Encounter	- Encounter
Encourage	- Motivate
Encroach	- Encroach
Endeavour	- Attempt, Try
Endorse	- Approve
Endow	- Demise
Endure	- Tolerate
Enervated	- Lazy
Enfranchise	- Discharge
Engender	- Create
Engross	- Hold
Engrossed	- Involved
Enhance	- Elevate
Enigma	- Puzzle
Enigmatic	- Mysterious
Enlarge	- Discharge
Ennui	- Boredom
Enormous	- Terrible
Enrage	- Anger
Ensconce	- Hide
Enshrine	- Enshrine
Ensnare	- Ensnare
Entangle	- Ensnare
Enter	- Enter
Entertain	- Entertain
Enthusiasm	- Enthusiasm
Enthrall	- Hold
Entice	- Lure, Entice

For Synonyms of	See
Entrap	- Ensnare
Entreat	- Request (earnestly)
Entrust	- Commit
Entwine	- Ensnare
Ephemeral	- Ephemeral
Epithalamium	- Anthem
Epithet	- Epithet
Epitome	- Apotheosis
Epoch	- Turning Point
Equality	- Equality
Equivalence	- Equality, Similarity
Equivocate	- Prevaricate
Eradicate	- Eradicate
Erect	- Erect
Error	- Mistake
Ersatz	- Bogus, Fake
Eructate	- Disgorge
Erudite	- Learned
Escape	- Abscond
Escheat	- Confiscate
Eschew	- Abstain, Avoid
Esoteric	- Mysterious
Esprit d' corps	- Allegiance
Espy	- Look
Essential	- Essential
Esteem	- Reverence
Estimate	- Appraise
Estrangement	- Alienation
Ethics	- Ethics
Eulogize	- Praise
Evade	- Avoid
Evaluate	- Appraise
Evanesce	- Disappear
Evanescent	- Ephemeral

For Synonyms of	See
Event	- Occurrence
Evince	- Demonstrate
Evoke	- Elicit
Examine	- Examine
Example	- Example
Exasperate	- Annoy
Exasperation	- Annoyance
Excavate	- Digout
Exception (Take)	- Object
Excessive	- Abundant
Exchange	- Exchange
Exchequer	- Treasury
Exclusive	- Exclusive
Excommunicate	- Boycott, Banish
Excoriate	- Abrade
Exculpate	- Aquit
Excursion	- Journey
Excuse	- Alibi
Execrate	- Denounce; detest
Exemption	- Concession
Exhausted	- Exhausted
Exhibit	- Demonstrate
Exhort	- Appeal
Exhume	- Digout
Exile	- Banish
Exonerate	- Aquit
Exotic	- Exclusive
Expanse	- Spread
Expatiate	- Explain
Expedition	- Journey
Expiate	- Amend
Explain	- Explain
Expostulate	- Reason
Expound	- Explain
Expunge	- Amend

For Synonyms of	See
Expurgate	- Amend
Exquisite	- Exquisite, Exclusive
Extemporaneous	- Extempore
Extempore	- Spontaneous, Extempore
Extent	- Spread
Extenuate	- Extenuate
Exterminate	- Eradicate
Extinguish	- Extinguish
Extirpate	- Eradicate
Extol	- Praise
Extradite	- Banish
Extraordinary	- Extraordinary
Extravagant	- Unrestrained, Extravagant
Exude	- Emit

F

For Synonyms of	See
Fabricate	- Devise
Facade	- Face
Face	- Face
Facet	- Face, Aspect
Facetious	- Facetious
Fad	- Craze
Faggot	- Bundle
Failure	- Failure
Fake	- Fake
Falter	- Falter
Famous	- Famous
Fan	- Admirer
Fanatic	- Bigot
Fanciful	- Fanciful, Strange
Fare	- Fare
Fart	- Emit
Fascinate	- Hold
Fashion	- Devise
Fasten	- Tie
Fastidious	- Fastidious
Fatal	- Fatal
Fathomless	- Abysmal
Fatigued	- Exhausted
Fault	- Mistake, Defect
Faux pas	- Mistake
Fawn	- Flatter
Faze	- Agitate, Perplex
Fealty	- Allegiance, Loyalty
Fear	- Fear
Fecund	- Fertile
Fee	- Fare
Feign	- Affect, Pretend
Feint	- Bait, Ruse
Fence	- Dodge
Ferocious	- Cruel
Fertile	- Fertile
Fervour	- Enthusiasm, Passion
Fetid	- Bad smelling, Malodorous
Fiat	- Order
Fib	- Prevaricate
Fidelity	- Allegiance, Loyalty
Fight	- Fight
Filch	- Steal
Finnicky	- Fastidious
Fisc	- Treasury
Fissure	- Crack
Fisticuff	- Fight

For Synonyms of	See
Fit	- Fit
Flabbergast	- Amaze
Flabby	- Limp
Flaccid	- Limp
Flag	- Flag
Flagitious	- Wicked (grossly; shamefully)
Flagrant	- Egregious
Flatter	- Flatter
Flatterer	- Sycophant
Flaunt	- Demonstrate
Flavour	- Aroma, Smell
Flaw	- Defect
Fleer	- Laugh, Ridicule
Fleet	- While away
Fleeting	- Ephemeral
Flexuous	- Flexuous
Flicker	- Tremble
Flinch	- Flinch
Fling	- Throw
Flippant	- Facetious
Flirt	- Trifle
Flock	- Herd
Floppy	- Limp
Flotsam	- Debris, Wreckage
Flounder	- Falter
Flurry	- Ado
Flush	- Clean
Foible	- Folly
Follower	- Follower
Folly	- Folly
Foment	- Instigate
Fondle	- Caress
Forage	- Delve

For Synonyms of	See
Forbid	- Forbid, Ban
Foreboding	- Inkling
Forebears	- Ancestor
Forecast	- Foretell
Forefathers	- Ancestor
Foresight	- Foresight
Foretell	- Foretell
Forfeit	- Confiscate
Forge	- Devise
Forlorn	- Sad, Alone
Formidable	- Awesome
Forsake	- Abandon
Forswear	- Abandon, Backtrack
Fortitude	- Courage
Fortuitous	- Casual
Fortune	- Property
Foster	- Foster
Fracas	- Quarrel
Fractious	- Irritable
Fragment	- Disintegrate, Scrap
Fragrance	- Aroma, Smell
Fraility	- Folly
Franchise	- Franchise
Fraud	- Cheat
Free	- Free
Freight	- Fare
Fret	- Abrade
Fretful	- Irritable
Friend	- Friend
Fright	- Fear
Frighten	- Frighten
Frightening	- Terrifying

For Synonyms of	*See*
Frisk	- Delve
Frivolous	- Facetious
Frolic	- Caper
Froward	- Disobedient
Frugal	- Miser
Fumble	- Falter
Funny	- Ridiculous
Fury	- Anger
Fussy	- Fastidious
Fusty	- Bad smelling, Malodorous
Futility	- Failure
G	
Gad	- Wander
Gaff	- Mistake; blunder
Gaggle	- Flock (of geese)
Gall	- Arrogance, Abrade
Gallivant	- Wander
Galore	- Abundant
Gambol	- Caper
Gape	- Gaze, Crack
Garb	- Dress
Garbage	- Garbage
Garment	- Dress
Garner	- Collect
Garnish	- Decorate
Garrulous	- Talkative
Gather	- Collect
Gaze	- Gaze, Look
Gender	- Class
Generate	- Create
Generous	- Rapacious
Genocide	- Genocide

For Synonyms of	*See*
Genre	- Class
Genuflect	- Kneel (bended)
Genus	- Class
Germane	- Appropriate, Apposite, Relevant
Get rid of	- Get rid of
Ghastly	- Horrible, Terrible
Giggle	- Laugh
Gimmick	- Ruse
Gird	- Tie
Glance	- Gaze, Look
Glare	- Gaze, Look, Shine
Gleam	- Dazzle, Shine
Glib	- Talkative
Glimmer	- Shine
Glisten	- Shine
Glitter	- Sparkle (with light); reflection of light with brilliance
Gloat	- Look; to gaze with a wicked or malicious joy
Gloomy	- Sad
Gloss	- A false or deceptive appearance
Glower	- Look
Gloze	- Extenuate
Glut	- Abound
Goad	- Stimulate
Gobble	- Devour
Gobbledegook	- Language characterised by circumlocution and jargon

For Synonyms of	See
Gore	- Pierce (with bones or tusks)
Gorge	- Devour, Gorge
Gourmet	- A connoisseur of delicacies of food and beverages
Grab	- Catch
Gradation	- Gradation
Grant	- Aid
Grasp	- Catch
Grate	- Scrape
Graze	- Scrape
Greenhorn	- Novice
Grieve	- Lament
Grimace	- Facial expression, often ugly or contorted, that indicates disapproval, pain etc.
Grin	- Smile
Grind	- Grind
Grisly	- Horrible
Grit	- Determination
Grope	- Delve; Search
Grotesque	- Absurd, Strange
Grouse	- Malice; ill will; spite
Grovel	- Cringe
Growl	- Growl
Grudge	- Malice
Gruesome	- Horrible
Grumble	- Complain, Growl
Guess	- Guess
Guffaw	- Laugh
Guide	- Guide

For Synonyms of	See
Gull	- Cheat
Gulp	- Drink
Guts	- Courage
Guzzle	- Drink
Gyrate	- Spin

H

For Synonyms of	See
Habiliment	- Dress; attire
Habituate	- Acclimatize
Hack	- Mercenary
Haggard	- Cadaverous, Exhausted
Hail	- Admire
Handicap	- Defect
Hanker	- Crave
Haphazard	- Indiscriminate
Happening	- Occurrence
Happenstance	- Occurrence; chance
Harangue	- A loud speech addressed to a multitude
Harass	- Harass
Harbinger	- Announcer pioneer/ forerunner
Harbour	- Shelter
Hardihood	- Boldness; audacity; robustness
Harness	- Tie
Harry	- Harass
Harsh	- Austere
Hasty	- Hasty
Haven	- Shelter
Hazard	- Risk, Danger
Healthful	- Healthful

For Synonyms of	*See*
Heave	- Elevate
Hector	- Chide
Hegemony	- Dominance
Heist	- Theft
Henchman	- Follower
Herald	- Announce, Announcer Declare
Herd	- Herd
Heresy	- Sacrilege
Hesitate	- Hesitate
Hiatus	- Crack
Hibernating	- Dormant
Hide	- Hide
Hinder	- Block
Hindrance	- Deadlock, Obstacle
Hint	- Hint
Hireling	- Mercenary
Hirsel	- Herd
Hoist	- Elevate
Hold	- Hold, Catch
Holy	- Holy
Homage	- Reverence
Homily	- Speech
Hoodwink	- Cheat
Hoot	- Scream
Horrendous	- Terrible
Horrible	- Horrible, Terrible
Horrid	- Terrible
Horrify	- Frighten
Horrifying	- Terrifying
Horror	- Fear
Hosannah	- Anthem
Host	- Abundant

For Synonyms of	*See*
Hubris	- Pride
Huff	- Annoyance, Irritation
Hug	- Affix, Embrace
Hum	- Din
Humane	- Kind
Humbug	- Quack
Humdrum	- Dull
Hunch	- Inkling
Hurdle	- Obstacle
Hurl	- Hurl, Throw
Hurt	- Damage
Hygienic	- Healthful
Hypochondria	- Anxiety
Hypochondriac	- Atrabilious

I

Idea	- Idea
Idle away	- While away
Ignoble	- Abject, Miserable
Ignoming	- Infamy
Ignoramus	- Ignoramus
Ignore	- Ignore
Imbibe	- Absorb
Imbue	- Inculcate
Imitate	- Emulate
Immense	- Terrific
Immerse	- Dip, Sink
Immure	- Confine, Imprison
Immanent	- Inherent
Impair	- Damage
Impale	- Pierce
Impart	- Demise
Impassive	- Impassive
Impatient	- Hasty

For Synonyms of	See
Impeach	- Accuse
Impecunious	- Poor
Impel	- Stimulate
Impersonate	- Disguise
Impediment	- Obstacle
Impertinent	- Arrogant, Rude, Impertinent
Impetuous	- Hasty
Impinge	- Impinge
Impious	- Impious
Implicate	- Ensnare
Implication	- Effect (implied)
Implore	- Request
Imposter	- Cheat
Impression	- Influence
Impound	- Confiscate, Imprison
Impoverish	- Degenerate
Impoverished	- Poor
Imprecate	- Curse
Impromptu	- Extempore, Spontaneous
Improvised	- Spontaneous
Imprison	- Imprison
Impudent	- Arrogant, Rude, Shameless
Impugn	- Object
Impulsive	- Hasty
Impute	- Credit
Inauspicious	- Ominous
Inborn	- Congenital
Incarcerate	- Confine, Imprison
Incense	- Smell, Anger
Incentive	- Prize
Incidence	- Occurrence

For Synonyms of	See
Incident	- Occurrence
Incidental	- Casual
Incipient	- Nascent
Incite	- Instigate
Inclination	- Inclination
Inchoate	- Nascent
Incredibility	- Disbelief
Incriminate	- Accuse
Inculcate	- Inculcate
Incumbent	- Contingent
Indecent	- Indecent
Indefatigable	- Untiring
Indemnify	- Indemnify, Compensate
Independent	- Free
Indict	- Accuse
Indigenous	- Aborigine
Indigent	- Poor
Indigence	- Poverty
Indiscriminate	- Indiscriminate
Indispensable	- Essential
Indoctrinate	- Inculcate
Indolent	- Lazy
Indomitable	- Invincible
Induce	- Motivate
Inducement	- Motive
Indulged	- Involved
Inept	- Awkward
Infamy	- Infamy
Infer	- Infer
Infiltrate	- Enter
Inflate	- Swell
Inflict	- Afflict
Influence	- Dominance, Influence

For Synonyms of	See
Inform	- Inform
Infraction	- Violation
Infringe	- Encroach
Infringement	- Violation
Infuriate	- Anger
Infuse	- Inculcate
Ingress	- Enter
Inherent	- Inherent
Inhibit	- Ban, Forbid
Injunction	- Order, Instruction
Inhuman	- Cruel
Inimical	- Injurious
Injurious	- Injurious
Iniquitous	- Wicked
Inkling	- Inkling
Innate	- Congenital
Innovate	- Innovate
Innuendo	- Hint
Inquisitive	- Eager; arious
Insert	- Insert
Insidious	- Treacherous
Insinuate	- Inculcate, Insert
Insinuation	- Hint
Insolent	- Rude
Inspect	- Examine
Inspire	- Motivate
Inspiration	- Motive
Instance	- Example, Occurrence
Instantly	- Extemporily
Instigate	- Instigate
Instil	- Inculcate
Instruction	- Instruction
Insult	- Insult

For Synonyms of	See
Insulting	- Insulting
Intensify	- Aggravate
Insurmountable	- Invincible
Intercede	- Interject
Insurrection	- Revolt
Insurgency	- Revolt
Interject	- Interject
Intermediary	- Mediator
Intern	- Confine, Imprison
Interpose	- Interject
Interpret	- Infer
Interruption	- Deadlock
Intervene	- Interject
Intimidate	- Frighten
Intrinsic	- Inherent
Introspect	- Cogitate
Intrude	- Enter
Intrusive	- Impertinent
Intuition	- Inkling
Inundate	- Sink, Dip
Inure	- Acclimatise
Invective	- Criticism
Invate	- Enter
Inveigh	- Criticize
Inveigle	- Entice, Lure, Persuade
Investigate	- Examine
Invincible	- Invincible, Inexorable
Involved	- Involved
Irascible	- Irritable
Ironic	- Sarcastic
Irony	- Paradox
Irritation	- Irritation

For Synonyms of	See
Irritate	- Annoy
Irritable	- Irritable
Isolate	- Seclude
J	
Jabber	- Chatter
Jam	- Block
Jargon	- Cant
Jaunt	- Journey
Jeer	- Ridicule
Jeopardy	- Danger, Risk
Jetsam	- Wreckage
Jettison	- Discard, Throw
Jib	- Disobey, Hesitate
Jilt	- Discard
Journey	- Journey
Junket	- Journey
Jurisdiction	- Domain
Jurist	- Lawyer
Justify	- Justify
Jutout	- Jutout
K	
Keen	- Cry
Ken	- Domain, Eager
Kill	- Kill
Kind	- Kind
Kindred	- Agnate
Kneel	- Kneel
Knock	- Strike
Kowtow	- Kneel
L	
Lack	- Dearth
Lackadaisical	- Dull
Lackey	- Sycophant

For Synonyms of	See
Lacklustre	- Dull
Laconic	- Uncommunicative
Lacuna	- Defect
Lagan	- Debris, Wreckage
Laity	- Ignoramus
Lampoon	- Deride, Ridicule, Satire
Lament	- Lament, Regret
Lamentation	- Lamentation
Languid	- Exhausted, Lazy
Languishing	- Lazy
Languor	- Laziness
Languorous	- Lazy
Larceny	- Theft
Largesse	- Prize
Lascivious	- Lewd
Lassitude	- Laziness
Latent	- Dormant
Laud	- Praise
Laugh	- Laugh
Lawyer	- Lawyer
Lay off	- Retrench
Laziness	- Laziness
Lazy	- Lazy
Learned	- Learned
Lee	- Shelter
Leer	- Look
Lees	- Dregs
Legate	- Bequeath
Legion	- Abundant
Lengthen	- Elongate
Lesemajeste	- Revolt
Lethal	- Fatal
Levigate	- Grind
Levitate	- Ascend, Lift

For Synonyms of	See
Lewd	- Lewd
Lextalionis	- Recrimination
Libel	- Defame
Libertine	- Unrestrained
Libidinous	- Lewd
Licentious	- Unrestrained
Lie down	- Lie down
Lie prone	- Lie down
Lie prostrate	- Lie down (facing the earth)
Lie recumbent	- Lie down
Lie supine	- Lie down
Lift	- Elevate, Lift
Ligate	- Tie
Limp	- Limp
Linger	- Stay
Lingo	- Cant
Listless	- Lazy
Listlessness	- Laziness
Litter	- Garbage, Herd
Loaf	- Wander
Lob	- Hurl, Throw
Loll	- While away
Lonely	- Alone, Lonely
Long	- Crave
Look	- Look
Loot	- Loot
Lop	- Droop, Trim
Loquacious	- Talkative
Loud	- Loud
Lounge	- While away
Loyalty	- Loyalty, Allegiance
Ludicrous	- Ridiculous; Absurd

For Synonyms of	See
Lugubrious	- Sad
Lure	- Lure
Luscious	- Tasty
Lustful	- Lewd
Lustrate	- Clean

M

For Synonyms of	See
Macabre	- Horrible, Weird
Magnanimous	- Kind
Magnate	- Baron
Maladroit	- Awkward
Malaprop	- Mistake
Malevolence	- Malice
Malice	- Malice
Malign	- Defame
Malinger	- Affect, Pretend
Malodour	- Malodour, Smell
Malodorous	- Malodorous
Mammoth	- Colossal
Mandate	- Order
Manifest	- Apparent, Demonstrate
Mania	- Craze
Mannequin	- Effigy
Marionette	- Effigy
Mark	- Mark
Maroon	- Surround
Marsh	- Mire
Marshall	- Set one's thoughts in sequence
Marvel	- Marvel
Mash	- Mash
Mask	- Hide
Masquerade	- Disguise
Massacre	- Genocide, Massacre

For Synonyms of	See
Mast	- Pillar
Matins	- Prayer
Mausoleum	- Memorial
Meandering	- Flexuous
Mediator	- Mediator
Meditate	- Cogitate
Medley	- Pot pourie
Melancholic	- Sad, Atrabilious
Melange	- Pot pourie
Melee	- Babel, Quarrel
Memento	- Memento
Memorabilia	- Memento
Memorial	- Memorial
Menacing	- Awesome
Mend	- Repair
Mercenary	- Mercenary
Metier	- Profession
Mettle	- Determination
Midget	- Dwarf
Mien	- Face
Mighty	- Powerful
Mime	- Emulate
Mimic	- Emulate
Minatory	- Awesome
Miracle	- Marvel
Mire	- Mire
Misappropriate	- Defalcate
Miscarriage	- Failure
Miser	- Miser
Miserable	- Miserable
Mistake	- Mistake
Mistrust	- Disbelief
Mitigate	- Extenuate, Relieve, Abate

For Synonyms of	See
Moat	- Boundary
Mock	- Deride, Ridicule
Modest	- Shy
Mollify	- Appease
Molt	- Discard
Monolith	- Colossal
Monotonous	- Dull
Montage	- Pot pourie
Monument	- Memorial
Mop	- Clean
Morality	- Ethics
Morals	- Ethics
Mordant	- Acerbic
Mortal remains	- Deadbody
Mortify	- Abash
Motive	- Motive
Motivate	- Motivate
Mottle	- Spot
Moult	- Discard
Mount	- Climb
Mourn	- Lament
Mull	- Cogitate
Munch	- Chew
Murder	- Kill
Murmur	- Din
Muster	- Collect
Musty	- Bad smelling, Malodorous
Mutiny	- Revolt
Muzzle	- Face
Mysterious	- Mysterious
Mystic	- Mysterious

For Synonyms of	See
N	
Nab	- Catch
Nap	- Nap
Nascent	- Nascent
Native	- Aborigine
Necessary	- Essential
Nefarious	- Wicked
Neglect	- Ignore
Neglected	- Abandoned
Neophyte	- Novice
Nexus	- Understanding
Nickname	- Epithet
Niggardly	- Miser
Noisome	- Bad smelling, Malodorous
Non-pareil	- Apotheosis
Nonsense	- Nonsense
Notion	- Idea
Novice	- Novice
Noxious	- Injurious
Nuance	- Delicate, Gradation
Nurture	- Foster
O	
Obeisance	- Reverence
Object	- Object
Objurgate	- Criticize, Rebuke
Obloquy	- Criticism, Infamy
Obsequious	- Servile
Obsession	- Craze
Obsolete	- Outdated
Obstacle	- Obstacle
Obstinate	- Arrogant
Obstruct	- Block

For Synonyms of	See
Obstruction	- Deadlock, Obstacle
Obtrusive	- Impertinent
Obviate	- Avert
Occupation	- Profession
Occurrence	- Occurrence
Odium	- Infamy
Odour	- Smell
Offence	- Insult
Ogle	- Look
Omen	- Omen
Ominous	- Ominous
Omnipresent	- Ubiquitous
Ooze	- Disgorge
Opposite	- Opposite
Opprobrium	- Infamy
Opulent	- Rich
Oration	- Speech
Ordainment	- Order
Order	- Order
Orgasm	- Climax
Outcaste	- Banish, Boycott
Outdated	- Outdated
Outrage	- Anger, Encroach
Outstanding	- Extraordinary
Overture	- Overture
Overwhelm	- Sink
P	
Palliate	- Extenuate
Palter	- Prevaricate
Pandemonium	- Babel
Panegyrize	- Praise
Panel	- Clique
Panic	- Frighten

For Synonyms of	See
Parade	- Demonstrate
Paradigm	- Example
Paradox	- Paradox
Paragon	- Apotheosis
Paranoia	- Anxiety
Parapet	- Boundary
Pare	- Trim
Pariah	- Anathema
Parity	- Equality, Similarity
Parley	- Consult
Paroxysm	- Fit
Parry	- Avert, Dodge
Parsimonious	- Miser
Passion	- Enthusiasm, Passion
Paternoster	- Prayer
Patriotism	- Loyalty
Pay damages	- Indemnify
Peak	- Peak
Pedant	- Learned
Peek	- Peep
Peel	- Bark
Peep	- Peep
Peer	- Gaze, Look
Peevish	- Irritable
Pelt	- Throw, Hurl
Penchant	- Inclination
Penetrate	- Insert
Penitence	- Repentance, Attrition
Penurious	- Miser, Poor
Penury	- Poverty
Perception	- Idea
Peril	- Risk, Danger

For Synonyms of	See
Pernicious	- Injurious
Perpetually	- Continuously
Perplex	- Perplex, Baffle
Persecute	- Harass
Persevere	- Try
Persevering	- Assiduous
Persistent	- Assiduous
Perspicacious	- Clever
Persuade	- Persuade
Pertinent	- Apposite, Relevant
Perturb	- Perplex
Pet	- Caress
Petrify	- Benumb
Pettifog	- Quibble
Petulant	- Irritable
Phenomenal	- Extraordinary
Phenomenon	- Marvel
Philippic	- Criticism, Speech
Phlegmatic	- Impassive
Physiognomy	- Face
Pierce	- Insert, Pierce
Pilfer	- Steal
Pilgrimage	- Journey
Pillage	- Loot
Pillar	- Pillar
Pillory	- Deride, Ridicule
Pinched	- Cadaverous
Pinnacle	- Peak
Pioneer	- Guide
Pique	- Irritation
Piracy	- Theft
Pirouette	- Spin
Pitiable	- Miserable

For Synonyms of	See
Placate	- Appease
Placebo	- Bogus
Placid	- Calm
Plagiarise	- Steal
Platitude	- Cliche
Plea	- Alibi
Plead	- Appeal, Request
Plenty	- Abundant
Plethora	- Abundant
Plight	- Dilemma
Ploy	- Ruse
Plummet	- Descend
Plunder	- Loot
Plunge	- Descend
Pogrom	- Genocide, Massacre
Pole	- Pillar
Politic	- Politic
Poll	- Trim
Pollute	- Adulterate
Poor	- Poor
Poppycock	- Nonsense
Popular	- Famous
Pore	- Look
Portend	- Augur, Foretell
Portent	- Omen
Portentous	- Ominous
Possum (Play)	- Pretend
Posterity	- Descendant
Pot pouri	- Pot pouri
Postpone	- Adjourn
Potent	- Powerful
Potentate	- Powerful
Pound	- Beat

For Synonyms of	See
Poverty	- Poverty
Powerful	- Powerful
Practice	- Tradition
Praise	- Praise
Prattle	- Chatter
Prayer	- Prayer
Pragmatic	- Politic
Precedence	- Precedence
Precedent	- Example, Precedence
Preclude	- Avert
Predicament	- Dilemma
Predict	- Foretell
Predilection	- Inclination, Bias
Predisposition	- Bias, Inclination
Pre-empt	- Arrogate
Preen	- Caress
Premonition	- Inkling
Preposterous	- Absurd, Strange
Prescience	- Inkling
Prescription	- Instruction
Presentiment	- Inkling
Preserve	- Conserve
Presumptuous	- Arrogant
Pretend	- Affect, Pretend
Pretext	- Alibi
Prevail	- Dominate
Prevaricate	- Prevaricate
Prick	- Impinge
Prickle	- Impinge
Pride	- Pride
Primitive	- Archaic
Principle	- Principle
Priority	- Precedence

For Synonyms of	See
Pristine	- Archaic
Privation	- Poverty
Prize	- Prize
Proclaim	- Announce, Declare
Proclivity	- Inclination
Procrastinate	- Dilly-dally
Prodigal	- Extravagant
Prodigious	- Extraordinary
Prodigy	- Marvel
Profane	- Impious
Profanity	- Sacrilege
Profess	- Pretend
Profession	- Profession
Proficient	- Adroit
Profligate	- Unrestrained
Progenitor	- Ancestor
Progeny	- Descendant
Prognosticate	- Foretell
Prohibit	- Ban, Forbid
Project	- Jut out
Prolapse	- Buckle
Prolific	- Fertile
Prolong	- Elongate
Promulgate	- Announce
Prop	- Pillar
Propensity	- Inclination
Property	- Property
Prophesy	- Foretell
Propinquity	- Closeness; proximity
Propitiate	- Appease
Propitious	- Auspicious
Prorogue	- Adjourn

For Synonyms of	See
Proscribe	- Forbid
Proselyte	- Defector
Protest	- Object
Protract	- Elongate; prolong
Protuberate	- Jut out
Provident	- Politic
Province	- Domain
Provoke	- Stimulate
Prowl	- Wander
Proximity	- Closeness
Prudent	- Politic; wise
Prune	- Trim
Pry	- Peep
Pugnacious	- Quarrelsome
Puisant	- Powerful
Pulvarise	- Grind
Pummel	- Beat
Puppet	- Effigy
Purloin	- Steal
Purr	- Growl
Putrid	- Bad smelling, Malodorous
Putsch	- Revolt
Puzzle	- Puzzle
Pygmy	- Dwarf
Pylon	- Pillar (in bridge)

Q

For Synonyms of	See
Quack	- Quack
Quaff	- Drink
Quagmire	- Mire
Quail	- Extinguish, Flinch
Quake	- Tremble
Qualm	- Hesitation

For Synonyms of	See
Quandary	- Dilemma
Quarantine	- Seclude
Quarrel	- Quarrel
Quarrelsome	- Quarrelsome
Quaver	- Tremble
Queer	- Strange
Quell	- Extinguish
Quench	- Extinguish
Quibble	- Quibble
Quiver	- Tremble
Quixotic	- Fanciful
Quotidian	- Circadian

R

For Synonyms of	See
Rabble	- Herd
Rage	- Anger
Raise	- Elevate
Ramification	- Aspect
Rampant	- Unrestrained
Rampart	- Boundary
Ramshackled	- Decrepit
Rancid	- Bad smelling, Malodorous
Rancour	- Malice
Random	- Indiscriminate
Rank	- Malodorous
Ransom	- Restore
Rapacious	- Generous
Rapprochement	- Rehabilitation
Rash	- Hasty
Rationalise	- Justify
Rattle	- Frighten, Perplex, Agitate
Raucus	- Loud
Ravage	- Destroy
Raven	- Devour
Raze	- Demolish
Realm	- Domain
Realty	- Property
Rear	- Foster, Elevate
Reason	- Reason
Rebate	- Concession
Rebel	- Disobey
Rebellion	- Revolt
Rebound	- Bounce, Rebound
Rebuff	- Rebuff
Rebuke	- Rebuke
Recant	- Retract, Backtract
Recede	- Recede
Reciprocate	- Retaliate
Rcite	- Chant
Reclaim	- Restore
Recommend	- Suggest
Recompense	- Compensate, Indemnify
Recon	- Regard
Recondite	- Mysterious
Recover	- Restore
Recrimination	- Recrimination
Recrudesce	- Aggravate
Rectify	- Repair
Recumbent	- Condingent
Recuperate	- Restore
Recusant	- Disobedient
Redeem	- Restore
Redolence	- Smell, Aroma
Redound	- Rebound
Reek	- Disgorge
Refractory	- Disobedient

For Synonyms of	See
Refrain	- Abstain
Refuge	- Shelter
Refuse	- Reject, Garbage
Refute	- Confute
Regale	- Entertain
Regalia	- Dress
Regard	- Regard
Regressive	- Backward
Regret	- Regret
Regurgitate	- Disgorge
Rehabilitation	- Rehabilitation
Re-imburse	- Indemnify
Re-instatement	- Rehabilitation
Reject	- Deny, Reject
Rejuvenate	- Restore
Relaxation	- Concession
Relegate	- Commit
Relevant	- Apposite, Relevant
Relict	- Relic
Relief	- Relief
Relieve	- Relieve
Relic	- Relic
Relinquish	- Cede; abandon
Reliquiae	- Relic
Remembrance	- Memento
Remains	- Relic
Remonstrate	- Chide, Reason
Remorse	- Attrition, Repentance
Rencontre	- Encounter
Rend	- Tear
Rendezvous	- Assignation
Renegade	- Defector
Renege	- Retract, Backtrack

For Synonyms of	See
Renounce	- Abandon
Renovate	- Innovate
Renowned	- Famous
Rent	- Crack, Fare
Repair	- Repair
Reparation	- Indemnify
Repartee	- Recrimination
Repay	- Indemnify
Repeal	- Annul
Repent	- Amends, Regret
Repentance	- Repentance
Repercuss	- Rebound
Replace	- Replace
Replenish	- Restore
Replicate	- Emulate
Reprehend	- Chide
Reprieve	- Relief
Reprimand	- Reprimand
Reprisal	- Revenge
Reproach	- Reprimand
Reprove	- Reprimand
Repudiate	- Deny
Reputed	- Famous
Request	- Request
Requiem	- Lamentation
Requisite	- Essential
Requite	- Retaliate
Rescind	- Annul
Resemblance	- Equality, Similarity
Resentment	- Irritation, Malice
Resolute	- Adamant
Resolve	- Determination
Restitute	- Restore
Restore	- Restore

For Synonyms of	See
Restrain	- Stop
Resurge	- Resurrect
Resurrect	- Resurrect
Resuscitate	- Resurrect
Retaliate	- Avenge, Retaliate
Retaliation	- Recrimination
Reticent	- Uncommunicative
Retort	- Recrimination
Retract	- Backtrack, Retract
Retreat	- Recede
Retrench	- Retrench
Retribution	- Revenge
Retrieve	- Restore
Retrofit	- Innovate
Retrograde	- Backward
Retrogress	- Recede
Retrogressive	- Backward
Retrospect	- Cogitate
Revamp	- Innovate
Reveal	- Disclose
Reverberate	- Bounce, Rebound
Revenge	- Revenge, Avenge
Reverence	- Reverence
Revive	- Resurrect
Revoke	- Annul
Revolt	- Disobey, Revolt
Revolve	- Spin
Reward	- Prize
Ribald	- Indecent
Rich	- Rich
Rickety	- Decrepit
Ricochet	- Rebound
Riddance	- Relief

For Synonyms of	See
Riddle	- Puzzle
Ridicule	- Deride, Ridicule
Ridiculous	- Ridiculous; ludicrous
Rigorous	- Strict
Rind	- Bark
Riposte	- Recrimination
Risible	- Ridiculous
Risk	- Risk, Danger
Risque	- Indecent
Rive	- Tear
Roam	- Wander
Robe	- Dress
Rock	- Shake
Rogue	- Vagabond
Rotate	- Spin
Rout	- Herd, Defeat
Rove	- Wander
Row	- Quarrel
Rubbish	- Garbage
Rubble	- Debris
Rude	- Rude
Rudimentary	- Nascent
Rue	- Repent
Ruffled	- Disorderly, Untidy
Ruminate	- Chew, Cogitate
Rummage	- Delve
Rumpus	- Babel
Ruse	- Bait, Ruse
Rut	- Mark

S

For Synonyms of	See
Sack	- Loot
Sacred	- Holy

For Synonyms of	*See*
Sacrilege	- Sacrilege
Sacrilegious	- Impious
Sacrosanct	- Holy
Sad	- Sad
Sag	- Buckle
Sagacious	- Clever, Politic
Salubrious	- Healthful
Salutary	- Healthful
Salvation	- Deliverance
Sanctify	- Enshrine
Sanction	- Approve
Sanitary	- Healthful
Sarcastic	- Sarcastic
Sardonic	- Sarcastic
Sate	- Gorge
Satiate	- Gorge
Satire	- Satire
Satirical	- Sarcastic
Savage	- Cruel
Scald	- Burn
Scarcity	- Dearth
Scare	- Frighten
Scarecrow	- Effigy
Scatter	- Scatter
Scholarly	- Learned
Scintillate	- Shine
Scoff	- Deride, Ridicule
Scold	- Chide
Scorch	- Burn
Scorn	- Contempt
Scour	- Clean
Scrabble	- Delve
Scrap	- Scrap, Quarrel
Scrape	- Scrape

For Synonyms of	*See*
Scratch	- Scrape
Scream	- Scream
Screech	- Scream
Scrutinize	- Examine
Scuffle	- Fight, Quarrel
Scum	- Dregs
Scurrilous	- Indecent
Secede	- Dissociate
Seclude	- Seclude
Secrete	- Hide
Sedition	- Revolt
Seduce	- Entice, Lure
See	- Look
Segregate	- Seclude, Classify
Seize	- Catch
Separate	- Dissociate
Serene	- Calm
Serious	- Serious
Sermon	- Speech
Servile	- Servile
Severe	- Austere
Shade	- Gradation
Shake	- Shake
Sham	- Bogus, Fake
Shameless	- Shameless
Shard	- Scrap
Shatter	- Disintegrate
Sheaf	- Bundle
Shed	- Discard
Shelter	- Shelter
Shimmer	- Shine
Shine	- Shine
Shiver	- Tremble
Shoal	- Herd

For Synonyms of	See
Shortchange	- Cheat
Shortcoming	- Defect
Show	- Demonstrate
Shrapnel	- Scrap
Shrick	- Scream
Shrill	- Scream, Loud
Shrink	- Shrink
Shrivel	- Shrink
Shudder	- Tremble
Shun	- Abstain
Shy	- Shy
Siesta	- Nap
Similarity	- Similarity
Simper	- Smile
Simulate	- Emulate
Singe	- Burn
Sink	- Drown, Sink
Sinuous	- Flexuous
Sip	- Drink
Skein	- Bunch
Skit	- Satire
Skive	- Abscond
Slander	- Defame
Slap	- Slap
Slatternly	- Untidy
Slaughter	- Kill, Massacre
Slavish	- Servile
Slipshod	- Untidy
Sliver	- Scrap
Slither	- Crawl
Slog	- Beat, Strike
Sloppy	- Untidy
Slough	- Discard
Slovenly	- Untidy

For Synonyms of	See
Slug	- Beat, Strike
Sluggish	- Lazy
Sluggishness	- Laziness
Smell	- Smell
Smile	- Smile
Smirk	- Smile
Smite	- Beat, Strike
Smother	- Suffocate
Smug	- Complacent
Snappish	- Irritable
Snarl	- Growl
Sneer	- Deride, Ridicule
Snigger	- Laugh
Snub	- Rebuff
Snuff	- Extinguish
Soar	- Ascend
Sobriquet	- Epithet
Soil	- Defile
Solemn	- Serious
Solicit	- Request
Solicitor	- Lawyer
Solitary	- Alone, Lonely
Somber	- Serious
Sordid	- Abject
Sort	- Classify, Seclude
Souvenir	- Memento
Sovereign	- Free
Spangle	- Spot
Sparkle	- Dazzle, Shine
Speckle	- Spot
Speech	- Speech
Spendthrift	- Extravagant
Spin	- Spin
Spite	- Contempt, Malice

For Synonyms of	See	For Synonyms of	See
Spleen	- Contempt, Malice	Stentorian	- Loud
Splinter	- Scrap	Stern	- Strict
Split	- Disintegrate, Tear	Stertorous	- Loud
Spoils	- Spoils	Stickout	- Jut out
Spontaneous	- Spontaneous	Stiffle	- Suffocate
Spoor	- Mark	Stigma	- Infamy
Spot	- Spot	Stimulate	- Stimulate
Spouse	- Companion	Stingy	- Miser
Spout	- Eject	Stink	- Malodour, Smell
Spread	- Scatter, Spread	Stint	- Conserve
Spur	- Incite or urge on	Stipple	- Spot
Spurious	- Fake	Stoic	- Impassive
Spurn	- Deny, Rebuff	Stolid	- Impassive
Spurt	- Eject	Stoop	- Cringe, Stoop
Squabble	- Quarrel	Stop	- Stop
Squash	- Mash	Strange	- Strange
Squib	- Satire	Strangle	- Suffocate
Squirm	- Writhe	Stratagem	- Ruse
Stab	- Pierce	Stress	- Emphasize
Stagger	- Falter	Strict	- Strict
Stagnate	- Stay	Strident	- Loud
Staid	- Serious	Strike	- Strike
Stake	- Pillar	Stringent	- Strict
Stance	- Bias	Strive	- Attempt, Try
Standard	- Flag	Struggle	- Attempt, Struggle
Stare	- Gaze, Look	Stub	- Stub
Startle	- Amaze	Stubble	- Stub
Staunch	- Stop	Stubborn	- Arrogant
Stave off	- Avert, Dodge	Stump	- Stub
Stay	- Stay	Stun	- Baffle, Benumb
Steal	- Steal	Stunt	- Stop
Stein	- Boundary	Stupefy	- Baffle, Benumb
Stem	- Stop	Subliminal	- Delicate
Stench	- Malodour, Smell	Submerge	- Sink, Dip

For Synonyms of	See
Submit	- Surrender
Suborn	- Entice, Motivate
Subscribe	- Assent
Subservient	- Servile
Subsidy	- Aid
Substitute	- Replace
Subterfuse	- Ruse
Subtle	- Delicate
Subvention	- Aid
Succulent	- Tasty
Succumb	- Surrender
Suffocate	- Suffocate
Suggest	- Suggest
Sullage	- Garbage
Sully	- Tarnish
Summon	- Collect
Sunder	- Tear
Supercilious	- Fastidious
Superfluous	- Abundant
Supersede	- Replace
Supplant	- Arogate
Supplicate	- Request
Surfeit	- Abundant, Gorge
Surmise	- Guess
Surrender	- Surrender
Surround	- Surround
Suspicion	- Apprehension
Suspire	- Crave, Surprise
Swag	- Bundle, Spoils
Swamp	- Mire
Swarm	- Herd
Swat	- Strike, Beat
Sway	- Shake, Dominance

For Synonyms of	See
Swell	- Swell
Swill	- Clean
Swindle	- Cheat
Swivel	- Spin
Swoop	- Descend
Sycophant	- Sycophant
Sympathy	- Sympathy

T

For Synonyms of	See
Taciturn	- Uncommunicative
Taint	- Adulterate, Blend
Talk	- Speech
Talkative	- Talkative; loquacious
Tantalise	- Harass
Tariff	- Fare
Tarnish	- Tarnish
Tarry	- Stay
Tassel	- Bunch (of threads)
Tasty	- Tasty
Taunt	- Ridicule
Tear	- Tear
Tedium	- Boredom
Teem	- Abound
Teeter	- Shake
Temerity	- Arrogance
Tempt	- Lure
Tenacity	- Determination
Tendency	- Bias
Tender	- Overture
Tenet	- Principle
Terrible	- Terrible
Terrific	- Terrific
Terrify	- Frighten
Terrifying	- Terrifying

For Synonyms of	See
Testy	- Irritable
Tether	- Tie (a rope or chain for confining a beast within certain limits)
Theft	- Theft
Thrash	- Beat
Threat	- Threat
Threaten	- Frighten
Threnody	- Lamentation (through ode or song)
Thress	- Beat
Throw	- Throw
Tie	- Tie
Timid	- Coward
Timorous	- Coward
Tinge	- Adulterate
Tirade	- Speech
Titter	- Laugh (restrainedly)
Toddle	- Shake
Token	- Memento
Tolerate	- Tolerate
Tomb	- Memorial
Topsyt-turvy	- Upheaval
Torment	- Harass
Tortuous	- Flexuous
Toss	- Hurl, Throw
Totter	- Shake
Tough	- Austere
Tour	- Journey
Toy	- Effigy, Trifle
Tract	- Spread
Trade	- Profession

For Synonyms of	See
Tradition	- Tradition
Trail	- Mark
Traiblazer	- Guide
Traipse	- Wander
Trait	- Peculiarity; Attribute; Property
Tramp	- Vagabond
Trance	- A deep sleep like state
Tranquil	- Calm
Transgress	- Encroach
Transgression	- Violation
Transient	- Ephemeral
Transitory	- Ephemeral
Transude	- Emit, ooze out
Trash	- Garbage
Treasure	- Treasure
Treasure-trove	- Treasure
Treasury	- Treasury
Treat	- Consult, Entertain
Tremble	- Tremble
Tremendous	- Terrific
Trespass	- Enter unlawfully upon another's land
Tribute	- Reverence
Trick	- Ruse
Trifle	- Trifle
Trifling	- Facetious; Witty; Humorous
Trim	- Trim
Trip	- Journey
Triturate	- Grind
Troupe	- Clique
Trousseau	- Dress (for bride)

For Synonyms of	See
Truckle	- Cringe (to shrink, bend or crouch, esp. in fear or servility)
Truculent	- Cruel
Truncate	- Trim
Try	- Try
Tryst	- Assignation
Tuft	- Bunch
Turbulence	- Upheaval
Turmoil	- Upheaval
Turncoat	- Defector
Turning point	- Turning point
Twaddle	- Chatter, Utter nonsense
Twinkle	- Shine
Twirl	- Spin
Twist	- Twist
Tycoon	- Baron
Tyrant	- Autocrat
Tyro	- Novice

U

For Synonyms of	See
Ubiquitous	- Ubiquitous
Umbrage	- Offence; annoyance or displeasure
Unabashed	- Shameless
Unbelief	- Disbelief
Uncanny	- Weird; (Happening through the intervention of unnatural)
Uncommunicative	- Uncommunicative
Unconquerable	- Invincible
Understanding	- Understanding
Unflagging	- Untiring
Universal	- Catholic, Ubiquitous
Unkempt	- Disorderly, Untidy
Unpropitious	- Ominous
Unrestrained	- Unrestrained
Unsatisfied	- Dis-satisfied
Untidy	- Disorderly, Untidy
Untiring	- Untiring
Upbraid	- Rebuke; Reproach
Upheaval	- Upheaval (A strong or violent change or disturbance as in a society)
Upright	- Erect
Uprising	- Revolt
Uproar	- Babel; Confusion; Commotion
Upset	- Upset, Perplex
Urge	- Appeal
Usher	- Guide
Usurp	- Arrogate

V

For Synonyms of	See
Vacant	- Vacant
Vacillate	- Waver
Vacuous	- Vacant
Vacuum	- Vacant
Vagabond	- Vagabond
Vagary	- Caprice
Vagrant	- Vagabond
Vainglory	- Pride

For Synonyms of	See
Vanish	- Disappear
Vanity	- Empty ostentation; Character or quality of being vain
Vanquish	- Defeat
Venal	- Mercenary
Veneer	- Hide (To overlay with a thin sheet of wood or other material)
Veneration	- Reverence
Vengeance	- Revenge
Verify	- Verify
Vertex	- Peak
Vespers	- Prayer
Vet	- Examine
Vex	- Irritate; Annoy; Provoke
Vicinity	- Closeness
Vicissitude	- Caprice
Vilify	- Defame
Vindicate	- Justify
Violate	- Breach
Violation	- Breach, Infringement; Transgression Violation
Visage	- Face
Vision	- Foresight
Vitriolic	- Acerbic; A hydrous sulphate of metal e.g. copper, iron and zinc
Vocation	- Profession

For Synonyms of	See
Void	- Vacant
Volition	- Desire, Will
Vomit	- Disgorge
Vouch	- Verify
Voyage	- Journey
Voyeur	- Peeping Tom (A sexual pervert who derives gratification from surreptitiously watching sexual acts or objects)
Vulgar	- Indecent

W

For Synonyms of	See
Wad	- Bundle
Wages	- Prize
Wail	- Cry
Wake	- Mark
Wallow	- Roll about in mud
Wander	- Wander
Wane	- Deplete
Wanton	- Egregious, Unrestrained
Ward off	- Avert, Dodge
Warning	- Warning
Wary	- Cautious
Wash	- Clean
Waspish	- Irritable
Wasted	- Done to no avail useless; physicaliy or psychologically wasted by long illness
Wastrel	- Extravagant
Watch	- Look

For Synonyms of	See
Watershed	- Turning point
Waver	- Waver; vacillate; unsteady
Wealth	- Property
Wealthy	- Rich
Weary	- Exhausted
Weeds	- Dress; clothing
Weep	- Cry
Weird	- Weird; fate; happening
Welsh	- Backtrack; to dodge fulfilling an obligation
Welter	- Writhe; lie in a state of turmoil or confusion
Wheedle	- Persuade
While away	- While away
Whirl	- Spin
Wholesome	- Healthful
Whorl	- Spin
Wicked	- Wicked; evil; cruel in practice
Will	- Desire, Will
Wilt	- Droop; loose self confidence/ courage
Wilted	- Limp
Wince	- Flinch; to drawback or shrink from what is dangerous difficult or unpleasant
Winding	- Flexuous; bend or turn; sinuous
Wish	- Desire
Wither	- Shrink; wilt; fade
Wizen	- Shrink; shrivel; dry up
Wobble	- Shake; more unsteadily
Worn	- Exhausted
Worry	- Anxiety
Wrangle	- Quarrel; dispute
Wreck	- Demolish
Wreckage	- Wreckage, Debris
Wrench	- Wring or pull with a twist
Wrest	- Twist
Wretched	- Miserable
Wriggle	- Writhe
Wring	- Twist
Writhe	- Writhe; twist

Y

For Synonyms of	See
Yearn	- Crave
Yield	- Surrender
Yoke	- Tie

Z

For Synonyms of	See
Zeal	- Enthusiasm
Zealot	- Bigot
Zenith	- Peak

❑❑❑